A MANUAL

OF THE

DIRECT AND EXCISE TAX SYSTEM

OF THE

UNITED STATES;

INCLUDING THE

FORMS AND REGULATIONS ESTABLISHED BY THE COMMISSIONER OF INTERNAL REVENUE,

THE

DECISIONS AND RULINGS OF THE COMMISSIONER,

TOGETHER WITH

EXTRACTS FROM THE CORRESPONDENCE OF THE OFFICE.

BY

GEORGE S. BOUTWELL.

LATE COMMISSIONER OF INTERNAL REVENUE.

FOURTH EDITION.

BOSTON:
LITTLE, BROWN AND COMPANY.
NEW YORK:
FITCH, ESTEE AND COMPANY.
1864.

PREFACE.

It has been my design in the preparation of this Manual to furnish to the officers of the revenue, to business men, and to members of the legal profession, such authority and information for the transaction of business, as can be derived from the proceedings, experience, and decisions of the Office of Internal Revenue. In the execution of this design I have received the aid and counsel of Commissioner Lewis, Deputy Commissioner McPherson, and of the clerks of the largest experience in the administration of the excise system. Among these I mention Messrs. George Parnell, William Richards, W. F. Downs, A. B. Johnson, and W. J. Gilbert.

I am also indebted to Mr. George G. W. Morgan for constant, intelligent, and faithful aid in the labor of compilation.

I do not claim that the treatise is either accurate or complete; but it is the best which, under the circumstances, it was practicable for me to prepare.

The following correspondence with the Hon. the Secretary of the Treasury indicates the plan of the work, and is the authority for the undertaking:

"Treasury Department,
"*Office of Internal Revenue, Washington, March* 30, 1863.

"Sir: Authority was given by Congress at the recent session for the publication of an edition of the Excise Laws, with such an index as might be prepared by the Commissioner of Internal Revenue. The index is now so far advanced that the printing may be commenced without delay.

"Many of the decisions which have been made from time to time have been printed by the office, in the newspapers, and by various persons who have prepared works upon the excise system; but these decisions have never been revised, and several of them are changed by the act of the third of March instant. There are also in the office many letters that were prepared by the Commissioner, relating to the application of the law to the pursuits and business of the people. It would be agreeable to me to prepare a hand-book, which shall contain the law, including sections from acts which do not relate exclusively to the internal revenue system, the decisions of the office, extracts from correspondence concerning the assessment and collection of taxes, together with the forms and regulations which have been established.

"I should undertake the labor without compensation, and with the understanding that the government might freely print the work for the use of its officers or for gratuitous distribution.

"It is my desire, however, to enter the work for copyright in my own name, with the privilege of publication, if there shall appear to be a demand therefor.

"With great respect, your obedient servant,

"GEORGE S. BOUTWELL."

"Hon. S. P. Chase,
"*Secretary of the Treasury.*"

"TREASURY DEPARTMENT, *April* 1, 1863.

"SIR: I have received your letter of the 30th ultimo, suggesting the preparation by you of a Hand-book of Internal Revenue, which shall contain the acts and parts of acts relating to the subject, the decisions of the office, extracts from correspondence concerning the assessment and collection of taxes, together with the forms and regulations which have been established; the work to be prepared (without compensation) by you for the use of the department or for gratuitous distribution, the copy-right to be taken out in your name, and you to have the privilege of publishing the work, if there should appear to be a demand therefor.

"I approve the plan as set forth above, and hereby authorize its execution.

"I am, very respectfully,

"S. P. CHASE,

"*Secretary of the Treasury.*

"Hon. GEORGE S. BOUTWELL."

INTRODUCTION.

Among the historical events, originating in the present civil war, is the passage of the act "to provide internal revenue to support the government and to pay interest on the public debt," approved July 1, 1862. It was my privilege to organize the Office of Internal Revenue; and in my attempt to perform the duty I was sustained by the generous confidence and unwavering support of the Secretary of the Treasury.

I received notice of my appointment while I was at Cairo in the service of the War Department. I arrived at Washington on the 16th of July, and entered upon my duties on the following day. My first labor was to read the excise law, which I had not before seen. Within a few days the Secretary assigned me a single clerk, then a second, then a third, and from time to time additions were made, till the clerical force now numbers one hundred and forty persons.

I examined the records of the Excise Bureau, established during the war of 1812; but they furnished no aid whatever in the execution of the work that was before me. I had neither time nor opportunity to study the excise system of Great Britain; and hence the organization of the system of the United States was based upon, and grew out of, the requirements of the law. I do not deem this a misfortune. The preliminary work of the office consisted in the division of the States into collection districts, the examination of the papers filed in behalf of applicants for the places of assessor and collector, the preparation of forms and books, and of instructions to collectors and assessors.

The public anxiety in regard to the construction of the law induced a large amount of correspondence with persons in various parts of the country, and, in the month of October, the letters sent numbered, occasionally, eight hundred per day. A considerable portion of these letters were formal, and others were repetitions of opinions previously given; but each day compelled attention to a large number of new questions. The correspondence of the office was arranged in eight divisions, and a competent and experienced clerk was placed at the head of each. In the beginning the Commissioner read each letter, and indicated, briefly, the answer to be returned. As the business increased, a clerk was charged with the work of separating those letters which corresponded to letters answered previously from those that contained new inquiries. The latter were considered by the Commissioner, answers dictated, and the letters and answers referred to the clerks charged, respectively, with the several branches of business to which the letters pertained.

The preparation of revenue stamps early engaged the attention of the Com missioner. By the provisions of the law it was necessary that each stamp should indicate upon its face the nature of the paper or instrument to which it was to be applied. This requisition involved the preparation of a large number of engravings and dies, which were to be dissimilar in design or in appearance. As the time was limited, and in case an attempt should be made to procure stamps of various designs, the risk of failure in some instances, at least, would be great, it was thought that the leading feature in each should be the same. Upon consultation with the Secretary of the Treasury, and with his approval, the head of Washington, after Stuart's painting, was adopted. By the first of January, 1863, more than ninety stamps, of different designs and denominations, had been engraved and prepared for use.

It was contemplated by the law that stamped paper should be furnished, on which might be written the various instruments subject to stamp duty. It has not yet been found practicable to comply with this requisition.

A system of bookkeeping was established in conformity to the requirements of the law, the purpose being to enable the office to furnish at any time a statement of the amount of revenue derived from every article subject to taxation in each and every district throughout the country.

The assessment lists returned to the office are carefully examined in detail, and all errors in the rate of taxation, or in computation, are noted, and the assessor informed thereof. Inasmuch as the office is in possession of the name and residence of every assistant assessor, and the limits of every division or subassessment district, each officer can be made responsible at once for any error which he may have committed.

The practice of the office in the construction of the law has been controlled by a few leading principles.

First. To levy a tax in those cases only which are clearly provided for by the statute, and, consequently, whenever a reasonable doubt exists, to rule against the government and in favor of the individual.

Second. In deciding whether an article is or is not a manufacture, to ascertain how it was regarded by business men at the time the excise law was passed; in all cases abstaining from inquiry as to the mode of preparation, or the nature or extent of the change produced. If the article in question was regarded by the makers and by business men as a new article of commerce, and it was produced by hand or machinery, it has been the practice to treat it as a manufacture under the law, unless specially exempt.

Third. To assess the tax upon articles manufactured and removed for consumption by the manufacturer, precisely as the tax would have been assessed if the articles had been removed for sale.

Fourth. In considering the law relating to the use of stamps it has been the practice of the office to give that signification to the names used in the statute descriptive of various instruments subject to stamp tax, which is ordinarily given to such descriptive terms by business and professional men.

Guided by these rules, and sustained by the patriotic sentiments of the people, it is a matter for congratulation that the taxes assessed have, with few unimportant exceptions, been paid with cheerfulness, and in no portion of the country with more alacrity than in the States of Maryland, Missouri, and Kentucky. The receipts thus far have not corresponded with the anticipations of the framers of the law, nor sustained the estimate made by the Commissioner in December last. It is believed, however, that the deficiency is in a large degree temporary, and that the average monthly receipts of the fiscal year 1863–'4 will be considerably in excess of the average monthly receipts from the 1st of September, 1862, to the 1st July, 1863.

The act of March 3, 1863, reduced the revenues of the country, and to the extent, probably, of several millions per annum. The difference between the actual receipts and estimates made is due in part to the action of Congress, and in part to circumstances connected with the business of the country, which were either unknown to the Commissioner or not sufficiently appreciated when the estimates were made. Congress also imposed new taxes, but the results have not yet been felt in the revenue receipts.

The estimate of the revenue to be derived from the tax on manufactures was based upon the product of the year ending 1st October, 1862. The product was necessarily large, growing, in part, out of the impetus given to that branch of business by the passage of the excise law, leading manufacturers to increase their operations to the greatest possible extent, in anticipation of the almost certain advance of prices consequent upon the imposition of the tax after the 31st of August.

The activity thus given to manufacturing industry at once supplied the market with goods and consumed the stock of raw cotton on hand. Hence it happened that the first year of the operation of the excise law found the country well supplied with goods and destitute of the material for continuing the manufacture upon a large scale. The revenue was thus diminished in amount by circumstances which were not clearly foreseen, or which were not sufficiently considered when the estimates of December were made.

A corresponding impetus was given to every other branch of manufacturing industry during the months of May, June, July, and August, 1862, followed by a decrease, more or less considerable, from September to the present time.

The stamp tax took effect, nominally, on the 1st of October, 1862, but the office was unable to furnish a supply of all denominations of stamps until the 1st day of the following January, and their use was not made imperative by law until the 1st day of June, 1863. It may therefore be assumed that the revenue from all sources has been less than it will be in future.

It is reasonable to expect an increase in the revenue for the fiscal year 1863–'4; and upon the return of peace the receipts will enable the government to pay the interest upon a debt twice as great as the present national debt, and to set aside a large sum for the payment of the principal.

From time to time additional sources of internal revenue will appear; and there ought to be no doubt of the ability of the nation to meet its liabilities, even if the war should continue upon its present gigantic scale till the year 1866.

The stability of the system is in the equal imposition of taxes, and in a just and impartial administration of the law.

GEO. S. BOUTWELL.

WASHINGTON, *July* 17, 1863.

CONTENTS.

A MANUAL

OF THE

DIRECT AND EXCISE TAX SYSTEM

OF

THE UNITED STATES.

DIRECT TAX.

AN ACT

To provide increased revenue from imports to pay interest on the public debt, and for other purposes.

* Sec. 8. *And be it further enacted,* That a direct tax of twenty millions of dollars be, and is hereby, annually laid upon the United States, and the same shall be and is hereby apportioned to the States, respectively, in manner following: Direct tax of $20,000,000, how apportioned.

To the State of Maine, four hundred and twenty thousand eight hundred and twenty-six dollars. Maine.

To the State of New Hampshire, two hundred and eighteen thousand four hundred and six and two-third dollars. New Hampshire.

To the State of Vermont, two hundred and eleven thousand and sixty-eight dollars. Vermont.

To the State of Massachusetts, eight hundred and twenty-four thousand five hundred and eighty-one and one-third dollars. Massachusetts

To the State of Rhode Island, one hundred and sixteen thousand nine hundred and sixty-three and two-third dollars. Rhode Island.

To the State of Connecticut, three hundred and eight thousand two hundred and fourteen dollars. Connecticut.

To the State of New York, two million six hundred and three thousand nine hundred and eighteen and two-third dollars. New York.

To the State of New Jersey, four hundred and fifty thousand one hundred and thirty-four dollars. New Jersey.

To the State of Pennsylvania, one million nine hundred and forty-six thousand seven hundred and nineteen and one-third dollars. Pennsylvania.

To the State of Delaware, seventy-four thousand six hundred and eighty-three and one-third dollars. Delaware.

To the State of Maryland, four hundred and thirty-six thousand eight hundred and twenty-three and one-third dollars. Maryland.

To the State of Virginia, nine hundred and thirty-seven thousand five hundred and fifty and two-third dollars. Virginia.

To the State of North Carolina, five hundred and seventy-six thousand one hundred and ninety-four and two-third dollars. North Carolina.

To the State of South Carolina, three hundred and sixty-three thousand five hundred and seventy and two-third dollars. South Carolina.

To the State of Georgia, five hundred and eighty-four thousand three hundred and sixty-seven and one-third dollars. Georgia.

To the State of Alabama, five hundred and twenty-nine thousand three hundred and thirteen and one-third dollars. Alabama.

To the State of Mississippi, four hundred and thirteen thousand eighty-four and two-third dollars. Mississippi.

---

* The preceding sections of this act relate to the tariff and they are therefore omitted.

Louisiana. To the State of Louisiana, three hundred and eighty-five thousand eight hundred and eighty-six and two-third dollars.

Ohio. To the State of Ohio, one million five hundred and sixty-seven thousand eighty-nine and one-third dollars.

Kentucky. To the State of Kentucky, seven hundred and thirteen thousand six hundred and ninety-five and one-third dollars.

Tennessee. To the State of Tennessee, six hundred and sixty-nine thousand four hundred and ninety-eight dollars.

Indiana. To the State of Indiana, nine hundred and four thousand eight hundred and seventy-five and one third dollars.

Illinois. To the State of Illinois, one million one hundred and forty-six thousand five hundred and fifty-one and one-third dollars.

Missouri To the State of Missouri, seven hundred and sixty-one thousand one hundred and twenty-seven and one-third dollars.

Kansas. To the State of Kansas, seventy-one thousand seven hundred and forty-three and one-third dollars.

Arkansas. To the State of Arkansas, two hundred and sixty-one thousand eight hundred and eighty-six dollars.

Michigan. To the State of Michigan, five hundred and one thousand seven hundred and sixty-three and one-third dollars.

Florida. To the State of Florida, seventy-seven thousand five hundred and twenty-two and two-third dollars.

Texas. To the State of Texas, three hundred and fifty-five thousand one hundred and six and two-third dollars.

Iowa To the State of Iowa, four hundred and fifty-two thousand and eighty-eight dollars.

Wisconsin. To the State of Wisconsin, five hundred and nineteen thousand six hundred and eighty-eight and two-third dollars.

California. To the State of California, two hundred and fifty-four thousand five hundred and thirty-eight and two-third dollars.

Minnesota. To the State of Minnesota, one hundred and eight thousand five hundred and twenty-four dollars.

Oregon. To the State of Oregon, thirty-five thousand one hundred and forty and two-third dollars.

New Mexico. To the Territory of New Mexico, sixty-two thousand six hundred and forty-eight dollars.

Utah. To the Territory of Utah, twenty-six thousand nine hundred and eighty-two dollars.

Washington. To the Territory of Washington, seven thousand seven hundred and fifty-five and one-third dollars.

Nebraska. To the Territory of Nebraska, nineteen thousand three hundred and twelve dollars.

Nevada. To the Territory of Nevada, four thousand five hundred and ninety-two and two-third dollars.

Colorado. To the Territory of Colorado, twenty-two thousand nine hundred and five and one-third dollars.

Dakota. To the Territory of Dakota, three thousand two hundred and forty-one and one-third dollars.

District of Columbia. To the District of Columbia, forty-nine thousand four hundred and thirty-seven and one-third dollars.

Collection districts for assessing and collecting the tax. SEC. 9. *And be it further enacted*, That, for the purpose of assessing the above tax and collecting the same, the President of the United States be, and he is hereby, authorized to divide, respectively, the States and Territories of the United States and the District of Columbia into convenient collection districts, and to nominate and, by and with the advice of the Senate, to appoint an assessor and a collector for each such district, who shall be freeholders and resident within the same: *Provided*, That any of said States and Territories, as well as the District of Columbia, may, if the President shall deem it proper, be erected into one district: *And provided, further*, That the appointment of said assessors and collectors, or any of them, shall not be made until on or after the second Tuesday in February, one thousand eight hundred and sixty-two.

Assessors and Collectors.

Proviso.

Date of appointment of assessors and collectors.

SEC. 10. *And be it further enacted*, That before any such collector shall enter upon the duties of his office he shall execute a bond for such amount as shall be prescribed by the Secretary of the Treasury, with sureties to be approved as sufficient by the Solicitor of the Treasury, containing the condition that said collector shall justly and faithfully account for to the United States, and pay over, in compliance with the order or regulations of the Secretary of the Treasury, all public moneys which may come into his hands or possession; which bond shall be filed in the office of the First Comptroller of the Treasury, to be by him directed to be put in suit upon any breach of the condition thereof. And such collectors shall, from time to time, renew, strengthen, and increase their official bonds, as the Secretary of the Treasury may direct.

Collectors to give bond before entering upon duty.

Details thereof.

SEC. 11. *And be it further enacted*, That each of the assessors shall divide his district into a convenient number of assessment districts, within each of which he shall appoint one respectable freeholder to be assistant assessor; and each assessor and assistant assessor so appointed, and accepting the appointment, shall, before he enters on the duties of his appointment, take and subscribe before some competent magistrate, or some collector to be appointed by this act, (who is hereby empowered to administer the same,) the following oath or affirmation, to wit: "I, A B, do swear, or affirm, (as the case may be,) that I will, to the best of my knowledge, skill, and judgment, diligently and faithfully execute the office and duties of assessor for, (naming the assessment district,) without favor or partiality, and that I will do equal right and justice in every case in which I shall act as assessor." And a certificate of such oath or affirmation shall be delivered to the collector of the district for which such assessor or assistant assessor shall be appointed. And every assessor or assistant assessor acting in the said office without having taken the said oath or affirmation shall forfeit and pay one hundred dollars, one moiety thereof to the use of the United States, and the other moiety thereof to him who shall first sue for the same; to be recovered, with costs of suit, in any court having competent jurisdiction.

Collection district to be divided into assessment districts.

Assistant assessors.

Oath.

Certificate.

Penalty for assessors, &c., acting without taking oath.

SEC. 12. *And be it further enacted*, That the Secretary of the Treasury shall establish regulations suitable and necessary for carrying this act into effect; which regulations shall be binding on each assessor and his assistants in the performance of the duties enjoined by or under this act, and shall also frame instructions for the said assessors and their assistants; pursuant to which instructions the said assessors shall, on the first day of March next, direct and cause the several assistant assessors in the district to inquire after and concerning all lands, lots of ground, with their improvements, buildings, and dwelling-houses, made liable to tax-

Secretary of Treasury to establish regulations under this act, and frame instructions.

Duty of assessors and assistants.

ation under this act by reference as well to any lists of assessment or collection taken under the laws of the respective States, as to any other records or documents, and by all other lawful ways and means, and to value and enumerate the said objects of taxation in the manner prescribed by this act, and in conformity with the regulations and instructions above mentioned.

Direct tax.

Real estate. Valuation to be as of April 1, 1862.

Exemptions.

Regard to be had to State valuations

SEC. 13. *And be it further enacted*, That the said direct tax laid by this act shall be assessed and laid on the value of all lands and lots of ground, with their improvements and dwelling-houses, which several articles subject to taxation shall be enumerated and valued, by the respective assessors, at the rate each of them is worth in money on the first day of April, eighteen hundred and sixty-two: *Provided, however*, That all property, of whatever kind, coming within any of the foregoing descriptions, and belonging to the United States or any State, or permanently or specially exempted from taxation by the laws of the State wherein the same may be situated at the time of the passage of this act, together with such property belonging to any individual, who actually resides thereon, as shall be worth the sum of five hundred dollars, shall be exempted from the aforesaid enumeration and valuation, and from the direct tax aforesaid: *And provided, further*, That in making such assessment due regard shall be had to any valuation that may have been made under the authority of the State or Territory at any period nearest to said first day of April.

Property owners to furnish lists upon request.

SEC. 14. *And be it further enacted*, That the respective assistant assessors shall, immediately after being required as aforesaid by the assessors, proceed through every part of their respective districts, and shall require all persons owning, possessing, or having the care or management of any lands, lots of ground, buildings, or dwelling-houses, lying and being within the collection district where they reside, and liable to a direct tax as aforesaid, to deliver written lists of the same; which lists shall be made in such manner as may be directed by the assessor, and, as far as practicable, conformably to those which may be required for the same purpose under the authority of the respective States.

If owner has no list and will disclose, officer to make list.

SEC. 15. *And be it further enacted*, That if any person owning, possessing, or having the care or management of property liable to a direct tax, as aforesaid, shall not be prepared to exhibit a written list when required, as aforesaid, and shall consent to disclose the particulars of any and all the lands and lots of ground, with their improvements, buildings, and dwelling-houses, taxable as aforesaid, then, and in that case, it shall be the duty of the officer to make such list, which, being distinctly read and consented to, shall be received as the list of such person.

Penalty for delivering or disclosing fraudulent list.

Lists, how to be made in such cases.

SEC. 16. *And be it further enacted*, That if any such person shall deliver or disclose to any assessor or assistant assessor appointed in pursuance of this act, and requiring a list or lists, as aforesaid, any false or fraudulent list, with intent to defeat or evade the valuation or enumeration hereby intended to be made, such person so offending, and being thereof convicted before any court having competent jurisdiction, shall be fined in a sum not exceeding five hundred dollars, at the discretion of the court, and shall pay all costs and charges of prosecution; and the valuation and enumeration required by this act shall, in all such cases, be made, as aforesaid, upon lists, according to the form above described, to be made out by the assessors and assistant assessors, respectively; which lists the said assessors are hereby authorized and required to make according to the best information they can obtain, and for the purpose of making which they are hereby authorized to enter into and upon all and singular the premises, respectively; and from the valuation and enumeration so made there shall be no appeal.

No appeal from valuation, &c.

Notice to owner to furnish list in certain cases.

SEC. 17. *And be it further enacted*, That in case any person shall be absent from his place of residence at the time an assessor shall call to receive the list of such person, it shall be the duty of such assessor or assistant assessor to leave at the house or place of residence of such person, with some person of suitable age and discretion, a written note or memorandum, requiring him to present to such assessor the list or lists required by this act within ten days from the date of such note or memorandum.

Assessors to make out list when it is not given upon notice or request.

SEC. 18. *And be it further enacted*, That if any person, on being notified or required as aforesaid, shall refuse or neglect to give such list or lists as aforesaid within the time required by this act, it shall be the duty of the assessor for the assessment district within which such person shall reside, and he is hereby authorized and required, to enter into and upon the lands, buildings, dwelling-houses, and premises, if it be necessary, of such persons so refusing or neglecting, and to make, according to the best information which he can obtain, and on his own view and information, such lists of the lands and lots of ground, with their improvements, buildings, and dwelling-houses, owned or possessed, or under the care or management of such person, as are required by this act; which lists, so made and subscribed by such assessor, shall be taken and reputed as good and sufficient lists of the persons and property for which such person is to be taxed for the purposes of this act.

Property of absent owners, list how made.

SEC. 19. *And be it further enacted*, That whenever there shall be in any assessment district any property, lands, and lots of ground, buildings, or dwelling-houses, not owned or possessed by, or under the care and management of, any person or persons within such district, and liable to be taxed as aforesaid, and no list of which shall be transmitted to the assessor in the manner provided by this act, it shall be the duty of the assessor for such district, and he is hereby authorized and required, to enter into and upon the real estate, if it be necessary, and take such view thereof, and make lists of the same, according to the form prescribed; which lists, being subscribed by the said assessor, shall be taken and reputed as good and sufficient lists of such property, under and for the purposes of this act.

Lists how made of property in another collection district.

SEC. 20. *And be it further enacted*, That the owners, possessors, or persons having the care or management of lands, lots of ground, buildings, and dwelling-houses, not lying or being within the assessment district in which they reside, shall be permitted to make out and deliver the lists thereof required by this act, (provided the assessment district in which the said objects of taxation lie or be is therein distinctly stated,) at the time and in the manner prescribed, to the assessor of the assessment district wherein such persons reside. And it shall be the duty of the assessors, in all such cases, to transmit such lists, at the time and in the manner prescribed for the transmission of the lists of the objects of taxation lying and being within their respective assessment districts, to the assessor of the collection district wherein the said objects of taxation shall lie or be immediately after the receipt thereof; and the said lists shall be valid and sufficient for the purposes of this act; and on the delivery of such list, the person making and delivering the same shall pay to the assessor one dollar, which he shall retain to his own use.

Lists to be taken in reference to a day certain.

SEC. 21. *And be it further enacted*, That the lists aforesaid shall be taken with reference to the day fixed for that purpose by this act, as aforesaid; and the assistant assessors, respectively, after collecting the said lists, shall proceed to arrange the same, and to make two general lists, the first of which shall exhibit, in alphabetical order, the names of all persons liable to pay a tax under this act, residing within the assessment district, together with the value and assessment of the objects liable to taxation within such district for which each such person is liable, and, whenever so required by the assessor, the amount of direct tax payable by each person on such objects under the State laws imposing direct taxes; and the second list shall exhibit, in alphabetical order, the names of all persons residing out of the collection district, owners of property within the district, together with the value and assessment thereof, with the amount of direct tax payable thereon as aforesaid. The forms of the said general list shall be devised and prescribed by the assessor, and lists taken according to such form shall be made out by the assistant assessors and delivered to the assessor within sixty days after the day fixed by this act, as aforesaid, requiring lists from individuals. And if any assistant assessor shall fail to perform any duty assigned by this act within the time prescribed by his precept, warrant, or other legal instructions, not being prevented therefrom by sickness or other unavoidable accident, every such assistant assessor shall be discharged from office, and shall, moreover, forfeit and pay two hundred dollars, to be recovered for the use of the United States in any court having competent jurisdiction, with costs of suit.

List of residents, of non-residents

Assessor to devise form of lists.

Penalty on assistant assessor for neglect of duty.

Notice to be given when lists, valuations, &c., are completed.

SEC. 22. *And be it further enacted*, That immediately after the valuations and enumerations shall have been completed as aforesaid, the assessor in each collection district shall, by advertisement in some public newspaper, if any there be in such district, and by written notifications to be publicly posted up in at least four of the most public places in each collection district, advertise all persons concerned of the place where the said lists, valuations, and enumerations may be seen and examined; and that during twenty-five days after the publication of the notifications, as aforesaid, appeals will be received and determined by him relative to any erroneous or excessive valuations or enumerations by the assessor. And it shall be the duty of the assessor in each collection district, during twenty-five days after the date of publication to be made as aforesaid, to submit the proceedings of the assistant assessors and the list by them received or taken as aforesaid to the inspection of any and all persons who shall apply for that purpose; and the said assessors are hereby authorized to receive, hear, and determine, in a summary way, according to law and right, upon any and all appeals which may be exhibited against the proceedings of the said assessors: *Provided always*, That it shall be the duty of said assessor to advertise and attend, not

Assessors to submit proceedings of assistants to inspection of parties interested.

To hear and determine appeals.

less than two successive days of the said twenty-five, at the court-house of each county within his collection district, there to receive and determine upon the appeals aforesaid: *And provided, also,* That the question to be determined by the assessor, on an appeal respecting the valuation of property, shall be, whether the valuation complained of be or be not in a just relation or proportion to other valuations in the same collection district. And all appeals to the assessors, as aforesaid, shall be made in writing, and shall specify the particular cause, matter, or thing respecting which a decision is requested; and shall, moreover, state the ground or principle of inequality or error complained of. And the assessor shall have power to re-examine and equalize the valuations as shall appear just and equitable; but no valuation shall be increased without a previous notice, of at least five days, to the party interested, to appear and object to the same, if he judge proper; which notice shall be given by a note in writing, to be left at the dwelling-house of the party by such assessor or an assistant assessor.

How valuations are to be determined.

Appeals to be in writing, what to contain.

Valuations may be re-examined and equalized,

not to be increased without notice, &c.

SEC. 23. *And be it further enacted,* That whenever a State, Territory, or the District of Columbia, shall contain more than one collection district, the assessors shall have power, on examination of the lists rendered by the assistant assessors, according to the provisions of this act, to revise, adjust, and equalize the valuation of lands and lots of ground, with their improvements, buildings, and dwelling-houses, between such collection districts, by deducting from or adding to either such a rate per centum as shall appear just and equitable.

If more than one collection district in a State, &c., the assessors may equalize, &c.

SEC. 24. *And be it further enacted,* That the assessors shall, immediately after the expiration of the time for hearing and deciding appeals, make out correct lists of the valuation and enumeration in each collection district, and deliver the same to the board of assessors hereinafter constituted in and for the States respectively. And it shall be the duty of the assessors in each State to convene in general meeting at such time and place as shall be appointed and directed by the Secretary of the Treasury. And the said assessors, or a majority of them, so convened, shall constitute, and they are hereby constituted, a board of assessors for the purposes of this act, and shall make and establish such rules and regulations as to them shall appear necessary for carrying such purposes into effect, not being inconsistent with this act or the laws of the United States.

Assessors to make out lists of valuations and deliver to board of assessors.

Board, how constituted.

SEC. 25. *And be it further enacted,* That the said board of assessors, convened and organized as aforesaid, shall and may appoint a suitable person or persons to be their clerk or clerks, but not more than one for each collection district, who shall hold his or their office or offices at the pleasure of said board of assessors, and whose duty it shall be to receive, record, and preserve all tax lists, returns, and other documents delivered and made to the said board of assessors, and who shall take an oath (or affirmation if conscientiously scrupulous of taking an oath) faithfully to discharge his or their trust; and in default of taking such oath or affirmation, previous to entering on the duties of such appointment, or on failure to perform any part of the duties enjoined on him or them respectively by this act, he or they shall respectively forfeit and pay the sum of two hundred dollars for the use of the United

Board of assessors to appoint clerks.

Number and duty of clerks.

Penalty for acting without taking oath.

States, to be recovered in any court having competent jurisdiction, and shall also be removed from office.

Duty of clerks.

SEC. 26. *And be it further enacted*, That it shall be the duty of the said clerks to record the proceedings of the said board of assessors, and to enter on the record the names of such of the assessors as shall attend any general meeting of the board of assessors for the purposes of this act. And if any assessor shall fail to attend such general meeting, his absence shall be noted on the said record, and he shall, for every day he may be absent therefrom, forfeit and pay the sum of ten dollars for the use of the United States. And if any assessor shall fail or neglect to furnish the said board of assessors with the lists of valuation and enumeration of each assessment district within his collection district within three days after the time appointed as aforesaid for such general meeting of the said board of assessors, he shall forfeit and pay the sum of five hundred dollars for the use of the United States, and, moreover, shall forfeit his compensation as assessor. And it shall be the duty of the clerks of the said board of assessors to certify to the Secretary of the Treasury an extract of the minutes of the board, showing such failures or neglect, which shall be sufficient evidence of the forfeiture of such compensation, to all intents and purposes: *Provided always*, That it shall be in the power of the Secretary of the Treasury to exonerate such assessor or assessors from the forfeiture of the said compensation, in whole or in part, as to him shall appear just and equitable.

Penalty on assessor for not attending general meeting of board.

for failing to furnish lists.

Certified copy of minutes of the board to be furnished Secretary of the Treasury, who may exonerate assessor.

Board to make out equalization and apportionment.

SEC. 27. *And be it further enacted*, That if the said board of assessors shall not, within three days after the first meeting thereof as aforesaid, be furnished with all the lists of valuation of the several counties and State districts of any State, they shall nevertheless proceed to make out the equalization and apportionment by this act directed, and they shall assign to such counties and State districts the valuation lists of which shall not have been furnished, such valuation as they shall deem just and right; and the valuation thus made to such counties and State districts by the board of assessors shall be final, and the proper quota of direct tax shall be, and is hereby, declared to be imposed thereon accordingly.

Their valuation to be final, and the basis of taxation.

Board of assessors to revise and adjust lists.

SEC. 28. *And be it further enacted*, That it shall be the duty of the said board of assessors diligently and carefully to consider and examine the said lists of valuation, and they shall have power to revise, adjust, and equalize the valuation of property in any county or State district, by adding thereto, or deducting therefrom, such a rate per centum as shall, under the valuation of the several counties and State districts, be just and equitable: *Provided*, The relative valuation of property in the same county shall not be changed, unless manifest error or imperfection shall appear in any of the lists of valuation, in which case the said board of assessors shall have power to correct the same, as to them shall appear just and right. And if, in consequence of any revisal, change, and alteration of the said valuation, any inequality shall be produced in the apportionment of the said direct tax to the several States as aforesaid, it shall be the duty of the Secretary of the Treasury to report the same to Congress, to the intent that provision may be made by law for rectifying such inequality.

Relative valuation not to be changed unless error appears.

Inequalities of taxation to be reported to Congress.

SEC. 29. *And be it further enacted*, That as soon as the said board of assessors shall have completed the adjustment and equalization of the valuation aforesaid, they shall proceed to apportion to each county and State district its proper quota of direct tax. And the said board of assessors shall, within twenty days after the time appointed by the Secretary of the Treasury for their first meeting, complete the said apportionment, and shall record the same; they shall thereupon further deliver to each assessor a certificate of such apportionment, together with the several lists by the assessors respectively presented to the board as aforesaid, and transmit to the Secretary of the Treasury a certificate of the apportionment by them made as aforesaid; and the assessors, respectively, shall thereupon proceed to revise their respective lists, and alter and make the same in all respects conformable to the apportionment aforesaid by the said board of assessors; and the said assessors, respectively, shall make out lists containing the sums payable according to the provisions of this act upon every object of taxation in and for each collection district; which lists shall contain the name of each person residing within the said district, owning or having the care or superintendence of property lying within the said district which is liable to the said tax, when such person or persons are known, together with the sums payable by each; and where there is any property within any collection district liable to the payment of the said tax, not owned or occupied by or under the superintendence of any person resident therein, there shall be a separate list of such property, specifying the sum payable, and the names of the respective proprietors, where known. And the said assessors shall furnish to the collectors of the several collection districts, respectively, within thirty-five days after the apportionment is completed, as aforesaid, a certified copy of such list or lists for their proper collection districts, and in default of performance of the duties enjoined on the board of assessors and assessors, respectively, by this section, they shall severally and individually forfeit and pay the sum of five hundred dollars to the use of the United States, to be recovered in any court having competent jurisdiction. And it is hereby enacted and declared that the valuation, assessment, equalization, and apportionment made by the said board of assessors, as aforesaid, shall be and remain in full force and operation for laying, levying, and collecting, yearly and every year, the annual direct tax by this act laid and imposed, until altered, modified, or abolished by law.

Board to apportion tax. *Duties of.* *Assessors to make their lists conform.* *Contents of lists.* *Lists to be given to collectors.* *Penalty on assessor, &c., under this section.* *Valuation and apportionment to continue until altered.*

SEC. 30. *And be it further enacted*, That there shall be allowed and paid to the several assessors and assistant assessors, for their services under this act: to each assessor two dollars per day for every day employed in making the necessary arrangements and giving the necessary instructions to the assistant assessors for the valuation, and three dollars per day for every day employed in hearing appeals, revising valuations, and making out lists agreeably to the provisions of this act, and one dollar for every hundred taxable persons contained in the tax list, as delivered by him to said board of assessors; to each assistant assessor two dollars for every day actually employed in collecting lists and making valuations, the number of days necessary for that purpose to be certified by the assessor and approved by the commis-

Pay of assessors and assistant assessors.

sioner of taxes, and one dollar for every hundred taxable persons contained in the tax lists, as completed and delivered by him to the assessor; to each of the assessors constituting the board of assessors, as aforesaid, for every day's actual attendance at said board, the sum of three dollars, and for travelling to and from the place designated by the Secretary of the Treasury, ten cents for each mile, by the most direct and usual route; and to each of the clerks of said board two dollars for every day's actual attendance thereon. And the said board of assessors, and said assessors, respectively, shall be allowed their necessary and reasonable charges for stationery and blank books used in the execution of their duties; and the compensation herein specified shall be in full for all expenses not otherwise particularly authorized, and shall be paid at the treasury, and such amount as shall be required for such payment is hereby appropriated.

Allowed for stationery and blank books.

Collector on receiving list to give three receipts.

SEC. 31. *And be it further enacted,* That each collector, on receiving a list, as aforesaid, from the said assessors, respectively, shall subscribe three receipts; one of which shall be given on a full and correct copy of such list, which list shall be delivered by him to, and shall remain with, the assessor of his collection district, and shall be open to the inspection of any person who may apply to inspect the same; and the other two receipts shall be given on aggregate statements of the lists aforesaid, exhibiting the gross amount of taxes to be collected in each county or State district contained in the collection district, one of which aggregate statements and receipts shall be transmitted to the Secretary, and the other to the First Comptroller of the Treasury.

Collector to give bond before receiving list.

Form, penalty, &c., of bond.

Proviso that present bond shall remain operative.

SEC. 32. *And be it further enacted,* That each collector, before receiving any list, as aforesaid, for collection, shall give bond with one or more good and sufficient sureties, to be approved by the Solicitor of the Treasury, in the amount of the taxes assessed in the collection district for which he has been or may be appointed; which bond shall be payable to the United States, with condition for the true and faithful discharge of the duties of his office according to law, and particularly for the due collection and payment of all moneys assessed upon such district, and the said bond shall be transmitted to the Solicitor of the Treasury, and, after approval by him, shall be deposited in the office of the First Comptroller of the Treasury: *Provided always,* That nothing herein contained shall be deemed to annul or in anywise impair the obligation of the bond heretofore given by any collector; but the same shall be and remain in full force and virtue, anything in this act to the contrary thereof in anywise notwithstanding.

Tax assessed to be a lien for two years.

SEC. 33. *And be it further enacted,* That the annual amount of the taxes so assessed shall be and remain a lien upon all lands and other real estate of the individuals who may be assessed for the same during two years after the time it shall annually become due and payable; and the said lien shall extend to each and every part of all tracts or lots of land or dwelling-houses, notwithstanding the same may have been divided or alienated in part.

Collector may appoint deputies, and revoke appointments, &c.

SEC. 34. *And be it further enacted,* That each collector shall be authorized to appoint, by an instrument of writing under his hand and seal, as many deputies as he may think proper, to be by him compensated for their services, and also to revoke the powers of any deputy, giving public notice thereof in that portion of the district assigned to such deputy; and each such deputy shall have the like authority, in every respect, to collect the direct tax so assessed within the portion of the district assigned to him which is by this act vested in the collector himself; but each collector shall, in every respect, be responsible both to the United States and to individuals, as the case may be, for all moneys collected, and for every act done as deputy collector by any of his deputies whilst acting as such: *Provided*, That nothing herein contained shall prevent any collector from collecting himself the whole or any part of the tax so assessed and payable in his district.

Authority of deputy.

Collector responsible for moneys collected by self and deputies.

SEC. 35. *And be it further enacted*, That each of the said collectors shall, within ten days after receiving his collection list from the assessors, respectively, as aforesaid, and annually, within ten days after he shall be so required by the Secretary of the Treasury, advertise in one newspaper printed in his collection district, if any there be, and by notifications, to be posted up in at least four public places in his collection district, that the said tax has become due and payable, and state the times and places at which he or they will attend to receive the same, which shall be within twenty days after such notification; and with respect to persons who shall not attend, according to such notifications, it shall be the duty of each collector, in person or by deputy, to apply once at their respective dwellings within such district, and there demand the taxes payable by such persons, which application shall be made within sixty days after the receipt of the collection list, as aforesaid, or after the receipt of the requisition of the Secretary of the Treasury, as aforesaid, by the collectors; and if the said taxes shall not be then paid, or within twenty days thereafter, it shall be lawful for such collector, or his deputies, to proceed to collect the said taxes by distraint and sale of the goods, chattels, or effects of the persons delinquent as aforesaid. And in case of such distraint, it shall be the duty of the officer charged with the collection to make, or cause to be made, an account of goods or chattels which may be distrained, a copy of which, signed by the officer making such distraint, shall be left with the owner or possessor of such goods, chattels, or effects, or at his or her dwelling, with some person of suitable age and discretion, with a note of the sum demanded, and the time and place of sale; and the said officer shall forthwith cause a notification to be publicly posted up at two of the taverns nearest to the residence of the person whose property shall be distrained, or at the court-house of the same county, if not more than ten miles distant, which notice shall specify the articles distrained, and the time and place for the sale thereof, which time shall not be less than ten days from the date of such notification, and the place proposed for sale not more than five miles distant from the place of making such distraint: *Provided*, That in any case of distraint for the payment of the tax aforesaid, the goods, chattels, or effects so distrained shall and may be restored to the owner or possessor if, prior to the sale thereof, payment or tender thereof shall be made to the proper officer charged with the collection, of the full amount demanded, together with such fee for levying, and such sum for the necessary and reasonable expense of removing and keeping the goods, chattels, or effects so distrained, as may be allowed in like cases by the laws or practice of the State wherein the distraint shall have

Collector to advertise that tax is due and payable, &c.

to demand at dwellings taxes not paid.

to distrain, if not paid within, &c.

Duty of officer in case of distraint.

Property may be restored after distraint, on payment &c., of tax, &c.

If tax not paid, property to be sold.

been made; but in case of non-payment or tender, as aforesaid, the said officers shall proceed to sell the said goods, chattels, or effects, at public auction, and shall and may retain from the proceeds of such sale the amount demandable for the use of the United States, with the necessary and reasonable expenses of distraint and sale, and a commission of five per centum thereon for his own use, rendering the overplus, if any there be, to the person whose goods, chattels, or effects shall have been distrained: *Provided*, That it shall not be lawful to make distraint of the tools or implements of a trade or profession, beasts of the plough necessary for the cultivation of improved lands, arms, or household furniture, or apparel necessary for a family.

Exemptions from distraint.

When personal property cannot be found sufficient to satisfy tax and costs, the real estate to be sold.

SEC. 36. *And be it further enacted*, That whenever goods, chattels, or effects sufficient to satisfy any tax upon buildings, dwelling-houses, or lands and their improvements, owned, occupied, or superintended by persons known or residing within the same collection district, cannot be found, the collector having first advertised the same for thirty days, in a newspaper printed within the collection district, if such there be, and having posted up, in at least ten public places within the same, a notification of the intended sale, thirty days previous thereto, shall proceed to sell at public sale so much of the said property as may be necessary to satisfy the taxes due thereon, together with an addition of twenty per centum to the said taxes. But in all cases where the property liable to a direct tax under this act may not be divisible, so as to enable the collector by a sale of part thereof to raise the whole amount of the tax, with all costs, charges, and commissions, the whole of such property shall be sold, and the surplus of the proceeds of the sale, after satisfying the tax, costs, charges, and commissions, shall be paid to the owner of the property, or his legal representatives, or if he or they cannot be found, or refuse to receive the same, then such surplus shall be deposited in the treasury of the United States, to be there held for the use of the owner or his legal representatives, until he or they shall make application therefor to the Secretary of the Treasury, who, upon such application, shall, by warrant on the treasury, cause the same to be paid to the applicant. And if the property advertised for sale as aforesaid cannot be sold for the amount of the tax due thereon, with the said additional twenty per centum thereto, the collector shall purchase the same in behalf of the United States for the amount aforesaid: *Provided*, that the owner or superintendent of the property aforesaid, after the same shall have been, as aforesaid, advertised for sale, and before it shall have been actually sold, shall be allowed to pay the amount of the tax thereon with an addition of ten per centum on the same, on the payment of which the sale of the property shall not take place: *Provided, also*, That the owners, their heirs, executors, or administrators, or any person on their behalf, shall have liberty to redeem the lands and other property sold, as aforesaid, within two years from the time of sale, upon payment to the collector for the use of the purchaser, his heirs or assigns, of the amount paid by said purchaser, with interest for the same, at the rate of twenty per centum per annum; and no deed shall be given in pursuance of such sale until the time of redemption shall have expired. And the collector shall render a distinct account of the charges incurred in

Provisions as to sale.

If real estate will not sell for enough to pay tax, the United States to take it.

Proviso empowering owners to redeem prior to sale on payment of taxes, with addition of ten per cent.

Right of redemption.

Deed not to be given until time for redemption has expired.

offering and advertising for sale such property, and shall pay into the treasury the surplus, if any there be, of the aforesaid addition of twenty per centum, or ten per centum, as the case may be, after defraying the charges. And in every case of the sale of real estate which shall be made under the authority of this act by the collectors, respectively, or their lawful deputies, respectively, the deeds for the estate so sold shall be prepared, made, executed, and proved or acknowledged at the time and times prescribed in this act by the collectors, respectively, within whose collection district such real estate shall be situated, in such form of law as shall be authorized and required by the laws of the United States, or by the law of the State in which such real estate lies, for making, executing, proving, and acknowledging deeds of bargain and sale or other conveyances for the transfer and conveyance of real estate; and for every deed so prepared, made, executed, proved, and acknowledged, the purchaser or grantee shall pay to the collector the sum of two dollars, for the use of the collector or other person effecting the sale of the real estate thereby conveyed.

Collector to render account of sale and pay surplus into treasury.

Form, &c., of deed.

Cost thereof.

SEC. 37. *And be it further enacted*, That with respect to property lying within any collection district not owned or occupied or superintended by some person residing in such collection district, and on which the tax shall not have been paid to the collector within ninety days after the day on which he shall have received the collection lists from the said assessors, respectively, as aforesaid, or the requisition of the Secretary of the Treasury, as aforesaid, the collector shall transmit lists of the same to one of the collectors within the same State, to be designated for that purpose by the Secretary of the Treasury; and the collector, who shall have been thus designated by the Secretary of the Treasury, shall transmit receipts for all the lists received, as aforesaid, to the collector transmitting the same; and the collectors, thus designated in each State by the Secretary of the Treasury, shall cause notifications of the taxes due as aforesaid, and contained in the lists thus transmitted to them, to be published for sixty days in at least one of the newspapers published in the State; and the owners of the property, on which such taxes may be due, shall be permitted to pay to such collector the said tax, with an addition of ten per centum thereon; *Provided*, that such payment is made within one year after the day on which the collector of the district where such property lies had notified that the tax had become due on the same.

Method for collection of tax on property of non residents.

SEC. 38. *And be it further enacted*, That when any tax, as aforesaid, shall have remained unpaid for the term of one year, as aforesaid, the collector in the State where the property lies, and who shall have been designated by the Secretary of the Treasury, as aforesaid, having first advertised the same for sixty days in at least one newspaper in the State, shall proceed to sell, at public sale, so much of the said property as may be necessary to satisfy the taxes due thereon, together with an addition of twenty per centum thereon; or if such property is not divisible, as aforesaid, the whole thereof shall be sold, and accounted for in the manner hereinbefore provided. If the property advertised for sale cannot be sold for the amount of the tax due thereon, with the said addition thereon, the collector shall purchase the same in behalf of the United States for such amount and addition. And the collector

Property may be sold when tax has remained unpaid one year.

Provision as to sale, &c.

shall render a distinct account of the charges incurred in offering and advertising for sale such property, and pay into the treasury the surplus, if any, of the aforesaid addition of ten or twenty per centum, as the case may be, after defraying the said charges.

Collectors to deposit with clerk of court lists of property sold.

SEC. 39. *And be it further enacted*, That the collectors, designated as aforesaid by the Secretary of the Treasury, shall deposit with the clerks of the district court of the United States in the respective States, and within which district the property lies, correct lists of the tracts of land or other real property sold by virtue of this act for non-payment of taxes, together with the names of owners or presumed owners, and of the purchasers of the same at the public sales aforesaid, and of the amount paid by said purchasers for the same; the owners, their heirs, executors, or administrators, or any person in their behalf, shall have liberty to redeem the lands or other property sold, as aforesaid, within two years from the time of sale, upon payment to the clerk aforesaid, for the use of the purchaser, his heirs, or assigns, of the amount paid by such purchaser for the said land, or other real property, with interest for the same at the rate of twenty per centum per annum, and of a commission of five per centum on such payment for the use of the clerk aforesaid. The clerks shall, on application, pay to the purchasers the moneys thus paid for their use; and the collectors, respectively, shall give deeds for the lands or property aforesaid to the purchasers entitled to the same, in all cases where the same shall not have been redeemed within two years, as aforesaid, by the original owners thereof, or their legal representatives, or any person in their behalf, and deposit such deeds with such clerk. And the said clerk shall be entitled to receive from the purchaser, for his own use, the sum of one dollar, in addition to the sum hereinbefore made payable to the collector, for every such deed, to be paid on the delivery thereof to such purchasers. And in all cases where lands may be sold under this act for the payment of taxes, belonging to infants, persons of insane mind, married women, or persons beyond sea, such persons shall have the term of two years after their respective disabilities shall have been removed, or their return to the United States, to redeem lands thus sold, on their paying into the clerk's office aforesaid the amount paid by the purchaser, with fifty per centum addition thereto, together with ten per centum interest per annum on the aggregate sum, and on their payment to the purchaser of the land aforesaid a compensation for all improvements he may have made on the premises subsequent to his purchase, the value of which improvements to be ascertained by three or more neighboring freeholders, to be appointed by the clerk aforesaid, who, on an actual view of the premises, shall assess the value of such improvements, on their oaths, and make return of such valuation to the clerk immediately. And the clerk of the court shall receive such compensation for his services herein, to be paid by and received from the parties, like costs of suit, as the judge of the district court shall in that respect tax and allow.

Right of redemption.

Proceedings.

Clerk's fees.

In regard to property of infants, insane, married women, and persons beyond the sea, sold for taxes.

Redemption, how made.

Improvements

Pay of clerk.

Collector to transmit monthly to Secretary of the Treasury statement of collections, pay over quarterly, &c.

SEC. 40. *And be it further enacted*, That the several collectors shall, at the expiration of every month after they shall, respectively, commence their collections in the next and every ensuing year, transmit to the Secretary of the Treasury a statement of the collections made by them, respectively, within the month, and pay over quarterly, or sooner, if required by the Secretary of the Treasury, the moneys by them respectively collected within the said term; and each of the said collectors shall complete the collection of all sums annually assigned to him for collection, as aforesaid, shall pay over the same into the treasury, and shall render his final account to the Treasury Department, within six months from and after the day when he shall have received the collection lists from the said board of assessors or the said requisition of the Secretary of the Treasury, as aforesaid: *Provided, however*, That the period of one year and three months from the said annual day shall be annually allowed to the collector designated in each State, as aforesaid, by the Secretary of the Treasury, with respect to the taxes contained in the list transmitted to him by the other collectors, as aforesaid.

Final accounts to be rendered half yearly.

Proviso granting fifteen months for taxes on lists transmitted to him by the collector.

SEC. 41. *And be it further enacted*, That each collector shall be charged with the whole amount of taxes by him receipted, whether contained in the lists delivered to him by the principal assessors, respectively, or transmitted to him by other collectors; and shall be allowed credit for the amount of taxes contained in the lists transmitted in the manner above provided to other collectors, and by them receipted as aforesaid; and also for the taxes of such persons as may have absconded, or become insolvent, subsequent to the date of the assessment, and prior to the day when the tax ought, according to the provisions of this act, to have been collected: *Provided*, That it shall be proved to the satisfaction of the First Comptroller of the Treasury that due diligence was used by the collector, and that no property was left from which the tax could have been recovered; and each collector, designated in each State, as aforesaid, by the Secretary of the Treasury shall receive credit for the taxes due for all tracts of land which, after being offered by him for sale in manner aforesaid, shall or may have been purchased by him in behalf of the United States.

To be charged with amount of taxes receipted for by him, and credited with taxes of absconding or insolvent persons.

Secretary of the Treasury to receive credit for taxes on land puchased for the United States.

SEC. 42. *And be it further enacted*, That if any collector shall fail either to collect or to render his account, or to pay over in the manner or within the times hereinbefore provided, it shall be the duty of the First Comptroller of the Treasury, and he is hereby authorized and required, immediately after such delinquency, to report the same to the Solicitor of the Treasury, who shall issue a warrant of distress against such delinquent collector and his sureties, directed to the marshal of the district, therein expressing the amount of the taxes with which the said collector is chargeable, and the sums, if any, which have been paid. And the said marshal shall, himself, or by his deputy, immediately proceed to levy and collect the sum which may remain due, by distress and sale of the goods and chattels, or any personal effects of the delinquent collector; and for want of goods, chattels, or effects aforesaid, sufficient to satisfy the said warrant, the same may be levied on the person of the collector, who may be committed to prison, there to remain until discharged in due course of law; and furthermore, notwithstanding the commitment of the collector to prison, as aforesaid, or if he abscond, and goods, chattels, and effects cannot be found sufficient to satisfy the said warrant, the said marshal or his deputy shall and may proceed to levy and collect the sum which remains due, by

Proceedings to be taken against delinquent collectors.

Personal property to be seized and sold.

Arrest.

Sale of personal effects of collector and sureties.

distress and sale of the goods and chattels, or any personal effects, of the surety or sureties of the delinquent collector. And the amount of the sums due from any collector, as aforesaid, shall, and the same are hereby declared to be a lien upon the lands and real estate of such collector and his sureties, until the same shall be discharged according to law. And for want of goods and chattels, or other personal effects of such collector or his sureties, sufficient to satisfy any warrant of distress, issued pursuant to the preceding section of this act, the lands and real estate of such collector and his sureties, or so much thereof as may be necessary for satisfying the said warrant, after being advertised for at least three weeks in not less than three public places in the collection district, and in one newspaper printed in the county or district, if any there be, prior to the proposed time of sale, may and shall be sold by the marshal or his deputy; and for all lands and real estate sold in pursuance of the authority aforesaid, the conveyances of the marshals or their deputies, executed in due form of law, shall give a valid title against all persons claiming under delinquent collectors or their sureties aforesaid. And all moneys that may remain of the proceeds of such sale, after satisfying the said warrant of distress, and paying the reasonable costs and charges of sale, shall be returned to the proprietor of the lands or real estate sold as aforesaid.

Sums due from collector to be a lien on his lands, and those of his sureties.

Real estate may be sold.

Title under tax deed.

Balance, if any, after satisfying warrant of distress, &c., to be returned to proprietor.

Penalty on collector and deputy for extortion, &c.

SEC. 43. *And be it further enacted*, That each and every collector, or his deputy, who shall exercise or be guilty of any extortion or oppression, under color of this act, or shall demand other or greater sums than shall be authorized by this act, shall be liable to pay a sum not exceeding two thousand dollars, to be recovered by and for the use of the party injured, with costs of suit, in any court having competent jurisdiction; and each and every collector, or his deputies, shall give receipts for all sums by them collected and retained in pursuance of this act.

Accounts, how to be kept at Treasury Department, of moneys received.

Secretary of the Treasury to report accounts to Congress annually.

SEC. 44. *And be it further enacted*, That separate accounts shall be kept at the treasury of all moneys received from the direct tax, and from the internal duties, or income tax, in each of the respective States, Territories, and District of Columbia, and collection districts; and that separate accounts shall be kept of the amount of each species of duty that shall accrue, with the moneys paid to the collectors, assessors, and assistant assessors, and to the other officers employed in each of the respective States, Territories, and collection districts, which accounts it shall be the duty of the Secretary of the Treasury, annually, in the month of December, to lay before Congress.

Assessors to make out lists of transfers and changes of real estate.

SEC. 45. *And be it further enacted*, That the assessors, respectively, shall, yearly and in every year, after the expiration of one year from the second Tuesday of February next, inquire and ascertain, in the manner by the fourteenth section of this act provided, what transfers and changes of property in lands, lots of ground, buildings, and dwelling-houses have been made and effected in their respective districts, subsequent to the next preceding valuation, assessment, and apportionment of the direct tax by this act laid; and within twenty days thereafter they shall make out three lists of such transfers and changes, and transmit one list to the Secretary of the Treasury, another list to the commissioner of taxes, and the third shall be delivered to the collector of the collection district. And it shall yearly, and every year, after the said year one thousand eight hundred and sixty-two, be the duty of the Secretary of the Treasury to notify the collectors of the several collection districts the day on which it shall be the duty of the said collectors to commence laying and collecting the annual direct tax by this act laid and imposed, according to the assessment of the tax lists to them delivered by the said assessors, as aforesaid, subject only to such alterations therein as shall be just and proper, in the opinion of the Secretary of the Treasury, to conform to the transfers and changes aforesaid, ascertained by the assessors aforesaid; and the said collectors shall, annually, in all respects, proceed in and conclude the collection of the said direct tax in the same manner and within the time hereinbefore provided and prescribed.

Duty of collectors.

SEC. 46. *And be it further enacted*, That in case any State, Territory, or the District of Columbia, after notice given of its intention to assume and pay, or to levy, collect, and pay said direct tax herein provided for and apportioned to said State, Territory, or District, shall, in any year after the taking effect of this act, fail to pay the amount of said direct tax, or any part thereof, as provided in this act, in such cases it shall be lawful for the Secretary of the Treasury of the United States to appoint United States assessors, assistant assessors, and collectors, as in this act provided, whose duty it shall be to proceed forthwith, under such regulations as the said Secretary of the Treasury shall prescribe, to collect all or any part of said direct tax the same as though said State, Territory, or District had not given notice, nor assumed to levy, collect, and pay said taxes, or any part thereof.

Proceedings if any State fails to pay, &c., her quota of the tax

SEC. 47. *And be it further enacted*, That any person who shall be convicted of wilfully taking a false oath or affirmation in any of the cases in which an oath or affirmation is required to be taken by this act, shall be liable to the pains and penalties to which persons are liable for wilful and corrupt perjury, and shall, moreover, forfeit the sum of five hundred dollars.

Penalty for taking false oath or affirmation.

SEC. 48. *And be it further enacted*, That there shall be allowed to the collectors appointed under this act, in full compensation for their services and that of their deputies in carrying this act into effect, a commission of four per centum upon the first hundred thousand dollars, one per centum upon the second one hundred thousand dollars, and one half of one per centum upon all sums above two hundred thousand dollars; such commissions to be computed upon the amounts by them respectively paid over and accounted for under the instructions of the Treasury Department: *Provided*, That in no case shall such commissions exceed the sum of four thousand dollars for a principal officer, and two thousand dollars for an assistant. And there shall be further allowed to each collector their necessary and reasonable charges for stationery and blank books used in the performance of their official duties, which, after being duly examined and certified by the commissioner of taxes, shall be paid out of the treasury.

Pay of collectors and deputies.

Commissions.

Proviso limiting salary.

Allowance for stationery, blank books, &c.

SEC. 49. *And be it further enacted*, That, from and after the first day of January next, there shall be levied, collected, and paid, upon the annual income of every person residing in the United States, whether such income is derived from any kind of property, or from any profession, trade, employment, or vocation carried on in the United States or elsewhere, or from any other source whatever, if such annual income exceeds the sum of eight hundred dollars, a tax of three per centum on the amount of such excess of such income above eight hundred dollars: *Provided*, That upon such portion of said income as shall be derived from interest upon treasury notes or other securities of the United States, there shall be levied, collected, and paid a tax of one and one-half per centum. Upon the income, rents, or dividends accruing upon any property, securities, or stocks owned in the United States by any citizen of the United States residing abroad, there shall be levied, collected, and paid a tax of five per centum, excepting that portion of said income derived from interest on treasury notes and other securities of the government of the United States, which shall pay one and one-half per centum. The tax herein provided shall be assessed upon the annual income of the persons hereinafter named for the year next preceding the time for assessing said tax, to wit, the year next preceding the first of January, eighteen hundred and sixty-two; and the said taxes, when so assessed and made public, shall become a lien on the property or other sources of said income for the amount of the same, with the interest and other expenses of collection until paid: *Provided*, That, in estimating said income, all national, State, or local taxes assessed upon the property, from which the income is derived, shall be first deducted.

Excess over $800 to be taxed three per cent.

Proviso imposing a tax on income from treasury notes of one and a half per cent.

Citizens of the United States residing abroad to pay a tax of five per cent. on income, excepting as above.

Assessment, when made.

Lien

Income, how to be estimated.

SEC. 50. *And be it further enacted*, That it shall be the duty of the President of the United States, and he is hereby authorized, by and with the advice and consent of the Senate, to appoint one principal assessor and one principal collector in each of the States and Territories of the United States, and in the District of Columbia, to assess and collect the internal duties or income tax imposed by this act, with authority in each of said officers to appoint so many assistants as the public service may require, to be approved by the Secretary of the Treasury. The said taxes to be assessed and collected under such regulations as the Secretary of the Treasury may prescribe. The said collectors, herein authorized to be appointed, shall give bonds, to the satisfaction of the Secretary of the Treasury, in such sums as he may prescribe, for the faithful performance of their respective duties. And the Secretary of the Treasury shall prescribe such reasonable compensation for the assessment and collection of said internal duties or income tax as may appear to him just and proper; not, however, to exceed in any case the sum of two thousand five hundred dollars per annum for the principal officers herein referred to, and twelve hundred dollars per annum for an assistant. The assistant collectors herein provided shall give bonds to the satisfaction of the principal collector for the faithful performance of their duties. The Secretary of the Treasury is further authorized to select and appoint one or more depositaries in each State for the deposit and safe-keeping of the moneys arising from the taxes herein imposed when collected, and the receipt of the proper officer of such depositary to the collector for the moneys deposited by him shall be the proper voucher for such collector in the settlement of his account at the Treasury Department. And he is further authorized and empowered to make such officer or depositary the disbursing agent of the treasury for the payment of all interest due to the citizens of such State upon the treasury notes or other

Mode of assessing and collecting income tax.

Collector to give bond.

Pay.

Assistant collector's bond.

Depositaries.

Depositaries to be disbursing agents.

government securities issued by authority of law. And he shall also prescribe the forms of returns to be made to the department by all assessors and collectors appointed under the authority of this act. He shall also prescribe the form of oath or obligation to be taken by the several officers authorized or directed to be appointed and commissioned by the President under this act, before a competent magistrate duly authorized to administer oaths, and the form of the return to be made thereon to the Treasury Department.

Form of return.

Form of oath.

SEC. 51. *And be it further enacted*, That the tax herein imposed by the forty-ninth section of this act shall be due and payable on or before the thirtieth day of June, in the year eighteen hundred and sixty-two, and all sums due and unpaid at that day shall draw interest thereafter at the rate of six per centum per annum; and if any person or persons shall neglect or refuse to pay after due notice, said tax assessed against him, her, or them, for the space of more than thirty days after the same is due and payable, it shall be lawful for any collector or assistant collector charged with the duty of collecting such tax, and they are hereby authorized, to levy the same on the visible property of any such person, or so much thereof as may be sufficient to pay such tax, with the interest due thereon, and the expenses incident to such levy and sale, first giving thirty days' public notice of the time and place of the sale thereof; and in case of the failure of any person or persons authorized to act as agent or agents for the collection of the rents or other income of any person residing abroad shall neglect or refuse to pay the tax assessed thereon (having had due notice) for more than thirty days after the thirtieth of June, eighteen hundred and sixty-two, the collector or his assistant, for the district where such property is located, or rents or income is payable, shall be and hereby is authorized to levy upon the property itself, and to sell the same, or so much thereof as may be necessary to pay the tax assessed, together with the interest and expenses incident to such levy and sale, first giving thirty days' public notice of the time and place of sale. And in all cases of the sale of property herein authorized, the conveyance by the officer authorized to make the sale, duly executed, shall give a valid title to the purchaser, whether the property sold be real or personal. And the several collectors and assistants appointed under the authority of this act may, if they find no property to satisfy the taxes assessed upon any person by authority of the forty-ninth section of this act, and which such person neglects to pay as hereinbefore provided, shall have power, and it shall be their duty, to examine under oath the person assessed under this act, or any other person, and may sell at public auction, after ten days' notice, any stock, bonds, or choses in action, belonging to said person, or so much thereof as will pay such tax and the expenses of such sale; and in case he refuses to testify, the said several collectors and assistants shall have power to arrest such person and commit him to prison, to be held in custody until the same shall be paid, with interest thereon, at the rate of six per centum per annum, from the time when the same was payable as aforesaid, and all fees and charges of such commitment and custody. And the place of custody shall in all cases be the same provided by law for the custody of persons committed for any cause by the authority of the United States, and the warrant

When income tax is payable.

Proceedings to enforce payment.

Levy.

Sale after notice

Title under tax sale.

Examinations

Sales of stocks, &c.

Penalty for refusing to testify.

Place of custody

of the collector, stating the cause of commitment, shall be sufficient authority to the proper officer for receiving and keeping such person in custody until the amount of said tax and interest, and all fees and the expense of such custody, shall have been fully paid and discharged; which fees and expenses shall be the same as are chargeable under the laws of the United States in other cases of commitment and custody. And it shall be the duty of such collector to pay the expenses of such custody, and the same, with his fees, shall be allowed on settlement of his accounts. And the person so committed shall have the same right to be discharged from such custody as may be allowed by the laws of the State or Territory, or the District of Columbia, where he is so held in custody, to persons committed under the laws of such State or Territory, or District of Columbia, for the non-payment of taxes, and in the manner provided by such laws; or he may be discharged at any time by order of the Secretary of the Treasury.

Custody, fees and expense of.

Custody, discharge from.

If any State is in rebellion, when this act goes into operation, act to be executed, when, &c

SEC. 52. *And be it further enacted*, That should any of the people of any of the States or Territories of the United States, or the District of Columbia, be in actual rebellion against the authority of the government of the United States at the time this act goes into operation, so that the laws of the United States cannot be executed therein, it shall be the duty of the President, and he is hereby authorized, to proceed to execute the provisions of this act within the limits of such State or Territory, or District of Columbia, so soon as the authority of the United States therein is re-established, and to collect the sums which would have been due from the persons residing or holding property or stocks therein, with the interest due, at the rate of six per centum per annum thereon until paid in the manner and under the regulations prescribed in the foregoing sections of this act.

Each State may collect and pay its quota of the direct tax in its own way.

Proceedings in such case.

SEC. 53. *And be it further enacted*, That any State or Territory and the District of Columbia may lawfully assume, assess, collect, and pay into the treasury of the United States the direct tax, or its quota thereof, imposed by this act upon the State, Territory, or the District of Columbia, in its own way and manner, by and through its own officers, assessors, and collectors; that it shall be lawful to use for this purpose the last or any subsequent valuation, list, or appraisal made by State or territorial authority for the purpose of State or territorial taxation therein, next preceding the date when this act takes effect, to make any laws or regulations for these purposes, to fix or change the compensation to officers, assessors, and collectors; and any such State, Territory or District, which shall give notice by the governor, or other proper officer thereof, to the Secretary of the Treasury of the United States, on or before the second Tuesday of February next, and in each succeeding year thereafter, of its intention to assume and pay, or to assess, collect, and pay into the treasury of the United States, the direct tax imposed by this act, shall be entitled, in lieu of the compensation, pay per diem and percentage herein prescribed and allowed to assessors, assistant assessors, and collectors of the United States, to a deduction of fifteen per centum on the quota of direct tax apportioned to such State, Territory or the District of Columbia levied and collected by said State, Territory, and District of Columbia through its said officers: *Provided, however*, That the deduction shall only be made to

Deduction in such case of 15 per cent. if paid by June 30.

apply to such part or parts of the same as shall have been actually paid into the treasury of the United States on or before the last day of June in the year to which such payment relates, and a deduction of ten per centum to such part or parts of the same as shall have been actually paid into the treasury of the United States on or before the last day of September in the year to which such payment relates, such year being regarded as commencing on the first day of April: *And provided further*, That whenever notice of the intention to make such payment by the State, or Territory and the District of Columbia shall have been given to the Secretary of the Treasury, in accordance with the foregoing provisions, no assessors, assistant assessors, or collectors, in any State, Territory, or District, so giving notice, shall be appointed, unless said State, Territory, or District shall be in default: *And provided, further*, That the amount of direct tax apportioned to any State, Territory, or the District of Columbia, shall be liable to be paid and satisfied, in whole or in part, by the release of such State, Territory, or District, duly executed, to the United States, of any liquidated and determined claim of such State, Territory, or District, of equal amount against the United States: *Provided*, That, in case of such release, such State, Territory, or District shall be allowed the same abatement of the amount of such tax as would be allowed in case of payment of the same in money.

Ten per cent. if paid by September 30.

No assessors to be appointed in such case.

State may pay its tax by releasing claim against the United States.

Proviso allowing abatement as in case of payment.

SEC. 54. *And be it further enacted*, That it shall be the duty of the collectors aforesaid in their respective districts, and they are hereby authorized, to collect the duties imposed by this act, and to prosecute for the recovery of the same, and for the recovery of any sum or sums which may be forfeited by virtue of this act; and all fines, penalties, and forfeitures which shall be incurred by force of this act, shall and may be sued for and recovered in the name of the United States or of the collector within whose district any such fine, penalty, or forfeiture shall have been incurred, by bill, plaint, or information; one moiety thereof to the use of the United States, and the other moiety thereof to the use of such collector.

Duty of collectors.

Fines and penalties, how recovered.

SEC. 55. *And be it further enacted*, That the amount of all debts due to the United States by any collector, under this act, whether secured by bond or otherwise, shall and are hereby declared to be a lien upon the lands and real estate of such collector, and of his sureties, if he shall have given bond, from the time when suit shall be instituted for recovering the same; and, for want of goods and chattels and other personal effects of such collector or his sureties to satisfy any judgment which shall or may be recovered against them, respectively, such lands and real estate may be sold at public auction, after being advertised for at least three weeks in not less than three public papers within the collection district, and in one newspaper printed in the county, if any there be, at least six weeks prior to the time of sale; and for all lands or real estate sold in pursuance of the authority aforesaid, the conveyances of the marshals or their deputies, executed in due form of law, shall give a valid title against all persons claiming under such collector or his sureties, respectively.

Debts due from collector to the United States to be a lien on his real estate and that of his sureties

SEC. 56. *And be it further enacted*, That, for superintending the collection of the direct tax and internal duties or income tax laid by this act, an officer is hereby authorized in the Treasury

Office of commissioner of taxes created.

Department, to be called "Commissioner of Taxes," who shall be charged, under the direction of the Secretary, with preparing all the forms necessary for the assessment and collection of the tax and duties aforesaid, with preparing, signing, and distributing all such licenses as are required, and with the general superintendence of all the officers employed in assessing and collecting said tax and duties; said commissioner shall be appointed by the President, upon the nomination of the Secretary of the Treasury, and he shall receive an annual salary of three thousand dollars. The Secretary of the Treasury may assign the necessary clerks to the office of said commissioner, whose aggregate salaries shall not exceed six thousand dollars per annum, and the amount required to pay the salaries of said commissioner and clerks is hereby appropriated.

Authority, duty, salary.

Clerks.

If a collector is sick, deputy may act, &c.

SEC. 57. *And be it further enacted*, That in case of the sickness or temporary disability of a collector to discharge such of his duties as cannot, under existing laws, be discharged by a deputy, they may be devolved by him upon a deputy: *Provided*, Information thereof be immediately communicated to the Secretary of the Treasury, and shall not be disapproved by him: *And provided*, That the responsibility of the collector or his sureties to the United States shall not be thereby affected or impaired.

If collector dies, resigns, &c., who to act in his place.

SEC. 58. *And be it further enacted*, That in case a collector shall die, resign, or be removed, the deputy of such collector longest in service at the time immediately preceding, who shall have been longest employed by him, may and shall, until a successor shall be appointed, discharge all the duties of said collector, and for whose conduct, in case of the death of the collector, his estate shall be responsible to the United States.

Approved August 5, 1861.

AN ACT

For the collection of direct taxes in insurrectionary districts within the United States, and for other purposes.

CHAP. XCVIII.
June 7, 1862.

Be it enacted by the Senate and House of Representatives of the United States of America in Congress assembled, That when in any State or Territory, or in any portion of any State or Territory, by reason of insurrection or rebellion, the civil authority of the government of the United States is obstructed, so that the provisions of the act entitled "An act to provide increased revenue from imports to pay interest on the public debt, and for other purposes," approved August fifth, eighteen hundred and sixty-one, for assessing, levying, and collecting the direct taxes therein mentioned, cannot be peaceably executed, the said direct taxes, by said act apportioned among the several States and Territories, respectively, shall be apportioned and charged in each State and Territory, or part thereof, wherein the civil authority is thus obstructed, upon all the lands and lots of ground situate therein, respectively, except such as are exempt from taxation by the laws of said State or of the United States, as the said lands or lots of ground were enumerated and valued under the last assessment

Act Aug. 5, 1861.

Direct tax to be charged in insurrectionary districts to all lands.

Lands to be valued.

and valuation thereof made under the authority of said State or Territory previous to the first day of January, anno Domini eighteen hundred and sixty-one; and each and every parcel of the said lands, according to said valuation, is hereby declared to be, by virtue of this act, charged with the payment of so much of the whole tax laid and apportioned by said act upon the State or Territory wherein the same is respectively situate, as shall bear the same direct proportion to the whole amount of the direct tax apportioned to said State or Territory as the value of said parcels of land shall respectively bear to the whole valuation of the real estate in said State or Territory according to the said assessment and valuation made under the authority of the same; and in addition thereto a penalty of fifty per centum of said tax shall be charged thereon.

Lands to be charged with the tax according to valuation.

Penalty.

SEC. 2. *And be it further enacted*, That on or before the first day of July next, the President, by his proclamation, shall declare in what States and parts of States said insurrection exists, and thereupon the said several lots or parcels of land shall become charged respectively with their respective portions of said direct tax, and the same together with the penalty shall be a lien thereon, without any other or further proceeding whatever.

Proclamation declaring the districts in insurrection.

SEC. 3. *And be it further enacted*, That it shall be lawful for the owner or owners of said lots or parcels of lands, within sixty days after the tax commissioners herein named shall have fixed the amount, to pay the tax thus charged upon the same, respectively, into the Treasury of the United States, or to the commissioners herein appointed, and take a certificate thereof, by virtue whereof the said lands shall be discharged from said tax.

Owners may pay tax in sixty days after the amount is fixed.

SEC. 4. *And be it further enacted*, That the title of, in, and to each and every piece or parcel of land upon which said tax has not been paid as above provided, shall thereupon become forfeited to the United States, and, upon the sale hereinafter provided for, shall vest in the United States or in the purchasers at such sale, in fee simple, free and discharged from all prior liens, encumbrances, right, title, and claim whatsoever.

Title forfeited to United States or in purchasers under this act.

SEC. 5. *And be it further enacted*, That the President of the United States, by and with the advice and consent of the Senate, may appoint a board of three tax commissioners for each of said States in which such insurrection exists, with a salary of three thousand dollars each per annum, to give security in the sum of fifty thousand dollars each, in such form as the Secretary of the Treasury shall direct, and to be approved by him, for the faithful performance of all their duties as such, and to account for and pay over all moneys and other property coming to their hands: *Provided*, That said commissioners shall not receive pay under the provisions of this act until they shall have entered upon the discharge of their duties.

Tax commissioners appointed

Salary.

Security.

Salary to commence on entry upon duties.

SEC. 6. *And be it further enacted*, That the said board of tax commissioners shall enter upon the discharge of the duties of their office whenever the commanding general of the forces of the United States, entering into any such insurrectionary State or district, shall have established the military authority of the United States throughout any parish or district or county of the same, and they shall open one or more offices for the transaction of business.

Time of commissioners entering upon duty.

SEC. 7. *And be it further enacted*, That the said board of com-

Commissioners to give notice of sale of lands.

Act Feb. 6, 1863.

missioners shall be required, in case the taxes charged upon the said lots and parcels of land shall not be paid as provided for in the third section of this act, to cause the same to be advertised for sale in a newspaper published in the town, parish, district, or county where situate, and if there be no such newspaper published in said county, or if the publisher thereof refuse to publish the same, then in any other newspaper to be selected by said commissioners in said district, or in the city of Washington, for at least four weeks, and by posting notices of said sale in three public places in the town, parish, district, or county within which said lands are situate, at least four weeks previous to the day of sale; and at the time and place of sale to cause the same to be severally sold to the highest bidder for a sum not less than the taxes, penalty, and costs, and ten per centum per annum interest on said tax pursuant to said notice; and the said commissioners shall, at said sale, strike off the same severally to the United States at that sum, unless some person shall bid the same or a larger sum; who shall, upon paying the purchase money in gold and silver coin, or in treasury notes of the United States, or in certificates of indebtedness against the United States, be entitled to receive from said commissioners their certificate of sale; which said certificate shall be received in all courts and places as prima facie evidence of the regularity and validity of said sale, and of the title of said purchaser or purchasers under the same: *Provided*, That the owner of said lots of ground, or any loyal person of the United States, having any valid lien upon or interest in the same, may, at any time, within sixty days after said sale, appear before the said board of tax commissioners in his or her own proper person, and, if a citizen, upon taking an oath to support the Constitution of the United States, and paying the amount of said tax and penalty, with interest thereon from the date of the said proclamation of the President mentioned in the second section of this act, at the rate of fifteen per centum per annum, together with the expenses of the sale and subsequent proceedings to be determined by said commissioners, may redeem said lots of land from said sale; and any purchaser, under the same, having paid moneys, treasury notes, or other certificates of indebtedness of the United States, shall, upon such redemption being made, be entitled to have the same, with the interest accruing after said sale, returned to him by the said commissioners, upon surrendering up the certificates of sale: *And provided, further*, That if the owner of said lots of ground shall be a minor, a non-resident alien, or loyal citizen beyond seas, a person of unsound mind, or under a legal disability, the guardian, trustee, or other person having charge of the person or estate of such person may redeem the same at any time within two years after the sale thereof, in the manner above provided, and with like effect: *And provided, further*, That the certificate of said commissioners shall only be affected as evidence of the regularity and validity of sale by establishing the fact that said property was not subject to taxes, or that the taxes had been paid previous to sale, or that the property had been redeemed according to the provisions of this act.

Conditions of sale.

Land may be redeemed within sixty days.

Conditions of redemption.

Two years allowed for aliens, minors, and loyal citizens abroad.

Certificate of commissioners evidence of regularity and validity of sale.

SEC. 8. *And be it further enacted*, That at any time within one year after the said sale by said commissioners, any person being the owner of any lot or parcel of ground at the passage of this act, who shall, by sufficient evidence, prove to the satisfaction of said board of commissioners that he or she, after the passage of this act, has not taken part in the present insurrection against the United States, or in any manner aided or abetted the same; and that, by reason of said insurrection, he or she has been unable to pay said tax, or to redeem said lands from sale within the time above provided for, the said board of commissioners may allow him or her further time to redeem the same, not exceeding two years from the day of sale; and for this purpose they may take the testimony of witnesses, and shall reduce the same to writing; and the United States, or any person claiming an interest in said lands, may appear and oppose the said application. From their decision the United States or any party in interest may appeal to the district court of the United States for said district, which is hereby authorized to take jurisdiction of the same, as in other cases involving the equity of redemption. And in case said board of commissioners should, for any cause, cease to act before the expiration of one year after said sales, the said district court shall have original jurisdiction of the proceeding for redemption, as herein provided, to take place before the said board of commissioners.

Commissioners may allow two years for redemption.

May appeal to district court.

SEC. 9. *And be it further enacted*, That in cases where the owners of said lots and parcels of ground have abandoned the same, and have not paid the tax thereon as provided for in the third section of this act, nor paid the same, nor redeemed the said land from sale as provided for in the seventh section of this act, and the said board of commissioners shall be satisfied that said owners have left the same to join the rebel forces or otherwise to engage in and abet this rebellion, and the same shall have been struck off to the United States at said sale, the said commissioners shall, in the name of the United States, enter upon and take possession of the same, and may lease the same, together or in parcels, to any person or persons who are citizens of the United States, or may have declared on oath their intention to become such, until the said rebellion and insurrection in said State shall be put down, and the civil authority of the United States established, and until the people of said State shall elect a legislature and State officers, who shall take an oath to support the Constitution of the United States, to be announced by the proclamation of the President, and until the first day of March next thereafter, said leases to be in such form and with such security as shall, in the judgment of said commissioners, produce to the United States the greatest revenue.

Proceedings in case of abandonment of land and non-payment of tax.

Commissioners to lease lands.

SEC. 10. *And be it further enacted*, That the said commissioners shall from time to time make such temporary rules and regulations, and insert such clauses in said leases as shall be just and proper to secure proper and reasonable employment and support, at wages or upon shares of the crop, of such persons and families as may be residing upon the said parcels or lots of land, which said rules and regulations are declared to be subject to the approval of the President.

To make rules and regulations for support of families.

SEC. 11. *And be it further enacted*, That the said board of commissioners, under the direction of the President, may be authorized, instead of leasing the said lands vested in the United States, as above provided, to cause the same, or any portion thereof, to be subdivided and sold in parcels not to exceed three hundred and twenty acres to any one purchaser, at public sale, after giving due

May sell lands to officers, soldiers, sailors, and marines

notice thereof, as upon the sale of other public lands of the United States, for sixty days, and to issue a certificate therefor; and that, at any such sale, any loyal citizen of the United States, or any person who shall have declared on oath his intention to become such, or any person who shall have faithfully served as an officer, musician, or private soldier or sailor in the army or navy or marine service of the United States, as a regular or volunteer, for the term of three months, may become the purchaser; and if upon such sale any person serving in the army or navy or marine corps shall pay one-fourth part of the purchase money, a certificate shall be given him, and he shall have the term of three years in which to pay the remainder, either in money or in certificates of indebtedness from the United States; and any citizen of the United States, or any person who shall have declared his intention to become such, being the head of a family, and residing in the State or district where said lands are situate, and not the owner of any other lands, may, under such rules as may be established by said board of commissioners, have the right to enter upon and acquire the rights of pre-emption in such lands as may be unimproved and vested in the United States, and as may be selected by said board of commissioners, under the direction of the President, from time to time, for such purpose.

Terms of sale.

Disposition of the proceeds.

SEC. 12. *And be it further enacted,* That the proceeds of said leases and sales shall be paid into the treasury of the United States, one-fourth of which shall be paid over to the governor of said State wherein said lands are situated, or his authorized agent, when such insurrection shall be put down, and the people shall elect a legislature and State officers who shall take an oath to support the Constitution of the United States, and such fact shall be proclaimed by the President, for the purpose of reimbursing the loyal citizens of said State, or for such other purpose as said State may direct; and one-fourth shall also be paid over to said State as a fund to aid in the colonization or emigration from said State of any free person of African descent who may desire to remove therefrom to Hayti, Liberia, or any other tropical State or colony.

Commissioners authorized to take evidence of value.

SEC. 13. *And be it further enacted,* That in case the records of assessment and valuation of the lots of land mentioned in the first section of this act shall be destroyed, concealed, or lost, so as not to come within the possession of the said boards of commissioners, they shall be authorized to take evidence of the same, or to value and assess the same in their own judgment upon such evidence as may appear before them; and no mistake in the valuation of the same, or in the amount of tax thereon, shall, in any manner whatever, affect the validity of the sale of the same or of any of the proceedings preliminary thereto.

Commissioners to keep record of tax assessed.

SEC. 14. *And be it further enacted,* That the said tax commissioners shall keep a book or books, in which they shall enter or cause to be entered the amount or quota of said direct tax assessed on each tract or parcel of land; which said amounts shall be distinctly stated in the advertisement, or notice of sale, together with a description of the tract to be sold, and an entry shall be made in said book, or books, of each tract sold, together with the name of the purchaser, and the sum for which the same may have been sold. A transcript or transcripts of said book or books, duly verified by said commissioners, and said books when said commission shall

Entry of sale and amount sold for.

Transcript to be sent to Secretary of the Treasury.

expire, shall be filed in the office of the Secretary of the Treasury of the United States, and said books and transcripts, and copies of said books and transcripts, duly certified by the Secretary of the Treasury, shall be evidence in any court in the United States. The said commissioners may employ a clerk, whose compensation shall be twelve hundred dollars per annum. **Clerk's salary.**

SEC. 15. *And be it further enacted*, That the thirteenth section of the act of August fifth, eighteen hundred and sixty-one, entitled "An act to provide increased revenue from imports, to pay interest on the public debt, and for other purposes," shall be so construed as not to exempt from taxation property above the value of five hundred dollars, but to exempt from taxation property of the value of five hundred dollars, or less, owned by individuals, notwithstanding the provisions of said act. **$500 exempt from taxation.**

SEC. 16. *And be it further enacted*, That this act shall take effect from and after its passage.

Approved, June 7, 1862.

AN ACT

To amend an act entitled "An act to provide increased revenue from imports, to pay interest on the public debt, and for other purposes, approved August five, eighteen hundred and sixty-one.

CHAP. LXVI.
May 13, 1862.

Be it enacted by the Senate and House of Representatives of the United States of America in Congress assembled, That the provision in the fifty-third section of the act "to provide increased revenue from imports, to pay interest on the public debt, and for other purposes," approved August five, eighteen hundred and sixty-one, allowing such portion of the tax as may be assessed by any State, Territory, or the District of Columbia "to be paid and satisfied, in whole or in part, by the release of such State, Territory, or District, duly executed, to the United States, of any liquidated and determined claim of such State, Territory, or District of equal amount against the United States: *Provided*, That in case of such release, such State, Territory, or District shall be allowed the same abatement of the amount of such tax as would be allowed in case of the payment of the same in money," shall be construed as applying to such claims of States for reimbursement of expenses incurred by them in enrolling, subsisting, clothing, supplying, arming, equipping, paying, and transporting its troops employed in aiding to suppress the present insurrection against the United States, as shall be filed with the proper officers of the United States before the thirtieth of July next. And in such cases the abatement of fifteen per centum shall be made on such portion of said tax as may be paid by the allowance of such claims, in whole or in part, the same as if the final settlement and liquidation thereof had been made before the thirtieth of June.

1861, ch. 45, § 53. Provision of former act, that State may pay its tax by release of its claims upon the United States — to apply to claims for expenses of volunteers filed before July 30, 1862.

Abatement in such case.

Approved, May 13, 1862.

3*

BY THE PRESIDENT OF THE UNITED STATES OF AMERICA:

A PROCLAMATION.*

Preamble.

Whereas, in and by the second section of an act of Congress passed on the 7th day of June, A. D. 1862, entitled "An act for the collection of direct taxes in insurrectionary districts within the United States and for other purposes," it is made the duty of the President to declare, on or before the first day of July then next following, by his proclamation, in what States and parts of States insurrection exists:

Certain States and parts of States proclaimed to be in rebellion.

Now, therefore, be it known that I, Abraham Lincoln, President of the United States of America, do hereby declare and proclaim that the States of South Carolina, Florida, Georgia, Alabama, Louisiana, Texas, Mississippi, Arkansas, Tennessee, North Carolina, and the State of Virginia, except the following counties: Hancock, Brooke, Ohio, Marshall, Wetzel, Marion, Monongalia, Preston, Taylor, Pleasants, Tyler, Ritchie, Doddridge, Harrison, Wood, Jackson, Wirt, Roane, Calhoun, Gilmer, Barbour, Tucker, Lewis, Braxton, Upshur, Randolph, Mason, Putnam, Kanawha, Clay, Nicholas, Cabell, Wayne, Boone, Logan, Wyoming, Webster, Fayette, and Raleigh, are now in insurrection and rebellion, and by reason thereof the civil authority of the United States is obstructed so that the provisions of the "Act to provide increased revenue from imports, to pay the interest on the public debt and for other purposes," approved August fifth, eighteen hundred and sixty-one, cannot be peaceably executed, and that the taxes legally chargeable upon real estate under the act last aforesaid, lying within the States and parts of States' as aforesaid, together with a penalty of fifty per centum of said taxes, shall be a lien upon the tracts or lots of the same, severally charged, till paid.

In witness whereof, I have hereunto set my hand and caused the seal of the United States to be affixed.

Done at the city of Washington, this first day of July, in the year of our Lord one thousand eight hundred and sixty-two, and of the independence of the United States of America the eighty-sixth.

[L. S.]

ABRAHAM LINCOLN.

By the President:

F. W. SEWARD, *Acting Secretary of State.*

---

* See act of June 7, 1862, § 2, p. 28.

AMENDATORY ACTS.

CHAP. 196. — An act to authorize payments in stamps, and to prohibit circulation of notes of less denomination than one dollar.

Be it enacted by the Senate and House of Representatives of the United States of America in Congress assembled, That the Secretary of the Treasury be, and he is hereby directed to furnish to the assistant treasurers, and such designated depositaries of the United States as may be by him selected, in such sums as he may deem expedient, the postage and other stamps of the United States, to be exchanged by them, on application, for United States notes; and from and after the first day of August next such stamps shall be receivable in payment of all dues to the United States less than five dollars, and shall be received in exchange for United States notes when presented to any assistant treasurer or any designated depositary selected as aforesaid in sums not less than five dollars.

Postage and other stamps to be furnished in exchange for U. S. notes, and to be received for dues less than $5.

SEC. 2. *And be it further enacted,* That from and after the first day of August, eighteen hundred and sixty-two, no private corporation, banking association, firm, or individual shall make, issue, circulate, or pay any note, check, memorandum, token, or other obligation, for a less sum than one dollar, intended to circulate as money or to be received or used in lieu of lawful money of the United States; and every person so offending shall, on conviction thereof in any district or circuit court of the United States, be punished by fine not exceeding five hundred dollars, or by imprisonment not exceeding six months, or by both, at the option of the court.

Circulation, &c. of notes less than $1, as money, prohibited.

Approved, July 17, 1862.

CHAP. 21. — An act to amend an act entitled "An act for the collection of direct taxes in insurrectionary districts within the United States and for other purposes," approved June seven, eighteen hundred and sixty-two.

Be it enacted by the Senate and House of Representatives of the United States of America in Congress assembled, That the seventh section of an act entitled "An act for the collection of direct taxes in insurrectionary districts within the United States and for other purposes," approved June seven, eighteen hundred and sixty-two, be amended so as to read as follows: SECTION 7. *And be it further enacted,* That the said board of commissioners shall be required, in case the taxes charged upon the said lots and parcels of land shall not be paid as provided for in the third section of this act, to cause the same to be advertised for sale in a newspaper published in the town, parish, district, or county where situate; and if there be no such newspaper published in said town,

Amendment of act 1862, chap. 98, sec. 7.

Tax commissioners to advertise for sale lands on which taxes are unpaid.

parish, district, or county, or if the publisher thereof refuse to publish the same, then in any other newspaper to be selected by said commissioners in said district, or in the city of Washington, for at least four weeks, and by posting notices of said sale in three public places in the town, parish, district, or county within which said lands are situate, at least four weeks previous to the day of sale; and at the time and place of sale to cause the same to be severally sold to the highest bidder for a sum not less than the taxes, penalty, and costs, and ten per centum per annum interest on said tax, pursuant to said notice; in all cases where the owner of said lots or parcels of ground shall not, on or before the day of sale, appear in person before the said board of commissioners and pay the amount of said tax, with ten per centum interest thereon, with the cost of advertising the same, or request the same to be struck off to a purchaser for a less sum than two-thirds of the assessed value of said several lots or parcels of ground, the said commissioners shall be authorized at said sale to bid off the same for the United States at a sum not exceeding two-thirds of the assessed value thereof, unless some person shall bid a larger sum; and in that case the same shall be struck off to the highest bidder, who shall, upon paying the purchase-money in gold and silver coin, or in the treasury notes of the United States, or in United States notes, or in certificates of indebtedness against the United States, be entitled to receive from said commissioners their certificate of sale; which said certificate shall be received in all courts and places as *prima facie* evidence of the regularity and validity of said sale, and of the title of the said purchaser or purchasers under the same: *Provided*, That the owner of said lots of ground, or any loyal person of the United States, having any valid lien upon or interest in the same, may at any time, within sixty days after said sale, appear before the said board of tax commissioners in his or her own proper person, and, if a citizen, upon taking an oath to support the Constitution of the United States, and paying the amount of said tax and penalty, with interest thereon from the date of the said proclamation of the President mentioned in the second section of this act, at the rate of fifteen per centum per annum, together with the expenses of the sale and subsequent proceedings, to be determined by said commissioners, may redeem said lots of land from said sale; and any purchaser under the same having paid moneys, treasury notes, or other certificates of indebtedness of the United States, shall, upon such redemption being made, be entitled to have the same, with the interest accruing after said sale, returned to him by the said commissioners, upon surrendering up the certificates of sale: *And provided further*, That if the owner of said lots of ground shall be a minor, a non-resident alien or loyal citizen beyond seas, a person of unsound mind, or under a legal disability, the guardian, trustee, or other person having charge of the person or estate of such person, may redeem the same at any time within two years after the sale thereof, and in the manner above provided, and with like effect: *And provided, further*, That at such sale any tracts, parcels, or lots of land which may be selected under the direction of the President for government use, for war, military, naval, revenue, charitable, educational, or police purposes, may, at said sale, be bid in by said commissioners, under the direction of the President, for, and struck off to the

And sell the same to highest bidder.

Payment, how made.

Certificate of sale, effect of

Owner or loyal person may redeem.

Proceedings for

Redemption where the owner is a minor, &c.

Certain tracts may be bid off for government use.

United States: *And provided, further,* That the certificate of said commissioners shall only be affected as evidence of the regularity and validity of sale, by establishing the fact that said property was not subject to taxes, or that the taxes had been paid previous to sale, or that the property had been redeemed according to the provisions of this act.

Certificate of commissioners, how impeached.

Approved, February 6, 1863.

The following extracts are incorporated among the excise laws, although it is not certain that all the provisions can be construed as appertaining to the system.

CHAP. 76. — An act to prevent and punish frauds upon the revenue, to provide for the more certain and speedy collection of claims in favor of the United States, and for other purposes.

March 3, 1863.

SEC. 5. *And be it further enacted,* That the collectors of the several districts of the United States, in all cases of seizure of any goods, wares, or merchandise, for violation of the revenue laws, the appraised value of which, in the district wherein such seizure shall be made, shall not exceed one thousand dollars, be, and they are hereby, authorized, subject to the approval of the Secretary of the Treasury, to release such goods on payment of the appraised value thereof.

Collectors may release goods upon payment of, &c.

SEC. 9. *And be it further enacted,* That, for the purpose of realizing as much as may properly be done from unproductive lands, and other property of the United States acquired under judicial proceedings or otherwise in the collection of debts, the Solicitor of the Treasury be, and he is hereby, authorized, with the approval of the Secretary of the Treasury, to rent, for a period not exceeding three years, or sell any such lands or other property at public sale, after advertising the time, place, and conditions of such sale, for three months preceding the same, in some newspaper published in the vicinity thereof, in such manner and upon such terms as may, in his judgment, be most advantageous to the public interests.

Solicitor, with the approval of the secretary, may rent lands, or sell them at public auction.

SEC. 10. *And be it further enacted,* That upon a report by a district attorney or any special attorney or agent having charge of any claim in favor of the United States, showing in detail the condition of such claim and the terms upon which the same may be compromised, and recommending that the same be compromised upon the terms so offered, and upon the recommendation of the Solicitor of the Treasury, the Secretary of the Treasury be, and he is hereby, authorized to compromise such claim accordingly.

United States claims may be compromised, by whom.

SEC. 11. *And be it further enacted,* That there shall be taxed and paid to district attorneys two per centum upon all moneys collected or realized in any suit or proceeding arising under the revenue laws conducted by them in which the United States is a party. The act in relation to costs, approved February twenty-sixth, one thousand eight hundred and fifty-three, shall not apply to such allowances, and the same shall be in lieu of all costs and fees in such suit or proceedings.

District attorneys to be allowed two per centum in lieu of fees.

Fees of district attorneys for defending suits against collectors, &c., for official acts.

SEC. 12. *And be it further enacted,* That in all suits or proceedings against collectors or other officers of the revenue for any act done by them, or for the recovery of any money exacted by or paid to such officer and by him paid into the treasury of the United States, in the performance of his official duty, in which any district or other attorney shall be directed to appear on behalf of such officer by the Secretary or Solicitor of the Treasury, or by any other proper officer of the government, such attorney shall be allowed such compensation for his services therein as shall be certified by the court in which such suit or proceedings shall be had, to be reasonable and proper, and approved by the Secretary of the Treasury. And where a recovery shall be had in any such suit or proceedings, and the court shall certify that there was probable cause for the act done by the collector or other officer, or that he acted under the directions of the Secretary of the Treasury or other proper officer of the government, no execution shall issue against such collector or other officer, but the amount so recovered shall, upon final judgment, be provided for and paid out of the proper appropriation from the treasury.

When execution may not be issued.

District attorneys to appear in suits against collectors unless otherwise instructed by secretary, and make returns annually to the solicitor of nature of returns.

SEC. 13. *And be it further enacted,* That in all suits or proceedings against collectors, or other officers of the revenue, for any act done by them, or for the recovery of any money exacted by or paid to such officers, which shall have been paid into the treasury of the United States, it shall be the duty of the respective district attorneys within the district where such suit or proceedings shall be had, unless otherwise instructed by the Secretary of the Treasury, to appear on behalf of such officers. And it shall be the duty of the several district attorneys, on the first of October of each year, to make returns to the Solicitor of the Treasury of the number of proceedings and suits commenced, pending, and determined within his district during the fiscal year next preceding the date of such returns, which returns shall show the date when such proceedings or suits in each case commenced; and if, for any reason, the determination of such proceedings or suits shall have been delayed or continued beyond the usual or reasonable period, such reasons shall be set forth, together with a statement of the measures taken by the district attorneys to press such proceedings or suits to a close. And the returns hereby directed shall be embraced in a report by the Solicitor to the Secretary of the Treasury, to be by him annually transmitted to Congress, with a statement of all moneys received by the Solicitor, and by each district attorney under the provisions of this act.

Secretary of the Treasury to transmit report to Congress annually.

Repealing limitations for commencing suits.

SEC. 14. *And be it further enacted,* That the seventeenth section of the act entitled "An act increasing temporarily the duties on imports, and for other purposes," approved July fourteenth, eighteen hundred and sixty-two, and so much of the eighty-ninth section of the act entitled "An act to regulate the collection of duties on imports and tonnage," approved March second, seventeen hundred and ninety-nine, and so much of the third section of the act entitled "An act in addition to the act for the punishment of certain crimes against the United States," approved March twenty-six, eighteen hundred and four, as impose any limitation upon the commencement of any action or proceeding for the recovery of any fine, penalty, or forfeiture incurred by reason of the violation of any law of the United States relating to the importation or entry of goods, wares, or merchandise, are hereby repealed.

Approved, March 3, 1863.

EXCISE TAX.

AN ACT

To provide internal revenue to support the government, to pay interest on the public debt, and for other purposes.

Be it enacted by the Senate and House of Representatives of the United States of America in Congress assembled, That, for the purpose of superintending the collection of internal duties, stamp duties, licenses, or taxes, imposed by this act, or which may hereafter be imposed, and of assessing the same, the Commissioner of Internal Revenue, whose annual salary shall be four thousand dollars, shall be charged, under the direction of the Secretary of the Treasury, with preparing all the instructions, regulations, directions, forms, blanks, stamps, and licenses, and distributing the same, or any part thereof, and all other matters pertaining to the assessment and collection of the duties, stamp duties, licenses, and taxes which may be necessary to carry this act into effect, and with the general superintendence of his office, as aforesaid, and shall have authority, and hereby is authorized and required, to provide cotton marks, hydrometers, and proper and sufficient adhesive stamps, and stamps or dies for expressing and denoting the several stamp duties, or the amount thereof in the case of percentage duties, imposed by this act, and to alter and renew or replace such stamps, from time to time, as occasion shall require. He may also contract for or procure the printing of requisite forms, decisions, regulations, and advertisements; but the printing of such forms, decisions, and regulations shall be done at the public printing office, unless the public printer shall be unable to perform the work. And the Secretary of the Treasury may, at any time prior to the first day of July, eighteen hundred and sixty-five, assign to the office of the Commissioner of Internal Revenue such number of clerks as he may deem necessary, or the exigencies of the public service may require; and the privilege of franking all letters and documents pertaining to the duties of his office, and of receiving free of postage all such letters and documents, is hereby extended to said Commissioner.

Commissioner of Internal Revenue.
Salary.

Duties and powers.

Secretary of the Treasury to assign clerks.
Commissioner may frank letters pertaining to the business of the office.

GENERAL PROVISIONS.

SEC. 2. *And be it further enacted*, That it shall be the duty of the Commissioner of Internal Revenue to pay over daily to the Treasurer of the United States all public moneys which may come into his possession, for which the Treasurer shall give proper receipts and keep a faithful account; and at the end of each month

Commissioner to pay over moneys daily.

Accounts to be rendered monthly

of all moneys received or paid out. the said Commissioner shall render true and faithful accounts of all public moneys received or paid out, or paid to the Treasurer of the United States, exhibiting proper vouchers therefor, and the same shall be received and examined by the Fifth Auditor of the Treasury, who shall thereafter certify the balance, if any, and transmit the accounts, with the vouchers and certificate, to the First Comptroller for his decision thereon; and the said Commissioner, when such accounts are settled as herein provided for, shall transmit a copy thereof to the Secretary of the Treasury. He shall at all times submit to the Secretary of the Treasury and the Comptroller, or either of them, the inspection of moneys in his hands, and shall, prior to the entering upon the duties of his office, execute a bond, with sufficient sureties, to be approved by the Secretary of the Treasury and by the First Comptroller, in a sum of not less than one hundred thousand dollars, payable to the United States, conditioned that said Commissioner shall faithfully perform the duties of his office according to law, and shall justly and faithfully account for and pay over to the United States, in obedience to law and in compliance with the order or regulations of the Secretary of the Treasury, all public moneys which may come into his hands or possession, and for the safekeeping and faithful account of all stamps, adhesive stamps, or vellum, parchment or paper bearing a stamp denoting any duty thereon, which bond shall be filed in the office of the First Comptroller of the Treasury. And such Commissioner shall, from time to time, renew, strengthen, and increase his official bond as the Secretary of the Treasury may direct.

Auditing of accounts.

Copy of each account when settled to be sent to Secretary.

Secretary and Comptroller may inspect moneys in Commissioners' hands.

Commissioner to give bond.

Deputy Commissioner.

Salary.

Duties and powers.

SEC. 3. *And be it further enacted,* That the Deputy Commissioner of Internal Revenue, whose annual salary shall be twenty-five hundred dollars, shall be charged with such duties in the Bureau of Internal Revenue as may be prescribed by the Secretary of the Treasury, or as may be required by law, and shall act as Commissioner of Internal Revenue in the absence of that officer, and exercise the privilege of franking all letters and documents pertaining to the office of Internal Revenue.

Revenue agents.

Duties.

Compensation.

SEC. 4. *And be it further enacted,* That the Secretary of the Treasury may appoint not exceeding five revenue agents, whose duties shall be, under the direction of the Secretary of the Treasury, to aid in the prevention, detection, and punishment of frauds upon the internal revenue, and in the enforcement of the collection thereof, who shall be paid, in addition to the expenses necessarily incurred by them such compensation as the Secretary of the Treasury may deem just and reasonable, not exceeding two thousand dollars per annum. The above salaries to be paid in the same manner as are other expenses for collecting the revenue.

Inspectors.

Duties.

Compensation

SEC. 5. *And be it further enacted,* That the Secretary of the Treasury may appoint inspectors in any assessment district where in his judgment it may be necessary for the purposes of a proper enforcement of the internal revenue laws or the detection of frauds, and such inspectors and revenue agents aforesaid shall be subject to the rules and regulations of the said Secretary, and have all the powers conferred upon any other officers of internal revenue in making any examination of persons, books, and premises which may be necessary in the discharge of the duties of their office. And the compensation of such inspectors shall be fixed and paid for such time as they may be actually employed, not exceeding four dollars per day, and their just and proper travelling expenses.

SEC. 6. *And be it further enacted,* That the cashier of internal duties, who shall hereafter be called cashier of internal revenue, and whose annual salary shall be twenty-five hundred dollars, shall perform such duties as may be assigned to his office by the Commissioner of Internal Revenue, under the regulations of the Secretary of the Treasury, and shall give a bond, with sufficient sureties to be approved by the Secretary of the Treasury and by the Solicitor, that he will faithfully account for all the moneys or other articles of value belonging to the United States which may come into his hands, and perform all the duties enjoined upon his office, according to law and regulations, as aforesaid; which bond shall be deposited with the First Comptroller of the Treasury.

Cashier. Salary. Duties and powers. To give a bond.

SEC. 7. *And be it further enacted,* That the second section of an act entitled "An act to provide internal revenue to support the government and to pay interest on the public debt," approved July one, eighteen hundred and sixty-two, shall remain and continue in full force; and the President is hereby authorized to alter the respective collection districts provided for in said section as the public interests may require.

Collection districts and appointment of assessors and collectors. Districts may be altered.

SEC. 8. *And be it further enacted,* That each assessor shall divide his district into a convenient number of assessment districts, which may be changed as often as may be deemed necessary, subject to such regulations and limitations as may be imposed by the Commissioner of Internal Revenue, within each of which the Secretary of the Treasury, whenever there shall be a vacancy or the public interest shall require, shall appoint, with the approval of the said Commissioner, one assistant assessor, who shall be a resident of the district of said assessor; and in case of a vacancy occurring in the office of assessor by reason of death or any other cause, the assistant assessor of the assessment district in which the assessor resided at the time of the vacancy occurring shall act as assessor until an appointment filling the vacancy shall be made. And each assessor and assistant assessor so appointed shall, before he enters on the duties of his office, take and subscribe, before some competent magistrate, or some collector, to be appointed by virtue of this act, (who is hereby empowered to administer the same,) the following oath or affirmation, to wit: "I, A B, do swear (or affirm, as the case may be) that I will bear true faith and allegiance to the United States of America, and will support the Constitution thereof, and that I will diligently and faithfully perform the duties of assessor (or assistant assessor) for (naming the assessment district) according to my best skill and judgment." And a certificate of such oath or affirmation shall be delivered to the collector of the district for which such assessor or assistant assessor shall be appointed.

Assessors to divide their districts into assessment districts. Appointment of asist't assessors. In case of vacancy in the office of assessor. Oath. Certificate thereof to be transmitted to collector.

SEC. 9. *And be it further enacted,* That before any collector shall enter upon the duties of his office, he shall execute a bond for such amount as shall be prescribed by the Commissioner of Internal Revenue, under the direction of the Secretary of the Treasury, with not less than five sureties to be approved by the Solicitor of the Treasury, conditioned that said collector shall faithfully perform the duties of his office according to law, and shall justly and faithfully account for and pay over to the United States, in compliance with the order or regulations of the Secre-

Collectors to give bonds. Conditions thereof.

4

tary of the Treasury, all public moneys which may come into his hands or possession; which bond shall be filed in the office of the First Comptroller of the Treasury. And such collector shall, from time to time, renew, strengthen, and increase his official bond, as the Secretary of the Treasury may direct, with such further conditions as the said Commissioner shall prescribe.

Bond may be renewed.

Deputy collectors.

SEC. 10. *And be it further enacted,* That each collector shall be authorized to appoint, by an instrument of writing under his hand, as many deputies as he may think proper, to be by him compensated for their services, and also to revoke any such appointment, giving such notice thereof as the Commissioner of Internal Revenue shall prescribe; and may require bonds or other securities, and accept the same from such deputy; and each such deputy shall have the like authority, in every respect, to collect the duties and taxes levied or assessed within the portion of the district assigned to him which is by this act vested in the collector himself; but each collector shall, in every respect, be responsible both to the United States and to individuals, as the case may be, for all moneys collected, and for every act done by any of his deputies whilst acting as such, and for every omission of duty.

Bonds may be required.

Duties and powers.

Collector responsible for acts of deputies.

Persons liable to taxation to make list or return.

SEC. 11. *And be it further enacted,* That it shall be the duty of any person, partnership, firm, association, or corporation, made liable to any duty, license, stamp, or tax imposed by law when not otherwise provided for, on or before the first Monday of May in each year, and in other cases before the day of levy, to make a list or return, verified by oath or affirmation, to the assistant assessor of the district where located, of the amount of annual income, the articles or objects charged with a special duty or tax, the quantity of goods, wares, and merchandise made or sold, and charged with a specific or ad valorem duty or tax, the several rates and aggregate amount, according to the respective provisions of this act, and according to the forms and regulations to be prescribed by the Commissioner of Internal Revenue, under the direction of the Secretary of the Treasury, for which such person, partnership, firm, association, or corporation is liable to be assessed.

Return to be made on oath.

Nature of return.

Regulations of Commiss'ner binding on all persons.

SEC. 12. *And be it further enacted,* That the instructions, regulations, and directions, as hereinbefore mentioned, shall be binding on each assessor and his assistants, and on each collector and his deputies, and on all other persons, in the performance of the duties enjoined by or under this act; pursuant to which instructions the said assessors shall, on the first Monday of May in each year, and from time to time thereafter, in accordance with this act, direct and cause the several assistant assessors to proceed through every part of their respective districts, and inquire after and concerning all persons being within the assessment districts where they respectively reside, owning, possessing, or having the care or management of any property, goods, wares, and merchandise, articles or objects liable to pay any duty, stamp, or tax, including all persons liable to pay a license or other duty, under the provisions of this act, and to make a list of the owners, and to value and enumerate the said objects of taxation respectively, by reference to any lists of assessment or collection taken under the laws of the respective States, to any other records or documents, to the written list, schedule, or return required to be made out and delivered to the assistant assessor, and by all other lawful ways

Assistant assessors to canvass districts.

Duties of assistant assessors.

and means, in the manner prescribed by this act, and in conformity with the regulations and instructions before mentioned.

SEC. 13. *And be it further enacted,* That if any person liable to pay any duty or tax, or owning, possessing, or having the care or management of property, goods, wares, and merchandise, articles or objects liable to pay any duty, tax, or license, shall fail to make and exhibit a list or return required by law, but shall consent to disclose the particulars of any and all the property, goods, wares, and merchandise, articles and objects liable to pay any duty or tax, or any business or occupation liable to pay any license, as aforesaid, then, and in that case, it shall be the duty of the officer to make such list or return, which being distinctly read, consented to, and signed and verified by oath or affirmation by the person so owning, possessing, or having the care and management as aforesaid, may be received as the list of such person.

Assistant assessor to make list for person disclosing.

List to be read to, and consented to by the person liable to tax.

To be signed and verified by oath or affirmation.

SEC. 14. *And be it further enacted,* That in case any person shall be absent from his or her residence or place of business at the time an assistant assessor shall call to receive the annual list or return, it shall be the duty of such assistant assessor to leave at such place of residence or business, with some one of suitable age and discretion, if such be present, otherwise to deposit in the nearest post office, a note or memorandum, addressed to such person, requiring him or her to present to such assessor the list or return required by law within ten days from the date of such note or memorandum, verified by oath or affirmation. And if any person, on being notified or required as aforesaid, shall refuse or neglect to give such list or return within the time required as aforesaid, or if any person shall not deliver a monthly or other list or return without notice at the time required by law, or if any person shall deliver or disclose to any assessor or assistant assessor any list, statement, or return, which, in the opinion of the assessor, is false or fraudulent, or contains any understatement or undervaluation, it shall be lawful for the assessor to summon such person, his agent, or other person having possession, custody, or care of books of account containing entries relating to the trade or business of such person, or any other persons as he may deem proper, to appear before such assessor and produce such book, at a time and place therein named, and to give testimony or answer interrogatories under oath or affirmation respecting any objects liable to duty or tax as aforesaid, or the lists, statements, or returns thereof, or any trade, business, or profession liable to any tax or license as aforesaid. Such summons may be served by any assistant assessor of the district. In case any person so summoned shall neglect or refuse to obey such summons according to its exigency, or to give testimony, or to answer interrogatories as required, it shall be lawful for the assessor, upon affidavit proving the facts, to apply to the judge of the district court, or a commissioner authorized to perform the duties of such judge at chambers, for an attachment against such person as for a contempt. It shall be the duty of such judge or commissioner to hear such application, and, if satisfactory proof be made, to issue an attachment directed to some proper officer for the arrest of such person, and upon his being brought before him to proceed to a hearing of the case, and upon such hearing the judge or commissioner shall have power to make such order as he shall deem proper to enforce obedience to the requirements of the summons and punish such person for his

Notice to be left for absent persons.

To be deposited in the post office in certain cases.

Persons neglecting to make return,

Or making fraudulent return,

May be summoned before the assessor.

Proceedings in case of failure to obey summons.

Authority and duty of judge of district court.

default or disobedience. It shall be the duty of the assessor or assistant assessor of the district within which such person shall have taxable property to enter into and upon the premises, if it be necessary, of such person so refusing or neglecting, or rendering a false or fraudulent list or return, and to make, according to the best information which he can obtain, including that derived from the evidence elicited by the examination of the assessor, and on his own view and information, such list or return, according to the form prescribed, of the property, goods, wares, and merchandise, and all articles or objects liable to duty or tax, owned or possessed or under the care or management of such person, and assess the duty thereon, including the amount, if any, due for license and income; and in case of the return of a false or fraudulent list or valuation, he shall add one hundred per centum to such duty; and in case of a refusal or neglect, except in cases of sickness or absence, to make a list or return, or to verify the same as aforesaid, he shall add fifty per centum to such duty; and in case of neglect occasioned by sickness or absence as aforesaid, the assessor may allow such further time for making and delivering such list or return as he may judge necessary, not exceeding thirty days; and the amount so added to the duty shall, in all cases, be collected by the collector at the same time and in the same manner with the duties; and the lists or returns so made and subscribed by such assessors or assistant assessors shall be taken and reputed as good and sufficient lists or returns for all legal purposes.

Assessors may enter upon premises.

May make list or return.

Penalties to be assessed.

Return of the assessor good and sufficient.

SEC. 15. *And be it further enacted*, That if any person shall deliver or disclose to any assessor or assistant assessor appointed in pursuance of law any false or fraudulent list, return, account, or statement, with intent to defeat or evade the valuation, enumeration, or assessment intended to be made, or if any person who being duly summoned to appear to testify, or to appear and produce such books as aforesaid, shall neglect to appear or to produce said books, he shall, upon conviction thereof before any circuit or district court of the United States, be fined in any sum not exceeding one thousand dollars, or be imprisoned for not exceeding one year, or both, at the discretion of the court, with costs of prosecution.

Penalty for making fraudulent return.

Or for refusing to appear and produce books.

SEC. 16. *And be it further enacted*, That whenever there shall be in any assessment district any property, goods, wares, and merchandise, articles or objects, not owned or possessed by, or under the care or management of, any person within such district, and liable to be taxed as aforesaid, and no list of which shall have been transmitted to the assistant assessor in the manner provided by this act, it shall be the duty of the assistant assessor for such district to enter into and upon the premises where such property is situated, and take such view thereof as may be necessary, and to make lists of the same, according to the form prescribed, which lists, being subscribed by the said assessor, shall be taken and reputed as good and sufficient lists of such property, goods, wares, and merchandise, articles or objects as aforesaid, for all legal purposes.

Taxable property owned by nonresident.

SEC. 17. *And be it further enacted*, That any owner or person having the care or management of property, goods, wares, and merchandise, articles or objects, not lying or being within the assessment district in which he resides, shall be permitted to make out and deliver the lists thereof required by this act (provided the

Person having taxable property in another district may make return in the district where he resides.

assessment district in which the said objects of duty or taxation are situated is therein distinctly stated) at the time and in the manner prescribed to the assistant assessor of the assessment district wherein such person resides. And it shall be the duty of the assistant assessor who receives any such list to transmit the same to the assistant assessor where such objects of taxation are situate, who shall examine such list; and if he approves the same, he shall return it to the assistant assessor from whom he received it, with his approval thereof; and if he fails to approve the same, he shall make such alterations therein and additions thereto as he may deem to be just and proper, and shall then return the said list to the assistant assessor from whom it was received, who shall proceed, in making the assessment of the tax upon the list by him so received, in all respects as if the said list had been made out by himself.

List to be transmitted to other district for examination.

SEC. 18. *And be it further enacted*, That the lists aforesaid shall, where not otherwise specially provided for, be taken with reference to the day fixed for that purpose by this act, as aforesaid, and, where duties accrue at other and different times, the lists shall be taken with reference to the time when said duties become due, and shall be denominated annual, monthly, and special lists. And the assistant assessors, respectively, after collecting the said lists, shall proceed to arrange the same, and to make two general lists—the first of which shall exhibit, in alphabetical order, the names of all persons, firms, companies, or corporations liable to pay any duty, tax, or license under this act, residing within the assessment district, together with the value and assessment or enumeration, as the case may require, of the objects liable to duty or taxation within such districts for which each such person is liable, or for which any firm, company, or corporation is liable, with the amount of duty or tax payable thereon; and the second list shall exhibit, in alphabetical order, the names of all persons residing out of the collection district, who own property within the district, together with the value and assessment or enumeration thereof, as the case may be, with the amount of duty or tax payable thereon as aforesaid. The forms of the said general list shall be devised and prescribed by the assessor, under the direction of the Commissioner of Internal Revenue, and lists taken according to such forms shall be made out by the assistant assessors and delivered to the assessor within thirty days after the day fixed by this act as aforesaid, requiring lists from individuals; or where duties, licenses, or taxes accrue at other and different times, the lists shall be delivered from time to time as they become due.

Annual, monthly, and special lists.

Two general lists to be made.

Alphabetical list of residents.

And of non-residents.

Form to be prescribed by Commissioner.

Lists to be returned by assistant within thirty days.

Other lists to be delivered from time to time.

SEC. 19. *And be it further enacted*, That the assessors for each collection district shall, by advertisement in some public newspaper published in each county within said district, if any such there be, if not, then in some newspaper in the collection district nearest thereto, and by notifications to be posted up in at least four public places within each assessment district, advertise, by not less than ten days' notice, all persons concerned, of the time and place within said county when and where appeals will be received and determined relative to any erroneous or excessive valuations, assessments, or enumerations by the assessor or assistant assessor returned in the annual list. And it shall be the duty of the assessor for each collection dis-

Annual list to be advertised.

Assessor to hold appeals.

trict, at the time fixed for hearing such appeal, as aforesaid, to submit the proceedings of the assessors and assistant assessors, and the annual lists taken and returned as aforesaid, to the inspection of any and all persons who may apply for that purpose. And the said assessor for each collection district is hereby authorized at any time to hear and determine in a summary way, according to law and right, upon any and all appeals which may be exhibited against the proceedings of the said assessors or assistant assessors: *Provided*, That no appeal shall be allowed to any party after he shall have been duly assessed, and the annual list containing the assessment has been transmitted to the collector of the district. And all appeals to the assessor, as aforesaid, shall be made in writing, and shall specify the particular cause, matter, or thing respecting which a decision is requested, and shall, moreover, state the ground or principle of error complained of. And the assessor shall have power to re-examine and determine upon the assessments and valuations and rectify the same as shall appear just and equitable; but no valuation, assessment, or enumeration shall be increased without a previous notice of at least five days to the party interested to appear and object to the same, if he judge proper, which notice shall be given by a note in writing to be left at the dwelling-house, office, or place of business of the party by such assessor, assistant assessor, or other person, or sent by mail to the nearest or usual post office address of said party: *Provided, further*, That on the hearing of appeals it shall be lawful for the assessor to require by summons the attendance of witnesses and the production of books of account in the same manner and under the same penalties as are provided in cases of refusal or neglect to furnish lists or returns. The bills for the attendance and mileage of said witnesses shall be taxed by the assessor and paid by the delinquent parties, or otherwise by the collector of the district, on certificate of the assessor, at the rates usually allowed in said district for witnesses in courts of justice.

Annual lists to be submitted to the inspection of any and all persons.

No appeal after list has been transmitted to collector.

Appeals to be made in writing.

Power of assessor.

Assessment not to be increased without five days' notice.

Witnesses may be summoned.

Books produced.

Penalties for neglect.

Fees of witnesses.

SEC. 20. *And be it further enacted*, That the said assessors of each collection district, respectively, shall, immediately after the expiration of the time for hearing appeals concerning taxes returned in the annual list, and from time to time as duties, taxes, or licenses become liable to be assessed, make out lists containing the sums payable according to law upon every object of duty or taxation for each collection district; which lists shall contain the name of each person residing within the said district, or owning or having the care or superintendence of property lying within the said district which is liable to any tax or duty, or engaged in any business or pursuit requiring a license, when such person or persons are known, together with the sums payable by each; and where there is any property within any collection district liable to the payment of the said duty or tax, not owned or occupied by or under the superintendence of any person resident therein, there shall be a separate list of such property, specifying the sum payable, and the names of the respective proprietors, when known. And the assessor making out any such separate list shall transmit to the assessor of the district, where the persons liable to pay such tax reside, or shall have their principal place of business, copies of the list of property held by persons so liable to pay such tax, to the end that the taxes assessed under the provisions of this act may be paid within the collection district where the persons

Time and method for assessors to make lists.

Contents of lists.

List of property owned by non-resident

To be transmitted to the assessor of the district where the person liable resides or has his place of business.

liable to pay the same reside, or may have their principal place of business. And in all other cases the said assessor shall furnish to the collectors of the several collection districts, respectively, within ten days after the time of hearing appeals concerning taxes returned in the annual list, and from time to time thereafter as required, a certified copy of such list or lists for their proper collection districts. And in case it shall be found or discovered by any assessor that the annual list so furnished to the proper collector, as aforesaid, is imperfect or incomplete, owing to the names of persons, firms, corporations, or objects liable to tax or duty being omitted therefrom, the said assessor may from time to time, at any time thereafter, enter on a special list all such objects of duty or taxation, with the names of persons owning or having the care or superintendence of property lying within said district liable to said tax or duty, or engaged in any business or pursuit requiring a license, with the sums payable by each, as he shall discover to have been omitted as aforesaid; and the same proceedings shall obtain and be had with respect to such objects of duty or tax as are by this act required in respect to objects of duty or taxes, and persons liable to tax regularly entered and returned on any monthly or special list: *Provided,* That the office or principal place of business of the said assessor shall be always open when he is not necessarily absent therefrom during the business hours of each day, for the hearing of appeals by parties who shall appear voluntarily before him: *Provided, further,* That it shall be in the power of the Commissioner of Internal Revenue to exonerate any assessor as aforesaid from forfeitures, in whole or in part, as to him shall appear just and equitable.

Annual lists to be sent to collectors within ten days after hearing appeals.

Amount omitted from annual list to be returned in special list.

Assessor's office to be opened during business hours

Commissioner may relieve assessors of forfeitures.

SEC. 21. *And be it further enacted,* That every assessor or assistant assessor who shall enter upon and perform the duties of his office without having taken the oath or affirmation prescribed by this act, or who shall wilfully neglect to perform any of the duties prescribed by this act at the time and in the manner herein designated, or who shall knowingly make any false or fraudulent list or valuation or assessment, or shall demand or receive any compensation, fee, or reward other than those provided for herein for the performance of any duty, or shall be guilty of extortion or wilful oppression in office, shall, upon conviction thereof in any circuit or district court of the United States having jurisdiction thereof, be subject to a fine of not exceeding one thousand dollars, or to imprisonment for not exceeding one year, or both, at the discretion of the court, and shall be dismissed from office, and shall be forever disqualified from holding any office under the government of the United States. And one half of the fine so imposed shall be for the use of the United States, and the other half for the use of the informer, who shall be ascertained by the judgment of the court; and the said court shall also render judgment against the said assessor or assistant assessor for the amount of damages sustained in favor of the party injured, to be collected by execution.

Penalty for misconduct on part of assessor or assistant.

Disposition of penalties.

SEC. 22. *And be it further enacted,* That there shall be allowed and paid to the several assessors a salary of fifteen hundred dollars per annum, payable quarterly. And in addition thereto, where the receipts of the collection district shall exceed the sum of one hundred thousand dollars and shall not exceed the sum of four hundred thousand dollars annually, one-half of one per centum upon the excess of receipts over one hundred thousand dollars.

Compensation of assessors.

Salary.

Commissions.

Where the receipts of a collection district shall exceed four hundred thousand dollars and shall not exceed six hundred thousand, one-fifth of one per centum upon the excess of receipts over four hundred thousand dollars. Where the receipts shall exceed six hundred thousand dollars, one-tenth of one per centum upon such excess; but the salary of no assessor shall, in any case, exceed the sum of four thousand dollars. And the several assessors shall be allowed and paid the sums actually and necessarily expended, with the approval of the Commissioner of Internal Revenue; but no account for such rent shall be allowed or paid until it shall have been verified in such manner as the Commissioner shall require, and shall have been audited and approved by the proper officer of the Treasury Department, for office rent, not exceeding the rate of five hundred dollars per annum. And the several assessors shall be paid, after the account thereof shall have been rendered to and approved by the proper officers of the treasury, their necessary and reasonable charges for clerk hire; but no such account shall be approved unless it shall state the name or names of the clerk or clerks employed, and the precise periods of time for which they were respectively employed, and the rate of compensation agreed upon, and shall be accompanied by an affidavit of the assessor stating that such service was actually required by the necessities of his office, and was actually rendered; and also by the affidavit of each clerk, stating that he has rendered the service charged in such account on his behalf, the compensation agreed upon, and that he has not paid, deposited, or assigned, or contracted to pay, deposit, or assign any part of such compensation to the use of any other person, or in any way, directly or indirectly, paid or given, or contracted to pay or give any reward or compensation for his office or employment, or the emoluments thereof. And the chief clerk of any such assessor is hereby authorized to administer, in the absence of the assessor, such oaths or affirmations as are required by this act. And there shall be allowed and paid to each assistant assessor four dollars for every day actually employed in collecting lists and making valuations, the number of days necessary for that purpose to be certified by the assessor; and three dollars for every hundred persons assessed contained in the tax list, as completed and delivered by him to the assessor; and twenty-five cents for each permit granted to any tobacco, snuff, or cigar manufacturer; and the said assessors and assistant assessors, respectively, shall be paid after the account thereof shall have been rendered to and approved by the proper officers of the treasury, their necessary and reasonable charges for stationery and blank books used in the discharge of their duties, and for postage actually paid on letters and documents received or sent, and relating exclusively to official business: *Provided*, That no such account shall be approved unless it shall state the date and the particular item of every such expenditure, and shall be verified by the oath or affirmation of such assessor or assistant assessor; and the compensation herein specified shall be in full for all expenses not otherwise particularly authorized. *Provided, further*, That the Secretary of the Treasury shall be, and he is hereby, authorized to fix such additional rates of compensation to be made to assessors and assistant assessors in cases where a collection district embraces more than a single congressional district, and to assessors and assistant assessors, revenue agents and inspectors, in Louisiana, North Carolina, Mississippi,

Not to exceed $4,000.

Office rent.

Clerk hire.

Chief clerk may administer oaths.

Compensation of assistant assessors.

Stationery, blank books and postage.

Accounts to be verified by oath.

Secretary may allow additional compensation in certain cases.

Tennessee, Missouri, California, and Oregon, and the Territories, as may appear to him to be just and equitable, in consequence of the greater cost of living and travelling in those States and Territories, and as may, in his judgment, be necessary to secure the services of competent officers; but the rates of compensation thus allowed shall not exceed the rates paid to similar officers in such States and Territories respectively.

Limit of compensation.

SEC. 23. *And be it further enacted,* That if any assessor shall demand of, or receive directly or indirectly from, any assistant assessor, as a condition of his appointment to or continuance in his said office of assistant assessor, any portion of the compensation herein allowed, such assistant assessor, or any other consideration, such assessor so offending shall be summarily dismissed from office, and shall be liable to a fine of not less than five hundred dollars upon conviction of said offence in any district or circuit court of the United States of the district in which such offence may be committed.

Fraud in appointment of assistant assessor.

Penalty.

SEC. 24. *And be it further enacted,* That assistant assessors shall make out their accounts for pay and charges allowed by law monthly, specifying each item and including the date of each day of service, and shall transmit the same verified by oath or affirmation to the assessor of the district, who shall thereupon examine the same, and, if it appear just and in accordance with law, he shall indorse his approval thereon, but otherwise shall return the same with objections. Any such account so approved may be presented by the assistant assessor to the collector of the district for payment, who shall thereupon pay the same, and, when receipted by the assistant assessor, be allowed therefor upon presentation to the Commissioner of Internal Revenue. Where any account, so transmitted to the assessor, shall be objected to, in whole or in part, the assistant assessor may appeal to the Commissioner of Internal Revenue, whose decision on the case shall be final. And should it appear, at any time, that any assessor has knowingly or negligently approved any account, as aforesaid, allowing any assistant assessor a sum larger than was due according to law, it shall be the duty of the Commissioner of Internal Revenue, upon proper proof thereof, to deduct the sum so allowed from any pay which may be due to such assessor; or the Commissioner as aforesaid may direct a suit to be brought in any court of competent jurisdiction against the assessor or assistant assessor in default, for the recovery of the amount knowingly or negligently allowed, as hereinbefore mentioned: *Provided,* That in estimating the allowance to be made to assistant assessors for periods of service less than a day, each ten hours shall be deemed the equivalent of a day.

Assistant assessors to make out accounts.

Account to be approved by assessor,

And paid by collector.

Assistant assessor may appeal to Commissioner.

Amount negligently approved by assessor to be deducted from his pay.

Ten hours to be the equivalent of a day in certain cases.

SEC. 25. *And be it further enacted,* That there shall be allowed to collectors, in full compensation for their services and that of their deputies, a salary of fifteen hundred dollars per annum, to be paid quarterly, and in addition thereto a commission of three per centum upon the first hundred thousand dollars, and a commission of one per centum upon all sums above one hundred thousand dollars and not exceeding four hundred thousand dollars, and a commission of one-half of one per centum on all sums above four hundred thousand dollars, such commissions to be computed upon the amounts by them respectively collected and paid over and accounted for under the instructions of the Treasury Department. And there shall be further paid, after the account thereof has been rendered to and approved by the proper officers of the

Compensation of collectors.

Salary.

Commissions.

treasury, to each collector his necessary and reasonable charges for stationery and blank books used in the performance of his official duties, and for postage actually paid on letters and documents received or sent, and exclusively relating to official business; but no such account shall be approved unless it shall state the date and the particular items of every such expenditure, and shall be verified by the oath or affirmation of the collector: *Provided,* That the salary and commissions of no collector, exclusive of stationery, blank books, and postage, shall exceed ten thousand dollars in the aggregate, nor more than five thousand dollars exclusive of the expenses for rent, stationery, blank books, and postage, and pay of deputies and clerks, to which such collector is actually and necessarily subjected in the administration of his office: *And provided, further,* That the Secretary of the Treasury be authorized to make such further allowances, from time to time, as may be reasonable in cases in which, from the territorial extent of the district, or from the amount of internal duties collected, or from other circumstances, it may seem just to make such allowances.

Stationery, blank books, and postage.

Not to exceed $10,000 nor more than $5,000 exclusive of expenses.

Secretary may make further allowance in certain cases.

Fiscal year to be observed in adjusting accounts.

SEC. 26. *And be it further enacted,* That in the adjustment of the accounts of assessors and collectors of internal revenue which shall accrue after the thirtieth of June, eighteen hundred and sixty-four, and in the payment of their compensation for services after that date, the fiscal year of the treasury shall be observed; and where such compensation, or any part of it, shall be by commissions upon assessments or collections, and shall during any year, in consequence of a new *apportionment* [appointment,] be due to more than one assessor or collector in the same district, such commissions shall be apportioned between such assessors or collectors according to the amounts collected by them respectively; but in no case shall a greater amount of the commissions be allowed to two or more assessors or collectors in the same district than is or may be authorized by law to be allowed to one assessor or collector. And the salary and commissions of assessors and collectors heretofore earned and accrued shall be adjusted, allowed, and paid in conformity to the provisions of this section, and not otherwise.

When new appointment is made during the fiscal year.

Salaries and commissions heretofore earned.

Collector to sign triplicate receipts of lists received from assessor.

SEC. 27. *And be it further enacted,* That each collector, on receiving, from time to time, lists and returns from the said assessors, shall subscribe three receipts: one of which shall be made upon a full and correct copy of each list or return, and be delivered by him to, and shall remain with, the assessor of his collection district, and shall be open to the inspection of any person who may apply to inspect the same; and the other two shall be made upon aggregate statements of the lists or returns aforesaid, exhibiting the gross amount of taxes to be collected in his collection district, one of which aggregate statements and receipts shall be transmitted to the Commissioner of Internal Revenue, and the other to the First Comptroller of the Treasury.

Collectors to advertise when and where taxes are payable.

SEC. 28. *And be it further enacted,* That each of said collectors shall, within twenty days after receiving his annual collection list from the assessors, give notice, by advertisement published in each county in his collection district, in one newspaper printed in such county, if any such there be, and by notifications to be posted up in at least four public places in each county in his collection district, that the said duties have become due and payable, and state the time and place within said county at which he or his deputy will attend to receive the same, which time shall not be less than *than* ten days after such notification; and all persons who shall neglect to pay the duties and taxes so as aforesaid assessed within the time specified, shall be liable to pay ten per centum additional upon the amount thereof, the fact of which liability shall be stated in the advertisement and notifications aforesaid. And if any person shall neglect to pay as aforesaid for more than ten days, it shall be the duty of the collector or his deputy to issue to such person a notice to be left at his dwelling or usual place of business, or be sent by mail, demanding the payment of said duties or taxes, stating the amount thereof, with a fee of twenty cents for the issuing and service of such notice, and with four cents for each mile actually and necessarily travelled in serving the same. And if such persons shall not pay the duties or taxes, with the penalty aforesaid, and the fee of twenty cents and mileage as aforesaid, within ten days after the service or the sending by mail of such notice, it shall be the duty of the collector or his deputy to collect the said duties or taxes, and fee of twenty cents and mileage, with ten per centum penalty as aforesaid. And with respect to all such duties or taxes as are not included in the annual lists aforesaid, and all taxes and duties the collection of which is not otherwise provided for in this act, it shall be the duty of each collector, in person or by deputy, to demand payment thereof, in the manner last mentioned, within ten days from and after receiving the list thereof from the assessor, or within twenty days from and after the expiration of the time within which such duty or tax should have been paid; and if the annual or other duties shall not be paid within ten days from and after such demand therefor, it shall be lawful for such collector, or his deputies, to proceed to collect the said duties or taxes, with ten per centum additional thereto, as aforesaid, by distraint and sale of the goods, chattels, or effects of the persons delinquent as aforesaid. And in case of distraint, it shall be the duty of the officer charged with the collection to make, or cause to be made, an account of the goods or chattels distrained, a copy of which, signed by the officer making such distraint, shall be left with the owner or possessor of such goods, chattels, or effects, or at his or her dwelling, or usual place of business, with some person of suitable age and discretion, with a note of the sum demanded, and the time and place of sale; and the said officer shall forthwith cause a notification to be published in some newspaper within the county wherein said distraint is made, if there is a newspaper published in said county, or to be publicly posted up at the post office, if there be one within five miles, nearest to the residence of the person whose property shall be distrained, and in not less than two other public places, which notice shall specify the articles distrained, and the time and place for the sale thereof, which time shall not be less than ten nor more than twenty days from the date of such notification, and the place proposed for sale not more than five miles distant from the place of making such distraint: *Provided*, That in any case of distraint for the payment of the duties or taxes aforesaid the goods, chattels, or effects so distrained shall and may be restored to the owner or possessor, if prior to the sale payment of the amount due or tender thereof shall be made to the proper officer charged with the collection of the full amount demanded, together with such fee for levying, and such sum for the necessary and reasonable expense of removing, ad-

Penalty for neglect to pay taxes.

Collector to demand payment personally, or by mail.

If duties are not paid within ten days after demand.

Duties and taxes not included in annual lists.

Collector to make distraint.

Proceedings in case of distraint.

Length of notice previous to sale.

Property to be restored on payment of tax and fees.

vertising, and keeping the gooas, chattels, or effects so distrained, as may be prescribed by the Commissioner of Internal Revenue; but in case of non-payment or tender, as aforesaid, the said officers shall proceed to sell the said goods, chattels, or effects at public auction, and shall and may retain from the proceeds of such sale the amount demandable for the use of the United States, with the necessary and reasonable expenses of distraint and sale, and a commission of five per centum thereon for his own use, rendering the overplus, if any there be, to the person whose goods, chattels, or effects shall have been distrained: *Provided, further*, That there shall be exempt from distraint the tools or implements of a trade or profession, one cow, arms, and provisions, and household furniture kept for use, and apparel necessary for a family.

Sale of goods in certain cases.

Property exempt from distraint.

Sale of property and disposition of surplus proceeds.

SEC. 29. *And be it further enacted*, That in all cases where the property liable to distraint for duties or taxes under this act may not be divisible, so as to enable the collector by a sale of part thereof to raise the whole amount of the tax, with all costs, charges, and commissions, the whole of such property shall be sold, and the surplus of the proceeds of the sale, after satisfying the duty or tax, costs, and charges, shall be paid to the owner of the property, or his, her, or their legal representatives; or if he, she, or they cannot be found, or refuse to receive the same, then such surplus shall be deposited in the treasury of the United States, to be there held for the use of the owner, or his, her, or their legal representatives, until he, she, or they shall make appication therefor to the Secretary of the Treasury, who, upon such application, shall, by warrant on the treasury, cause the same to be paid to the applicant. And if the property advertised for sale as aforesaid cannot be sold for the amount of the duty or tax due thereon, with the costs and charges, the collector shall purchase the same in behalf of the United States for an amount not exceeding the said tax or duty, with the costs and charges thereon. And all property so purchased may be sold by said collector under such regulations as may be prescribed by the Commissioner of Internal Revenue. And the collector shall render a distinct account of all charges incurred in the sale of such property to the Commissioner of Internal Revenue, who shall, by regulation, determine the fees and costs to be allowed in cases of distraint and other seizures; and the said collector shall pay into the treasury the surplus, if any there be, after defraying the charges.

Property may be purchased for the United States by the collector and resold under regulations of the commissioner.

Collector to render account.

Sale of real estate.

SEC. 30. *And be it further enacted*, That in any case where goods, chattels, or effects sufficient to satisfy the duties imposed by this act upon any person liable to pay the same shall not be found by the collector or deputy collector whose duty it may be to collect the same, he is hereby authorized to collect the same by seizure and sale of real estate; and the officer making such seizure and sale shall give notice to the person whose estate is proposed to be sold, by giving him in hand, or leaving at his last and usual place of abode, if he has any such within the collection district where said estate is situated, a notice, in writing, stating what particular estate is proposed to be sold, describing the same with reasonable certainty, and the time when and place where said officer proposes to sell the same; which time shall not be less than twenty nor more than forty days from the time of giving said notice. And the said officer shall also cause a notification to the same effect to be published in some newspaper within the county where

Notice to be given of time and place of sale.

Time and method of advertising.

such seizure is made, if any such there be, and shall also cause a like notice to be posted up at the post office nearest to the estate so seized, and in two other public places within the county. And the place of said sale shall not be more than five miles distant from the estate seized, except by special order of the Commissioner of Internal Revenue. At the time and place appointed, the officer making such seizure shall proceed to sell the said estate at public auction, offering the same at a minimum price, including the amount of duties with the ten per centum additional thereon, the expense of making such levy and all charges for advertising, and an officer's fee of ten dollars. And if no person offers for said estate the amount of said minimum, the officer shall declare the same to be purchased by him for the United States, and shall deposit with the district attorney of the United States a deed thereof, as hereinafter specified and provided; otherwise, the same shall be declared to be sold to the highest bidder. And said sale may be adjourned by said officer for a period not exceeding five days, if he shall think it advisable so to do. If the amount bid shall not be then and there paid, the officer shall forthwith proceed to again sell said estate in the same manner. If the amount bid shall be then and there paid, the officer shall give his receipt therefor, if requested, and within five days thereafter he shall make out a deed of the estate so sold to the purchaser thereof, and execute the same in his official capacity, in the manner prescribed by the laws of the State in which said estate may be situated, in which said deed shall be recited the fact of said seizure and sale, with the cause thereof, the amount of duty for which said sale was made, and of all charges and fees, and the amount paid by the purchaser, and all his acts and doings in relation to said seizure and sale, and shall have the same ready for delivery to said purchaser, and shall deliver the same accordingly, upon request therefor. And said deed shall be prima facie evidence of the truth of the facts stated therein, and, if the proceedings of the officer as set forth have been substantially in pursuance of the provisions of this act, shall be considered and operate as a conveyance to the purchaser of the title to said estate, but shall not affect the rights of innocent parties acquired previously to the claim of the United States under this act. The surplus, if any, arising from such sale shall be disposed of as provided in this act for like cases arising upon sales of personal property. And any person whose estate may be seized for duties, as aforesaid, shall have the same right to pay or tender the amount due, with all proper charges thereon, prior to the sale thereof, and thereupon to relieve his said estate from sale as aforesaid, as is provided in this act for personal property similarly situated. And any collector or deputy collector may, for the collection of duties imposed upon any person or for which any person may be liable by this act, and committed to him for collection, seize and sell the lands of such person situated in any other collection district within the State in which said officer resides; and his proceedings in relation thereto shall have the same effect as if the same were had in his proper collection district. And the owners, their heirs, executors, or administrators, or any person having an interest therein or a lien thereon, or any person on their behalf, shall have liberty to redeem the land sold as aforesaid, within one year from and after recording the said deed, upon payment to the purchaser, or, in case he cannot be found in the county where the lands are situate, to the col-

Place of sale.

Method of sale.

Estate may be purch'd for United States and deed deposited with district attorney.

Sale may be adjourned five days.

Property may be resold on failure of purchaser to complete purchase.

Deed to be made according to State laws.

Deed to recite fact of seizure and sale.

And to be prima facie evidence thereof.

Rights of innocent parties not to be affected.

Surplus, how disposed of.

Collector may seize land in any other district in the State.

Owners may redeem within one year.

lector, for the use of the purchaser, his heirs or assigns, of the amount paid by the purchaser, with interest on the same at the rate of twenty per centum per annum. And it shall be the duty of every collector to keep a record of all sales of land made in his collection district, whether by himself or his deputies, in which shall be set forth the tax for which any such sale was made, the dates of seizure and sale, the name of the party assessed, and all proceedings in making said sale, the amount of fees and expenses, the name of the purchaser, and the date of the deed; which record shall be certified by the officer making the sale. And it shall be the duty of any deputy making sale, as aforesaid, to return a statement of all his proceedings to the collector, and to certify the record thereof. And in case of the death or removal of the collector, or the expiration of his term of office from any other cause, said record shall be deposited in the office of the clerk of the district court of the United States for the district within which the said collector resided; and a copy of every such record, certified by the collector, or by the clerk, as the case may require, shall be evidence in any court of the truth of the facts therein stated. And when any lands sold, as aforesaid, shall be redeemed as hereinbefore provided, the collector or clerk, as the case may be, shall make an entry of the fact upon the record aforesaid, and the said entry shall be evidence of such redemption. And the claim of the government to lands sold under and by virtue of the foregoing provisions shall be held to have accrued at the time of seizure thereof.

Rate of interest to be paid on redemption.

Collector to keep record of sales of land.

Deputies to return certified statements of sales to collectors.

Record to be deposited with clerk of district court when collect'r goes out of office.

Duty of collector in case of redemption.

Claim of the government to accrue at time of seizure.

Taxes returned against non-residents.

SEC. 31. *And be it further enacted*, That if any collector shall find, upon any list of taxes returned to him for collection, property lying within his district which is charged with any specific or ad valorem tax or duty, but which is not owned, occupied, or superintended by some person known to such collector to reside or to have some place of business within the United States, and upon which the duty or tax has not been paid within the time required by law, such collector shall forthwith take such property into his custody, and shall advertise the same, and the tax charged upon the same, in some newspaper published in his district, if any shall be published therein, otherwise in some newspaper in an adjoining district, for the space of thirty days; and if the taxes thereon, with all charges for advertising, shall not be paid within said thirty days, such collector shall proceed to sell the same, or so much as is necessary, in the manner provided for the sale of other goods distrained for the non-payment of taxes, and out of the proceeds shall satisfy all taxes charged upon such property, with the costs of advertising and selling the same. And like proceedings to those provided in the preceding section for the purchase and resale of property which cannot be sold for the amount of duty or tax due thereon shall be had with regard to property sold under the provisions of this section. And any surplus arising from any sale herein provided for shall be paid into the treasury, for the benefit of the owner of the property. And the Secretary of the Treasury is authorized, in any case where money shall be paid into the treasury for the benefit of any owner of property sold as aforesaid, to repay the same, on proper proof being furnished that the person applying therefor is entitled to receive the same.

How collected.

Sale in case of non-payment.

Proceedings.

Surplus to be paid into treasury.

Secretary may refund to owner.

SEC. 32. *And be it further enacted*, That whenever a collector shall have on any list duly returned to him the name of any person not within his collection district who is liable to tax, or of any person so liable to tax who shall have, in the collection district in which he resides, no sufficient property subject to seizure or distraint from which the money due for duties or tax can be collected, it shall and may be lawful for such collector to transmit a copy or statement containing the name of the person liable to such duty as tax aforesaid, with the amount and nature thereof, duly certified under his hand, to the collector of any district to which said person shall have removed, or in which he shall have property, real or personal, liable to be seized and sold for duty or tax; and the collector of the district to whom the said certified copy or statement shall be transmitted shall proceed to collect the said duty or tax in the same way as if the name of the person and objects of tax contained in the said certified copy or statement were on any list furnished to him by the assessor of his own collection district; and the said collector, upon receiving said certified copy or statement as aforesaid, shall transmit his receipt for it to the collector sending the same to him.

Collector may transmit list to another district where person liable resides, or where he has property.

Duty of collector receiving such list.

SEC. 33. *And be it further enacted*, That the several collectors shall, at the expiration of each and every month after they shall, respectively, commence their collections, transmit to the Commissioner of Interval Revenue a statement of the collections made by them, respectively, within the month, and pay over monthly, or at such time or times as may be required by the Commissioner of Internal Revenue, the moneys by them respectively collected within the said term, and at such places as may be designated and required by the Commissioner of Internal Revenue; and each of the said collectors shall complete the collection of all sums assigned to him for collection, as aforesaid, shall pay over the same into the treasury, and shall render his accounts to the Treasury Department as often as he may be required. And the Secretary of the Treasury is authorized to designate one or more depositories in each State, for the deposit and safe-keeping of the moneys collected by virtue of this act; and the receipt of the proper officer of such depository to a collector for the money deposited by him shall be a sufficient voucher for such collector in the settlement of his accounts at the Treasury Department. And the Commissioner of Internal Revenue may, under the direction of the Secretary of the Treasury, prescribe such regulations with reference to such deposits as he may deem necessary.

Collect'rs to transmit monthly statements of collections to Commissioner, and pay over moneys collect'd at such times as he may designate.

Final account to be rendered as often as required.

Depositories.

Regulations in reference to deposits to be prescribed.

SEC. 34. *And be it further enacted*, That each collector shall be charged with the whole amount of taxes, whether contained in lists delivered to him by the assessors, respectively, or delivered or transmitted to him by assistant assessors from time to time, or by other collectors, and with the additions thereto, with the par value of all stamps deposited with him, and with all moneys collected for passports, penalties, forfeitures, fees, or costs, and he shall be credited with all payments made as provided by law, with all stamps returned by him uncancelled to the treasury, with the salary, fees, commissions, and charges allowed by law, and with the amount of duties or taxes contained in the lists transmitted in the manner above provided to other collectors, and by them receipted as aforesaid; and also with the amount of the

Collectors to be charged with taxes receipted for, with par val'e of stamps, &c.

To be credited with payments, commissions, &c.

Taxes of absconding persons.

duties or taxes of such persons as may have absconded, or become insolvent, prior to the day when the duty or tax ought, according to the provisions of this act, to have been collected: *Provided,* That it shall be proved to the satisfaction of the Commissioner of Internal Revenue that due diligence was used by the collector, and that no property was left from which the duty or tax could have been recovered, who shall certify the facts to the First Comptroller of the Treasury. And each collector shall also be credited with the amount of all property purchased by him for the use of the United States, provided he shall faithfully account for and pay over the proceeds thereof upon a resale of the same as required by this act.

Collector to prove that he has used due diligence.

Collectors failing to account for taxes due.

SEC. 35. *And be it further enacted,* That if any collector shall fail either to collect or to render his account, or to pay over in the manner or within the times hereinbefore provided, it shall be the duty of the First Comptroller of the Treasury, and he is hereby authorized and required, immediately after evidence of such delinquency, to report the same to the Solicitor of the Treasury, who shall issue a warrant of distress against such delinquent collector, directed to the marshal of the district, therein expressing the amount with which the said collector is chargeable, and the sums, if any, which have been paid over by him, so far as the same are ascertainable. And the said marshal shall, himself, or by his deputy, immediately proceed to levy and collect the sum which may remain due, with five per centum thereon, and all the expenses and charges of collection, by distress and sale of the goods and chattels, or any personal effects of the delinquent collector, giving at least five days' notice of the time and place of sale, in the manner provided by law for advertising sales of personal property on execution in the State wherein such collector resides. And the bill of sale of the officer of any goods, chattels, or other personal property, distrained and sold as aforesaid, shall be conclusive evidence of title to the purchaser, and prima facie evidence of the right of the officer to make such sale, and of the correctness of his proceedings in selling the same. And for want of goods and chattles, or other personal effects of such collector, sufficient to satisfy any warrant of distress, issued pursuant to the preceding section of this act, the lands and real estate of such collector, or so much thereof as may be necessary for satisfying the said warrant, after being advertised for at least three weeks in not less than three public places in the collection district, and in one newspaper printed in the county or district, if any there be, prior to the proposed time of sale, shall be sold at public auction by the marshal or his deputy, who, upon such sale, shall, as such marshal or deputy marshal, make and deliver to the purchaser of the premises so sold a deed of conveyance thereof, to be executed and acknowledged in the manner and form prescribed by the laws of the State in which said lands are situated, which said deed so made shall invest the purchaser with all the title and interest of the defendant or defendants named in said warrant, existing at the time of the seizure thereof. And all moneys that may remain of the proceeds of such sale after satisfying the said warrant of distress, and paying the reasonable costs and charges of sale, shall be returned to the proprietor of the lands or real estate sold as aforesaid.

Duty of the First Comptroller thereon.

Solicitor of the Treasury to issue a warrant.

Marshal to levy on the property of the collector.

Bill of sale to be conclusive evidence of title, and prima facie evidence of right of officer to make sale.

Levy on real estate.

Notice of sale.

Marshal to execute deed.

Surplus to be returned to proprietor of lands sold.

SEC. 36. *And be it further enacted,* That each and every collector, or his deputy, who shall be guilty of any extortion or wilful oppression, under color of law, or shall knowingly demand other or greater sums than shall be authorized by law, or shall receive any fee, compensation, or reward, except as herein prescribed, for the performance of any duty, or shall wilfully neglect to perform any of the duties enjoined by this act, shall, upon conviction, be subject to a fine of not exceeding one thousand dollars, or to be imprisoned for not exceeding one year, or both, at the discretion of the court, and be dismissed from office and be forever thereafter incapable of holding any office under the government; and one-half of the fine so imposed shall be for the use of the United States, and the other half for the use of the informer, who shall be ascertained by the judgment of the court; and the said court shall also render judgment against said collector or deputy collector for the amount of damages accruing to the party injured, to be collected by execution. And each and every collector, or his deputies, shall give receipts for all sums by them collected.

Penalty upon collectors for extortion or oppression.

Disposal of fines.

SEC. 37. *And be it further enacted,* That a collector or deputy collector, assessor, assistant assessor, revenue agent, or inspector, shall be authorized to enter, in the daytime, any brewery, distillery, manufactory, building, or place where any property, articles, or objects, subject to duty or taxation under the provisions of this act, are made, produced, or kept, within his district, so far as it may be necessary for the purpose of examining said property, articles, or objects, or inspecting the accounts required by this act from time to time to be made or kept by any manufacturer or producer, relating to such property, articles, or objects. And every owner of such brewery, distillery, manufactory, building, or place, or persons having the agency or superintendence of the same, who shall refuse to admit such officer, or to suffer him to examine said property, articles, or objects, or to inspect said accounts, shall, for every such refusal, forfeit and pay the sum of five hundred dollars: *Provided, however,* That when such premises shall be open at night, such officers may enter while so open in the performance of their official duties.

Revenue officers may enter brewery, &c., in the daytime,

Penalty for refusing to admit officers.

And at night when premises are open.

SEC. 38. *And be it further enacted,* That if any person shall forcibly obstruct or hinder any assessor or assistant assessor, or any collector or deputy collector, revenue agent or inspector, in the execution of this act, or of any power and authority hereby vested in him, or shall forcibly rescue, or cause to be rescued, any property, articles, or objects, after the same shall have been seized by him, or shall attempt or endeavor so to do, the person so offending shall, upon conviction thereof, for every such offence, forfeit and pay the sum of five hundred dollars, or double the value of property so rescued, or be imprisoned for a term not exceeding two years, at the discretion of the court: *Provided,* That if any such officer shall divulge to any party, or make known in any manner other than as provided in this act, the operations, style of work or apparatus of any manufacturer or producer visited by him in the discharge of his official duties, he shall be subject to the penalties prescribed in section *thirty-five* [thirty-six] of this act.

Penalty for obstructing revenue officer.

Penalty for officer divulging the operations of any person visited.

SEC. 39. *And be it further enacted,* That in case of the sickness or temporary disability of a collector to discharge such of his

Collector may devolve his duties upon a deputy in case of sickness.

5*

duties as cannot under existing laws be discharged by a deputy, they may be devolved by him upon one of his deputies; and for the official acts and defaults of such deputy the collector or his sureties shall be held responsible to the United States.

Oldest deputy collector to act in case of vacancy.

Bond of deputy available to heirs, &c., in case of loss.

SEC. 40. *And be it further enacted*, That in case a collector shall die, resign, or be removed, the deputies of such collector shall continue to act until his successor is appointed; and the deputy of such collector longest in service at the time immediately preceding shall, until a successor shall be appointed, discharge all the duties of said collector; and for the official acts and defaults of such deputy a remedy shall be had on the official bond of the collector, as in other cases; and of two or more deputy collectors, appointed on the same day, the one residing nearest the residence of the collector at the time of his death, resignation, or removal, shall discharge the said duties until the appointment of a successor. And any bond or security taken from a deputy by such collector, pursuant to this act, shall be available to his legal representatives and sureties to indemnify them for loss or damage accruing from any act of the deputy so continuing or succeeding to the duties of such collector.

Collectors to collect duties and taxes, and to sue for fines and penalties.

Suits to be in the name of the United States.

Penalties to be divided between the government and the informer.

Employment of counsel to be authorized by commissioner.

SEC. 41. *And be it further enacted*, That it shall be the duty of the collectors aforesaid, or their deputies, in their respective districts, and they are hereby authorized, to collect all the duties and taxes imposed by this act, however the same may be designated, and to prosecute for the recovery of any sum or sums which may be forfeited by virtue of this act; and all fines, penalties, nd forfeitures which may be incurred or imposed by virtue of this ct shall be sued for and recovered, in the name of the United tates, in any proper form of action, or by any appropriate form of proceeding, qui tam, or otherwise, before any circuit or district court of the United States for the district within which said fine, penalty, or forfeiture may have been incurred, or before any other court of competent jurisdiction; and where not otherwise and differently provided for, one moiety thereof shall be to the use of the United States, and the other moiety thereof to the use of the person, to be ascertained by the judgment of the court, who shall first inform of the cause, matter, or thing whereby any such fine, penalty, or forfeiture was incurred: *Provided*, That in case of any suit brought upon information received from any person, other than a collector, deputy collector, assessor, assistant assessor or inspector, of internal revenue, the United States shall not be subject to any costs of suit, nor shall the fees of any attorney or counsel employed by any such officer be allowed in the settlement of his account unless the employment of such attorney or counsel shall be authorized by the Commissioner of Internal Revenue, either express or by general regulations.

False swearing to be deemed perjury.

SEC. 42. *And be it further enacted*, That if any person, in any case, matter, hearing, or other proceeding in which an oath or affirmation shall be required to be taken or administered under and by virtue of this act, shall, upon the taking of such oath or affirmation, knowingly and wilfully swear or affirm falsely, every person so offending shall be deemed guilty of perjury, and shall, on conviction thereof, be subject to the like punishment and penalties now provided by the laws of the United States for the crime of perjury.

SEC. 43. *And be it further enacted*, That separate accounts shall be kept at the treasury of all moneys received from internal duties or taxes in each of the respective States, Territories, and collection districts; and that separate accounts shall be kept of the amount of each species of duty or tax that shall accrue, so as to exhibit, as far as may be, the amount collected from each source of revenue, with the moneys paid as compensation and for allowances to the collectors and deputy collectors, assessors and assistant assessors, inspectors, and other officers employed in each of the respective States, Territories, and collection districts, an abstract in tabular form, of which accounts it shall be the duty of the Secretary of the Treasury, annually, in the month of December, to lay before Congress.

Separate accounts to be kept of moneys received from the several districts, and the several sources of revenue.

Abstract to be laid before Congress.

SEC. 44. *And be it further enacted*, That the Commissioner of Internal Revenue, subject to regulations prescribed by the Secretary of the Treasury, shall be, and is hereby, authorized, on appeal to him made, to remit, refund, and pay back all duties erroneously or illegally assessed or collected, and all duties that shall appear to be unjustly assessed or excessive in amount, or in any manner wrongfully collected, and also repay to collectors or deputy collectors the full amount of such sums of money as shall or may be recovered against them or any of them *them* in any court, for any internal duties or licenses collected by them, with the costs and expenses of suit, and all damages and costs recovered against assessors, assistant assessors, collectors, deputy collectors, and inspectors, in any suit which shall be brought against them or any of them by reason of anything that shall or may be done in the due performance of their official duties, and also compromise such suits and all others relating to internal revenue: And all judgments and moneys recovered or received for taxes, costs, forfeitures, and penalties shall be paid to the collector as internal duties are required to be paid; and all sums of money which the Commissioner is authorized to pay by virtue of this section shall be paid by drafts drawn on collectors of internal revenue.

Commissioner authorized to refund taxes illegally collected.

Commissioner to repay to collectors any moneys recovered of them in any courts for acts done in due performance of duties of office.

Commis'ner may compromise suits. All penalties to be paid to collectors.

SEC. 45. *And be it further enacted*, That in all cases of distraint and sale of goods or chattels for non-payment of taxes, duties, or licenses, as provided for, the bill of sale of such goods or chattels given by the officer making such sale, to the purchaser thereof, shall be prima facie evidence of the right of the officer to make such sale, and conclusive evidence of the regularity of his proceedings in selling the same.

Bill of sale given by collector to be prima facie evidence of right to make sale, and conclusive evidence of regularity of his proceedings.

SEC. 46. *And be it further enacted*, That if, for any cause, at any time after this act goes into operation, the laws of the United States cannot be executed in a State or Territory of the United States, or any part thereof, or within the District of Columbia, it shall be the duty of the President, and he is hereby authorized, to proceed to execute the provisions of this act within the limits of such State or Territory, or part thereof, or District of Columbia, so soon as the authority of the United States therein shall be reestablished, and to collect the taxes, duties, and licenses, in such States and Territories under the regulations prescribed in this act, so far as applicable; and where not applicable, the assessment and levy shall be made, and the time and manner of collection regulated, by the instructions and directions of the Commissioner of Internal Revenue, under the direction of the Secretary of the Treasury.

Duty of the President in States and Territories where this act cannot be executed.

Officers appointed under this act to perform necessary duties for the collection of any direct tax

SEC. 47. *And be it further enacted,* That the officers who may be appointed under this act, except within those districts within any State or Territory which have been or may be otherwise especially provided for by law, shall be, and hereby are, authorized, in all cases where the payment of such tax shall not have been assumed by the State, to perform all the duties relating to or regarding the assessment and collection of any direct tax imposed, or which may be imposed by law.

Articles held by any person with intent to defraud the revenue, may be seized by any collector.

The articles forfeited to the United States.

Forfeiture to be enforced by proceeding *in rem.*

Penalty for fraud $500, or double the amount of duties.

SEC. 48. *And be it further enacted,* That all goods, wares, merchandise, articles or objects on which duties are imposed by the provisions of law, which shall be found in the possession or custody or within the control of any person or persons, for the purpose of being sold or removed by such person or persons in fraud of the internal revenue laws, or with design to avoid payment of said duties, may be seized by any collector or deputy collector, who shall have reason to believe that the same are possessed, had, or held for the purpose or design aforesaid, and the same shall be forfeited to the United States; and also all articles of raw materials found in the possession of any person or persons intending to manufacture the same for the purpose of being sold by them in fraud of said laws, or with design to evade the payment of said duties, and also all tools, implements, instruments, and personal property whatsoever, in the place or building, or within any yard or enclosure where such articles on which duties are imposed, as aforesaid, and intended to be used by them in the fraudulent manufacture of such raw materials, shall be found, may also be seized by any collector or deputy collector, as aforesaid, and the same shall be forfeited as aforesaid; and the proceedings to enforce said forfeiture shall be in the nature of a proceeding in rem in the circuit or district court of the United States for the district where such seizure is made, or in any other court of competent jurisdiction. And any person who shall have in his custody or possession any such goods, wares, merchandise, articles or objects subject to duty as aforesaid, for the purpose of selling the same with the design of avoiding payment of the duties imposed thereon, shall be liable to a penalty of five hundred dollars, or not less than double the amount of duties fraudulently attempted to be evaded, to be recovered in any court of competent jurisdiction; and the goods, wares, merchandise, articles or objects which shall be so seized by any collector or deputy collector, may, at the option of the collector, during the pendency of such proceedings, be delivered to the marshal of said district, and remain in his care and custody and under his control until final judgment in such proceeding shall be rendered: *Provided, however,* That when the property so seized may be liable to perish or become greatly reduced in value by keeping, or when it cannot be kept without great expense, the owner thereof, the collector, or the marshal of the district, may apply to the assessor of the district to examine said property; and if, in the opinion of said assessor, it shall be necessary that the said property should be sold to prevent such waste or expense, he shall appraise the same; and the owner thereupon shall have said property returned to him upon giving bond in such form as may be prescribed by the Commissioner of Internal Revenue, and in an amount equal to the appraised value, with such sureties as the said assessor shall deem good and sufficient, to abide the final order, decree, or judgment of the court

Custody of goods may be given to U. S. marshal.

Perishable property may be appraised and returned to owner, he giving bond for same.

having cognizance of the case, and to pay the amount of said appraised value to the collector, marshal, or otherwise, as he may be ordered and directed by the court, which bond shall be filed by said assessor with the Commissioner of Internal Revenue. But if said owner shall neglect or refuse to give said bond, the assessor shall issue to the collector or marshal aforesaid an order to sell the same; and the said collector or marshal shall thereupon advertise and sell the said property at public auction in the same manner as goods may be sold on final execution in said district; and the proceeds of the sale, after deducting the reasonable costs of the seizure and sale, shall be paid to the court aforesaid, to abide its final order, decree, or judgment.

If bond not given property may be sold at auction.

SEC. 49. *And be it further enacted,* That all the provisions hereinafter made for the delivery of returns, lists, statements, and valuations, and for additions to the duty in case of false or fraudulent lists or returns, or in case of undervaluation or understatement on lists or returns, or in case of refusal or neglect to deliver lists or returns, and for the imposition of fines, penalties, and forfeitures, shall be held and taken to apply to all persons, associations, corporations, or companies liable to pay duty or tax; and any additions to duties, fines, penalties, or forfeitures hereinafter imposed for failure to perform any duty required to be performed, shall be held and taken to be additional to those hereinbefore provided.

Provisions hereinafter made for delivery of returns, &c., imposition of fines, &c., apply to all persons, corporations, &c.

Fines hereinafter imposed additional to those hereinbefore provided.

SEC. 50. *And be it further enacted,* That the provisions of the act entitled "An act further to provide for the collection of duties on imports," approved March second, one thousand eight hundred and thirty-three, now in force, shall be taken and deemed as extending to and embracing all cases arising under the laws for the collection of internal duties, stamp duties, licenses, or taxes, which have been or may be hereafter enacted; and all persons duly authorized to assess, receive, or collect such duties or taxes under such laws are hereby declared to be and to have been revenue officers within the true intent and meaning of the said act, and entitled to all the exemptions, immunities, benefits, rights, and privileges therein enumerated or conferred.

Act of March 2, 1833, for the removal of suits from State courts to federal courts, to apply to internal revenue cases.

Officers of internal revenue declared to be revenue officers under said act.

SEC. 51. *And be it further enacted,* That the provisions of the sixteenth section of the act approved August sixth, eighteen hundred and forty-six, entitled "An act to provide for the better organization of the treasury, and for the collection, safe-keeping, transfer, and disbursement of the public revenue," are hereby applied to, and shall be construed to include, all officers of the internal revenue charged with the safe-keeping, transfer, or disbursement of the public moneys arising therefrom, and to all other persons having actual charge, custody, or control of moneys or accounts arising from the administration of the internal revenue.

Section 16, act of August 6, 1846, applied to internal revenue officers.

SEC. 52. [*And be it further enacted,*] That all assessors and their assistants, all collectors and their deputies, and all inspectors, are hereby authorized to administer oaths and take evidence touching any part of the administration of this law with which they are respectively charged, and where such oaths and evidence are by law authorized to be taken; and any perjury therein shall be punished in the like manner, and to the same degree, as in the case of perjury committed in proceedings in the courts of the United States.

Assessors and their assistants, collectors and their deputies, and inspectors, authorized to administer oaths.

SPIRITS, ALE, BEER, AND PORTER.

Distillers must apply for licenses.

SEC. 53. *And be it further enacted,* That any person required by law to be licensed as a distiller, shall, in addition to what is required by other provisions of law, make an application therefor to the assessor of the district, and before the same is issued the person so applying shall give bond to the United States, in such sum as shall be required by the collector, and with one or more sureties, to be approved by said collector, conditioned that in case any additional still or stills, or other implements to be used as aforesaid, shall be erected by him, his agent or superintendent, he will, before using, or causing, or permitting the same to be used, report in writing to the said assessor the capacity thereof, and information from time to time of any change in the form, capacity, ownership, agency, or superintendence, which all or either of the said stills or other implements may undergo, and that he will from day to day enter, or cause to be entered, in a book to be kept for that purpose, the number of gallons of spirits that may be distilled by said still or stills, or other implements, and also of the quantities of grain or other vegetable productions, or other substances put into the mash tub, or otherwise used by him, his agent or superintendent, for the purpose of producing spirits; and said book shall be open at all times during the day (Sundays excepted) to the inspection of the said assessor, assistant assessor, collector, deputy collector, or inspector, who may make any memorandums or transcripts therefrom; and also that he will render to the said assessor or assistant assessor, on the first, eleventh, and twenty-first days of each and every month, or within five days thereafter, during the continuance of said license, an exact account in writing, of the number of gallons of spirits distilled, and also of the number of gallons placed in warehouse and the number sold or removed for consumption or sale by him, his agent or superintendent, and the proof thereof, and also of the quantities of grain or other vegetable productions, or other substances, put into the mash tub, or otherwise used by him, his agent or superintendent, for the purpose of producing spirits, for the period or fractional part of a month then next preceding the date of said report, which said report shall be verified by affidavit in the manner prescribed by law; that he will not sell or permit to be sold, or removed for consumption or sale, any spirits distilled by him under and by virtue of his said license, until the same shall have been inspected, gauged, and proved, and the quantity thereof duly entered upon his books as aforesaid; and that he will, at the time of rendering said account, pay to the said collector, or his deputy, the duties which by law are imposed on the spirits so distilled. And the said bond may be renewed or changed from time to time, in regard to the amount and sureties thereof, according to the discretion of the collector.

Must give bond. Additional still or stills. Keep record of gallons distilled, and quantity of grain used. Book to be open at all times, Sundays excepted. Render to assessor tri-monthly accounts. Will not sell or remove spirits before inspection. Will pay duties to collector. Bond may be renewed.

Application for license to distil to state full details.

SEC. 54. *And be it further enacted,* That the application in writing made by any person for a license for distilling as aforesaid, shall state the place of distilling, the number and capacity of the still or stills, boiler or boilers, and the name of the person, firm, company, or corporation using the same; and any person making a false statement in either of the said particulars shall forfeit and pay the sum of one hundred dollars, to be recovered with costs of suit.

Penalty of $100 for false statement.

Duty on spirits distilled on and after July 1, 1864, $1 50. Duty on and after February 1, 1865, $2. Spirits in possession of distiller on which duty not paid, to be held as distilled on those days. Duty to be paid within five days after rendering account. Duty a lien on distillery, &c. First proof the basis. Penalty for distilling and using spirits without license.

SEC. 55. *And be it further enacted,* That in addition to the duties payable for licenses herein provided, there shall be levied, collected, and paid on all spirits that may be distilled and sold, or distilled and removed for consumption or sale, of first proof, on and after the first day of July, eighteen hundred and sixty-four, and prior to the first day of February, eighteen hundred and sixty-five, a duty of one dollar and fifty cents on each and every gallon; and on and after February first, eighteen hundred and sixty-five, a duty of two dollars on each and every gallon. And all spirits which may be in the possession of the distiller or in public store or bonded warehouse, on either the first day of July or February aforesaid, no duty having been paid thereon, shall be held and treated as if distilled on those days respectively, and said duties shall be paid by the owner, agent, or superintendent of the still or other vessel in which the said spirits shall have been distilled, within five days after the time of rendering the accounts of spirits so chargeable with duty, required to be rendered by law. And the said duties shall be a lien on the distillery used for distilling the same, with the stills, vessels, fixtures, and tools therein, and on the lot or tract of land whereon the said distillery is situated, until the said duty shall be paid: *Provided,* That the duty on all spirits shall be collected at no lower rate than the basis of first proof, and shall be increased in proportion for any greater strength than the strength of first proof: *Provided, further,* That any person who shall distil spirits and use the same in the manufacture of any other article without having taken out a license and paid such duties as are prescribed by law in relation thereto, shall, in addition to all other penalties and forfeitures, be liable to pay one hundred per centum additional duties thereon.

Standard of first proof. Tralles hydrometer. Tables of Prof. McCulloh adopted until otherwise ordered by Secretary of Treasury, who is authorized to adopt hydrometers, &c.

SEC. 56. *And be it further enacted,* That the term first proof used in this act and in the laws of the United States shall be construed and is hereby declared to mean that proof of a liquor which corresponds to fifty degrees of Tralles centesimal hydrometer, adopted by regulation of the Treasury Department, of August twelfth, eighteen hundred and fifty, at the temperature of sixty degrees Fahrenheit's thermometer. And in levying duties on liquors above and below proof, the table contained in the manual for inspectors of spirits, prepared by Professor McCulloch, under the superintendency [e] of Professor Bache, and adopted by the Treasury Department, shall be used and taken as giving the proportions of absolute alcohol in the liquids gauged and proved according to which duties shall be levied, until otherwise ordered by the Secretary of the Treasury, who is hereby authorized to adopt such hydrometers and prescribe such rules and regulations as he may deem necessary to insure a uniform system of inspection and gauging of spirits subject to duties throughout the United States.

Record of quantity of spirits made, sold, &c., placed in bonded warehouse, &c.

SEC. 57. *And be it further enacted,* That every person who shall be the owner of any still, boiler, or other vessel, used or intended to be used for the purpose of distilling spirituous liquors, as hereinbefore provided, or who shall have such still, boiler, or other vessel under his superintendence, either as agent for the owner or on his own account; and every person who shall use any still, boiler, or other vessel, as aforesaid, either as owner, agent, or otherwise, shall from day to day make true and exact entry, or cause to be entered in a book to be kept for that purpose, the number of gallons of spirits distilled, and also the number of gallons placed in warehouse, and also the number sold, or removed for consumption or sale, and the proof thereof; which book shall always be open in the daytime, (Sundays excepted,) for the inspection of the said assessor, assistant assessor, collector, deputy collector, or inspector, who may take any minutes, memorandums, or transcripts thereof; and shall render to said assessor or assistant assessor, on the first, eleventh, and twenty-first days of each and every month in each year, or within five days thereafter, an account in duplicate, taken from his books, of the number of gallons of spirits distilled, and also the number of gallons sold, or removed for consumption or sale, and the proof thereof, not before accounted for; and shall also keep a book, or books, in a form to be prescribed by the Commissioner of Internal Revenue, and to be open at all seasonable hours for inspection by the assessor, assistant assessor, collector, deputy collector, or inspector of the district, wherein shall be entered, from day to day, the quantities of grain, or other vegetable productions, or other substances put into the mash tub by him, his agent or superintendent, for the purpose of producing spirits; and shall verify or cause to be verified the said entries, reports, books, and accounts, by oath or affirmation, to be taken before the assessor or assistant assessor, or other competent officer, according to the form required by law, and shall immediately forward to the collector of the district one of the said duplicate accounts duly verified as aforesaid; and shall also pay to the collector the duties on the spirits so distilled and sold, or removed for consumption or sale, and in said accounts mentioned at the time of rendering the duplicate account thereof: *Provided*, That distillers who distil or manufacture less than one hundred and fifty barrels of spirits per year may make returns and pay duties on the first day of each and every month in lieu of the first, eleventh, and twenty-first days of the month, and furnish bonds correspondingly, anything to the contrary notwithstanding: *And provided further*, That brandy distilled from grapes shall pay a tax of twenty-five cents per gallon.

Render tri-monthly accounts to assessor.

Record of quantity of grain, &c., used.

Record open to officers.

Record to be verified by oath.

Pay duties to collector tri-monthly.

Distillers who distil less than 150 barrels per year to make monthly returns.

Tax on brandy made from grapes.

Secretary of the Treasury shall appoint inspectors.

SEC. 58. *And be it further enacted*, That there shall be appointed by the Secretary of the Treasury, in every collection district where the same may be necessary, one or more inspectors of spirits, refined coal oil or other oil, tobacco, cigars, and other articles, who shall take an oath faithfully to perform their duties, in such form as the Commissioner of Internal Revenue shall prescribe, and who shall be entitled to receive such fees as may be fixed and prescribed by said Commissioner, to be paid by the owner or manufacturer of the articles inspected, gauged, or proved. And any manufacturer of spirits, refined coal oil or other oil, tobacco, cigars, or other articles which may by law be required to be inspected, who shall refuse to admit an inspector upon his premises, so far as it may be necessary for the performance of his duties, or who shall obstruct an inspector in the performance of his duties, shall forfeit the sum of one hundred dollars, to be recovered in the manner provided for other penalties imposed by this act.

Commis'er shall prescribe form of oath and fees.

Penalty of $100 for refusal to admit inspectors, &c.

All spirits to be inspected before used or removed.

SEC. 59. *And be it further enacted*, That all spirits distilled as aforesaid by any person licensed as aforesaid shall, before the same are used, or removed for any purpose, be inspected, gauged, and proved by some inspector appointed for the performance of such duties, who shall mark upon the cask or other package containing such spirits, in a manner to be prescribed by said Commissioner, the quantity and proof of the contents of such cask or package, with the date of inspection and the name of the inspector, and shall make a return of all spirits so inspected, and the name of the distiller, to the collector, and a duplicate thereof to the assessor of the district; and the duty imposed by law shall be paid on all spirits so inspected and not removed forthwith to a bonded warehouse. And any person who shall attempt fraudulently to evade the payment of duties upon any spirits distilled as aforesaid, by changing in any manner the mark upon any such cask or package, shall forfeit the sum of one hundred dollars for each cask or package so altered or changed, to be recovered as hereinbefore provided. And any such inspector who shall knowingly put upon any such cask or package any false or fraudulent mark shall be liable to the same penalty hereinbefore provided for each cask or package so fraudulently marked. And any person who shall purchase or sell any empty cask with the inspection marks thereon, or who shall fraudulently use any cask or package so marked, for the purpose of selling any other spirits than that so inspected, or for selling spirits of a quality or quantity different from that so inspected, shall be subject to a like penalty for each cask or package so purchased, sold, or used.

Inspection marks.

Inspector to make returns to collector and assessor.

Tax to be paid unless spirits are removed to bonded warehouse.

Penalty of $100 per cask for fraudulent marking, or for purchasing or using branded casks fraudulently.

Penalty for buying or selling casks with inspection marks thereon.

SEC. 60. *And be it further enacted*, That the owner or owners of any distillery or oil refinery, may provide, at his or their own expense, a warehouse, in conformity with such regulations as the Secretary of the Treasury may prescribe; and such warehouse, when approved by the collector, is hereby declared a bonded warehouse of the United States, and shall be used only for storing distilled spirits or refined coal oal, or naphtha, and to be under the custody of the collector or his deputy. And the duty on the spirits, coal oil, or naphtha stored in such warehouse shall be paid before it is removed from such warehouse, unless removed in pursuance of law.

Distillers and refiners of coal oil may erect warehouse.

Declared bonded warehouse.

Duty to be paid before removal from warehouse.

SEC. 61. *And be it further enacted*, That all distilled spirits and all refined coal oil and naphtha, upon which an excise duty is imposed by law, may, after being inspected, gauged, proved, and marked by the inspector according to the provisions of this act, be removed, without payment of the duty, under such rules and regulations, and upon the execution of such transportation bonds or other security as the Secretary of the Treasury may prescribe. The said spirits, oil, or naphtha so removed shall be transferred directly from the distillery or refinery to a bonded warehouse, established in conformity with law and treasury regulations, and may be transported from such warehouse to any one other bonded warehouse used for the storage of distilled spirits, coal oil, or naphtha. And after the arrival of such distilled spirits, coal oil, or naphtha, at the bonded warehouse within the district of the assessor to which it has been transferred, it shall be again inspected, and the duty shall be assessed and paid on any deficiency or reduction of the number of proof gallons beyond such allowance for leakage as may be established by the regulations of the Commissioner of Internal Revenue, received at the warehouse, from the number of proof gallons as stated in the bond given at the place of shipment. And any distilled spirits, coal oil, or naphtha in the public warehouses shall be

Distilled spirits, refined coal oil, and naphtha may be removed without payment of duty under bond, &c.

Transfer from one to another bonded warehouse

Reinspection and payment of duty required on any deficiency beyond the allowance for leakage.

Cost and expenses chargeable same as on imported goods deposited in bonded warehouse.

Spirits, oil, or naphtha in the custody of officer while in a bonded warehouse, and at the risk of the owner.

Owner to pay expense of labor upon goods in bonded warehouse.

No drawback to be allowed.

subject to the same rules and regulations, and be chargeable with the same costs and expenses in all respects to which imported goods deposited in public store or bonded warehouse may be subject; and shall be in charge of a proper officer, to be designated by the Secretary of the Treasury, who, with the owner and proprietor of the warehouse, shall have the joint custody of all the distilled spirits, oil, or naphtha so stored in said warehouse, which shall be at the risk of the owner of the said spirits, oil, or naphtha. And all labor on the same shall be performed by the owner or proprietor of the warehouse, under the supervision of the officer in charge of the same, and at the expense of said owner or proprietor of the warehouse. And no drawback shall in any case be allowed on any distilled spirits, coal oil, or naphtha, upon which an excise duty shall have been paid, either before or after it shall have been placed in a bonded warehouse: *Provided*, That any distilled spirits, coal oil, or naphtha may be withdrawn from the bonded warehouse after payment, to the collector of internal revenue for the district in which the warehouse is situated, of the duty imposed by law, or may be removed without payment of the duty for the purpose of being exported, or for the purpose of being redistilled for export, after the quantity and proof of the spirits, oil, or naphtha to be removed has been ascertained and inspected according to the provisions of law, under such rules and regulations and the execution of such bond or other security as the Secretary of the Treasury may prescribe. And any spirits, oil, or naphtha so removed for distillation shall be returned to the warehouse and shall be again inspected, and the duty shall be paid to the said collector on any deficiency or reduction beyond the allowance for loss by redistillation established by the Commissioner of Internal Revenue, in the number of proof gallons received at the warehouse for the purpose of being exported, as aforesaid. And nothing in this section shall be construed to prevent the manufacture for exportation, without payment of duty, of medicines, preparations, compositions, perfumery, cosmetics, cordials, and other liquors manufactured wholly or in part of domestic spirits, as provided for in this act.

Distilled spirits, coal oil, or naphtha may be withdrawn from bonded warehouse under certain circumstances

Spirits, &c., so removed for distillation to be returned to the warehouse and again inspected.

Medicines, &c., may be manufactured for exportation without payment of duty.

Entries on the distiller's books to be verified by oath or affirmation.

SEC. 62. *And be it further enacted*, That the entries required to be made in the books of the distiller, as aforesaid, shall, on the first, eleventh, and twenty-first days of each and every month, or within five days thereafter, be verified by oath or affirmation of the person or persons by whom such entries shall have been made, which oath or affirmation shall be certified at the end of such entries by the assessor, or assistant assessor, or officer administering the same, and shall be, in substance, as follows: "I do swear (or affirm) that the foregoing entries were made by me on the respective days specified, and that they state, according to the best of my knowledge and belief, the whole quantity of spirituous liquors distilled and sold, or removed for consumption or sale, at the distillery owned by ——— ———, in the county of ———, amounting to ——— gallons, according to proof prescribed by the laws of the United States."

Oath

When entries not made by owner, agent, or superintendent.

SEC. 63. *And be it further enacted*, That the owner, agent, or superintendent aforesaid, shall, in case the original entries required to be made in his books by this act shall not have been made by himself, subjoin to the oath or affirmation of the person by whom they were made the following oath or affirmation, to be taken as aforesaid: "I do swear (or affirm) that, to the best of my knowledge and belief, the foregoing entries are just and true, and that I have taken all the means in my power to make them so."

Subjoined oath of the owner, agent, or superintendent, in certain cases.

SEC. 64. *And be it further enacted,* That there shall be paid on all beer, lager beer, ale, porter, and other similar fermented liquors, by whatever name such liquors may be called, a duty of one dollar for each and every barrel containing not more than thirty-one gallons, and at a like rate for any other quantity, or for fractional parts of a barrel, which shall be brewed or manufactured and sold, or removed for consumption or sale, within the United States or the Territories thereof, or within the District of Columbia; which duty shall be paid by the owner, agent, or superintendent of the brewery or premises in which such fermented liquors shall be made, and shall be paid at the time of rendering the accounts of such fermented liquors so chargeable with duty, as hereinafter required: *Provided,* That fractional parts of a barrel shall be halves, thirds, quarters, sixths, eighths, and sixteenths; and any fractional part containing less than one-sixteenth shall be accounted one-sixteenth; more than one-sixteenth, and not more than one-eighth, shall be accounted one-eighth; more than one-eighth, and not more than one-sixth, shall be accounted one-sixth; more than one-sixth, and not more than one-quarter, shall be accounted one-quarter; more than one-quarter, and not more than one-third, shall be accounted one-third; more than one-third, and not more than one-half, shall be accounted one-half; more than one-half shall be accounted one barrel: *Provided, further,* That beer, lager beer, ale, porter, and other fermented liquors in bottles, shall be assessed, according to the quantity contained therein, at the rate of one dollar for thirty-one gallons, when the duty has not been previously paid on the liquors contained therein.

Duty on beer, lager beer, ale, porter, and other similar fermented liquors.

Duty paid at the time of rendering accounts.

Mode of reckoning fractional parts

Beer, &c., in bottles, to be assessed according to the quantity contain'd therein.

SEC. 65. *And be it further enacted,* That every person owning or occupying any brewery or premises used or intended to be used for the purpose of brewing or making such fermented liquors, or who shall have such premises under his control or superintendence as agent for the owner or occupant, or shall have in his possession or custody any vessel or vessels intended to be used on said premises in the manufacture of beer, lager beer, ale, porter, or other similar fermented liquors, either as owner, agent, or otherwise, shall, from day to day, enter or cause to be entered in a book to be kept by him for that purpose, and which shall be open at all times, (except Sundays,) between the rising and setting of the sun, for the inspection of said assessor, assistant assessor, collector, deputy collector, or inspector, who may take any minutes or memorandums or transcripts thereof, the quantity, packages, or number of barrels and fractional parts of barrels of fermented liquors made, and also the quantity sold, or removed for consumption or sale, keeping separate account of the several kinds and descriptions; and shall render to said assessor or assistant assessor, on the first day of each month in each year, or within ten days thereafter, a general account in writing, taking from his books, of the quantity or number of barrels and fractional parts of barrels of each kind of fermented liquors made, and also of the quantity sold, or removed for consumption or sale, for one month preceding said day; and shall verify, or cause to be verified, the said entries,

Persons owning or occupying any brewery, &c., shall keep a book where he shall enter the quantity, &c., of fermented liquors made, also the quantity sold or removed for consumption or sale; said book to be at all times open to the assistant assessor.

A general account to be rendered on the first day of each month.

Account to be verified by oath or affirmation before the assessor or assistant assessor.

Forward duplicate to collector and pay the duty.

reports, books, and general accounts, and the facts therein set forth, on oath or affirmation, to be taken before the assessor or assistant assessor, or other competent officer, according to the form required by law; and shall immediately forward to the collector of the district one of the said duplicate accounts, duly certified by the assessor or assistant assessor, and shall also pay to the said collector the duties which are imposed by law on the liquor made and sold, or removed for consumption or sale, and in the said accounts mentioned, at the time of rendering the duplicate account thereof as aforesaid. But where the manufacturer of any beer, lager beer, or ale, manufactures the same in one collection district, and owns or occupies a depot or warehouse for the storage and sale of such beer, lager beer, or ale in another collection district, he may, instead of paying to the collector of the district where the same was manufactured the duties chargeable thereon, present to such assessor or assistant assessor an invoice of the quantity or number of barrels about to be removed for the purpose of storage and sale, specifying in such invoice the depot or warehouse in which he intends to place such beer, lager beer, or ale; and thereupon such assessor or assistant assessor shall indorse on such invoice his permission for such removal, and the assessor or assistant assessor shall, at the same time, transmit to the collector of the district in which such depot or warehouse is situated a duplicate of such invoice; and thereafter the manufacturer of the beer, lager beer, or ale so removed shall render the same account, and pay the same duties, and be subject to the same liabilities and penalties as if the beer, lager beer, or ale had been manufactured in the district to which the same has been removed. The Commissioner of Internal Revenue may prescribe such rules as he may deem necessary for the purpose of carrying the provisions of this section into effect.

Where the manufacturer of beer, &c., manufactures the same in one district and has a depot for storage and sale of the same in another collection district.

Assessor or assistant assessor may grant permission for removal.

Duty to be paid in the district to which the same has been removed.

Commissioner may prescribe rules.

Entries made in brewer's book required to be verified by oath or affirmation of the person or persons by whom they were made, and the oath or affirmation certified by the assessor or assistant assessor.

SEC. 66. *And be it further enacted*, That the entries made in the books required to be kept by the foregoing section shall, on said first day of each and every month, or within ten days thereafter, be verified by the oath or affirmation of the person or persons by whom such entries shall have been made, which oath or affirmation shall be certified at the end of such entries by the assessor or assistant assessor, or other competent officer administering the same, and shall be, in substance, as follows: "I do swear (or affirm) that the foregoing entries were made by me on the respective days specified, and that they state, according to the best of my knowledge and belief, the whole quantity of fermented liquors either brewed, or brewed and sold at the brewery owned by ———, in the county of ———, amounting to ——— barrels."

Oath.

Entries made by other persons to be verified.

SEC. 67. *And be it further enacted*, That the owner, agent, or superintendent aforesaid, shall, in case the original entries required to be made in his books shall not have been made by himself, subjoin to the oath or affirmation the following oath or affirmation, to be taken as aforesaid: "I do swear (or affirm) that, to the best of my knowledge and belief, the foregoing entries are just and true, and that I have taken all the means in my power to make them so."

Oath.

Penalty for neglect to make true reports, &c.

SEC. 68. *And be it further enacted*, That the owner, agent, or superintendent of any vessel or vessels used in making fermented liquors, or of any still, boiler, or other vessel used in the distillation of spirits on which duty is payable, who shall neglect or refuse to make true and exact entry and report of the same, or to do or cause to be done any of the things by law required to be done as aforesaid, shall forfeit for every such neglect or refusal all the liquors and spirits made by or for him, and all the vessels used in making the same, and the stills, boilers, and other vessels used in distillation, together with the sum of five hundred dollars, to be recovered with costs of suits; which said liquors or spirits, with the vessels containing the same, with all the vessels used in making the same, may be seized by any collector or deputy collector of internal duties, and held by him until a decision shall be had thereon according to law: *Provided*, That such seizure be made within thirty days after the cause for the same shall have come to the knowledge of the collector or deputy collector, and that proceedings to enforce said forfeiture shall have [been] commenced by such collector within twenty days after the seizure thereof. And the proceedings to enforce said forfeiture of said property shall be in the *the* nature of a proceeding in rem, in the circuit or district court of the United States for the district where such seizure is made, or in any other court of competent jurisdiction.

Forfeiture of stills, &c.

As to time of seizure.

Proceedings in rem.

SEC. 69. *And be it further enacted*, That in all cases in which the duties aforesaid, payable on spirits distilled and sold, or removed for consumption or sale, or beer, lager beer, ale, porter, and other similar fermented liquors, shall not be paid at the time of rendering the account of the same, or at the time when they shall have become payable, as herein required, to the collector or deputy collector of the district, the person or persons chargeable therewith shall pay, in addition, ten per centum on the amount thereof; and, until such duties, with such addition, shall be paid, they shall be and remain a lien upon the distillery where such liquors have been distilled, and upon the brewery where such liquors have been brewed, and upon the stills, boilers, vats, and all other implements thereto belonging, and upon the lot or tract of land whereon the distillery or brewery is situate, until the same shall have been paid. And in case of refusal or neglect to pay said duties, with the addition, within ten days after the same shall have become payable, the amount thereof may be recovered by distraint and sale of the goods, chattels, and effects of the delinquent.

Ten per centum added for neglect to pay duties.

Duties a lien on distillery, &c.

Distraint.

SEC. 70. *And be it further enacted*, That every person licensed as aforesaid to distil spirits, or licensed as a brewer, who shall neglect or refuse to furnish the account and duplicate thereof, as hereinbefore provided, or who shall refuse to permit the said assessor, assistant assessor, collector or deputy collector, or inspector to examine the books in the manner provided for, when requested, shall, for every such refusal or neglect, forfeit the sum of three hundred dollars.

Penalty of $300 for neglect, &c.

LICENSES.

SEC. 71. *And be it further enacted*, That no person, firm, company, or corporation shall be engaged in, prosecute, or carry on any trade, business, or profession, hereinafter mentioned and described, until he or they shall have obtained a license therefor in the manner hereinafter provided.

Trades and occupations to be licensed.

SEC. 72. *And be it further enacted*, That every person, firm, company, or corporation required by this act to obtain a license to engage in any trade, business, or profession, for which a

Requirements to obtain license.

license is required by law, shall register with the assistant assessor of the assessment district, in which he shall design to carry on such trade, business, or profession, first, his or their name or style, and in case of a firm or company, the names of the several persons constituting such firm or company, and their places of residence; second, the trade, business, or profession for which a license is desired; third, the place where such trade, business, or profession is to be carried on; fourth, if a rectifier, the number of barrels he designs to rectify; if a peddler, whether he designs to travel on foot, or with one, two, or more horses; if an innkeeper, the yearly rental value of the house and property to be occupied for said purpose; if not rented, the assistant assessor shall value the same. All of which facts shall be returned duly certified by such assistant assessor, both to the assessor and collector of the district; and thereupon, upon payment to the collector or deputy collector of the district the amount as hereinafter provided, such collector or deputy collector shall make out and deliver a license for such trade, business, or profession.

Penalty for not taking out a license.

SEC. 73. *And be it further enacted,* That if any person or persons shall exercise or carry on any trade, business, or profession, or do any act hereinafter mentioned, for the exercising, carrying on, or doing of which trade, business, or profession, a license is required by this act, without taking out such license as in that behalf required, he, she, or they shall, for every such offence, besides being liable to the payment of the tax, be subject to imprisonment for a term not exceeding two years, or a fine not exceeding five hundred dollars, or both, one moiety of such fine to the use of the United States, the other moiety to the use of the person who shall first give information of the fact whereby said forfeiture was incurred.

Distribution of fines.

Conditions of license.

SEC. 74. *And be it further enacted,* That in every license to be taken out under or by authority of this act shall be contained and set forth the purpose, trade, business, or profession for which such license is granted, and the name and place of abode of the person or persons taking out the same; if for a rectifier, the quantity of spirits authorized to be rectified; if by a peddler, whether authorized to travel on foot, or with or [one,] or two, or more horses, the time for which such license is to run, and the date or time of granting such license, and (except in the case of auctioneers and peddlers) the place at which the trade, business, or profession for which such license is granted shall be carried on: *Provided,* That a license granted under this act shall not authorize the person or persons, (except lawyers, physicians, surgeons, dentists, cattle brokers, horse dealers, and auctioneers,) or firm, company, or corporation mentioned therein, to exercise or carry on the trade, business, or profession specified in such license in any other place than that mentioned therein, or otherwise provided; but nothing herein contained shall prohibit the storage of goods, wares, or merchandise in other places than the place of business nor the sale by manufacturers or producers of their own goods, wares, and merchandise, at the place of production or manufacture, or at their principal office or place of business, provided no goods, wares, or merchandise shall be kept for sale at said office. And every person exercising or carrying on any trade, business, or profession, or doing any act for which a license is required, shall, on demand of any officer of internal revenue, produce such

Proviso against carrying on business in any other place than described in license.

Must produce license on demand of officer.

license, and unless he shall do so may be taken and deemed to have no license. And in case any peddler shall refuse to produce his or her license when demanded by any officer of internal revenue, said officer may seize the horse, wagon, and contents, or pack, bundle, or basket of any person so refusing and hold the same until the license is produced. And all licenses granted after the first day of May in any year shall continue in force until the first day of May next succeeding, and shall be issued upon the payment of a ratable propotion of the whole amount of duty imposed for such license; and each license so granted shall be dated on the first day of the month in which the liability therefor accrued.

Penalty.

Licenses to expire May 1.

SEC. 75. *And be it further enacted,* That upon the death of any person or persons licensed under or by virtue of this act, or upon the removal of any person or persons from the house or premises at which the trade, business, or profession mentioned in such license, was authorized, it may and shall be lawful for the collector to authorize, by indorsement on such license, or otherwise, as the Commissioner of Internal Revenue shall direct, the person or persons so removing, as aforesaid, to any other place, to carry on the trade, business, or profession specified in such license, at the place to which such person may have removed, or the executors or administrators, or the wife or child of such deceased, person, or the assignee or assigns of such person or persons so removing as aforesaid, who shall be possessed of and occupy the house or premises before used for such purpose as aforesaid, in like manner to exercise or carry on the same trade, business, or profession mentioned in such license, in or upon the same house or premises at which said person or persons, as aforesaid, deceased or removing as before mentioned, by virtue of such license before exercised or carried on such trade, business, or profession, for or during the residue of the term for which such license was originally granted, without taking out any fresh license for the residue of such term, until the expiration thereof: *Provided, always,* That a fresh entry of the premises at which such trade, business, or profession shall continue to be exercised or carried on, as aforesaid, shall thereupon be made by and in the name or names of the person or persons to whom such authority, as aforesaid, shall be granted.

Removals authorized.

To be indorsed on license.

Exec'rs, &c., may carry on business.

Licenses may be transferred.

New entry of license to be made.

SEC. 76. *And be it further enacted,* That in every case where more than one of the pursuits, employments, or occupations, hereinafter described, shall be pursued or carried on in the same place by the same person at the same time, except as therein mentioned, license must be taken out for each according to the rates severally prescribed: *Provided,* That in cities and towns having a less population than six thousand persons according to the last preceding census, one license, if so applied for, may embrace the business of land warrant brokers, claim agents, and real estate agents, upon payment of the highest fee for licenses applicable to either one of said pursuits.

License to be taken for each pursuit, &c.

Proviso.

SEC. 77. *And be it further enacted,* That no auctioneer shall be authorized, by virtue of his license as such auctioneer, to employ any other person to act as auctioneer in his behalf, except in his own store or warehouse, or in his presence, or by virtue of said license to sell any goods or other property at private sale; and any auctioneer who shall sell any goods or commodities, other-

Auctioneers not to employ other persons, nor to sell at private sale.

Penalty

wise than by auction, without having taken out a license for that purpose, shall be subject and liable to the penalty imposed upon persons dealing in, or retailing, trading, or selling any such goods or commodities without license, notwithstanding any license granted, as aforesaid, for the purpose of exercising or carrying on the trade or business of an auctioneer; and where such goods or commodities are the property of any person or persons duly licensed to deal in, or retail, or trade in, or sell the same, such person or persons having made lawful entry of his, her, or their house or premises for such purpose, it shall and may be lawful for any person exercising or carrying on the trade or business of an auctioneer being duly licensed for that purpose, to sell such goods or commodities for and on behalf of such person or persons in said house or premises, without taking out a separate license for such sale. The provisions of this section shall not apply to judicial or executive officers making auction sales by virtue of any judgment or decree of any court, nor public sales made by executors and administrators.

Licensed auctioneer may sell goods of licensed dealer on premises.

Not to apply to sales by executive and judicial officers, &c.

No license to exempt from penalty provided by State laws for carrying on the trade, &c., nor authorize a trade, &c., prohibited by State laws.

SEC. 78. *And be it further enacted*, That no license hereinbefore provided for shall, if granted, be held, or construed to exempt any person carrying on the trade, business, or profession specified in said license from any penalty or punishment provided by the laws of any State for carrying on such trade, business, or profession, within such State, or in any manner to authorize the commencement or continuance of such trade, business, or profession, contrary to the laws of such State, or in places prohibited by municipal law; no[r] shall any such license be held or construed to prevent or prohibit any State from placing a duty or tax for State or other purposes on any trade, business, or profession, for which a license is required by this act; nor shall any person carrying on any trade, business, or profession, for which a license is required by this act, be exempted from procuring such license, or from any penalty or punishment herein provided, by, or in consequence of, any State law either authorizing or prohibiting such trade, business, or profession.

Business to be done at pl'ce nam'd in license, except by lawyers, &c.

SEC. 79. *And be it further enacted*, That there shall be paid annually for each license granted, the sum herein stated respectively. Any number of persons, except lawyers, conveyancers, claim agents, physicians, surgeons, dentists, cattle brokers, horse dealers, and peddlers, carrying on such business in copartnership may transact such business at the place specified in their license, and not otherwise, that is to say:

Bankers, $100.

For every $1,000 in excess of $50,000 $2.

Definition of.

One. Bankers using or employing a capital not exceeding the sum of fifty thousand dollars shall pay one hundred dollars for each license; when using or employing a capital exceeding fifty thousand dollars, for every additional thousand dollars in excess of fifty thousand dollars, two dollars. Every person, firm, or company, and every incorporated or other bank, having a place of business where credits are opened by the deposit or collection of money or currency, subject to be paid or remitted upon draft, check, or order, or where money is advanced or loaned on stocks, bonds, bullion, bills of exchange, or promissory notes, or where stocks, bonds, bullion, bills of exchange, or promissory notes are received for discount or sale, shall be regarded a banker under this act: *Provided*, That any savings bank having no capital stock, and whose business is confined to receiving deposits and

Savings banks exempted in certain cases.

loaning the same for the benefit of its depositors, and which does no other business of banking, shall not be liable to pay for a license as a banker.

Two. Wholesale dealers, whose annual sales do not exceed fifty thousand dollars, shall pay fifty dollars for each license; and if exceeding fifty thousand dollars, for every additional thousand dollars in excess of fifty thousand dollars, one dollar. Every person shall be regarded as a wholesale dealer under this act whose business it is to sell or offer to sell any goods, wares, or merchandise of foreign or domestic production, not including wines, spirits, or malt liquors, whose annual sales exceed twenty-five thousand dollars. And the license required by any wholesale dealer shall not be for a less amount than his sales for the previous year, unless he has made or proposes to make some change in his business that will in the judgment of the assessor or assistant assessor reduce the amount of his annual sales; nor shall any license as a wholesale dealer allow any such person to act as a commercial broker: *Provided,* That any license understated may and shall be again assessed, and that no person holding a license as a wholesale dealer in liquors shall be required to take an additional license on account of the sale of other goods, wares, or merchandise on the same premises.

Wholesale dealers, $50.

For every $1,000 in excess of $50,000 $1

Definition of.

Cannot act as commerc'l broker.

License understated may be again assessed.

Three. Retail dealers shall pay ten dollars for each license. Every person whose business or occupation it is to sell or offer for sale any goods, wares, or merchandise of foreign or domestic production, not including spirits, wines, ale, beer, or other malt liquors, and whose annual sales exceed one thousand and do not exceed twenty-five thousand dollars, shall be regarded as a retail dealer under this act.

Retail dealers, $10.

Definition of.

Four. Wholesale dealers in liquors whose annual sales do not exceed fifty thousand dollars shall pay fifty dollars for each license; and if exceeding fifty thousand dollars, for every additional one thousand dollars in excess of fifty thousand dollars, one dollar. Every person who shall sell or offer for sale any distilled spirits, fermented liquors, or wines of any kind in quantities of more than three gallons at one time to the same purchaser, or whose annual sales, including sales of other merchandise, shall exceed twenty-five thousand dollars, shall be regarded a wholesale dealer in liquors.

Wholesale liquor dealers, $50.

For every $1,000 in excess of $50,000 $1.

Definition of.

Five. Retail dealers in liquors shall pay twenty-five dollars for each license. Every person who shall sell or offer for sale foreign or domestic spirits, wines, ale, beer, or other malt liquors in quantities of three gallons or less, or whose annual sales, including all sales of other merchandise, do not exceed twenty-five thousand dollars, shall be regarded as a retail dealer in liquors under this act. But nothing herein contained shall authorize the sale of any spirits, wines, or malt liquors to be drank on the premises.

Retail liquor dealers, $25.

Definition of.

Six. Lottery-ticket dealers shall pay one hundred dollars for each license. Every person, association, firm, or corporation who shall make, sell, or offer to sell lottery tickets or fractional parts thereof, or any token, certificate, or device representing or intended to represent a lottery ticket or any fractional part thereof, or any policy of numbers in any lottery, or shall manage any lottery or prepare schemes of lotteries, or superintend the drawing of any lottery, shall be deemed a lottery-ticket dealer under this act.

Lottery ticket dealers, $100.

Definition of.

Seven. Horse dealers shall pay for each license the sum of ten

Horse dealers, $10.

Definition of. dollars. Any person whose business it is to buy or sell horses or mules shall be regarded a horse dealer under this act: *Provided*, That one license having been paid, no additional license shall be required of any horse dealer who keeps a livery stable, nor of any livery-stable keeper who may also be a horse dealer.

Livery stable keepers, $10. Definition of. Eight. Livery-stable keepers shall pay ten dollars for each license. Any person whose business it is to keep horses for hire, or to let, or to keep, feed, or board horses for others, shall be regarded as a livery-stable keeper under this act.

Brokers, $50. Definition of. Nine. Brokers shall pay fifty dollars for each license. Every person, firm, or company, except such as hold a license as a banker, whose business it is as a broker to negotiate purchases or sales of stocks, exchange, bullion, coined money, bank notes, promissory notes, or other securities, shall be regarded as a broker, under this act, and shall make oath or affirmation, according to the form to be prescribed by the Commissioner of Internal Revenue, that all their transactions are made for a commission: Bankers not subject to license as brokers. *Provided*, That any person holding a license as a banker shall not be required to take out a license as a broker.

Pawnbrokers, $50. Ten. Pawnbrokers using or employing a capital of not exceeding fifty thousand dollars shall pay fifty dollars for each license, and when using or employing a capital exceeding fifty thousand For every $1,000 in excess of $50,000, $2. dollars, for every additional thousand dollars in excess of fifty thousand dollars, two dollars. Every person whose business or Definition of. occupation it is to take or receive, by way of pledge, pawn, or exchange, any goods, wares, or merchandise, or any kind of personal property whatever, for the repayment or security of money lent thereon, shall be deemed a pawnbroker under this act.

Land warrant brokers, $25. Definition of. Eleven. Land-warrant brokers shall pay twenty-five dollars for each license. Any person shall be regarded as a land-warrant broker within the meaning of this act who makes a business of buying and selling land warrants, or of furnishing them to settlers or other persons.

Cattle brokers, $10. Twelve. Cattle brokers, whose annual sales do not exceed ten thousand dollars, shall pay for each license the sum of ten dollars; For every $1,000 in excess of $10,000, $1. and if exceeding the sum of ten thousand dollars, one dollar for each additional thousand dollars. Any person whose business it Definition of. is to buy, or sell, or deal in cattle, hogs, or sheep, shall be considered as a cattle broker.

Produce brokers, $10. Definition of. Thirteen. Produce brokers, whose annual sales do not exceed the sum of ten thousand dollars, shall pay ten dollars for each license. Every person, other than one holding a license as a broker, wholesale, or retail dealer, whose occupation it is to buy or sell agricultural or farm products and whose annual sales do not exceed ten thousand dollars, shall be regarded as a produce broker under this act.

Commercial brokers, $20. Definition of. Fourteen. Commercial brokers shall pay twenty dollars for each license. Any person or firm, whose business it is, as a broker, to negotiate sales or purchases of goods, wares, produce, or merchandise, not otherwise provided for in this act, or seek orders therefor in original or unbroken packages, or to negotiate freights and other business for the owners of vessels, or for the shippers or consignors or consignees of freight carried by vessels, shall be regarded a commercial broker under this act.

Custom-house brokers, $10. Fifteen. Custom-house brokers shall pay ten dollars for each license. Every person whose occupation it is, as the agent of others, to arrange entries and other custom-house papers, or transact business at any port of entry relating to the importation or exportation of goods, wares or merchandise, shall be regarded a custom-house broker under this act. Definition of.

Sixteen. Distillers shall pay fifty dollars for each license. Every person, firm, or corporation who distils or manufactures spirits for sale shall be deemed a distiller under this act: *Provided*, That any person, firm, or corporation, distilling or manufacturing less than three hundred barrels per year shall pay twenty-five dollars for a license: *And provided, further*, That no license shall be required for any still, stills, or other apparatus used by druggists and chemists for the recovery of alcohol for pharmaceutical and chemical or scientific purposes which has been used in those processes: *And provided, further*, That distillers of apples, grapes, and peaches, distilling or manufacturing less than one hundred and fifty barrels per year from the same, shall pay twelve and one-half dollars for a license for that purpose. Distillers, $50. Definition of. Distillers making less than 300 barrels per year, $25. Distillers of apples, grapes, and peaches, making less than 150 bbls. per year, $12 50.

Seventeen. Brewers shall pay fifty dollars for each license. Every person, firm, or corporation, who manufactures fermented liquors of any name or description, for sale, from malt, wholly or in part, or from any substitute therefor, shall be deemed a brewer under this act: *Provided*, That any person, firm, or corporation who manufactures less than five hundred barrels per year shall pay the sum of twenty-five dollars for a license. Brewers, $50. Definition of. Brewers making less than 500 bbls. per year, $25.

Eighteen. Rectifiers shall pay twenty-five dollars for each license to rectify any quantity of spirituous liquors, not exceeding five hundred barrels, packages or casks, containing not more than forty gallons to each barrel, package, or cask of liquor so rectified; and twenty-five dollars additional for each additional five hundred such barrels, packages or casks, or any fractional part thereof. Every person, firm, or corporation, who rectifies, purifies, or refines spirituous liquors or wines by any process, or mixes distilled spirits, whiskey, brandy, gin, or wine, with any materials for sale under the name of whiskey, rum, brandy, gin, wine, or any other name, shall be regarded as a rectifier under this act. Rectifiers, $25. For every additional 500 barrels, $25. Definition of.

Nineteen. Coal-oil distillers shall pay for each license the sum of fifty dollars. Any person, firm, or corporation, who shall refine, produce, or distil crude or refined petroleum or rock oil, or crude coal oil, or crude or refined oil made of asphaltum, shale, peat, or other bituminous substances, or shall manufacture coal illuminating oil, shall be regarded a coal-oil distiller under this act. Coal oil distillers, $50. Definition of.

Twenty. Hotels, inns, and taverns shall be classified and rated according to the yearly rental, or, if not rented, according to the estimated yearly rental, of the house and property intended to be occupied for said purposes, as follows, to wit: All cases where the rent or valuation of the yearly rental of said house and property shall be two hundred dollars, or less, shall pay ten dollars. And if exceeding two hundred dollars, for any additional one huudred dollars or fractional part thereof in excess of two hundred dollars, five dollars. Every place where food and lodging are provided for and furnished to travellers and sojourners, in view of payment therefor, shall be regarded as a hotel, inn, or tavern under this act: *Provided*, That nothing herein contained shall be construed to exempt keepers of hotels, taverns, and eating-houses in which liquors are sold by retail, to be Hotels, inns, and taverns. Where the yearly rental does not exceed $200, $10. For every additional $100, $5. Keepers of hotels, taverns, and eating-houses, selling liquors, must take additional license.

drank upon the premises, from taking out a license for such sale, for which license they shall pay a tax of twenty-five dollars. The yearly rental shall be fixed and established by the assessor of the proper district at its proper value, but if rented, at not less than the actual rent agreed on by the parties. All steamers and vessels, upon waters of the United States, on board of which passengers or travellers are provided with food or lodgings, shall be subject to and required to pay twenty-five dollars for each license: *Provided*, That if there be any fraud or collusion in the return of actual rent to the assessor, there shall be a penalty equal to double the amount of licenses required by this section, to be collected as other penalties under this act are collected.

Steamers and vessels, $25.

Penalty in case of fraud.

Eating-houses, $10.

Definition of.

Twenty-one. Eating-houses shall pay ten dollars for each license. Every place where food or refreshments of any kind, not including spirits, wines, ale, beer, or other malt liquors, are provided for casual visitors and sold for consumption therein, shall be regarded as an eating-house under this act. But the keeper of an eating-house having taken out a license therefor shall not be required to take out a license as a confectioner, anything in this act to the contra[r]y notwithstanding.

Confectioners, $10.

Definition of.

Twenty-two. Confectioners shall pay ten dollars for each license. Every person who sells at retail confectionery, sweetmeats, comfits, or other confects, in any building, shall be regarded as a confectioner under this act. But wholesale and retail dealers, having taken out a license therefor, shall not be required to take out a license as confectioner, anything in this act to the contrary notwithstanding.

Claim agents, $10.

Definition of.

Twenty-three. Claim agents and agents for procuring patents shall pay ten dollars for each license. Every person whose business it is to prosecute claims in any of the executive departments of the federal government, or procure patents, shall be deemed a claim or patent agent, as the case may be, under this act.

Patent-right dealers, $10.

Definition of.

Twenty-four. Patent-right dealers shall pay ten dollars for each license. Every person whose business it is to sell or offer for sale patent rights shall be regarded a patent-right dealer under this act.

Real-estate agents, $10.

Definition of.

Twenty-five. Real-estate agents shall pay ten dollars for each license. Every person whose business it is to sell or offer for sale real estate for others, or to rent houses, stores, or other buildings or real estate, or to collect rent for others, shall be regarded as a real-estate agent under this act.

Conveyancers, $10.

Definition of.

Twenty-six. Conveyancers shall pay ten dollars for each license. Every person, other than one holding a license as a lawyer or claim agent, whose business it is to draw deeds, bonds, mortgages, wills, writs, or other legal papers, or to examine titles to real estate, shall be regarded a conveyancer under this act.

Intelligence office keepers, $10.

Definition of.

Twenty-seven. Intelligence office keepers shall pay ten dollars for each license. Every person whose business it is to find or furnish places of employment for others, or to find or furnish servants, upon application in writing or otherwise, receiving compensation therefor, shall be regarded as an intelligence office keeper under this act.

Insurance agents, $10.

Definition of.

Twenty-eight. Insurance agents shall pay ten dollars for each license. Any person who shall act as agent of any fire, marine, life, mutual, or other insurance company or companies, shall be regarded as an insurance agent under this act: *Provided*, That no license shall be required of any insurance agent or broker whose receipts, as such agent, are less than the sum of three hundred dollars in any one year.

Foreign insurance agents, $50.

Definition of.

Twenty-nine. Foreign insurance agents shall pay fifty dollars for each license. Every person who shall act as agent of any foreign fire, marine, life, mutual, or other insurance company or companies, shall be regarded as a foreign insurance agent under this act.

Auctioneers whose annual sales do not exceed $10,000, $10.

Annual sales exceeding $10,000, $20.

Definition of.

Thirty. Auctioneers whose annual sales do not exceed ten thousand dollars, shall pay ten dollars for each license; auctioneers whose annual sales exceed ten thousand dollars, shall pay twenty dollars for each license. Every person shall be deemed an auctioneer within the meaning of this act whose business it is to offer property for sale to the highest or best bidder.

Manufacturers, $10.

Definition of.

Thirty-one. Manufacturers shall pay ten dollars for each license. Any person, firm, or corporation, who shall manufacture by hand or machinery any goods, wares, or merchandise, exceeding annually the sum of one thousand dollars, shall be regarded a manufacturer under this act.

Peddlers

1st class, $50

2d class, $25.

3d class, $15.

4th class, $10.

Definition of.

Thirty-two. Peddlers shall be classified and rated as follows, to wit: when travelling with more than two horses, or mules, the first class, and shall pay fifty dollars for each license; when travelling with two horses, or mules, the second class, and shall pay twenty-five dollars for each license; when travelling with one horse, or mule, the third class, and shall pay fifteen dollars for each license; when travelling on foot, the fourth class, and shall pay ten dollars for each license. Any person, except persons peddling only newspapers, Bibles, or religious tracts, who sells or offers to sell, at retail, goods, wares, or other commodities, travelling from place to place, in the street, or through different parts of the country, shall be regarded a peddler under this act: *Provided*, That any peddler who sells, or offers to sell, dry goods, foreign and domestic, by one or more original packages or pieces, at one time, to the same person or persons, shall pay fifty dollars for each license. And any person who peddles jewelry shall pay fifty dollars for each license: *Provided, further*, That manufacturers and producers of agricultural tools and implements, garden seeds, stoves, and hollow ware, brooms, wooden ware, and powder, delivering and selling at wholesale any of said articles, by themselves or their authorized agents, at places other than the place of manufacture, shall not be required, for any sale thus made, to take out any additional license therefor: *Provided, further*, That nothing contained in this paragraph shall authorize the sale of wine, spirits, or malt liquors.

Peddlers of dry goods, $50.

Peddlers of jewelry, $50.

Apothecaries, $10.

Definition of.

Thirty-three. Apothecaries shall pay ten dollars for each license. Every person who keeps a shop or building where medicines are compounded or prepared according to prescriptions of physicians, or where medicines are sold, shall be regarded an apothecary under this act. But wholesale and retail dealers, who have taken out a license therefor shall not be required to take out a license as apothecary, anything in this act to the contrary notwithstanding; nor shall apothecaries who have taken out a license as such be required to take out a license as retail dealers in liquor in consequence of selling alcohol.

Photographers whose receipts do not exceed $500, $10.

Thirty-four. Photographers shall pay ten dollars for each license when the receipts do not exceed five hundred dollars; when over

Over $500 and under $1,000, $15. Over $1,000, $25. five hundred dollars and under one thousand dollars, fifteen dollars; when over one thousand dollars, twenty-five dollars. Any person or persons who make for sale photographs, ambrotypes, daguerreotypes, or pictures, by the action of light, shall be regarded a photographer under this act. Definition of.

Tobacconists, $10. Thirty-five. Tobacconists shall pay ten dollars for each license. Any person, firm, or corporation whose business it is to sell, at retail, cigars, snuff, or tobacco in any form, shall be regarded a tobacconist under this act. But wholesale and retail dealers, and keepers of hotels, inns, taverns, and eating-houses, having taken out a license therefor, shall not be required to take out a license as tobacconists, anything in this act to the contrary notwithstanding. Definition of.

Butchers, $10. Thirty-six. Butchers shall pay ten dollars for each license. Every person whose business it is to sell butchers' meat at retail shall be regarded as a butcher under this act: *Provided*, That no butcher having taken out a license, and paid ten dollars therefor, shall be required to take out a license as retail dealer on account of selling other articles at the same store, stall, or premises: *Provided, further*, That butchers whose annual sales do not exceed one thousand dollars, and butchers who retail butchers' meat exclusively by themselves or agents, and persons who sell shell or other fish, or both, travelling from place to place, and not from any shop or stand, shall be required to pay five dollars only for each license, any existing law to the contrary notwithstanding; and having taken out a license therefor, shall not be required to take out a license as a peddler for retailing butchers' meat or fish, as aforesaid. And no license shall be required of persons who sell shell or other fish from handcarts or wheelbarrows exclusively. Definition of. Butchers retailing from carts, $5.

Theatres, museums, and concert halls, $100. Thirty-seven. Proprietors of theatres, museums, and concert halls receiving pay as entrance money shall pay one hundred dollars for each license. Every edifice used for the purpose of dramatic or operatic or other representations, plays, or performances, and not including halls rented or used occasionally for concerts or theatrical representations, shall be regarded as a theatre under this act: *Provided*, That when any such edifice is under lease at the passage of this act, the fee for license shall be paid by the lessee, unless otherwise stipulated between the parties to said lease. Definition of.

Circuses, $100. Thirty-eight. The proprietor or proprietors of circuses shall pay one hundred dollars for each license. Every building, tent, space, or area where feats of horsemanship or acrobatic sports or theatrical performances are exhibited, shall be regarded as a circus under this act: *Provided*, That no license procured in one State shall be held to authorize exhibitions in another State. And but one license shall be required under this act to authorize exhibitions within any one State. Definition of.

Jugglers, $20. Thirty-nine. Jugglers shall pay for each license twenty dollars. Every person who performs by sleight of hand shall be regarded as a juggler under this act. The proprietors or agents of all other public exhibitions or shows for money, not enumerated in this section, shall pay for each license ten dollars: *Provided*, That no license procured in one State shall be held to authorize exhibitions in another State. And but one license shall be required under this act to authorize exhibitions within any one State. Definition of. Exhibitions or shows, $10

Forty. Bowling alleys and billiard-rooms shall pay ten dollars for every alley or table in the building or place to be licensed. Every place or building where bowls are thrown or billiards played and open to the public with or without price, shall be regarded as a bowling alley or billiard-room, respectively, under this act.

Bowling alleys and billiard rooms, for each alley or table, $10.

Definition of.

Forty-one. Proprietors of gift enterprises shall pay fifty dollars for each license. Every person, firm, or corporation, who shall sell or offer for sale any article of merchandise of any description whatsoever, with a promise, express or implied, to give or bestow, or in any manner to hold out to the public the promise of gift or bestowal of any article or thing for and in consideration of the purchase by any person of any other article or thing shall be regarded a proprietor of a gift enterprise under this act: *Provided,* That no such proprietor, in consequence of being thus licensed, shall be exempt from paying any other license or tax required by law, and the license herein required shall be in addition thereto.

Gift enterprises, $50.

Definition of.

Forty-two. Owners of stallions and jacks shall pay ten dollars for each license. Every person who keeps a male horse or a jack for the use of mares, requiring or receiving pay therefor, shall be required to take out a license under this act, which shall contain a brief description of the animal, its age, and place or places where used or to be used: *Provided,* That all accounts, notes, or demands, for the use of any such horse or jack without a license, as aforesaid, shall be invalid and of no force in any court of law or equity.

Stallions and jacks, $10.

Persons liable to pay.

Forty-three. Lawyers shall pay ten dollars for each license. Every person who for fee or reward, shall prosecute or defend causes in any court of record or other judicial tribunal of the United States or of any of the States, or give legal advice in relation to any cause or matter whatever shall be deemed to be a lawyer within the meaning of this act.

Lawyers, $10.

Definition of.

Forty-four. Physicians, surgeons, and dentists shall pay ten dollars for each license. Every person (except apothecaries) whose business it is, for fee and reward, to prescribe remedies or perform surgical operations for the cure of any bodily disease or ailing, shall be deemed a physician, surgeon, or dentist, as the case may be, within the meaning of this act.

Physicians, surgeons, and dentists, $10.

Definition of.

Forty-five. Architects and civil engineers shall pay ten dollars for each license. Every person whose business it is to plan, design, or superintend the construction of buildings, or ships, or of roads, or bridges, or canals, or railroads, shall be regarded as an architect and civil engineer under this act: *Provided,* That this shall not include a practical carpenter who labors on a building.

Architects and civil engineers, $10.

Definition of.

Exemption.

Forty-six. Builders and contractors shall pay twenty-five dollars for each license; and if his said contracts in any one year exceed in amount twenty-five thousand dollars, he shall pay one dollar on every additional thousand dollars in excess thereof. Every person whose business it is to construct buildings, or ships, or bridges, or canals, or railroads by contract, shall be regarded as a builder and contractor under this act: *Provided,* That no license shall be required from any person whose building contracts do not exceed two thousand five hundred dollars in any one year.

Builders and contractors, $25.

For every $1,000 in excess of $25,000, $1.

Definition of.

Exemption.

Plumbers and gas-fitters, $10.

Forty-seven. Plumbers and gas-fitters shall pay ten dollars for each license. Every person, firm, or corporation, whose business it is to fit, furnish, or sell plumbing materials, gas-pipes, gas-burners, or other gas-fixtures, shall be regarded a plumber and gas-fitter within the meaning of this act.

Definition of.

Assayers, not exceeding $250,000, $100.

Forty-eight. Assayers, assaying gold and silver, or either, of a value not exceeding in one year two hundred and fifty thousand dollars, shall pay one hundred dollars for each license, and two hundred dollars when the value exceeds two hundred and fifty thousand dollars and does not exceed five hundred thousand dollars, and five hundred dollars when the value exceeds five hundred thousand dollars. Any person or persons or corporation whose business or occupation it is to separate gold and silver from other metals or mineral substances with which such gold or silver, or both, are alloyed, combined, or united, or to ascertain or determine the quantity of gold or silver in any alloy or combination with other metals, shall be deemed an assayer for the purpose of this act.

Exceeding $250,000 and not exceeding $500,000, $200.

Exceeding $500,000, $500.

Definition of.

General business, $10.

Forty-nine. A license fee of ten dollars shall be required of every person, firm, or corporation, engaged in any business, trade, or profession whatsoever, for which no other license is herein required, whose gross annual receipts therefrom exceed the sum of one thousand dollars per annum.

No license required in certain cases unless annual sales exceed $1,000.

SEC. 80. *And be it further enacted*, That where the annual gross receipts or sales of any apothecaries, confectioners, eating-houses, tobacconists, or retail dealers, except retail dealers in spirituous and malt liquors, shall not exceed the sum of one thousand dollars, such apothecaries, confectioners, eating-houses, tobacconists, and retail dealers shall not be required to take out or pay for license, anything in this act to the contrary notwithstanding; the amount or estimated amount of such annual sales to be ascertained or estimated in such manner as the Commissioner of Internal Revenue shall prescribe, and so of all other annual sales or receipts, where the rate of the license is graduated by the amount of sales or receipts; and where the amount of the license or the rate has been increased, or is liable to be increased, by law above the amount of any existing license to any person, firm, or company, or has been understated or underestimated, such person, firm, or company shall be again assessed and pay the amount of such increase, which shall be indorsed on the original license, which shall thereafter be held good and sufficient.

Annual sales to be estimated as Commission'r shall prescribe.

Reassessments to be made where rates have been increased.

License understated may be again assessed.

License not required to sell goods at the place of manufacture.

SEC. 81. *And be it further enacted*, That nothing contained in the preceding sections of this act, requiring licenses, shall be construed to require an additional license as a dealer for the sale of goods, wares, and merchandise made or produced, and sold by the manufacturer or producer at the manufactory or place where the same is made or produced, or at the principal office or place of business, as provided in section *seventy-three* [seventy-four] of this act; [nor] to *vinters* [vintners] who sell, at the place where the same is made, wine of their own growth; nor to apothecaries, as to wines or spirituous liquors which they use exclusively in the preparation or making up of medicines; nor shall any provisions be construed to prohibit physicians from keeping on hand medicines solely for the purpose of making up their own prescriptions for their own patients.

Nor to vintners.

Nor to apothecaries as to wines and liquors in certain circumstances

Nor to physicians making up their own prescriptions.

Manufactures, articles, and products.

Specific and ad valorem duty.

Sec. 82. *And be it further enacted,* That every individual, partnership, firm, association, or corporation, (and any word or words in this act indicating or referring to person or persons shall be taken to mean and include partnerships, firms, associations, or corporations, when not otherwise designated or manifestly incompatible with the intent thereof,) shall comply with the following requirements, that is to say: Definition of person or persons liable to tax under this act.

First. Before commencing, or, if already commenced, before continuing, any manufacture liable to be assessed, under the provisions of this act, and which shall not be differently provided for elsewhere, every person shall furnish, without previous demand therefor, to the assistant assessor a statement, subscribed and sworn to, or affirmed, setting forth the place where the manufacture is to be carried on, and the principal place of business for sales, the name of the manufactured article, the proposed market for the same, whether foreign or domestic, and generally the kind and quality manufactured or proposed to be manufactured. Manufacturer to furnish a sworn statement before commencing business as to place, articles manufactured, proposed market, &c.

Second. He shall within ten days after the first day of each and every month, or on or before a day prescribed by the Commissioner of Internal Revenue, make return under oath or affirmation of the products and sales or delivery of such manufacture in form and detail as may be required, from time to time, by the Commissioner of Internal Revenue. To make monthly return of products and sales in manner prescribed by Commissioner.

Third. All such returns, statements, descriptions, memoranda, oaths, and affirmations, shall be in form, scope, and detail as may be prescribed, from time to time, by the Commissioner of Internal Revenue. Returns made under oath.

Sec. 83. *And be it further enacted,* That upon the amounts, quantities, and values of produce, goods, wares, merchandise, and articles produced or manufactured, and sold or delivered, hereinafter enumerated, the manufacturer or producer thereof, whether manufactured or produced for himself or for others, shall pay to the collector of internal revenue within his district, monthly, or on or before a day to be prescribed by the Commissioner of Internal Revenue, the duties on such products or manufactures. Duties to be paid monthly. And for neglect to pay such duties within ten days after demand, in writing delivered to him in person, or left at his house or place of business, or manufactory, or sent by mail, the amount of such duties, with the additions hereinbefore prescribed, may be levied upon the real and personal property of any such producer or manufacturer. In case of neglect to pay duties within ten days after demand. And such duties and additions, and whatever shall be the expenses of levy, shall be a lien from the day prescribed by the Commissioner for their payment aforesaid, in favor of the United States, upon the said real and personal property of such producer or manufacturer; and such lien may be enforced by distraint, as provided in this act. Duties a lien upon the real and personal property of manufacturer or producer. And in all cases of goods manufactured or produced, in whole or in part upon commission, or where the material is furnished by one party and manufactured by another, if the manufacturer shall be required to pay under this act the tax hereby imposed, such person or persons so paying the same shall be entitled to collect the amount thereof of the owner Manufacturer paying the duty may have lien on goods.

or owners, and shall have a lien for the amount thus paid upon the produced or manufactured goods.

Proceedings for neglect or refusal to pay duties.

SEC. 84. *And be it further enacted*, That for neglect or refusal to pay the duties provided by law on manufactured articles, or articles produced, as aforesaid, the goods, wares, and merchandise manufactured or produced and unsold by or not passed out of the possession of such manufacturer or producer, shall be forfeited to the United States, and may be sold or disposed of for the benefit of the same, in manner as shall be prescribed by the Commissioner of Internal Revenue, under the direction of the Secretary of the Treasury. In such case the collector or deputy collector may take possession of said articles, and may maintain such possession in the premises and buildings where they may have been manufactured, or deposited, or may be. He shall summon, giving notice of not less than two nor more than ten days, the parties in possession of said goods, enjoining them to appear before the assessor or assistant assessor, at a day and hour in such summons fixed, then and there to show cause, if any there be, why, for such neglect or refusal, such articles should not be declared forfeited to the United States. The manufacturers or producers thereof shall be deemed to be the parties interested, if the articles shall be, at the time of taking such possession, upon the premises where manufactured or produced; if they shall at such time have been removed from the place of manufacture or production, the parties interested shall be deemed to be the persons or parties in whose custody or possession the articles shall be found. Such summons shall be served upon such parties in person, or by leaving a copy thereof at the place of abode or business of the party to whom the same may be directed. In case no such party or place can be found, which fact shall be determined by the collector's return on the summons, such notice, in the nature of a summons, shall be given by advertisement for the term of three weeks in one newspaper in the county nearest to the place of such sale. If at or before such hearing such duties shall not have been paid, and the assessor or assistant assessor shall adjudge the summons and notice, service and return of the same to be sufficient, the said articles shall be by him declared forfeit, and shall be sold, disposed of, or turned over by the collector to the use of any department of the government as may be directed by the Secretary of the Treasury, who may require of any officer of the government into whose possession the same may be turned over the proper voucher therefor; and the proceeds of sale of said articles, if any there be after deducting the duties and additions thereon, together with the fees, costs, and expenses of all proceedings incident to the seizure and sale, to be determined by said Commissioner, shall be refunded and paid to the owner, or, if he cannot be found, to the manufacturer or producer in whose custody the articles were when seized, as the said Commissioner may deem just, by draft on the same or some other collector; or if the said articles are turned over without sale to the use of any department of the government, the excess of the value of said articles, after deducting the amount of the duties, additions, fees, costs, and expenses accrued thereon when turned over as aforesaid, shall be refunded and paid by the said department to the owner, or, if he cannot be found, to the manufacturer or producer in whose custody or possession the said articles were when seized as aforesaid. The Commissioner of

Proceeds, after deducting duties and all expenses, to be paid to the owner.

Or to the manufacturer or producer.

Internal Revenue, with the approval of the Secretary of [the] Treasury, may review any such case of forfeiture and do justice in the premises. If the forfeiture shall have been wrongly declared, and sale made, the Secretary is hereby authorized, in case the specific articles cannot be restored to the party aggrieved in as good order and condition as when seized, to make up to such party in money his loss and damage from the contingent fund of his department. Immediate notice of any seizure of manufactured articles or products shall be given to the Commissioner of Internal Revenue by the collector or deputy collector, who shall also make return of his proceedings to the said Commissioner after he shall have sold or otherwise disposed of the articles or products so forfeited; and the assessor or assistant assessor shall also make return of his proceedings relating to such forfeiture to the said Commissioner. And any violation of, or refusal to comply with, the provisions of the *eighty-first* [eighty-second] section of this act, shall be good cause for seizure and forfeiture, substantially in manner as detailed in this section; but before forfeiture shall be declared by virtue of the provisions of this section, the amount of duties which may be due from the person whose manufactures or products are seized, shall first be ascertained in the manner prescribed in the *eighty-fourth* [eighty-fifth] section of this act; and such violation or refusal to comply shall further make any party so violating or refusing to comply liable to a fine or penalty of five hundred dollars, to be recovered in manner and form as provided in this act. Articles which the collector may adjudge perishable may be sold or disposed of before declaration of forfeiture. Said sales shall be made at public auction, and notice thereof shall be given as the said Commissioner shall prescribe.

Under certain circumstances the Commis'ner, with the approval of the Secretary, may review proceedings.

Immediate returns of seizures to be made to Commissioner.

Violation of 82d section good cause for seizure.

The amount of duties to be ascertained before seizure.

Penalty.

Perishable articles, how disposed of

SEC. 85. *And be it further enacted*, That in case of the manufacture and sale or production and sale, consumption or delivery of any goods, wares, merchandise, or articles as hereinafter mentioned, without compliance on the part of the party manufacturing or producing the same with all the requirements and regulations prescribed by law in relation thereto, the assistant assessor may, upon such information as he may have, assume and estimate the amount and value of such manufactures or products, and upon such assumed amount assess the duties and add thereto fifty per centum; and said duties shall be collected in like manner as in case the provisions of this act in relation thereto had been complied with, and to such articles all the foregoing provisions for liens, fines, penalties, and forfeitures, shall in like manner apply.

The assistant assessor to assume and estimate duties in certain cases.

SEC. 86. *And be it further enacted*, That any person, firm, company, or corporation, manufacturing or producing goods, wares, and merchandise, sold or removed for consumption or use, upon which duties or taxes are imposed by law, shall, in their return of the value and quantity, render an account of the full amount of actual sales made by the manufacturer, producer, or agent thereof, and shall state in a separate column the items and account of the deductions, if any, claimed; whether any part, and if so, what part, of said goods, wares, and merchandise has been consumed or used by the owner, owners, or agent, or used for the production of another manufacture or product, together with the market value of the same at the time of such use or consumption; whether such goods, wares, and merchandise were shipped for a foreign port or consigned to auction or commissioned

Manufacturers shall render an account of the full amount of actual sales.

Deduct'ns claimed.

Quantity consumed.

Quantity used for another manufacture.

Return to be made according to the market value.

merchants, other than agents, for sale; and shall make a return according to the value at the place of shipment, when shipped for a foreign port, or according to the value at the place of manufacture or production, when removed for use or consumption, or consigned to others than agents of the manufacturer or producer. The value and quantity of the goods, wares, and merchandise required to be stated as aforesaid, shall be estimated by the actual sales made by the manufacturer, or by his, her, or their agent, or person or persons acting in his, her, or their behalf. And where such goods, wares, and merchandise have been removed for consumption or for delivery to others, or placed on shipboard, or are no longer within the custody or control of the manufacturer or his agent, not being in his factory, store, or warehouse, the value shall be estimated at the average of the market value of the like goods, wares, and merchandise, at the time when the same became liable to duty. And when goods, wares, and merchandise are sold by the manufacturer or producer, or the agent thereof having the charge of the business, the following deductions only may be allowed, viz:

Deduct'ns which may be allowed under certain circumstances.

First. Freight from the place of deposit at the time of sale to the place of delivery.

Second. *That* [the] reasonable commission not exceeding three per centum, and other expenses of sale bona fide paid; and no commission shall be deducted when the sale is made at the place of manufacture or production: *Provided*, That no deduction shall be made on the market value at the place of manufacture or production, on goods, wares, and merchandise consigned to auction or commission merchants for sale, or placed on shipboard to be removed from the United States, or when consigned to other than agents having charge of the business of such manufacturer or producer, nor when used or consumed by the manufacturer, producer, or agent thereof.

Manufacturers of tobacco, snuff, or cigars required to make additional statement.

SEC. 87. *And be it further enacted*, That any person, firm, company, or corporation who shall now be engaged in the manufacture of tobacco, snuff, or cigars, or who shall hereafter commence or engage in such manufacture, before commencing, or, if already commenced, before continuing, such manufacture for which they may be liable to be assessed under the provisions of law, shall, in addition to a compliance with all other provisions of law, furnish to the assessor or assistant assessor a statement, subscribed under oath or affirmation, accurately setting for[th] the place, and if in a city, the street and number of the street where the manufacturing is, or is to be, carried on, the name and description of the manufactured article, the proposed market for the same, whether foreign or domestic, and if the same shall be manufactured for or to be sold and delivered to any other person or party, the name and residence and business or occupation of the person or party for whom the said article is to be manufactured or delivered, and penerally the kind and quality manufactured or proposed to be manufactured; and shall, within the time above mentioned, apply to and obtain from the assessor or assistant assessor of the district in which said manufacture is carried on, or proposed to be carried on, in addition to the license required by existing laws, a permit in writing, to be signed by said assessor or assistant assessor in such form as shall be prescribed by the Commissioner of Internal Revenue, which permit shall be kept by such manufacturer sus-

A permit required in form as prescribed by the Commissioner.

pended in some open and conspicuous place in the principal room in which such manufacturing is so carried on. And such manufacturer shall also give notice to the assessor [or] assistant assessor, in writing, of any and every change or removal made, accurately setting forth, as hereinbefore mentioned, the place where the said manufacture is to be carried on; and whenever such change or removal takes place, before it shall be lawful to commence such manufacture, a new permit in writing shall be applied for and obtained in manner aforesaid. And the assistant assessor of the proper assessment district shall be entitled to demand and receive from such manufacturer for each pe[r]mit so granted the sum of twenty-five cents. And if any person or agent of any firm, company, or corporation shall manufacture for sale tobacco, snuff, or cigars of any description without first obtaining the permit herein required, such person or agent shall be subject, upon conviction thereof, to a penalty of three hundred dollars, and in addition thereto shall be liable to imprisonment for a term not exceeding one year, at the discretion of the court.

Manufacturer to give notice of every change, &c.

New permit.

Fee for permit.

Penalty.

SEC. 88. *And be it further enacted*, That it shall be the duty of the assistant assessor of each district to keep a record in a book or books, to be provided for the purpose, to be open to the inspection of any person upon reasonable request, in which shall be arranged alphabetically the name of any and every person, firm, company, or corporation who may be engaged in the manufacture of tobacco, snuff, or cigars within his district to whom a permit has been issued, together with the place where such manufacture is carried on and place of residence of the person or persons engaged therein; a copy of which record shall be, by said assistant assessor, forwarded to the assessor of the district, who shall preserve the same in his office.

Assistant assessor to keep a book containing names of all persons in his district having permits.

SEC. 89. *And be it further enacted*, That in all cases where tobacco, snuff, or cigars, of any description, are manufactured, in whole or in part upon commission or shares, or where the material from which any such articles are made, or are to be made, is furnished by one party and manufactured by another, or where the material is furnished or sold by one party with an understanding or contract with another that the manufactured article is to be received in payment therefor or any part thereof, the duty or tax imposed by law thereon, when paid by the manufacturer, may be collected at the time, or at any time subsequently, of the party for whom the same was made or to whom the same was delivered, as aforesaid. And in case of any fraud or collusion by which the government shall be defrauded, or attempted to be defrauded, by a party who furnishes the material and the manufacturer of any of the articles aforesaid, such material shall be liable to forfeiture, and such articles shall be liable to be assessed the highest rates of duty imposed by law upon any article belonging to its grade or class.

Where the material is furnished by one party and manufactured by another.

Penalty in case of fraud or collusion.

SEC. 90. *And be it further enacted*, That any person, firm, company, or corporation, now or hereafter engaged in the manufacture of tobacco, snuff, or cigars of any description whatsoever, shall be, and hereby is, required to make out and deliver to the assistant assessor of the assessment district a true statement or inventory of the quantity of each of the different kinds of tobacco, snuff-flour, snuff, cigars, tin-foil, licorice and stems held or owned by him or them on the day this act takes effect or at the time of

Manufacturer required to make an inventory of the quantity owned by him on the day this act takes effect commencing business under this act, setting forth what portion of said goods was manufactured or produced by him or them, and what was purchased from others, whether chewing, smoking, fine-cut, shorts, pressed, plug, snuff-flour or prepared snuff, the several kinds of cigars and the market price thereof, which statement or inventory shall be verified by the oath or affirmation of such person or persons and be in manner and form as prescribed by the Commissioner of Internal Revenue; and the said person, firm, company, or corporation engaged as aforesaid, on the first day of January in every year hereafter, shall make out and deliver to the said assistant assessor a true statement or *or* inventory, in manner and form as aforesaid and verified as aforesaid, of all such articles, aforesaid, then held or owned by him or them, setting forth all and singular what is required to be set forth in the statement or inventory first aforesaid; and every such person, company, or corporation shall keep in a book, in such manner and form as said Commissioner may prescribe, an accurate account of all the articles aforesaid thereafter purchased by him or them, the quantity of tobacco, snuff, snuff-flour, or cigars, of whatever description sold, consumed, or removed for consumption or sale, or removed from the place of manufacture; and he or they shall, on Wednesday of each week, furnish to the assistant assessor of the district a true and accurate copy of the entries in said book during the week ending on the preceding Saturday, which copy shall be verified by oath or affirmation, on the receipt whereof an assessment of the duties due by said person, company, or corporation shall be immediately made and transmitted to the collector of the district, to whom said duties shall be paid within five days thereafter; and in case the duties shall not be paid within the said five days, the said collector may, on one day's notice, distrain for the same, with ten per centum additional on the amount thereof, subject to all the provisions of law relating to licenses, returns, assessments, payment of taxes, liens, fines, penalties, and forfeitures, not inconsistent herewith in the case of other manufacturers; and such duty shall be paid by the manufacturer or the person for whom the goods are manufactured as the assessor may deem best for the collection of the revenue: *Provided,* That it shall be the duty of any manufacturer or vender of tin-foil used in covering manufactured tobacco, on demand of any officer of internal revenue, to render to such officer a correct statement, verified by oath or affirmation, of the quantity and amount of tin-foil sold or delivered to any person or persons named in such demand; and in case of refusal or neglect to render such statement, or of cause to believe such statement to be incorrect or fraudulent, the assessor of the district may cause an examination of persons, books, and papers to be made in the same manner as provided in the fourteenth section of this act: *Provided,* That manufactured tobacco, snuff, or cigars, may be transferred, without payment of the duty, directly from the place of manufacture to a bonded warehouse established in conformity with law and treasury regulations, under such rules and regulations and upon the execution of such transportation bonds as the Secretary of the Treasury may prescribe; said bonds or other security to be taken by the assessor of the district from which such removal is made, and may be transported from such warehouse to a bonded warehouse used for the storage of merchandise at any port of entry and withdrawn

Inventory to be made on the first day of January in every year.

Account to be kept in a book in manner as prescribed by the Commissioner.

A copy of weekly entries to be furnished the assistant assessor.

Duties to be paid within five days.

Collector may distrain on one day's notice.

Duty may be collected of the manufacturer or owner.

Proviso with regard to tin foil used in covering tobacco.

In case of fraudulent statement how to proceed.

Transfer may be made to a bonded warehouse without payment of the duty.

therefrom for consumption *or* [on] payment of the duty or removed for export to a foreign country without payment of duty, in conformity with the provisions of this act relating to the removal of distilled spirits; all the rules, regulations, and conditions of which, so far as applicable, shall apply to tobacco, snuff, or cigars, in bonded warehouse. And no drawback shall in any case be allowed upon any manufactured tobacco, snuff, or cigars, upon which any excise duty has been paid either before or after it has been placed in bonded warehouse.

Regulations for the removal of distilled spirits to be observed in regard to the removal of tobacco so far as applicable.

No drawback to be allowed.

SEC. 91. *And be it further enacted,* That every manufacturer of tobacco, snuff, or cigars of any description, as hereinbefore mentioned, or his chief workman, agent, or superintendent, shall, at the end of each and every month, make and sign a declaration, in writing, that no such article or commodity, as aforesaid, has, during such preceding month or time when the last declaration was made, been removed, carried, or sent, or caused, or suffered, or known to have been removed, carried, or sent from the premises of such manufacturer other than such as have been duly assessed and the duties imposed by law paid thereon, on pain of forfeiting for every refusal or neglect to make such declaration, one hundred dollars. And if any such manufacturer or his chief workman, agent, or superintendent, shall make any false or untrue declaration, such manufacturer or chief workman, agent, or superintendent, making the same, upon conviction thereof, shall forfeit three hundred dollars, or, at the discretion of the court, be liable to imprisonment for a term not exceeding one year.

Manufacturers required to make and sign monthly a declaration, &c.

Penalty for neglect or refusal.

Penalty for making a false declaration.

SEC. 92. *And be it further enacted,* That if any person other than the manufacturer shall sell, or consign, or remove for sale, or part with the possession of any manufactured tobacco, snuff, or cigars, upon which the duties imposed by law have not been paid, with the knowledge thereof, such person shall be liable to a penalty of one hundred dollars for each and every offence. And any person who shall purchase or receive for sale any such tobacco, snuff, or cigars, which has not been inspected, branded, or stamped as required by this act, or upon which the tax has not been paid, if it has accrued or become payable with knowledge thereof, shall be liable to a penalty of fifty dollars for each and every offence. And any person who shall purchase or receive for sale any such tobacco, snuff, or cigars, from any manufacturer who has not a permit to manufacture, shall be liable for each and every offence to a penalty of one hundred dollars, and, in addition thereto, a forfeiture of all the articles, as aforesaid, so purchased or received, or the full value thereof.

Penalty when any one other than the manufacturer parts with the possession of tobacco, snuff, or cigars, on which duties imposed by law have not been paid.

Penalty for receiving tobacco, snuff, or cigars under certain circumstances.

Penalty for receiving tobacco, snuff, or cigars from a manufacturer who has no permit.

SEC. 93. *And be it further enacted,* That all goods, wares, and merchandise, or articles manufactured or made (except refined petroleum, refined coal oil, gold and silver, spirituous and malt liquors, manufactured tobacco, and snuff and cigars) by any person or firm, where the product shall not exceed the rate of six hundred dollars per annum, and shall be made or produced by the labor of such person or firm, or by his or their family, shall be, and are hereby, exempt from duty; where the product shall exceed such rate and not exceed the rate of one thousand dollars the duty shall be levied, assessed, and collected only upon the excess above the rate of six hundred dollars per annum; and in all other cases the whole annual product, (including any business or transaction where one party has been furnished with materials, or any part thereof, and

Manufactures where the product shall not exceed the rate of $600 per annum under certain circumstances exempt, except refined petroleum, refined coal oil, gold and silver, spirituous and malt liquors, manufactured tobacco, and snuff and cigars.

Duty when the rate exceeds $600, but does not exceed $1,000 per annum.

Duty in all other cases.

employed by another party to manufacture, make, or finish the goods, wares, and merchandise, or articles, paying or promising to pay therefor, and to whom the same are returned when so made and finished,) shall be assessed and the duty paid thereon by the producer or manufacturer: *Provided,* That whenever a producer or manufacturer shall use or consume, or shall remove for consumption or use any articles, goods, wares, or merchandise, which if removed for sale would be liable to taxation, he shall be assessed upon the salable value of the articles, goods, wares, or merchandise so used or so removed for consumption or use.

Duty to be assessed on the salable value of articles, &c., when removed for consumption or use.

Duties on manufactures.

SEC. 94. *And be it further enacted,* That upon the articles, goods, wares, and merchandise hereinafter mentioned, except where otherwise provided, which shall be produced and sold, or be manufactured or made and sold, or be consumed or used by the manufacturer or producer thereof, or removed for consumption, or for delivery to others than agents of the manufacturer or producer within the United States or Territories thereof, there shall be levied, collected, and paid the following duties, to be paid by the producer or manufacturer thereof, that is to say:

Candles.

On candles, of whatever material made, a duty of five per cent. ad valorem.

Mineral coals.

On mineral coals, except such as are known in the trade as pea coal and dust coal, a duty of five cents per ton: *Provided,* That in case of contracts of lease of coal lands made prior to the passage of this act the lessee shall pay the tax, if not otherwise agreed; and all duties or taxes on coal mined and delivered by coal operators on contracts heretofore made shall be paid by the purchasers thereof, if not otherwise agreed by the parties.

The lessee of coal lands to pay the tax in case of certain contracts.

Oils.

On lard oil, mustard-seed oil, linseed oil, and on all animal or vegetable oils, not exempted or provided for elsewhere, whether pure or adulterated, a duty of five cents per gallon.

Gas.

On gas, illuminating, made of coal, wholly or in part, or any other material, when the product shall not be above two hundred thousand cubic feet per month, a duty of ten cents per one thousand cubic feet; when the product shall be above two and not exceeding five hundred thousand cubic feet per month, a duty of fifteen cents per one thousand cubic feet; when the product shall be above five hundred thousand and not exceeding five millions of cubic feet per month, a duty of twenty cents per one thousand cubic feet; when the product shall be above five millions, a duty of twenty-five cents per one thousand cubic feet. And the general average of the monthly product for the year preceding the return required by this act shall regulate the rate of duty herein imposed. And where any gas-works have not been in operation for the next year preceding the return as aforesaid, then the rate shall be regulated upon the estimated average of the monthly product: *Provided,* That the product required to be returned by law by any gas company shall be understood to be the product charged in the bills actually rendered by the gas company during the month preceding the return; and all gas companies are hereby authorized to add the duty or tax imposed by law to the price per thousand cubic feet on gas sold: *Provided, further,* That all gas furnished for lighting street lamps, and not measured, and all gas made for and used by any hotel, inn, tavern, and private

Rate of duty regulated by the average monthly product.

Where gas works have not been in operation the preceding year.

The product to be returned to be the same as that charged in the bills actually rendered.

Companies may charge tax to consumers.

For lighting streets, &c.

dwelling-house shall be subject to duty whatever the amount of product, and may be estimated; and if the returns in any case shall be understated or under-estimated, it shall be the duty of the assistant assessor of the district to increase the same as he shall deem just and proper: *And provided, further,* That gas companies located within the corporate limits of any city or town, whether in the district or otherwise, or so located as to compete with each other, shall pay the rate imposed by law upon the company having the largest production: *And provided, further,* That coal tar produced in the manufacture of illuminating gas, and the products of the redistillation of coal tar thus produced, shall be exempt from duty.

Assistant assessor may increase the amount when underestimated.

Rate of tax where gas companies may compete with each other.

Coal tar exempt.

On coal illuminating oil, refined, and naphtha, benzine, and benzole, produced by the distillation of coal, asphaltum, shale, peat, petroleum, or rock oil, and all other bituminous substances used for like purposes, a duty of twenty cents per gallon: *Provided,* That such oil, refined and produced by the distillation of coal, asphaltum, or shale, exclusively, shall be subject to pay a duty of fifteen cents per gallon, anything to the contrary notwithstanding: *And provided, further,* That distillers of coal oil or naphtha, benzine, or benzole, shall be subject to all the provisions of law applicable to distillers of spirits, with regard to licenses, bonds, returns, assessments, liens, penalties, drawbacks, and all other provisions designed for the purpose of ascertaining the quantity distilled, and securing the payment of duties, so far as the same may, in the judgment of the Commissioner of Internal Revenue, and under regulations prescribed by him, be deemed necessary for that purpose: *And provided, also,* That naphtha of specific gravity exceeding eighty degrees, according to Baume's hydrometer, and of the kind usually known as gasoline, shall be subject to a tax of five per centum ad valorem.

Coal oil, naphtha, benzine, and benzole.

Proviso respecting distilled coal oil.

Distillers of coal oil subject to the provisions of law applicable to distillers of spirits so far as deemed necessary by the Commissioner.

Proviso in regard to naphtha.

On spirits of turpentine, a duty of twenty cents per gallon: *Provided,* That all the provisions of law relating to the assessment and collection of the duties on cotton, under rules and regulations to be prescribed by the Secretary of the Treasury, so far as the same may be deemed applicable thereto, shall apply to the assessment and collection of duties on spirits of turpentine.

Spirits of turpentine.

On ground coffee, and on all ground substitutes for coffee, or preparations of which coffee forms a part, and on all unground substitutes for coffee, a duty of one cent per pound.

Ground coffee

On ground pepper, ground mustard, ground pimento, ground cloves, and ground clove stems, ground cassia, and ground ginger, and all imitations of the same, a duty of one cent per pound.

Ground spices

On molasses produced from the sugar cane, and not from sorghum or imphee, a duty of five cents per gallon.

Molasses.

On sirup of molasses or sugar-cane juice, when removed from the plantation, concentrated molasses or melado, and cistern bottoms, of sugar produced from the sugar cane and not made from sorghum or imphee, a duty of one cent and one-fourth of one cent per pound.

Sugar-cane juice &c.

On brown or Muscovado sugar not above number twelve Dutch standard in color, produced from the sugar cane and not from sorghum or imphee, other than those produced by the refiner, a duty of two cents per pound.

Brown sugar.

On all clarified or refined sugars above number twelve and not above number eighteen Dutch standard in color, produced directly

Refined sugars

from the sugar cane and not from sorghum or imphee, a duty of two and one-half cents per pound.

Clarified or refined sugars. On all clarified or refined sugars above number eighteen Dutch standard in color, produced directly from the sugar cane and not from sorghum or imphee, a duty of three and one-half cents per pound.

Duty on gross amount of sales of sugar refiners. On the gross amount of the sales of sugar refiners, including all the products of their manufactories or refineries, a duty of two and a half of one per centum ad valorem: *Provided*, That every person shall be regarded as a sugar refiner, and pay the duties levied by law, whose business it is to advance the quality and value of sugar upon which a duty has been assessed and paid, by melting and recrystalization, or by liquoring, claying, or other washing process, or by any other chemical or mechanical means, or who shall advance the quality or value of molasses, concentrated molasses or melado, upon which a duty has been assessed and paid, by boiling or other process.

Who are sugar refiners.

Sugar candy and confectionery. On sugar candy and all confectionery made wholly or in part of sugar, valued at not exceeding twenty cents per pound, a duty of two cents per pound; exceeding twenty and not exceeding forty cents per pound, a duty of four cents per pound; when exceeding forty cents per pound, or sold by the box, package, or otherwise than by the pound, a duty of ten per centum ad valorem.

Chocolate. On chocolate and cocoa prepared, a duty of one and a half cent per pound.

Saleratus and bicarbonate of soda. On saleratus and bicarbonate of soda, a duty of five mills per pound.

Starch. On starch made of potatoes, a duty of two mills per pound; made of corn or wheat, a duty of three mills per pound; made of rice or any other material, a duty of one cent per pound.

Gunpowder. On gunpowder, and all explosive substances used for mining, blasting, artillery, or sporting purposes, when valued at twenty-eight cents per pound or less, a duty of one cent per pound; when valued at above twenty-eight cents per pound and not exceeding thirty-eight cents per pound, a duty of one and a half cent per pound; and when valued at above thirty-eight cents per pound, a duty of eight cents per pound.

White lead. On white lead, a duty of thirty-five cents per one hundred pounds.

Oxide of zinc. On oxide of zinc, a duty of thirty-five cents per one hundred pounds.

Sulphate of barytes. On sulphate of barytes, a duty of twelve cents per one hundred pounds: *Provided*, That white lead, oxide of zinc, and sulphate of barytes, paints and painters' colors, or any one of them, shall not be subject to any additional duty in consequence of being mixed or ground with linseed oil, when the duties upon all the materials so mixed or ground shall have been previously paid.

Paints and painters' colors. On all paints and painters' colors, dry or ground in oil, or in paste with water, not otherwise provided for, a duty of five per centum ad valorem.

Varnish or Japan. On varnish or Japan, made wholly or in part of gum copal, or other gums or substances, a duty of five per centum ad valorem.

Glue and gelatine. On glue and gelatine of all descriptions, in the solid state, a duty of one cent per pound.

On glue and cement, made wholly or in part of glue, to be sold in the liquid state, a duty of forty cents per gallon. Cement and glue.

On pins, solid head or other, a duty of five per centum ad valorem. Pins.

On screws, commonly called wood screws, a duty of ten per centum ad valorem. Wood screws.

On clocks and timepieces, and on clock movements, when sold without being cased, a duty of five per centum ad valorem. Clocks, time-pieces, and clock movements.

On umbrellas and parasols made of cotton or silk, or other material, a duty of five per centum ad valorem. Umbrellas and parasols.

On gold leaf, eighteen cents per pack, containing not more than twenty books of twenty-five leaves each. Gold leaf.

On gold foil, two dollars per ounce troy weight. Gold foil.

On paper of all descriptions, including pasteboard, binders' board, and tarred paper for roofing or other purposes, a duty of three per centum ad valorem. Paper.

On soap, castile, palm-oil, erasive, and soap of all other descriptions, white or colored, except softsoap and soap otherwise provided for, valued at not above five cents per pound, a duty of two mills per pound; valued at above five cents per pound, a duty of one cent per pound. Soap.

On soap, fancy, scented, honey, cream, transparent, and all descriptions of toilet and shaving soap, a duty of five cents per pound. Fancy soap.

On softsoap, a duty of five per centum ad valorem. Soft soap.

On all uncompounded chemical productions, not otherwise provided for, a duty of five per centum ad valorem. Uncompounded chemicals.

On essential oils, of all descriptions, a duty of five per centum ad valorem. Essential oils.

On pickles, preserved fruits, preserved vegetables, preserved meats, fish, and shellfish in cans, kegs, or air-tight packages, a duty of five per centum ad valorem. Pickles, &c.

On billheads, printed, printed cards and printed circulars, a duty of five per centum ad valorem. Billheads, &c.

On all printed books, magazines, pamphlets, reviews, and all other similar printed publications, except newspapers, a duty of five per centum ad valorem. Books, &c.

On productions of stereotypers, lithographers, and engravers, a duty of five per centum ad valorem. Productions of stereotypers, &c.

On photographs or any other sun picture, being copies of engravings or works of art, or used for the illustration of books, and on photographs so small in size that stamps cannot be affixed, a duty of five per centum ad valorem. Photographs.

On all repairs of engines, cars, carriages, or other articles, when such repairs increase the value of the articles so repaired ten per centum or over, a duty of three per centum on such increased value: *Provided*, That on such repairs made upon ships, steamboats, or other vessels, a duty of two per centum only on the increased value shall be assessed. Repairs of engines, &c., duty on increased value under certain circumstances.

On the hulls, as launched, of all ships, barks, brigs, schooners, sloops, sailboats, steamboats, canal boats, and all other vessels or water craft, (not including engines or rigging,) hereafter built, made, constructed, or finished, a duty of two per centum ad valorem. Ships, &c.

On slate, freestone, sandstone, marble, and building stone of any other description, when dressed, hewn, or finished, a duty of Building stone.

three per centum ad valorem: *Provided*, That the cost for the erection, fitting, adjusting, or setting building stone of any description, shall not be included in the assessment of any duties thereon.

Monumental stones.

On marble, and other monumental stones, with or without inscriptions, five per centum ad valorem.

Lime and cement.

On lime and Roman or water cement, a duty of three per centum ad valorem.

Brick, tiles, &c.

On brick, draining tiles, and earthen and stone water pipes, a duty of three per centum ad valorem.

Masts, spars, and vessel blocks.

On masts, spars, and ship or vessel blocks, whether made to order or for sale, a duty of two per centum ad valorem.

Furniture sold unfinished.

On all furniture, or other articles made of wood, sold in the rough or unfinished, a duty of five per centum ad valorem: *Provided*, That all furniture, or other articles made of wood, previously assessed, and a duty paid thereon, shall be assessed a duty of five per centum ad valorem upon the increased value only thereof when sold in a finished condition.

Proviso relative to finished furniture sold under certain circumstances.

Salt.

On salt, a duty of six cents per one hundred pounds.

Sails, tents, &c.

On sails, tents, shades, awnings, and bags, made of cotton, flax, or hemp, or part of either or other material, five per centum ad valorem: *Provided*, That when the material from which any of the foregoing articles are made was imported, or has been subject to and paid a duty, and the same is made by sewing, a duty shall be assessed only on the increased value thereof.

Proviso relative to.

Mineral and other waters.

On artificial mineral waters, soda waters, sarsaparilla water, and all beverages used for like purposes, sold in bottles, or from fountains, or otherwise, and not otherwise provided for, a duty of five per centum ad valorem.

Medicinal waters

On mineral or medicinal waters, or waters from springs impregnated with minerals, a duty of one-half cent for each bottle containing not more than one pint; when containing more than one pint and not more than one quart, one cent; when containing more than one quart, for each additional quart or fractional part thereof, one cent.

Pig iron.

On pig iron, a duty of two dollars per ton.

Blooms, &c., made under certain circumstances

On blooms, slabs, or loops, when made in forges or bloomeries, directly from the ore, a duty of three dollars per ton.

Railroad iron.

On railroad iron, a duty of three dollars per ton.

Rerolled.

On railroad iron, rerolled, a duty of two dollars per ton: *Provided*, That the term rerolled shall apply only to rails for which the manufacturer receives pay for remanufacturing, and not for new iron.

Iron not advanced beyond bars, &c.

On all iron advanced beyond blooms, slabs, or loops, and not advanced beyond bars, and band, hoop, and sheet iron, not thinner than number eighteen wire gauge, and plate iron not less than one-eighth of an inch in thickness, a duty of three dollars per ton: *Provided*, That a ton shall, for all the purposes of this act, be deemed and taken to be two thousand pounds.

Other iron.

On band, hoop, and sheet iron, thinner than number eighteen wire gauge, plate iron less than one-eighth of an inch in thickness, and cut nails and spikes, not including nails, tacks, brads, or finishing nails, usually put up and sold in papers, whether in papers or otherwise, nor horseshoe nails wrought by machinery, a duty of five dollars per ton: *Provided*, That bars, rods, axe-polls, bands, hoops, sheets, plates, nails, and spikes, not includ-

Proviso.

ing such as are usually put up in papers, nor horseshoe nails wrought by machinery, as before mentioned, manufactured from iron, upon which the duty of three dollars has been levied and paid, shall be subject only to a duty of two dollars per ton in addition thereto, anything in this act to the contrary notwithstanding.

On iron castings used for bridges or other permanent structures, a duty of three dollars per ton. Iron castings for bridges, &c.

On stoves and hollow-ware and castings of iron exceeding ten pounds in weight for each casting, not otherwise provided for, a duty of three dollars per ton. Stoves and hollow-ware.

On rivets exceeding one-fourth of an inch in diameter, nuts and washers not less than two ounces each in weight, and bolts exceeding five-sixteenths of one inch in diameter, a duty of five dollars per ton: *Provided*, That when *a duty upon* the iron from which rivets, nuts, washers, and bolts, as aforesaid, shall have been made, has paid a duty of not less than three dollars per ton, a duty only, in addition thereto, shall be paid of two dollars per ton: *Provided, further*, That castings of iron, and iron of all descriptions advanced beyond pig iron, blooms, slabs, or loops, upon which no duty has been assessed or paid in the form of pig iron, blooms, slabs, or loops, shall be assessed and pay, in addition to the foregoing rates of iron so advanced, a duty of three dollars per ton. Rivets, washers, &c. Proviso. Proviso.

On steel, in ingots, bars, sheets, or wire, not less than one-fourth of an inch in thickness, valued at seven cents per pound or less, a duty of five dollars per ton; valued at above seven cents per pound, and not above eleven cents per pound, a duty of ten dollars per ton; valued at above eleven cents, a duty of twelve dollars and fifty cents per ton: *Provided*, That steel rolled, and sheet, rod, or wire made of steel upon which a duty has been assessed and paid, shall be assessed and pay a duty of five per centum ad valorem upon the increased value only thereof. Steel. Proviso.

On steam-engines, including locomotive and marine engines, a duty of three per centum ad valorem. Steam-engines.

On quicksilver produced from the ore, a duty of two per centum ad valorem. Quicksilver.

On copper and lead ingots, pigs or bars, and spelter and brass, a duty of three per centum ad valorem. Copper and lead ingots, &c.

On rolled brass, copper rolled, yellow sheathing metal in rods or sheets, and shot, sheet lead, and lead pipes, a duty of three per centum ad valorm: *Provided*, That when any of the articles herein mentioned shall not have been assessed and a duty paid thereon of three per centum, in the form of ingots, pigs, or bars, a duty of five per centum shall be assessed and paid thereon. Rolled brass, &c. Proviso.

On goat, calf, kid, sheep, horse, hog, and dog skins, tanned or dressed in the rough, a duty of five per centum ad valorem Goat, &c., skins, in rough.

On goat, calf, kid, sheep, horse, hog, and dog skins, curried or finished, a duty of five per centum ad valorem: *Provided*, That all goat, calf, kid, sheep, horse, hog, and dog skins, previously assessed in the rough, and upon which duties have been actually paid, shall be assessed on the increased value only when curried or finished. Goat, &c., skins, finished. Proviso.

On patent, enamelled, and Japanned leather and skins of every description, a duty of five per centum ad valorem. Patent, enamelled, and Japanned leather.

On oil-dressed leather and deer skins, dressed or smoked, a duty of five per centum ad valorem: *Provided*, That when leather Oil-dressed leather, &c. Proviso.

or skins, upon which a duty has been previously assessed and paid, shall be manufactured into gloves, mittens or moccasins, the duty shall only be assessed upon the increased value thereof when so manufactured.

Leather in the rough.

On leather of all descriptions, tanned or partially tanned, in the rough, a duty of five per centum ad valorem.

Leather curried or finished. Proviso.

On leather of all descriptions, curried or finished, a duty of five per centum ad valorem: *Provided*, That all leather previously assessed in the rough and upon which duties have been actually paid shall be assessed on the increased value only when curried or finished.

Wine from grapes.

On wine made of grapes, a duty of five cents per gallon.

All other wine. Proviso. Penalty.

On all other wines or liquors known or denominated as wine, not made from currants, rhubarb, or berries, produced by being rectified or mixed with other spirits, or into which any matter whatever may be infused to be sold as wine, or by any other name, and not otherwise provided for in this act, a duty of fifty cents per gallon: *Provided*, That the returns, assessment, and collections of the duties on such wines shall be subject to the regulations of the Commissioner of Internal Revenue. And any person who shall willingly and knowingly sell or offer for sale any such wine made after the passage of this act, upon which the duty herein imposed has not been paid, or which has been fraudulently evaded, shall, upon conviction thereof, be subject to a penalty of one hundred dollars or to imprisonment not exceeding two years, at the discretion of the court.

Furs. Proviso.

On furs of all descriptions, when made up or manufactured, a duty of five per centum ad valorem: *Provided*, That all manufactured furs, on which a duty has been previously assessed and paid before manufacture, it shall be assessed only on the increased value thereof when so manufactured.

Cloth. Proviso in regard to thread and yarn.

On cloth and all textile or knitted or felted fabrics of cotton, wool, or other materials, before the same has been dyed, printed or bleached, and on all cloth painted, enamelled, shirred, tarred, varnished, or oiled, a duty of five per centum ad valorem: *Provided*, That thread and yarn, and warps for weaving shall be regarded as manufactures and be subject to a duty of five per centum ad valorem.

Ready-made clothing, &c. Proviso.

On ready-made clothing, boots and shoes, gloves, mittens, and moccasins, caps, hats and bonnets, or other articles of dress for the wear of men, women, or children, five per centum ad valorem: *Provided*, That any tailor, boot or shoemaker, hat, cap, or bonnet maker, milliner or dressmaker, exclusively engaged in manufacturing any of the foregoing articles to order as custom work and not for sale generally, who shall make affidavit to the assessor or assistant assessor, that the entire amount of such manufactures so made does not exceed the sum of six hundred dollars per annum, shall be exempt from duty; when exceeding six hundred dollars per annum, a duty of three per centum ad valorem on the excess above six hundred dollars.

Cotton.

On cotton upon which no duty has been levied, collected, or paid, and which is not exempted by law, a duty of two cents per pound, which shall be and remain a lien thereon, until said duty shall have been paid, in the possession of any person or persons whomsoever.

On all manufactures of cotton, wool, silk, worsted, flax, hemp, jute, India-rubber, gutta-percha, wood, willow, glass, pottery-ware, leather, paper, iron, steel, lead, tin, copper, zinc, brass, gold, silver, horn, ivory, bone, bristles, wholly or in part, or of other materials not in this act otherwise provided for, a duty of five per centum ad valorem: *Provided*, That on all cloths dyed, printed, or bleached, on which a duty or tax shall have been paid before the same were so dyed, printed, or bleached, the said duty or tax of five per centum shall be assessed only upon the increased value thereof: *And provided, further*, That any cloth or fabrics, as aforesaid, when made of thread, yarn or warps, upon which a duty, as aforesaid, shall have been assessed and paid, shall be assessed and pay a duty on the increased value only thereof. Manufactures of cotton, wool, &c. Proviso.

On all diamonds, emeralds, precious stones and imitations thereof, and all other jewelry, a duty of ten per centum ad valorem: *Provided*, That when diamonds, emeralds, precious stones or imitations thereof, imported from foreign countries, or upon which import duties have been paid, shall be set or reset in gold or any other material, the duty shall be assessed and paid upon the value only of the settings. Diamonds, &c. Proviso.

On cavendish, plug, twist, and all other kinds of manufactured tobacco, not herein provided for, from which the stem has been taken out in whole or in part, or which is sweetened, thirty-five cents per pound. Tobacco with the stem removed, or which is sweetened.

On smoking tobacco manufactured with all the stem in, the leaf not having been butted or stripped from the stem, and on refuse tobacco known as fine-cut shorts, twenty-five cents per pound. Smoking tobacco with all the stem in.

On smoking tobacco, made exclusively of stems and not mixed with leaf or leaf and stems, fifteen cents per pound. Smoking tobacco made exclusively of stems.

On snuff, manufactured of tobacco, or any substitute for tobacco, ground dry or damp, pickled, scented, or otherwise, of all descriptions, thirty-five cents per pound. Snuff.

On fine-cut chewing tobacco, whether manufactured with the stems in or not, or however sold, whether loose, in bulk, or in packages, papers, wrappers, or boxes, thirty-five cents per pound. Fine-cut chewing tobacco.

On cigarettes made of tobacco, enclosed in a paper wrapper, valued at not over five dollars per hundred packages, each containing not more than twenty-five cigarettes, one dollar per hundred packages. And all cigarettes made of tobacco enclosed in a paper wrapper, valued at over five dollars per hundred packages, as aforesaid, shall be subject to the same duties herein provided for cigars of like value. Cigarettes enclosed in paper wrappers, &c. Cigarettes valued at over $5 per 100 packages. subject to like tax as provided for cigars.

On cigarrettes made wholly of tobacco, and also on cigars known as cheroots, or short sixes, valued in each case at not over five dollars per thousand, three dollars per thousand. Cigarettes and cheroots.

On cigars, valued at over five dollars and not over fifteen dollars per thousand, eight dollars per thousand. Cigars valued at over $5 per M, &c.

On cigars, valued at over fifteen dollars and not over thirty dollars per thousand, fifteen dollars per thousand. Cigars valued at over $15 per M.

On cigars, valued at over thirty dollars per thousand and not over forty-five dollars, twenty-five dollars per thousand. Valued over $30 per M.

On cigars, at over forty-five dollars per thousand, forty dollars per thousand, and the valuation of cigars herein mentioned shall in all cases be the value of the cigars exclusive of the tax. Valued at over $45 per M.

All cigars to be labelled and stamped after inspection unless removed to a bonded warehouse for exportation.

And all cigars manufactured after the passage of this act shall be packed in bundles, boxes, or packages open to inspection, and correctly labelled with the number and kind contained therein, and after inspection, unless the same shall be removed to a bonded warehouse for exportation, shall be stamped by the inspector with stamps to be provided by the Commissioner of Internal Revenue, denoting the tax thereon, and so affixed that the bundle or box cannot be opened without effacing or destroying said stamp. And any bundle, box, or package of cigars which shall be sold or pass out of the hands of the manufacturer, except into a bonded warehouse, without such stamps so affixed by an inspector, shall be forfeited, and may be seized wherever found, and sold, one-half of the proceeds of such sale to be paid to the informer and the other to the United States. And every person, before making any cigars after the passage of this act, shall apply for and procure from the assistant assessor of the district in which he or she resides, a permit authorizing such persons to carry on the trade of cigar making, for which permit he or she shall pay said assistant assessor the sum of twenty-five cents. And every person employed, or working at the business of cigar making in any other district than that in which he or she is a resident, shall, before making any cigars in such other district, present said permit to the assistant assessor of the district where so employed or working, and procure the indorsement of said assistant assessor thereon, authorizing said business in said district, for which indorsement the assistant assessor shall be entitled to receive from the applicant the sum of ten cents. And it shall be the duty of every assistant assessor, upon application of any person residing in his district, to furnish a permit, or to indorse upon the permit of the applicant, if resident in another district, authority to pursue the trade of cigar making within the proper district of such assistant assessor; and said assistant assessor shall keep a record of all permits granted or indorsed by him, showing the date of each permit, the name, residence, and place of employment of the party named therein, the name and district of the officer who originally granted the same, or who may have made any subsequent indorsements thereon, and the name or names of the party or parties by whom the person named in such permit is employed, or, if working for himself or herself, stating such fact; and every person making cigars shall keep an accurate account of all the cigars made by him or her, for whom, and their kind or quality; and, if made for any other person, shall state in said account the name of the person or persons for whom the same were made, and his or their place of business, and shall, on the first Monday of every month, deliver to the assistant assessor of the district, if required by him, a copy of such account, verified by oath or affirmation that the same is true and correct. And if any person shall make any cigars without procuring such permit, or the proper indorsement thereon, he or she shall be punished by a fine of five dollars for each day he or she shall so offend, or by imprisonment for such time as the court may order for each day's offence, not exceeding thirty days in the whole upon any one conviction. And if any person making cigars shall fail to make the return herein required, or shall make a false return, he or she shall be punished by a fine not exceeding one hundred dollars, or by imprisonment not exceeding thirty days. And if any person,

May be forfeited and seized under certain circumstances.

Cigar makers to apply for a permit.

When the cigar maker works in any other district than the one where he received his permit he must procure an indorsement to his permit.

Fee for indorsing permit.

Assistant assessors required to indorse permits and keep a record of all permits granted or indorsed.

What this record must show.

Persons making cigars are to keep an accurate account, &c.

A copy to be given to the assistant assessor, if required, on the first Monday of every month.

Penalty for making cigars without permit.

Penalty for false return.

firm, company, or corporation shall employ or procure any person to make any cigars, who has not the permit or the indorsement thereon required by this act, he, she, or they shall be punished by a fine of ten dollars for each day he, she, or they shall so employ such person, or by imprisonment not exceeding ten days. And if any person shall be found making cigars without such permit, or the indorsement thereon, the collector of the district may seize any cigars, or tobacco for making cigars, which may be found in possession of such person, and the same shall be forfeited to the United States and sold; and one-half of the proceeds paid to the United States, one-fourth to the informer, and the other fourth to the collector making the seizure.

Penalty for employing any one to make cigars who has not a permit.

On bullion in lump, ingot, bar, or otherwise, a duty of one-half of one per centum ad valorem, to be paid by the assayer of the same, who shall stamp the product of the assay as the Commissioner of Internal Revenue, under the direction of the Secretary of the Treasury, may prescribe by general regulations. And every and all sales, transfers, exchanges, transportation, and exportation of gold or silver assayed at any mint of the United States, or by any private assayer, unless stamped as prescribed by general regulations, as aforesaid, is hereby declared unlawful; and every person or corporation who shall sell, transfer, transport, exchange, export or deal in the same, shall be subject to a penalty of one thousand dollars for each offence, and to a fine not exceeding that sum, and to imprisonment for a term not exceeding two years nor less than six months. No jeweler, worker or artificer in gold and silver, shall use either of those metals except it shall have first been stamped as aforesaid, as required by this act; and every violation of this section shall subject the offender to the penalties contained herein. No person or corporation shall take, transport, or cause to be transported, export, or cause to be exported from the United States any gold or silver in its natural state, uncoined or unassayed, and unstamped, as aforesaid; and for every violation of this provision every offender shall be subject to the penalties contained herein: *Provided*, That the foregoing subdivision of this section providing for a tax on gold and silver shall only be in force from and after sixty days after the passage of this act.

Bullion.

Gold and silver assayed to be stamped before sale or transfer of the same.

Penalty.

No jeweler allowed to use gold or silver unless the same has first been stamped.

No person allowed to export any gold or silver in its natural state.

Penalty.

SEC. 95. *And be it further enacted*, That whenever any manufactured articles, goods, wares, or merchandise on which an excise or impost duty has been paid, and which are not specially provided for, are increased in value by being polished, painted, varnished, waxed, oiled, gilded, electrotyped, galvanized, plated, framed, ground, pressed, colored, dyed, trimmed, ornamented, or otherwise more completely finished or fitted for use or sale, without changing the original character or purposes for which the same are intended to be used, there shall be levied, collected, and paid a tax of five per centum ad valorem upon the amount of such increased value, to be ascertained by deducting from the value of the finished article when sold, or removed for sale, delivery, or consumption, the cost or value of the original article to the person, firm, or company liable to the duty imposed upon the increased value thereof. The increasing of values in the manner aforesaid shall be deemed manufacturing, and any person, firm, company, or corporation engaged therein shall be liable to all the provisions of law for the collection of internal duties relating to

Tax on increased value in certain cases.

Increased value, how ascertained.

Increasing of values deemed manufacturing.

manufacturers as to licenses, returns, payment of taxes, liens, fines, penalties, and forfeitures.

Articles exempt from duty.

SEC. 96. *And be it further enacted,* That newspapers, boards, shingles, laths, and other lumber, staves, hoops, shooks, headings, and timber partially wrought and unfinished for chairs, tubs, pails, hubs, spokes, felloes, snaths, lasts, shovel and fork handles, match-wood, umbrella stretchers, alcohol made or manufactured of spirits or materials upon which the duties imposed by law shall have been paid, bone dust, plaster or gypsum, malt, burning fluid, printers' ink, flax prepared for textile or felting purposes until actually woven, marble and slate or other building stones in block, rough and unwrought, charcoal, coke, all flour and meal made from grain, bread and breadstuffs, butter, cheese, concentrated milk, paraffine, whale and fish oil, value of the bullion used in the manufacture of silver ware, silver bullion rolled or prepared for platers' use exclusively, materials prepared for the manufacture of hoop skirts exclusively and unfit for other use, (such as cut tapes and small wares for joining hoops together,) shall be, and hereby are, exempt from duty. And also all goods, wares, and merchandise, and articles made or manufactured from materials which have been subject to and upon which internal duties have been actually paid, or materials imported upon which duties have been paid or upon which no duties have been imposed by law, where the increased value of such goods, wares, or merchandise, and articles so made or manufactured, shall not exceed the amount of five per centum ad valorem, shall be, and hereby are, exempt from duty.

Manufactures exempt when the increased value does not exceed five per centum.

Manufacturers delivering goods under contract made prior to this act are allowed to add to the price of such goods so much as will be equivalent to the duty subsequently imposed.

SEC. 97. *And be it further enacted,* That every person, firm, or corporation, who shall have made any contract prior to the passage of this act, and without other provision therein for the payment of duties imposed by law enacted subsequent thereto, upon articles to be delivered under such contract, is hereby authorized and empowered to add to the price thereof so much money as will be equivalent to the duty so subsequently imposed on said articles, and not previously paid by the vendee, and shall be entitled by virtue hereof to be paid and to sue for and recover the same accordingly: *Provided,* That where the United States is the purchaser under such prior contract, the certificate of the proper officer of the department by which the contract was made, showing, according to regulations to be prescribed by the Secretary of the Treasury, the articles so purchased by the United States, and liable to such subsequent duty, shall be taken and received, so far as the same is applicable, in discharge of such subsequent duties on articles so contracted to be delivered to the United States and actually delivered according to such contract:

Proviso; when the United States is the purchaser.

AUCTION SALES.

Auction sales.

SEC. 98. *And be it further enacted,* That there shall be levied and collected and paid on all sales of real estate, goods, wares, merchandise, articles, or things at auction, including all sales of stocks, bonds, and other securities, a duty of one-fourth of one per centum on the gross amount of such sales; and every auctioneer or other person making such sales, as aforesaid, shall, at the end of each and every month, or within ten days thereafter, make a list or return to the assistant assessor of the district of the gross amount

Make monthly returns of gross amount of receipts

of such sales, made as aforesaid, with the amount of duty which has accrued or should accrue thereon, which list shall have annexed thereto a declaration under oath or affirmation, in form and manner as may be prescribed by the Commissioner of Internal Revenue, that the same is true and correct, and shall, at the same time, as aforesaid, pay to the collector or deputy collector the amount of duty or tax thereupon, as aforesaid, and in default thereof shall be subject to and pay a penalty of five hundred dollars. In all cases of delinquency in making said list or payment the assessment and collection shall be made in the manner prescribed in the general provisions of this act: *Provided*, That no duty shall be levied under the provisions of this section upon any sales by judicial or executive officers making auction sales by virtue of a judgment or decree of any court, nor to public sales made by guardians, executors, or administrators.

Penalty.

No duty levied on sales by judicial officers, &c.

BROKERS.

SEC. 99. *And be it further enacted*, That all brokers, and bankers doing business as brokers, shall be subject to pay the following duties and rates of duty upon the sales of merchandise, produce, gold and silver bullion, foreign exchange, uncurrent money, promissory notes, stocks, bonds, or other securities as hereinafter mentioned, and shall be subject to all the provisions, where not inapplicable thereto, for the returns, assessment, collection of the duties, and leins and penalties as are prescribed for the persons, firms, companies, or corporations, owning or possessing, or having the management of railroads, steamboats, and ferry-boats, that is to say: Upon all sales of merchandise, produce, or other goods, one-eighth of one per centum; upon all sales and contracts for sales of stocks and bonds, one-twentieth of one per centum on the par value thereof; and of gold and silver bullion and coin, foreign exchange, promissory notes, or other securities, one twentieth of one per centum on the amount of such sales, and of all contracts for such sales: *Provided*, That any person, firm, or company, not being licensed as a broker, or banker, or whole-sale or retail dealer, who shall sell or offer to sell any merchandise, produce, or gold and silver bullion, foreign exchange, uncurrent money, promissory notes, stocks, bonds, or other securities, not bona fide at the time his own property, and actually on hand, shall be liable, in addition to all other penalties provided in such cases, to pay fifty per centum in addition to the foregoing duties and rates of duty.

Brokers.

Per centum on sales.

Penalty for selling without license in certain cases.

SEC. 100. *And be it further enacted*, That there shall be levied annually, on every carriage, yacht, billiard table, gold watch, or pianoforte, or other musical instruments, and on all gold and silver plate the several duties or sums of money set down in figures against the same respectively, or otherwise specified and set forth in schedule A, hereto annexed, to be paid by the person or persons owning, possessing, or keeping the same on the first Monday of May in each year, and the same shall be and remain a lien thereon until paid.

Annual tax on carriages, &c.

SCHEDULE A.

Carriages, &c.	Carriage, gig, chaise, phæton, wagon, buggy wagon, carryall, rockaway, or other like carriage, and any coach, hackney coach, omnibus, or four-wheeled carriage, the body of which rests upon springs of any description, which may be kept for use, for hire, or for passengers, and which shall not be used exclusively in husbandry or for the transportation of merchandise, valued at fifty dollars and not exceeding one hundred dollars, including harness used therewith, each one dollar	$1 00
	Carriages of like description, valued at above one hundred dollars and not above two hundred dollars, each, two dollars	2 00
	Carriages of like description, valued at above two hundred dollars and not above three hundred dollars, each, three dollars	3 00
	Carriages of like description, valued above three hundred dollars and not above five hundred dollars, each, six dollars	6 00
	Carriages of like description, valued above five hundred dollars, each, ten dollars	10 00
Gold watches.	On gold watches, composed wholly or in part of gold or gilt, kept for use, valued at one hundred dollars or less, each, one dollar	1 00
	On gold watches, composed wholly or in part of gold or gilt, kept for use, valued at above one hundred dollars, each, two dollars	2 00
Pianofortes, &c.	On pianofortes, organs, melodions, or other parlor musical instruments, kept for use, not including those placed in churches or public edifices, valued at not less than one hundred dollars and not above two hundred dollars, each, two dollars	2 00
	When valued at above two hundred dollars and not above four hundred dollars, each, four dollars	4 00
	When valued above four hundred dollars, each, six dollars	6 00
Yachts.	On yachts, pleasure or racing boats, by sail or steam, measuring by custom-house measurement ten tons or less, each, five dollars	5 00
	Exceeding ten and not exceeding twenty tons, each, ten dollars	10 00
	Exceeding twenty and not exceeding forty tons, each, twenty-five dollars	25 00
	Exceeding forty and not exceeding eighty tons, each, fifty dollars	50 00
	Exceeding eighty and not exceeding one hundred and ten tons, each, seventy-five dollars	75 00
	Exceeding one hundred and ten tons, each, one hundred dollars	100 00
Billiard tables.	Billiard tables, kept for use, ten dollars	10 00
	Provided, That billard tables kept for hire, and upon which a license tax has been imposed, shall not be required to pay the tax on billiard tables kept for use as aforesaid, anything herein to the contrary notwithstanding.	
Plate of gold.	On plate, of gold, kept for use, per ounce troy, fifty cents	50
Plate of silver.	On plate, of silver, kept for use, per ounce troy, five cents	05
Proviso.	*Provided*, That silver spoons or plate of silver used by one family to an amount not exceeding forty ounces as aforesaid, belonging to any one person, plate belonging to religious societies, and souvenirs and keepsakes actually given and received as such and not kept for use; also, all premiums awarded as a token of merit by any agricultural society, corporation, or association of persons, for any purpose whatever, shall be exempt from duty.	

SLAUGHTERED CATTLE, SWINE, AND SHEEP.

SEC. 101. *And be it further enacted*, That there shall be paid by any person, firm, company, or agent or employé thereof, the following duties or taxes, that is to say:

Cattle and calves exceeding three months old. On all cattle and calves exceeding three months old, slaughtered, except when slaughtered for the hides and tallow exclusively, forty cents per head.

Cattle and calves under three mo's old. On all cattle and calves under three months old, slaughtered, five cents per head.

Swine. On all swine slaughtered, ten cents per head.

Sheep and lambs. On all sheep and lambs slaughtered, five cents per head.

Proviso. *Provided*, That cattle, not exceeding five in number, and calves, swine, sheep, and lambs, not exceeding in all twenty in number, slaughtered by any person for his or her own consumption, in any one year, shall be exempt from duty; and all sheep slaughtered for the pelts shall pay two cents only per head.

SEC. 102. *And be it further enacted,* That on and after the date on which this act shall take effect, any person or persons, firms, or companies, or agents or employés thereof, who shall slaughter for sale any cattle, calves, sheep, lambs, or swine, or who shall be the occupant of any building or premises in which such cattle, sheep, or swine shall be slaughtered, *any cattle, calves, sheep, lambs, or swine,* shall be required to make and render a list within ten days after the first day of each and every month to the assistant assessor of the district where the slaughtering is done, stating the number of cattle, calves, if any, the number of swine, if any, and the number of sheep and lambs, if any, slaughtered, as aforesaid, with the several rates of duty as fixed therein in this act, together with the whole amount thereof, which list shall have annexed thereto a declaration of said person or persons, agents or employés thereof, as aforesaid, under oath or affirmation, in such manner and form as may be prescribed by the Commissioner of Internal Revenue, that the same is true and correct, and shall, within the time and in the manner prescribed for the payment of duties on manufactures, pay the full amount of duties accruing thereon, as aforesaid, to the collector or deputy collector of the district, as aforesaid; and in case of default in making the return or payment of the duties, as aforesaid, the assessment and collection shall be made as in the provisions of this act required; and in case of fraud or evasion, the party offending shall forfeit and pay a penalty of ten dollars per head for any cattle, calves, swine, sheep, or lambs so slaughtered upon which the duty is fraudulently withheld, evaded, or attempted to be evaded; and the Commissioner of Internal Revenue may prescribe such further rules and regulations as he may deem necessary for ascertaining the correct number of cattle, calves, swine, sheep, and lambs liable to be taxed under the provisions of this act.

Persons who slaughter for sale required to make monthly returns.

Penalty for fraud or evasion.

RAILROADS, STEAMBOATS, FERRY-BOATS, AND BRIDGES.

SEC. 103. *And be it further enacted,* That every person, firm, company, or corporation owning or possessing or having the care or management of any railroad, canal, steamboat, ship, barge, canal boat, or other vessel, or any stage coach or other vehicle engaged or employed in the business of transporting passengers or property for hire, or in transporting the mails of the United States, or any canal, the water of which is used for mining purposes, shall be subject to and pay a duty of two and one-half per centum upon the gross receipts of such railroad, canal, steamboat, ship, barge, canal boat, or other vessel, or such stage coach or other vehicle: *Provided,* That the duty hereby imposed shall not be charged upon receipts for the transportation of persons or property, or mails, between the United States and any foreign port; and any person or persons, firms, companies, or corporations, owning, possessing, or having the care or management of any toll road, ferry, or bridge, authorized by law to receive toll for the transit of passengers, beasts, carriages, teams, and freight of any description, over such toll road, ferry, or bridge, shall be

Tax of 2½ per centum upon the gross receipts of railroads, canals steamboats, ships, barges, canal boats, vessels, stage coaches, and vehicles transporting passengers or property for hire.

Not chargable upon steamers and vessels plying between the United States and foreign ports.

Tax of three per centum on ferries and bridges receiving tolls for passengers and freight, on gross receipts.

subject to and pay a duty of three per centum on the gross amount of all their receipts of every description. But when the gross receipts of any such bridge or toll road shall not exceed the amount necessarily expended to keep such bridge or road in repair, no tax shall be imposed on such receipts: *Provided,* That all such persons, companies, and corporations shall have the right to add the duty or tax imposed hereby to their rates of fare whenever their liability thereto may commence, any limitations which may exist by law or by agreement with any person or company which may have paid or be liable to pay such fare to the contrary notwithstanding.

Not taxable when receipts are less than expenses of repairs.

May add the tax to the rates of fare.

EXPRESS COMPANIES.

A tax of three per centum upon gross receipts of express business.

SEC. 104. *And be it further enacted,* That any person, firm, company, or corporation carrying on or doing an express business, shall be subject to and pay a duty of three per centum on the gross amount of all the receipts of such express business.

INSURANCE COMPANIES.

Tax of 1½ per centum upon the gross receipts of premiums by inland, fire, and marine insurance companies.

SEC. 105. *And be it further enacted,* That there shall be levied, collected, and paid a duty of one and a half of one per centum upon the gross receipts of premiums, or assessments for insurance from loss or damage by fire or by the perils of the sea, made by every insurance company, whether inland or marine or fire insurance company, and by every association or individual engaged in the business of insurance against loss or damage by fire or by the perils of the sea; and by every person, firm, company, or corporation, who shall issue tickets or contracts of insurance against injury to persons while travelling by land or water; and a like duty shall be paid by the agent of any foreign insurance company having an office or doing business within the United States; and that in the account or return to be rendered, they shall state the amount insured, renewed, or continued, the gross amount of premiums received and assessments collected, and the duties by law accruing thereon for the quarter then next preceding.

To include tickets and contracts of insurance against injury to persons travelling.

Foreign companies to pay tax of 1½ per cent.

Returns to state the amount insured, &c., and gross amount of premiums and the duties thereon.

PASSPORTS.

Passports subject to a tax of $5.

May be paid to any collector.

Receipt and application to be forwarded to Secretary of State, who is to transmit the receipt to the Commissioner of Internal Revenue.

Moneys to be charged to collectors.

The same sum to be paid to ministers and consuls, who are to account therefor to the treasury.

SEC. 106. *And be it further enacted,* That for every passport issued from the office of the Secretary of State, there shall be paid the sum of five dollars; which amount may be paid to any collector appointed under this act, and his receipt therefor shall be forwarded with the application for such passport to the office of the Secretary of State, or any agent appointed by him, to be transmitted to the Commissioner of Internal Revenue, there to be charged to the account of such collector. And the collectors shall account for all moneys received for passports in the manner hereinbefore provided, and a like amount shall be paid for every passport issued by any minister or consul of the United States, who shall account therefor to the treasury.

TELEGRAPH COMPANIES.

SEC. 107. *And be it further enacted,* That any person; firm, company, or corporation owning or possessing or having the care or management of any telegraphic line by which telegraphic despatches or messages are received or transmitted, shall be subject to and pay a duty of five per centum on the gross amount of all receipts of such person, firm, company, or corporation.

Tax of five per centum upon the gross receipts of telegraph companies.

THEATRES, OPERAS, CIRCUSES, AND MUSEUMS.

SEC. 108. *And be it further enacted,* That any person, firm, or corporation, or the manager or agent thereof, owning, conducting, or having the care or management of any theatre, opera, circus, museum, or other public exhibition of dramatic or operatic representations, plays, performances, musical entertainments, feats of horsemanship, acrobatic sports, or other shows which are opened to the public for pay, but not including occasional concerts, school exhibitions, lectures, or exhibitions of works of art, shall be subject to and pay a duty of two per centum on the gross amount of all receipts derived by such person, firm, company, or corporation from such representations, plays, performances, exhibitions, shows, or musical entertainments.

Tax of two per centum upon the gross receipts of theatres, circuses, and other exhibitions and shows.

SEC. 109. *And be it further enacted,* That any person, firm, company, or corporation owning or possessing, or having the care or management of any railroad, canal, steamboat, ship, barge, canal boat, or other vessel, or any ferry, toll-road or bridge, as enumerated and described in section one hundred and *two* [three] of this act; or carrying on or doing an express business; or engaged in the business of insurance, as herein before described; or owning or having the care and management of any telegraph line, or owning, possessing, leasing, or having the control or management of any circus, theatre, opera, or museum, shall within twenty days after the end of each and every month, make a list or return in duplicate to the assistant assessor of the district, stating the gross amount of their receipts, respectively, for the month next preceding, which return shall be verified by the oath or affirmation of such owner, possessor, manager, agent, or other proper officer, in the manner and form to be prescribed from time to time by the Commissioner of Internal Revenue; and shall also pay to the collector the full amount of duties which have accrued on such receipts for the month aforesaid. And in case of neglect or refusal to make said lists or return for the space of ten days after such return should have been made as aforesaid, the assessor or assistant assessor shall proceed to estimate the amount received and the duties payable thereon, and shall add thereto ten per centum as hereinbefore provided in other cases of delinquency to make return for purposes of assessment; and for the purpose of making such assessment, or of ascertaining the correctness of any such return, the books of any such person, firm, company, or corporation shall be subject to the inspection of the assessor or assistant assessor on his demand or request therefor. And in case of neglect or refusal to pay the duties, with the addition aforesaid, when the same have been ascertained, for the space of ten days after the same shall have become payable, the owner, possessor, or person having the management as aforesaid, shall pay, in addition, ten per centum

Managers of railroads, canals, steamboats, ships, barges, canal boats, or other vessels, ferries, toll-roads, bridges, insurance companies, telegraphs, theatres, operas, circuses, shows, to make returns within twenty days after the end of each month to the assistant assessor, &c.

Return to state the gross receipts for the month, and to be verified by oath.

Form of return to be prescribed by Commissioner.

Duties to be paid to collector of the district.

In case of neglect or refusal to make returns for ten days, the assessor or assistant assessor to estimate receipts and taxes, and add ten per cent.

Books of owners or managers to be inspectsd by assessor or assistant assessor upon demand.

When payment is neglected or refused, a penalty of ten per cent. imposed.

on the amount of such duties and addition; and for any attempt knowingly to evade the payment of such duties, the said owner, possessor, or person having the care or management as aforesaid, shall be liable to pay a penalty of one thousand dollars for every such attempt, to be recovered as provided in this act for the recovery of penalties. And all provisions of this act in relation to liens and collections by distraint, not incompatible herewith, shall apply to this section and the objects therein embraced.

A penalty of $1,000 for any attempt knowingly to evade the payment of duties.

Lien and distraint as in other cases.

BANKS AND BANKING.

Monthly tax of one twenty-fourth of one per cent. upon deposits in banks or with any person engaged in banking.

Monthly duty of one twenty-fourth of one per cent. upon the capital of banks and persons engaged in banking.

Amount invested in United States bonds exempted.

Monthly duty of 1-12 of 1 per cent. upon average amount of circulation issued by any bank.

Additional monthly duty of 1-6 of 1 per cent. upon average amount of circulation beyond 90 per cent. of capital.

Additional monthly duty of 1-6 of 1 per cent. upon amount of circulation beyond the average for the 6 months preceding July 1, 1864.

Return to be made on the first of each month to the assessor of the district.

Return to be verified by the oath of the president or cashier in the form prescribed by the commissioner.

SEC. 110. *And be it further enacted*, That there shall be levied, collected, and paid a duty of one twenty-fourth of one per centum each month upon the average amount of the deposits of money, subject to payment by check or draft, or represented by certificates of deposit or otherwise, whether payable on demand or at some future day, with any person, bank, association, company or corporation engaged in the business of banking; and a duty of one twenty-fourth of one per centum each month as aforesaid, upon the average amount of the capital of any bank, association, company, or corporation, or person engaged in the business of banking beyond the amount invested in United States bonds; and a duty of one-twelfth of one per centum each month, upon the average amount of circulation issued by any bank, association, corporation, company, or person, including as circulation all certified checks and all notes and other obligations calculated or intended to circulate or to be used as money, but not including that in the vault of the bank, and redeemed and on deposit for said bank; and an additional duty of one-sixth of one per centum, each month, upon the average amount of such circulation, issued as foresaid, beyond the amount of ninety per centum of the capital of any such bank, association, corporation, company, or person, and upon any amount of such circulation, beyond the average amount of the circulation that had been issued as aforesaid by any such bank, association, corporation, company, or person, for the six months preceding the first day of July, 1864. And on the first Monday of August next, and of each month thereafter, a true and accurate return of the amount of circulation, of deposit and of capital as aforesaid for the previous month shall be made and rendered in duplicate by each of such banks, associations, corporations, companies, or persons to the assessor of the district in which any such bank, association, corporation, or company may be located, or in which such person may reside, with a declaration annexed thereto, and the oath or affirmation of such person, or of the president or cashier of such bank, association, corporation or company, in such form and manner as may be prescribed by the Commissioner of Internal Revenue that the same contains a true and faithful statement of the amount of circulation, deposits, and capital as aforesaid, subject to duty as aforesaid, and shall transmit the duplicate of said return to the Commissioner of Internal Revenue, and within twenty days thereafter, shall pay to the said Commissioner of Internal Revenue the duties hereinbefore prescribed upon the said amount of circulation, of deposits and of capital as aforesaid, and for any refusal or neglect to make or to render such return and payment as aforesaid, any such bank, association, corporation, company, or person so in default shall be subject to and pay a penalty of two

Duties to be paid to the Commissioner within 20 days.

Penalty for neglect.

hundred dollars, besides the additional penalty and forfeitures in other cases provided in this act; and the amount of circulation, deposit and capital, as aforesaid, in default of the proper return shall be estimated by the assessor or assistant assessor of the district as aforesaid, upon the best information he can obtain; and every such penalty, together with the duties as aforesaid, may be recovered for the use of the United States in any court of competent jurisdiction. And in the case of banks with branches, the duty herein provided for shall be imposed upon the circulation of each branch, severally, and the amount of capital of each branch shall be considered to be the amount allotted to such branch; and so much of an act entitled "An act to provide ways and means for the support of the government," approved March 3, 1863, as imposes any tax on banks, their circulation, capital, or deposits, other than is herein provided, is hereby repealed: *Provided,* That this section shall not apply to associations which are taxed under and by virtue of the act "to provide a national currency, secured by a pledge of United States bonds, and to provide for the circulation and redemption thereof;" nor to any savings bank having no capital stock, and whose business is confined to receiving deposits and loaning the same on interest for the benefit of the depositors only, and which do no other business of banking: *And provided, further,* That any bank ceasing to issue notes for circulation, and which shall deposit in the treasury of the United States, in lawful money, the amount of its outstanding circulation, to be redeemed at par, under such regulations as the Secretary of the Treasury may prescribe, shall be exempt from any tax upon such circulation.

Proceedings in case of neglect.

Banks with branches.

This section not to apply to national banks.

Nor to certain savings banks.

Banks ceasing to issue notes for circulation may be exempt from tax.

LOTTERIES.

SEC. 111. *And be it further enacted,* That every individual partnership, firm, and association, being proprietors, managers, or agents of lotteries, shall pay a tax of five per centum on the gross amount of the receipts from the said business; and all persons making such sales shall, within ten days after the first day of each and every month, make and render a list or return in duplicate to the assistant assessor of the gross amount of such sales, made as aforesaid, with the amount of duty which has accrued or should accrue thereon; which list shall have annexed thereto a declaration, under oath or affirmation, in such form and signed by such officer, agent, or clerk, as may be prescribed by the Commissioner of Internal Revenue, that the same is true and correct, and *that* the said proprietors, managers, and agents shall, on or before the twentieth day of each and every month, as aforesaid, pay the collector or deputy collector of the proper district the amount of the duty or tax as aforesaid. And in default of making such lists or returns, the said proprietors, managers, and agents, and all other persons making such sales, shall be subject to and pay a penalty of one thousand dollars, besides the additions, penalties, and forfeitures in other cases provided; and the said proprietors, managers, and agents shall, in default of paying the said duty or tax at the time herein required, be subject to and pay a penalty of one thousand dollars, or be imprisoned not exceeding one year. In all cases of delinquency in making said list, return, or payment, the assessments and collections shall be made in the man-

Tax of 5 per cent upon the gross receipts of lotteries.

Returns to be made monthly and in duplicate to the assistant assessor with the amount of duty.

To be verified by oath or affirmation.

Form of return to be prescribed by Commissioner.

Payment to be made to collector on or before the 20th day of each month.

Penalty of $1,000 in case of default to make lists in addition to ordinary penalties.

Penalty of $1,000 in case of non-payment and imprisonment not exceeding one year.

In case of delinquency the assessment and collections to be made as provided in sections 84 and 85.

Commissioner may grant free permits to managers of certain fairs whose proceeds are to be applied to the relief of sick and wounded soldiers or other charitable purpose.

Lotteries not legalized.

ner prescribed in the provisions of this act in relation to manufactures, articles, and products: *Provided*, That the managers of any sanitary fair, or of any charitable, benevolent, or religious association, may apply to the collector of the district and present to him proof that the proceeds of any contemplated lottery, raffle, or gift enterprise will be applied to the relief of sick and wounded soldiers, or to some other charitable use, and thereupon the Commissioner shall grant a permit to hold such lottery, raffle, or gift enterprise, and the said sanitary fair, or charitable or benevolent association, shall be exempt from all charge, whether from tax or license, in respect of such lottery, raffle, or gift enterprise: *Provided, further*, That nothing in this section contained shall be construed to legalize any lottery.

Lottery tickets to be stamped with name of vendor and date of sale.

Penalty for neglect of $50.

SEC. 112. *And be it further enacted*, That each lottery ticket or certificate supplementary thereto shall be legibly stamped at the time of sale with the name of the vendor and the date of such sale, under a penalty of fifty dollars, to be paid by the vendor of each lottery ticket or certificate supplementary thereto sold without being first stamped as aforesaid.

Sales without license subject the seller to a penalty of $500 additional to other penalties.

Purchasers of tickets from unlicensed lottery ticket vendors may recover twice the amount paid at any time within three years with costs.

SEC. 113. *And be it further enacted*, That in addition to all other penalties and forfeitures now imposed by law for the evasion of license fees or other taxes upon the lottery business, any person who shall hereafter sell or dispose of any lottery ticket or certificate supplementary thereto, or any device in the nature thereof, without having first duly obtained a license, as hereinbefore mentioned, shall incur a penalty of five hundred dollars for each and every such offence; and any person who shall purchase, obtain, or receive any lottery ticket, or any policy of numbers, tokens, certificate, wager, or device, representing or intended to represent a lottery ticket or fractional part thereof, from any person not having a license to deal in lottery tickets, as provided by law, may recover from such person of whom the same was purchased, obtained, or received, at any time within three years thereafter, before any court of competent jurisdiction, a sum equal to twice the amount paid for the same, with just and legal costs.

ADVERTISEMENTS.

Tax of 3 per cent. upon advertisements in newspapers, magazines, &c.

Owners and managers to make returns quarterly, giving the gross receipts and duties.

Return to be made to the assistant assessor and in duplicate.

To be verified by oath or affirmation.

SEC. 114. *And be it further enacted*, That there shall be levied, collected, and paid by any person or persons, firm, or company, publishing any newspaper, magazine, review, or other literary, scientific, or news publication issued periodically, on the gross receipts for all advertisements, or all matters for the insertion of which in said newspaper or other publication, as aforesaid, or in extras, supplements, sheets, or fly-leaves accompanying the same, pay is required or received, a duty of three per centum; and the person or persons, firm or company, owning, possessing, or having the care or management of any and every such newspaper or other publication, as aforesaid, shall make a list or return on the first day of January, April, July, and October of each year, containing the gross amount of receipts as aforesaid, and the amount of duties which have accrued thereon, and render the same in duplicate to the assistant assessor of the district where such newspaper, magazine, review, or other literary or news publication is or may be published; which list or return shall have annexed a declaration, under oath or affirmation, to be made according to the manner and form which may be from time to time prescribed by the Commissioner of Internal Revenue, of the owner, possessor, or person having the care or management of such newspaper, magazine, review, or other publication, as aforesaid, that the same is true and correct; and shall also, quarterly, within ten days after the time of making said list or return, pay to the collector or deputy collector of the district the full amount of said duties. And in case of neglect or refusal to comply with any of the provisions contained in this section, or to make and render said list or return, for the space of ten days after the time when said list or return ought to have been made, as aforesaid, the assistant assessors of the respective districts shall proceed to estimate the duties as heretofore provided in other cases of delinquency; and in case of neglect or refusal to pay the duties, as aforesaid, for the space of ten days after said duties become due and payable, and have been demanded, said owner, possessor, or person or persons having the care or management of said newspapers or publications, as aforesaid, shall pay, in addition thereto, a penalty of ten per centum on the amount due. And in case of fraud or evasion, whereby the revenue is attempted to be defrauded, or the duty withheld, said owners, possessors, or person or persons having the care or management of said newspapers or other publications, as aforesaid, shall forfeit and pay a penalty of one thousand dollars for each offence, or for any sum fraudulently unaccounted for. And all provisions in this act in relation to returns, additions, penalties, forfeitures, liens, assessments, and collection, not incompatible herewith, shall apply to this section and the objects herein embraced: *Provided*, That in all cases where the rate or price of advertising is fixed by any law of the United States, State, or Territory, it shall be lawful for the company, person or persons, publishing said advertisements, to add the duty or tax imposed by this act to the price of said advertisements, any law to the contrary notwithstanding; and that the receipts for advertisements to the amount of six hundred dollars annually, by any person or persons, firm, or company publishing any newspaper, magazine, review, or other literary, scientific, or news publication, issued periodically, shall be exempt from duty: *And provided further*, That all newspapers whose average circulation does not exceed two thousand copies shall be exempted from all taxes for advertisements.

Form to be prescribed by Commissioner.

Payment to be made to collector or deputy within ten days.

Assistant assessor to estimate duties in case of neglect or refusal for ten days.

Penalty of ten per cent. in case of neglect or refusal to pay the duties for ten days.

In case of attempt to defraud the revenue a penalty of $1,000 for each offence.

General provisions in regard to returns, additions, penalties, &c., applicable to this section.

When prices of advertising are fixed by law, proprietors may add the tax thereto.

Receipts to the amount of $600 annually exempt.

Newspapers whose average circulation does not exceed 2,000 copies exempt from tax.

SEC. 115. *And be it further enacted*, That whenever by this act any license, duty, or tax of any description has been imposed on any person or corporate body, or property of any person, or incorporated or unincorporated company, having more than one place of business, it shall be lawful for the Commissioner of Internal Revenue to prescribe and determine in what district such tax shall be assessed and collected, and to what officer thereof the official notices required in that behalf shall be given, and of whom payment of such tax shall be demanded: *Provided*, That all taxes on manufactures, manufacturing companies, and manufacturing corporations, shall be assessed, and the tax collected in the district within which the place of manufacture is located, unless otherwise provided.

When tax is imposed upon a person or corporation having more than one place of business, Commissioner may determine where and to what collector the tax shall be paid, also to whom the official notices shall be given.

Tax on manufactures to be paid in the district where the manufactory is situated, except as otherwise provided.

INCOME.

Income tax to be assessed annually upon every person in the U. States, and upon every citizen thereof residing abroad. Enumeration of sources of income taxable. Exceptions referred to. The sum of $600 exempt. Tax of 5 per cent. over $600 and not over $5,000. Tax of 7½ per cent. on excess of $5,000 and not exceeding $10,000. Tax of 10 per cent. on the excess over $10,000. Tax to be levied upon the income of the calendar year next preceding. Income from notes, bonds, and securities of the United States to be included. But one deduction of $600 from the income of a single family, unless separate income is derived from separate estate or labor. Profit and loss on sales of real estate purchased and sold within the year to be included in estimating income.

SEC. 116. *And be it further enacted,* That there shall be leveid, collected, and paid annually upon the annual gains, profits, or income of every person residing in the United States, or of any citizen of the United States residing abroad, whether derived from any kind of property, rents, interests, dividends, salaries, or from any profession, trade, employment, or vocation, carried on in the United States or elsewhere, or from any other source whatever, except as hereinafter mentioned, if such annual gains, profits, or income, exceed the sum of six hundred dollars, a duty of five per centum on the excess over six hundred dollars and not exceeding five thousand dollars; and a duty of seven and one-half of one per centum per annum on the excess over five thousand dollars, and not exceeding ten thousand dollars; and a duty of ten per centum on the excess over ten thousand dollars. And the duty herein provided for shall be assessed, collected, and paid upon the gains, profits, or income for the year ending the thirty-first day of December next, preceding the time for levying, collecting, and paying said duty: *Provided,* That income derived from interest upon notes, bonds, and other securities of the United States shall be included in estimating incomes under this section: *Provided,* That only one deduction of six hundred dollars shall be made from the aggregate incomes of all the members of any family composed of parents and minor children, or husband and wife, except in cases where such separate income shall be derived from the separate and individual estate, gains, or labor of the wife or child: *And provided, further,* That net profits realized by sales of real estate purchased within the year for which income is estimated, shall be chargeable as income; and losses on sales of real estate purchased within the year, for which income is estimated, shall be deducted from the income of such year.

In estimating income certain taxes assessed and paid to be deducted.

SEC. 117. *And be it further enacted,* That in estimating the annual gains, profits, or income of any person, all national, State, and municipal taxes, other than the national income tax, lawfully assessed within the year upon the property or sources of income of any person, as aforesaid, from which said annual gains, profits, or income is or should be derived, shall be deducted, in addition to six hundred dollars, from the gains, profits, or income of the person who has actually paid the same, whether owner, tenant, or mortgagor; also the salary or pay received for services in the civil, military, naval, or other service of the United States, including senators, representatives, and delegates in Congress, above the rate of six hundred dollars per annum; and there shall also be deducted the income derived from dividends on shares in the capital stock of any bank, trust company, savings institution, insurance, railroad, canal, turnpike, canal navigation, or slack-water company, and the interest on any bonds or other evidences of indebtedness of any such corporation or company, which shall have been assessed and the tax paid, as hereinafter provided; also the amount paid by any person for the rent of the homestead used or occupied by himself or his family, and the rental value of any homestead used or occupied by any person or by his family, in his own right or in the right of his wife, shall not be included and assessed as part of the income of such person. In estimating the annual gains, profits, or income of any person, the interest

Salaries and payments to public officers in excess of $600 to be deducted.

Also, income from certain shares and from interest on bonds of corporations, when the tax has been previously assessed upon such income and interest.

Also, rent paid for homestead or the rental value thereof, when used or occupied either in right of the party or in that of his wife.

over and above the amount of interest paid upon all notes, bonds, and mortgages, or other forms of indebtedness, bearing interest, whether due and paid or not, if good and collectable, shall be included and assessed as part of the income of such person for each year; and also all income or gains derived from the purchase and sale of stocks or other property, real or personal, and the increased value of live stock, whether sold or on hand, and the amount of sugar, wool, butter, cheese, pork, beef, mutton, or other meats, hay and grain, or other vegetable or other productions of the estate of such person sold, not including any part thereof unsold or on hand during the year next preceding the thirty-first of December, shall be included and assessed as part of the income of such person for each year, and the gains and profits of all companies, whether incorporated or partnership, other than the companies specified in this section, shall be included in estimating the annual gains, profits, or income of any person entitled to the same, whether divided or otherwise. In estimating deductions from income, as aforesaid, when any person rents buildings, lands, or other property, or hires labor to carry on land, or to conduct any other business from which such income is actually derived, or pays interest upon any actual incumbrance thereon, the amount actually paid for such rent, labor, or interest, shall be deducted; and also the amount paid out for usual or ordinary repairs, not exceeding the average paid out for such purposes for the preceding five years, shall be deducted, but no deduction shall be made for any amount paid out for new buildings, permanent improvements, or betterments, made to increase the value of any property or estate: *Provided*, That in cases where the salary or other compensation paid to any person in the employment or service of the United States, shall not exceed the rate of six hundred dollars per annum, or shall be by fees, or uncertain or irregular in the amount or in the time during which the same shall have accrued or been earned, such salary or other compensation shall be included in estimating the annual gains, profits, or income of the person to whom the same shall have been paid, in such manner as the Commissioner of Internal Revenue, under the direction of the Secretary of the Treasury, may prescribe.

Excess of interest receivable over amount of interest paid to be taxed, if it is collectable, whether collected or not.

Income derived from gains by purchase and sale of property, increasd value of live stock and agricultural products sold subject to tax.

Excluding articles on hand and not sold during the calendar year aforesaid.

Profits of companies not enumerated in this section subject to income tax, whether divided or not.

Payments for rents, labor, and interest upon incumbrances on property from which income is derived, to be deducted.

Also payments for repairs, not exceeding the average of last five years.

No deduction for new buildings, permanent improvemtnts, betterments, &c.

The pay of employés of the U.S. who receive less than $600 per year, or who are paid by fees, to be added to other income.

Manner of collection to be prescribed by Commissioner under direction of Secretary of Treasury.

SEC. 118. *And be it further enacted*, That it shall be the duty of all persons of lawful age, and all guardians and trustees, whether such trustees are so by virtue of their office as executors, administrators, or in other fiduciary capacity, to make a list or return under oath or affirmation, in such form and manner as may be prescribed by the Commissioner of Internal Revenue, to the assistant assessor of the district in which he resides, of the amount of his or her income, or the income of such minors or persons as may be held in trust as aforesaid, according to the requirements hereinbefore mentioned, stating the sources from which said income is derived, whether from any kind of property, or the purchase and sale of property, rents, interest, dividends, salaries, or from any profession, trade, employment, or vocation, or otherwise. And in case of neglect or refusal to make such return, the assessor or assistant assessor shall assess the amount of his or her income, and the duty thereon, in the same manner as is provided for in other cases of neglect and refusal to furnish lists or returns in the provisions of this act, where not otherwise incompatible; and the assistant assessor may increase the amount of the list or return, or

Returns to be made by all persons of lawful age, and by all guardians and trustees, to the assistant assessor of the district.

Form to be prescribed by the Commissioner.

Particulars to be stated in return.

In case of neglect or refusal, assessor or assistant assessor to make the assessment.

Assistant assessor may increase the return of any person if satisfied the same is understated.

Party may make a declaration under oath.

Form to be prescribed by the Commissioner of Internal Revenue.

Particulars to which the declaration may relate.

When return has been increased, the party may state under oath the amount of income.

of any party making such return, if he shall be satisfied that the same is understated: *Provided,* That any party, in his or her own behalf, or as guardian or trustee, as aforesaid, shall be permitted to declare, under oath or affirmation, the form and manner of which shall be prescribed by the Commissioner of Internal Revenue, that he or she was not possessed of an income of six hundred dollars, liable to be assessed according to the provisions of this act, or may declare that he or she has been assessed elsewhere in the same year for, and has paid an income duty, under authority of the United States, and shall thereupon be exempt from income duty in said district; or, if the list or return of any party shall have been increased by the assistant assessor, in manner as aforesaid, such party may be permitted to declare, under oath or affirmation, the amount of annual income, or the amount held in trust, as aforesaid, liable to be assessed, and the same, so declared, shall be received by such assistant assessor as true, and as the sum upon which duties are to be assessed and collected, except that the deductions claimed in such cases shall not be made or allowed until approved by the assistant assessor. But any person feeling aggrieved by the decision of the assistant assessor in such cases, may appeal to the assessor of the district, and his decision thereon shall be final; and the form, time, and manner of proceedings shall be subject to rules and regulations to be prescribed by the Commissioner of Internal Revenue.

The statement to be received as true.

Deducti'ns claimed must be approved by assistant assessor.

Right of appeal to assessor.

His decision final.

Commissioner to prescribe rules and regulations.

Income tax to be levied on the 1st of May in each year.

Payable on or before the 30th of June until and including the year 1870.

If payment not made within 30 days after 30th of June, and for ten days after demand, a penalty of 10 per cent. imposed, except in case of the estates of deceas'd and insolvent persons.

When demand has been made, the amount due a lien in favor of the United States from the time it was due upon all the property of the party in default.

Manner of enforcing lien.

Proceedings by collector.

Form of warrant to be prescribed by Commissioner.

Levy to be sufficient to cover fees, costs, and expenses of levy.

Collector's certificate to vest title in the purchaser.

SEC. 119. *And be it further enacted,* That the duties on incomes herein imposed shall be levied on the first day of May, and be due and payable on or before the thirtieth day of June, in each year, until and including the year eighteen hundred and seventy, and no longer; and to any sum or sums annually due and unpaid for thirty days after the thirtieth of June, as aforesaid, and for ten days after demand thereof by the collector, there shall be levied in addition thereto the sum of ten per centum on the amount of duties unpaid, as a penalty, except from the estates of deceased and insolvent persons. And if any person liable to pay such duty shall neglect or refuse to pay the same, after such demand, the amount due shall be a lien in favor of the United States from the time it was due until paid, with the interest, penalties, and costs that may accrue in addition thereto, upon all the property and rights to property belonging to such person; and in default of the payment of said duty aforesaid, said lien may be enforced by distraint upon such property, rights to property, stocks, securities, and evidences of debt, by whomsoever holden; and for this purpose the collector, after demands duly given, as aforesaid, shall issue a warrant, in form and manner to be prescribed by the Commissioner of Internal Revenue, under the directions of the Secretary of the Treasury, and by virtue of such warrant there may be levied on such property, rights to property, stocks, securities, and evidences of debt, a further sum, to be fixed and stated in such warrant, over and above the said annual duty, interest, and penalty for non-payment, sufficient for the fees, costs, and expenses of such levy. And in all cases of sale, as aforesaid, the certificate of such sale by the collector shall vest in the purchaser all right, title, and interest of such delinquent in and to such property, whether the property be real or personal; and where the subject of sale shall be stocks, the certificate of said sale shall be lawful authority and notice to the proper corporation, company, or asso ciation, to record the same on the books or records, in the same manner as if transferred or assigned by the person or party holding the same, to issue new certificates of stock therefor in lieu of any original or prior certificates, which shall be void whether cancelled or not. And said certificates of sale of the collector, where the subject of sale shall be securities or other evidences of debt, shall be good and valid receipts to the person holding the same, as against any person holding, or claiming to hold, possession of such securities or other evidences of debt.

Duty of 5 per cent. on dividends of banks, trust companies, savings institutions, and insurance companies.

SEC. 120. *And be it further enacted,* That there shall be levied and collected a duty of five per centum on all dividends in scrip or money thereafter declared due, and whenever the same shall be payable, to stockholders, policy-holders, or depositors, as part of the earnings, income, or gains of any bank, trust company, savings institution, and of any fire, marine, life, inland, insurance company, either stock or mutual, under whatever name or style known or called, in the United States or Territories, whether specially incorporated or existing under general laws, and on all undistributed sums, or sums made or added during the year to their surplus or contingent funds; and said banks, trust companies, savings institutions, and insurance companies shall pay the said duty, and are hereby authorized to deduct and withhold from all payments made on account of any dividends or sums of money that may be due and payable as aforesaid, the said duty of five per centum. And a list or return shall be made and rendered to the assessor or assistant assessor in duplicate, and one of said lists or returns shall be transmitted, and the duty paid to the Commissioner of Internal Revenue within thirty days after the time when any dividends or sums of money become due or payable as aforesaid; and said list or return shall contain a true and faithful account of the amount of duties as aforesaid; and there shall be annexed thereto a declaration of the president, cashier, or treasurer of the bank, trust company, savings institution, or insurance company, under oath or affirmation, in form and manner as may be prescribed by the Commissioner of Internal Revenue, that the same contains a true and faithful account of the duties as aforesaid. And for any default in the making or rendering of such list or return, with such declaration annexed, the bank, trust company, savings institution, or insurance company, making such default, shall forfeit as a penalty the sum of one thousand dollars; and in case of any default in making or rendering said list or return, or of any default in the payment of the duty as required, or any part thereof, the assessment and collection of the duty and penalty shall be in accordance with the general provisions of law in other cases of neglect and refusal: *Provided,* That the duty upon the dividends of life insurance companies shall not be deemed due or to be collected until such dividends shall be payable by such companies, nor shall the portion of premiums returned by mutual life insurance companies to their policy holders be considered as dividends or profits under this act.

Same duty on additions to surplus or contingent funds.

Duty to be withheld from all payments on account of such dividends.

Return to be made to assessor and duty paid to Commiss'ner within 30 days after dividend is payable.

Return to be verified by oath of president, cashier, or treasurer.

Penalty for default in rendering return.

In case of default, assessment and collection to be in accordance with general provisions.

Dividends of life insurance companies not due until payable.

Premiums returned by mutual life insurance companies, not dividends.

Bank neglecting to make dividend or addition to surplus as often as once in 6 months to make return on 1st of January and 1st of July

SEC. 121. *And be it further enacted,* That any bank legally authorized to issue notes as circulation which shall neglect or omit to make dividends or additions to its surplus or contingent fund as often as once in six months, shall make a list or return in duplicate, under oath or affirmation of the president or cashier, to the assessor or assistant assessor of the district in which it is located, on the first day of January and July in each year, or within thirty days thereafter, of the amount of profits which have accrued or been earned and received by said bank during the six months next preceding said first days of January and July; and shall present one of said lists or returns and pay to the collector of the district a duty of five per centum on such profits; and in case of default to make such list or return and payment within the thirty days as aforesaid, shall be subject to the provisions of the foregoing section of this act: *Provided,* That when any dividend is made which includes any part of the surplus or contingent fund of any bank, trust company, savings institution, insurance or railroad company, which has been assessed and the duty paid thereon, the amount of duty so paid on that portion of the surplus or contingent fund may be deducted from the duty on such dividend.

Duty of 5 per cent. to be paid to the collector.

Duty paid on surplus or contingent fund to be deducted from duty on future dividend.

SEC. 122. *And be it further enacted,* That any railroad, canal, turnpike, canal navigation, or slackwater company indebted for any money for which bonds or other evidence of indebtedness have been issued, payable in one or more years after date, upon which interest is stipulated to be paid, or coupons representing the interest, or any such company that may have declared any dividend in scrip, or money due or payable to its stockholders, as part of the earnings, profits, income, or gains of such company, and all profits of such company carried to the account of any fund, or used for construction, shall be subject to and pay a duty of five per centum on the amount of all such interest, or coupons, dividends, or profits, whenever the same shall be payable; and said companies are hereby authorized to deduct and withhold from all payments, on account of any interest, or coupons and dividends due and payable as aforesaid, the duty of five per centum; and the payment of the amount of said duty so deducted from the interest, or coupons, or dividends, and certified by the president or treasurer of said company, shall discharge said company from that amount of the dividend, or interest, or coupon, on the bonds or other evidences of their indebtedness so held by any person or party whatever, except where said companies may have contracted otherwise. And a list or return shall be made and rendered to the assessor or assistant assessor in duplicate, and one of said lists or returns shall be transmitted and the duty paid to the Commissioner of Internal Revenue within thirty days after the time when said interest, coupons, or dividends become due and payable, and as often as every six months; and said list or return shall contain a true and faithful account of the amount of the duty, and there shall be annexed thereto a declaration of the president or treasurer of the company, under oath or affirmation, in form and manner as may be prescribed by the Commissioner of Internal Revenue, that the same contains a true and faithful account of said duty. And for any default in making or rendering such list or return, with the declaration annexed, or of the payment of the duty as aforesaid, the company making such default shall forfeit as a penalty the sum of one thousand dollars; and in case of any default in making or rendering said list or return, or of the payment of the duty, or any part thereof, as aforesaid, the assessment and collection of the duty and penalty shall be made according to the provisions of law in other cases of neglect or refusal.

Duty of 5 per cent. on dividends and interest on bonds of railroad, canal, turnpike, canal navigation, and slackwater companies.

Companies to withhold duty from all payments.

Payment to discharge companies from that amount of indebtedness.

Return to be made to assessor and duty paid to Commissioner within 30 days.

Return to be verified by oath of president or treasurer.

Penalty for default in making return.

In case of default in making return, or payment of the duty, assessment, and collect'n, to be according to general provisions.

SEC. 123. *And be it further enacted,* That there shall be levied, collected, and paid on all salaries of officers, or payments for ser

Duty of 5 per cent. on salaries in excess of $600.

vices to persons in the civil, military, naval, or other employment or service of the United States, including senators and representatives and delegates in Congress, when exceeding the rate of six hundred dollars per annum, a duty of five per centum on the excess above the said six hundred dollars; and it shall be the duty of all paymasters, and all disbursing officers, under the government of the United States, or in the employ thereof, when making any payments to officers and persons as aforesaid, or upon settling and adjusting the accounts of such officers and persons, to deduct and withhold the aforesaid duty of five per centum, and shall, at the same time, make a certificate stating the name of the officer or person from whom such deduction was made, and the amount thereof, which shall be transmitted to the office of the Commissioner of Internal Revenue, and entered as part of the internal duties; and the pay-roll, receipts, or account of officers or persons paying such duty, as aforesaid, shall be made to exhibit the fact of such payment. And it shall be the duty of the several Auditors of the Treasury Department, when auditing the accounts of any paymaster or disbursing officer, or when settling or adjusting the accounts of any such officer, to require evidence that the duties or taxes mentioned in this section have been deducted and paid over to the Commissioner of Internal Revenue: *Provided*, That payments of prize money shall be regarded as income from salaries, and the duty thereon shall be adjusted and collected in like manner.

Disbursing officers to withhold amount and transmit to Commissioner.

Auditors of the Treas'y to require evidence that duties have been paid.

Payments of prize money to be regarded as salaries.

LEGACIES AND DISTRIBUTIVE SHARES OF PERSONAL PROPERTY.

SEC. 124. *And be it further enacted*, That any person or persons having in charge or trust, as administrators, executors, or trustees, any legacies or distributive shares arising from personal property, where the whole amount of such personal property, as aforesaid, shall exceed the sum of one thousand dollars in actual value, passing, after the passage of this act, from any person possessed of such property, either by will or by the intestate laws of any State or Territory, or any personal property or interest therein, transferred by deed, grant, bargain, sale, or gift, made or intended to take effect in possession or enjoyment after the death of the grantor or bargainor, to any person or persons, or to any body or bodies politic or corporate, in trust or otherwise, shall be, and hereby are, made subject to a duty or tax, to be paid to the United States, as follows, that is to say:

Administrators, executors, and trustees to pay tax on legacies and distributive shares, where the whole amount exceeds $1,000.

First. Where the person or persons entitled to any beneficial interest in such property shall be the lineal issue or lineal ancestor, brother or sister, to the person who died possessed of such property, as aforesaid, at the rate of one dollar for each and every hundred dollars of the clear value of such interest in such property.

Lineal issue or lineal ancestor, brother or sister, 1 per cent.

Second. Where the person or persons entitled to any beneficial interest in such property shall be a descendant of a brother or sister of the person who died possessed, as aforesaid, at the rate of two dollars for each and every hundred dollars of the clear value of such interest.

Descendant of brother or sister, 2 per cent.

Third. Where the person or persons entitled to any beneficial interest in such property shall be a brother or sister of the father or mother, or a descendant of a brother or sister of the father or

Brother or sister of father or mother or descendant of same, 4 per cent.

mother, of the person who died possessed, as aforesaid, at the rate of four dollars for each and every hundred dollars of the clear value of such interest.

Brother or sister of grandfather or grandmother, or descendant of same, 5 per cent.

Fourth. Where the person or persons entitled to any beneficial interest in such property shall be a brother or sister of the grandfather or grandmother, or a descendant of the brother or sister of the grandfather or grandmother, of the person who died possessed as aforesaid, at the rate of five dollars for each and every hundred dollars of the clear value of such interest.

Other degree of consanguinity, or stranger in blood, 6 per cent.

Fifth. Where the person or persons entitled to any beneficial interest in such property shall be in any other degree of collateral consanguinity than is hereinbefore stated, or shall be a stranger in blood to the person who died possessed, as aforesaid, or shall be a body politic or corporate, at the rate of six dollars for each and every hundred dollars of the clear value of such interest:

Husband or wife, exempt.

Provided, That all legacies or property passing by will, or by the laws of any State or Territory, to husband or wife of the person who died possessed, as aforesaid, shall be exempt from tax or duty.

Tax a lien upon the property for 20 years.

SEC. 125. *And be it further enacted*, That the tax or duty aforesaid shall be a lien and charge upon the property of every person who may die as aforesaid, for twenty years, or until the same shall, within that period, be fully paid to and discharged by the United States;

Executor, &c., to pay the tax before the payment of any legacy.

and every executor, administrator, or trustee, before payment and distribution to the legatees or any parties entitled to beneficial interest therein, shall pay to the collector or deputy collector of the district of which the deceased person was a resident, the amount of the duty or tax assessed upon such legacy or distributive share,

Return to be made to the assessor or assistant.

and shall also make and render to the assessor or assistant assessor of the said district a schedule, list, or statement, in duplicate, of the amount of such legacy or distributive share, together with the amount of duty which has accrued or shall accrue thereon,

Return to be under oath.

verified by his oath or affirmation, to be administered and certified thereon by some magistrate or officer having lawful power to administer such oaths, in such form and manner as may be prescribed by the Commissioner of Internal Revenue, which schedule, list, or statement shall contain the names of each and every person entitled to any beneficial interest therein, together with the clear value of such interest, the duplicate of which schedule, list, or statement shall be by him immediately delivered, and the tax thereon paid to such collector; and upon such payment and delivery of such schedule, list, or statement, said collector or deputy collector shall grant to such person paying such duty or tax a receipt or receipts for the same in duplicate, which shall be prepared as hereinafter provided.

Receipt of the collector to be sufficient evidence to entitle executor to credit in the settlement of his account.

Such receipt or receipts, duly signed and delivered by such collector or deputy collector, shall be sufficient evidence to entitle such executor, administrator, or trustee, to be credited and allowed such payment by every tribunal which, by the laws of any State or Territory, is, or may be, empowered to decide upon and settle the accounts of executors and administrators.

Proceedings in case of neglect.

And in case such executor, administrator, or trustee, shall refuse or neglect to pay the aforesaid duty or tax to the collector or deputy collector, as aforesaid, within the time hereinbefore provided, or shall neglect or refuse to deliver to said collector or deputy collector the duplicate of the schedule, list, or statement of such legacies, property, or personal estate, under oath, as aforesaid, or shall neglect or refuse to deliver the schedule, list, or statement of such legacies, property, or personal estate, under oath, as aforesaid, or shall deliver to said assessor or assistant assessor a false schedule or statement of such legacies, property, or personal estate, or give the names and relationship of the persons entitled to beneficial interests therein untruly, or shall not truly and correctly set forth and state therein the clear value of such beneficial interest, or where not administration upon such property or personal estate shall have been granted or allowed under existing laws, the assistant assessor shall make out such lists and valuation as in other cases of neglect or refusal, and shall assess the duty thereon; and the collector shall commence appropriate proceedings before any court of the United States, in the name of the United States, against such person or persons as may have the actual or constructive custody or possession of such property or personal estate, or any part thereof, and shall subject such property or personal estate, or any portion of the same, to be sold upon the judgment or decree of such court, and from the proceeds of such sale the amount of such tax or duty, together with all costs and expenses of every description to be allowed by such court, shall be first paid, and the balance, if any, deposited according to the order of such court, to be paid under its direction to such person or persons as shall establish title to the same. The deed or deeds, or any proper conveyance of such property or personal estate, or any portion thereof, so sold under such judgment or decree, executed by the officer lawfully charged with carrying the same into effect, shall vest in the purchaser thereof all the title of the delinquent to the property or personal estate sold under and by virtue of such judgment or decree, and shall release every other portion of such property or personal estate from the lien or charge thereon created by this act. And every person or persons who shall have in his possession, charge, or custody, any record, file, or paper containing or supposed to contain any information concerning such property or personal estate, as aforesaid, passing from any person who may die, as aforesaid, shall exhibit the same at the request of the assessor or assistant assessor of the district, and to any law officer of the United States, in the performance of his duty under this act, his deputy or agent, who may desire to examine the same. And if any such person, having in his possession, charge, or custody, *and* [any] such records, files, or papers, shall refuse or neglect to exhibit the same on request, as aforesaid, he shall forfeit and pay the sum of five hundred dollars: *Provided*, In all legal controversies where such deed or title shall be the subject of judicial investigation the recital in said deed shall be prima facie evidence of its truth, and that the requirements of the law had been complied with by the officers of the government.

Assistant assessor to make list and assess the duty.

Collector to commence proceedings in United States court.

Property to be sold.

Disposition of proceeds.

Deed of the proper officer to vest title in the purchaser.

Penalty for refusing to exhibit records, files, &c.

Recital in such deed to be *prima facie* evidence of its truth.

SUCCESSION TO REAL ESTATE.

SEC. 126. *And be it further enacted*, That for the purposes of this act the term "real estate" shall include all lands, tenements, and hereditaments, corporeal and incorporeal; that the term "succession" shall denote the devolution of title to any real estate; and that the term "person" shall be held to include persons, body corporate, company, or association.

"Real estate" defined.

"Succession" defined.

"Person" defined.

What shall be deemed a succession.

SEC. 127. *And be it further enacted,* That every past or future disposition of real estate by will, deed, or laws of descent, by reason whereof any perso[n] shall become beneficially entitled, in possession or expectancy, to any real estate, or the income thereof, upon the death of any person dying after the passing of this act, shall be deemed to confer, on the person entitled by reason of any such disposition, a "succession;" and the term "successor" shall denote the person so entitled; and the term "predecessor shall denote the grantor, testator, ancestor, or other person from whom the interest of the successor has been or shall be derived.

"Successor" and "predecessor."

Increase of benefit accruing upon the extinction of any estate by death to be deemed a succession.

SEC. 128. *And be it further enacted,* That where any real estate shall, at or after the passing of this act, be subject to any charge, estate, or interest, determinable by the death of any person, or at any period ascertainable only by reference to death, the increase of benefit accruing to any person upon the extinction or determination of such charge, estate, or interest, shall be deemed to be a succession accruing to the person then entitled, beneficially, to the real estate or the income thereof.

Persons taking succession jointly to pay in proportion to their respective interests.

Beneficial interests accruing by survivorship to be deemed a new succession.

SEC. 129. *And be it further enacted,* That where any persons, after the passing of this act, shall take any succession jointly, they shall pay the duty chargeable thereon by this act in proportion to their respective interests in the succession; and any beneficial interest in such succession, accruing to any of them by survivorship, shall be deemed to be a new succession, derived from the predecessor from whom the joint title shall have been derived.

Disposition of real estate with reservation of benefit for any term of life to be deemed to confer a succession at the time of the determination of such benefit.

SEC. 130. *And be it further enacted,* That where any disposition of real estate shall be accompanied by the reservation or assurance of, or contract for, any benefit to the grantor, or any other person, for any term of life, or for any period ascertainable only by reference to death, such disposition shall be deemed to confer at the time appointed for the determination of such benefit an increase of beneficial interest in such real estate, as a succession equal in annual value to the yearly amount or yearly value of the benefit so reserved, assured, or contracted for, on the person in whose favor such disposition shall be made.

Where beneficial ownership is reserved by secret trust, &c., for any term of life, such disposition to be deemed a succession.

SEC. 131. *And be it further enacted,* That where any disposition of real estate shall purport to take effect presently, or under such circumstances as not to confer succession, but, by the effect or in consequence of any engagement, secret trust, or arrangement capable of being enforced in a court of law or equity, the beneficial ownership of such real estate shall not, bona fide, pass according to the terms of such disposition, but shall, in fact, be reserved to the grantor or other person for some period ascertainable only by reference to death, the person shall be deemed, for the purposes of this act, to acquire the real estate so passing as a succession derived from the person making the disposition as the predecessor.

Conveyance, without valuable and adequate consideration to be deemed to confer a succession.

SEC. 132. *And be it further enacted,* That if any person shall, by deed of gift or other assurance of title, made without valuable and adequate consideration, and purporting to vest the estate either immediately or in the future, whether or not accompanied by the possession, convey any real estate to any person, such disposition shall be held and taken to confer upon the grantee a succession within the meaning of this act.

Duties on successions.

SEC. 133. *And be it further enacted,* That there shall be levied and paid to the United States in respect of every such succession as aforesaid, according to the value thereof, the following duties, that is to say:

Lineal issue, or lineal ancestor, 1 per centum.

Where the successor shall be the lineal issue or lineal ancestor of the predecessor, a duty at the rate of one dollar per centum upon such value.

Brother or sister, or descend't of the same, 2 per cent.

Where the successor shall be a brother or sister, or a descendant of a brother or sister of the predecessor, a duty at the rate of two dollars per centum upon such value.

Brother or sister of the father or mother, or descendant of the same, 4 per cent.

Where the successor shall be a brother or sister of the father or mother, or a descendant of a brother or sister of the father or mother of the predecessor, a duty at the rate of four dollars per centum upon such value.

Brother or sister of the grandfather or grandmother, or descendant of the same, 5 per cent.

Where the successor shall be a brother or sister of the grandfather or grandmother, or a descendent of the brother or sister of the grandfather or grandmother of the predecessor, a duty at the rate of five dollars per centum upon such value.

Any other degree of consanguinity, or stranger in blood, 6 per cent.

Where the successor shall be in any other degree of collateral consanguinity to the predecessor than is hereinbefore described, or shall be a stranger in blood to him, a duty at the rate of six dollars per centum upon such value.

When successor dies before becoming entitled in possession, but one duty shall be payable, but the duty to be at the highest rate chargeable upon either succession.

SEC. 134. *And be it further enacted*, That where the interest of any successor in any real estate shall, before he shall have become entitled thereto in possession, have passed by reason of death to any other successor or successors, then one duty only shall be paid in respect of such interest, and shall be due from the successor who shall first become entitled thereto in possession; but such duty shall be at the highest rate which, if every such successor had been subject to duty, would have been payable by any one of them.

Where succession is alienated before the successor becomes entitled in possession, duty to be paid at the same rate and time.

SEC. 135. *And be it further enacted*, That wherever, after the passing of this act, any succession shall, before the successor shall have become entitled thereto in possession, have become vested by alienation, or by any title not conferring a new succession, in any other person, then the duty payable in respect thereof shall be paid at the same rate and time as the same would have been payable if no such alienation had been made or derivative title created; and where the title to any succession shall be accelerated by the surrender or extinction of any prior interests, then the duty thereon shall be payable at the time of such surrender or *extension* [extinction] of prior title.

Where title is accelerated by surrender of prior interest, duty to be paid at the time of surrender.

Real estate subject to charitable trust under such disposit'n as would confer succession, to pay a duty at the highest rate.

SEC. 136. *And be it further enacted*, That where real estate shall become subject to a trust for any charitable or public purposes, under any past or future disposition, which, if made in favor of an individual, would confer on him a succession, there shall be payable in respect of such real estate upon its becoming subject to such trusts, a duty at the rate of six per centum upon the amount or principal value of such real estate.

Duty payable when the successor becomes entitled in possession.

SEC. 137. *And be it further enacted*, That the duty imposed by this act shall be paid at the time when the successor, or any person in his right or on his behalf, shall become entitled in possession to his succession, or to the receipt of the income and profits thereof, except that if there shall be any prior charge, estate, or interest, not created by the successor himself upon or in the succession, by reason whereof the successor shall not be presently entitled to the full enjoyment or value thereof, the duty, in respect of the increased value accruing upon the determination of such charge, estate, or interest, shall, if not previously paid, compounded for, or commuted, be paid at the time of such determination.

Interest of successor in moneys to arise from sale of real estate under trust, to be deemed a succession.

Duty to be paid by the trustee or executor.

SEC. 138. *And be it further enacted,* That the interest of any successor in moneys to arise from the sale of real estate under any trust for the sale thereof shall be deemed to be a succession chargeable with duty under this act, and the said duty shall be paid by the trustee, executor, or other person having control of the funds.

Interest of successor in personal property under trust to be converted into realty chargeable as a succession.

Duty to be paid by trustee or executor.

SEC. 139. *And be it further enacted,* That the interest of any successor in personal property, subject to any trust for the investment thereof in the purchase of real estate to which the successor would be absolutely entitled, shall be chargeable with duty under this act as a succession, and the tax shall be payable by the trustee, executor, or other person having control of the funds.

Contingent incumbrance not to be estimated in valuing a succession.

Where such incumbrance takes effect as an actual burden, a proportionate amount of the duty to be repaid.

SEC. 140. *And be it further enacted,* That in estimating the value of a succession no allowance shall be made in respect of any contingent incumbrance thereon; but in the event of such incumbrance taking effect as an actual burden on the interest of the successor, he shall be entitled to a return of a proportionate amount of the duty so paid by him in respect of the amount or value of the incumbrance when taking effect.

No allowance to be made for any contingency by which the estate may pass to another person.

If the estate thus passes, the proper amount to be repaid.

If the property is applied to the payment of the predeces'r's debts, the executor to repay the duties from the proceeds.

If the estate is defeated by any person claiming title under the predecessor, such person to be chargeable with the duties refunded.

SEC. 141. *And be it further enacted,* That in estimating the value of a succession no allowance shall be made in respect of any contingency upon the happening of which the real estate may pass to some other person; but in the event of the same so passing, the successor shall be entitled to a return of so much of the duty paid by him as will reduce the same to the amount which would have been payable by him if such duty had been assessed in respect of the actual duration or extent of his interest: ***Provided,*** That if the estate of the successor shall be defeated, in whole or in part, by its application to the payment of the debts of the predecessor, the executor, administrator, or trustee so applying it shall pay out of the proceeds of the sale thereof the amount so refunded: *And provided, also,* That if the estate of the successor shall be defeated, in whole or in part, by any person claiming title from and under the predecessor, such person shall be chargeable with the amount of duty so refunded, and such amounts shall be collected in the manner herein provided for the collection of duties.

Where a successor has not obtained the whole of his succession when duty becomes payable, he shall be charged on the value obtained.

Secretary of the Treasury may refund duties in certain cases.

SEC. 142. *And be it further enacted,* That where a successor shall not have obtained the whole of his succession at the time of the duty becoming payable, he shall be chargeable only with duty on the value thereof from time to time obtained by him; and whenever any duty shall have been paid on account of any succession, and it shall afterwards be proved, to the satisfaction of the Secretary of the Treasury, that such duty, not being due from the person paying the same, was paid by mistake, or was paid in respect of real estate, which the successor shall have been unable to recover, or of which he shall have been evicted, or deprived by any superior title, or that for any other reason it ought to be refunded, the Secretary of the Treasury shall thereupon refund the same to the person entitled thereto, by draft drawn on any collector of internal revenue.

SEC. 143. *And be it further enacted,* That where, in the opinion of the Commissioner of Internal Revenue, any succession shall be of such a nature, or so disposed or circumstanced, that the value thereof shall not be fairly ascertainable under any of the preceding directions, or where, from the complication of circumstances affecting the value of a succession, or affecting the assessment or recovery of the duty thereon, the Commissioner shall think it expedient to exercise this present authority, it shall be lawful for him to compound the duty payable on the succession upon such terms as he shall think fit, and to give discharges to the successor, upon payment of duty according to such composition; and it shall be lawful for him, in any special cases in which he may think it expedient so to do, to enlarge the time for payment of any duty.

Com'sioner may compound duties in certain cases.

SEC. 144. *And be it further enacted,* That it shall be lawful for the Commissioner, in his discretion, upon application made by any person who shall be entitled to a succession in expectancy, to commute the duty presumptively payable in respect of such succession for a certain sum to be presently paid, and for assessing the amount which shall be so payable he shall cause a present value to be set upon such presumptive duty, regard being had to the contingencies affecting the liability to such duty, and the interest of money involved in such calculation being reckoned at the rate for the time being allowed by the Commissioner in respect of duties paid in advance, and upon the receipt of such certain sum he shall give discharges to the successor accordingly.

Com'sioner may commute duties in certain cases.

SEC. 145. *And be it further enacted,* That the duty imposed by this act shall be a first charge on the interest of the successor, and of all persons claiming in his right, in all the real estate in respect whereof such duty shall be assessed for five years, unless sooner paid.

Duty to be a lien for five years.

SEC. 146. *And be it further enacted,* That the Commissioner shall, at the request of any successor, or any person claiming in his right, cause to be made so many separate assessments of the duty payable in respect of the interest of the successor in any separate tracts of real estate, or in defined portions of the same tract, as shall be reasonably required; and in such cases the respective tracts shall be chargeable only with the amount of duty separately assessed in respect thereof.

Com'sioner may cause separate tracts to be separately assessed.

SEC. 147. *And be it further enacted,* That any person liable to pay duty in respect to any succession, shall give notice to the assessor or assistant assessor of his liability to such duty, and shall at the same time deliver to the assessor or assistant assessor a full and true account of said succession, for the duty whereon he shall be accountable, and of the value of the real estate involved, and of the deductions claimed by him, together with the names of the successor and predecessor, and their relation to each other, and all such other particulars as shall be necessary or proper for enabling the assessor or assistant assessor fully and correctly to ascertain the duties due; and the assessor or assistant assessor, if satisfied with such account and estimate as originally delivered, or with any amendments that may be made therein upon his requisition, may assess the succession duty on the footing of such account and estimate; but it shall be lawful for the assessor or assistant

Return to be made to assessor or assistant assessor.

Assistant assessor, if dissatisfied with return, may assess upon such information as he may obtain.

assessor, if dissatisfied with such account, or if no account and estimate shall be delivered to him, to assess the duty on the best information he can obtain, subject to appeal as hereinafter provided; and if the duty so assessed shall exceed the duty assessible according to the return made to the assessor or assistant assessor, and with which he shall have been dissatisfied, or if no account and estimate has been delivered, and if no appeal shall be taken against such assessment, then it shall be in the discretion of the assessor, having regard to the merits of each case, to assess the whole or any part of the expenses incident to the taking of such assessment, in addition to such duty; and if there shall be an appeal against such last-mentioned assessment, then the payment of such expenses shall be in the discretion of the Commissioner of Internal Revenue.

In such case he may assess expenses of making assessment.

Penalty for neglect to make return or to pay duties.

SEC. 148. *And be it further enacted*, That if any person required to give any such notice or deliver such account, as aforesaid, shall wilfully neglect to do so for the period of ten days after being notified, he shall be liable to pay to the United States a sum equal to ten per centum upon the amount of duty payable by him; and if any person liable under this act to pay any duty in respect of his succession shall, after such duty shall have been finally ascertained, wilfully neglect to do so within ten days after being notified, he shall also be liable to pay to the United States a sum equal to ten per centum upon the amount of duty so unpaid, at the same time and in the same manner as the duty to be collected.

Appeal may be taken to the assessor.

SEC. 149. *And be it further enacted*, That it shall be lawful for any party, liable to pay duty in respect of his succession, who shall be dissatisfied with the assessment of the assistant assessor, within thirty days after the date of such ass[ess]ment, to appeal to the assessor from such assessment, who shall decide on such appeal, and give notice thereof to such party, who, if still dissatisfied, may, within twenty days after notice as aforesaid, appeal from such decision to the Commissioner of Internal Revenue, and furnish a statement of the grounds of such appeal to the Commissioner, whose decision upon the case, as presented by the statements of the assessor or assistant assessor and such party, shall be final.

or to the Commissioner.

By whom duties to be collected.

SEC. 150. *And be it further enacted*, That the duties levied and assessed upon successions by this act shall be collected by the same officers, in the same manner, and by the same processes as are or may be prescribed by law for the collection of direct taxes assessed upon lands under the authority of the United States.

STAMP DUTIES.

Stamp duties.

SEC. 151. *And be it further enacted*, That all laws in force at the time of the passage of this act in relation to stamp duties shall continue in force until the first day of August, eighteen hundred and sixty-four, and on and after the first day of August, eighteen hundred and sixty-four, there shall be levied, collected, and paid, for and in respect of the several instruments, matters, and things mentioned and described in the schedule (marked B) hereunto annexed, or for or in respect of the vel[l]um, parchment, or paper upon which such instruments,

Provisions of this act to take effect August 1, 1864, in reference to stamp duties.

Schedule B.

matters, or things, or any of them, shall be written or printed, by any person or persons, or party who shall make, sign, or issue the same, or for whose use or benefit the same shall be made, signed, or issued, the several duties or sums of money set down in figures against the same, respectively, or otherwise specified or set forth in the said schedule.

Instrument not to be recorded unless properly stamped.

SEC. 152. *And be it further enacted,* That it shall not be lawful to record any instrument, document, or paper required by law to be stamped, unless a stamp or stamps of the proper amount shall have been affixed; and the record of any such instrument, upon which the proper stamp or stamps aforesaid shall not have been affixed, shall be utterly void, and shall not be used in evidence.

No instrument to be invalid for want of particular stamp, if stamps of proper amount are affixed.

SEC. 153. *And be it further enacted,* That no instrument, document, writing, or paper of any description, required by law to be stamped, shall be deemed or held invalid and of no effect for the want of the particular kind or description of stamp designated for and denoting the duty charged on any such instrument, document, writing, or paper, provided a legal stamp, or stamps, denoting a duty of equal amount, shall have been duly affixed and used thereon: *Provided,* That the provisions of this section shall not apply to any stamp appropriated to denote the duty charged on proprietary articles, or articles enumerated in Schedule C.

Provisions of this section not to apply to proprietary stamps.

Official instruments issued or used by U. S. officers exempt.

SEC. 154. *And be it further enacted,* That all official instruments, documents, and papers, issued or used by the officers of the United States government, shall be, and hereby are, exempt from duty.

Penalty for forging, counterfeiting, or misusing stamps or dies.

SEC. 155. *And be it further enacted,* That if any person shall forge or counterfeit, or cause or procure to be forged or counterfeited, any stamp or die, or any part of any stamp or die, which shall have been provided, made, or used in pursuance of this act, or shall forge, counterfeit, or resemble, or cause or procure to be forged, counterfeited, or resembled, the impression, or any part of the impression, of any such stamp or die, as aforesaid, upon any vellum, parchment, or paper, or shall stamp or mark, or cause or procure to be stamped or marked, any vellum, parchment, or paper, with any such forged or counterfeited stamp or die, or part of any stamp or die, as aforesaid, with intent to defraud the United States of any of the duties hereby imposed, or any part thereof; or if any person shall utter, or sell, or expose to sale, any vellum, parchment, or paper, article, or thing, having thereupon the impression of any such counterfeited stamp or die, or any part of any stamp or die, or any such forged, counterfeited, or resembled impression, or part of impression, as aforesaid, knowing the same respectively to be forged, counterfeited, or resembled; or if any person shall knowingly use any stamp or die which shall have been so provided, made, or used, as aforesaid, with intent to defraud the United States; or if any person shall fraudulently cut, tear, or remove, or cause or procure to be cut, torn, or removed, the impression of any stamp or die which shall have been provided, made, or used in pursuance of this act, from any vellum, parchment, or paper, or any instrument or writing charged or chargeable with any of the duties hereby imposed; or if any person shall wilfully remove or cause to be removed from any stamped envelope the cancelling or defacing marks thereon, with intent to use the same or cause the use of the same the second time, or shall knowingly or wilfully sell or buy such washed or restored stamps, or offer the same for sale, or give or expose the same to any person for use, or knowingly use the same, or prepare the same with intent for the second use thereof, then, and in every such case, every person so offending, and every person knowingly and wilfully aiding, abetting, or assisting in committing any such offence as aforesaid, shall be deemed guilty of felony, and shall, on conviction thereof, forfeit the said counterfeit stamps and the articles upon which they are placed, and be punished by fine not exceeding one thousand dollars, or by imprisonment and confinement to hard labor not exceeding five years, or both, at the discretion of the court.

Mode of cancelling adhesive stamps.

SEC. 156. *And be it further enacted*, That in any and all cases where an adhesive stamp shall be used for denoting any duty imposed by this act, except as hereinafter provided, the person using or affixing the same shall write thereupon the initials of his name and the date upon which the same shall be attached or used, so that the same may not again be used. And if any person shall fraudulently make use of an adhesive stamp to denote any duty imposed by this act without so effectually cancelling and obliterating such stamp, except as before mentioned, he, she, or they shall forfeit the sum of fifty dollars: *Provided*, That any proprietor or proprietors of proprietary articles, or articles subject to stamp duty under Schedule C of this act, shall have the privilege of furnishing, without expense to the United States, in suitable form, to be approved by the Commissioner of Internal Revenue, his or their own dies or designs for stamps to be used thereon, to be made under the direction and to be retained in the possession of the Commissioner of Internal Revenue for his or their separate use, which shall not be duplicated to any other person. That in all cases where such stamp is used, instead of his or their writing the date thereon, the said stamp shall be so affixed on the box, bottle, or package, that in opening the same, or using the contents thereof, the said stamp shall be effectually destroyed; and in default thereof, shall be liable to the same penalty imposed for neglect to affix said stamp as hereinbefore prescribed in this act. Any person who shall fraudulently obtain or use any of the aforesaid stamps or designs therefor, and any person forging, or counterfeiting, or causing or procuring the forging or counterfeiting any representation, likeness, similitude, or colorable imitation of the said last mentioned stamp, or any engraver or printer who shall sell or give away said stamps, or selling the same, or, being a merchant, broker, peddler, or person dealing, in whole or in part, in similar goods, wares, merchandise, manufactures, preparations, or articles, or those designed for similar objects or purposes, shall have knowingly or fraudulently in his, her, or their possession, any such forged, counterfeited likeness, similitude, or colorable imitation of the said last-mentioned stamp, shall be deemed guilty of a felony, and, upon conviction thereof, shall be subject to all the penalties, fines, and forfeitures prescribed in the preceding section of this act.

Penalty for failure to cancel.

Proprietors of articles in schedule C may furnish private dies.

Mode of cancelling private stamps.

Penalty for forging or counterfeiting private stamps.

Commissioner may prescribe other method of cancellation.

SEC. 157. *And be it further enacted,* That the Commissioner of Internal Revenue be, and he is hereby, authorized to prescribe such method for the cancellation of stamps, as substitute for or in addition to the method now prescribed by law, as he may deem expedient and effectual. And he is further authorized in his discretion to make the application of such method imperative upon the manufacturers of proprietary articles, or articles included in Schedule C, and upon stamps of a nominal value exceeding twenty-five cents each.

Penalty for issuing instruments without proper stamps.

SEC. 158 *And be it further enacted,* That any person or persons who shall make, sign, or issue, or who shall cause to be made, signed, or issued, any instrument, document, or paper of any kind or description whatsoever, or shall accept or pay, or cause to be accepted or paid, any bill of exchange, draft, or order or promissory note, for the payment of money, without the same being duly stamped, or having thereupon an adhesive stamp for denoting the duty chargeable thereon, with intent to evade the provisions of this act, shall, for every such offence, forfeit the sum of two hundred dollars, and such instrument, document, or paper, bill, draft, order, or note shall be deemed invalid and of no effect: *Provided,* That the title of a purchaser of land by deed duly stamped, shall not be defeated or effected by the want of a proper stamp on any deed conveying said land by any person from, through, or under whom his grantor claims or holds title.

Unstamped instruments to be invalid.

Deeds of land.

Bills of exchange drawn abroad, but payable in the United States, to be stamped before payment.

SEC. 159. *And be it further enacted,* That the acceptor or acceptors of any bill of exchange or order for the payment of any sum of money drawn, or purporting to be drawn, in any foreign country, but payable in the United States, shall, before paying or accepting the same, place thereupon a stamp, indicating the duty upon the same, as the law requires for inland bills of exchange, or promissory notes, and no bill of exchange shall be paid or negotiated without such stamp; and if any person shall pay or negotiate, or offer in payment, or receive or take in payment, any such draft or order, the person or persons so offending shall forfeit the sum of two hundred dollars.

Papers relating to bounties, &c., exempt.

SEC. 160. *And be it further enacted,* That no stamp duty shall be required on powers of attorney or any other paper relating to applications for bounties, arrearages of pay, or pensions, or to the receipt thereof from time to time, or upon tickets or contracts of insurance when limited to injury to persons while travelling; nor on certificates *or* [of] the measurement or weight of animals, wood, coal, or other articles; nor on deposit notes to mutual insurance companies for insurance upon which policies subject to stamp duties have been or are to be issued; nor on any certificate of the record of a deed or other instrument in writing, or of the acknowledgment or proof thereof by attesting witnesses; nor to any indorsement of a negotiable instrument or on any warrant of attorney, accompanying a bond or note, when such bond or note shall have affixed thereto the stamp or stamps denoting the duty required; and whenever any bond or note shall be secured by a mortgage, but one stamp shall be required to be placed on such papers: *Provided,* That the stamp duty placed thereon shall be the highest rate required for said instruments, or either of them.

Insurance against injury while travelling.

Certificates of measurement and weight.

Mutual insurance deposit notes.

Certificates of record.

Acknowledgements of deeds, &c.

Bond, mortgage, &c., but one stamp.

Commissioner authorized to sell stamps and allow a commission of 5 per cent.

SEC. 161. *And be it further enacted*, That the Commissioner of Internal Revenue be, and is hereby, authorized to sell to and supply collectors, deputy collectors, postmasters, stationers, or any other persons, at his discretion, with adhesive stamps, or stamped paper, vellum, or parchment, as herein provided for, in amounts of not less than fifty dollars, upon the payment, at the time of delivery, of the amount of duties said stamps, stamped paper, vellum, or parchment, so sold or supplied, represent, and may allow, upon the aggregate amount of such stamps, as aforesaid, the sum of not exceeding five per centum as commission to the collectors, postmasters, stationers, or other purchasers; but the cost of any paper, vellum, or parchment shall be paid by the purchaser of such stamped paper, vellum, or parchment, as aforesaid: *Provided*, That any proprietor or proprietors of articles named in Schedule C, who shall furnish his or their own die or design for stamps, to be used especially for his or their own propietary articles, shall be allowed the following commission, namely: On amounts purchased at one time of not less than fifty nor more than five hundred dollars, five per centum; on amounts over five hundred dollars, ten per centum. The Commissioner of Internal Revenue may from time to time make regulations, upon proper evidence of the facts, for the allowance of such of the stamps issued under the provisions of this act as may have been spoiled, destroyed, or rendered useless or unfit for the purpose intended, or for which the owner may have no use, or which through mistake may have been improperly or unnecessarily used, or where the rates or duties represented thereby have been paid in error, or remitted; and such allowance shall be made either by giving other stamps in lieu of the stamps so allowed for, or by repaying the amount or value, after deducting therefrom, in case of repayment, the sum of five per centum to the owner thereof; but no allowance shall be made in any case until the stamps so spoiled or rendered useless shall have been returned to the Commissioner of Internal Revenue, or until satisfactory proof has been made showing the reason why said stamps cannot be so returned: *Provided*, That the Commissioner of Internal Revenue may, from time to time, furnish, supply, and deliver to any manufacturer of friction or other matches, cigar lights, or wax tapers, a suitable quantity of adhesive or other stamps, such as may be prescribed for use in such cases, without prepayment therefor, on a credit not exceeding sixty days, requiring, in advance, such security as he may judge necessary to secure payment therefor to the Treasurer of the United States, within the time prescribed for such payment. And upon all bonds or other securities taken by said Commissioner, under the provisions of this act, suits may be maintained by said Treasurer in the circuit or district court of the United States, in the several districts where any of the persons giving said bonds or other securities, reside or may be found, in any appropriate form of action.

Commission on private stamps.

Commissioner may make allowance for stamps spoiled, &c.

Manufacturers of matches may be supplied on credit.

Collectors to stamp instruments exempt from duty or subject to certain duty.

SEC. 162. *And be it further enacted*, That it shall be lawful for any person to present to the collector of the district, subject to the rules and regulation of the Commissioner of Internal Revenue, any instrument not previously issued or used, and require his opinion whether or not the same is chargeable with any stamp duty; and if the said collector shall be of opinion that such instrument is chargeable with any stamp duty, he shall, upon the payment therefor, affix and cancel the proper stamp; and if of the opinion that such instrument is not chargeable with any stamp duty, or is chargeable only with the duty by him designated, he is hereby required to impress thereon a particular stamp, to be provided for that purpose, with such words or device thereon as he shall judge proper, which shall denote that such instrument is not chargeable with any stamp duty, or is chargeable only with the duty denoted by the stamp affixed; and every such instrument upon which the said stamp shall be impressed shall be deemed to be not chargeable, or to be chargeable only with the duty denoted by the stamp so affixed, and shall be received in evidence in all courts of law or equity, notwithstanding any objections made to the same by reason of it being unstamped, or of it being insufficiently stamped.

Instruments heretofore issued without stamps not to be used or recorded until stamps are affixed.

SEC. 163. *And be it further enacted,* That no deed, instrument, document, writing, or paper, required by law to be stamped, which has been heretofore signed or issued without being duly stamped, or with a deficient stamp, nor any copy thereof, shall be recorded or admitted or used as evidence in any court until a legal stamp or stamps, denoting the amount of duty, shall have been affixed thereto, and the date, when the same is so used or affixed, with his initials, shall have been placed thereon by the person using or affixing the same; and the person desiring to use or record any such deed, instrument, document, writing, or paper as evidence, his agent or attorney, is authorized in the presence of the court, register, or recorder, respectively, to affix the stamp or stamps thereon required:

Stamps may be affixed to instruments previously issued.

Provided, That no instrument, document, or paper made, signed, or issued prior to the passage of this act without being duly stamped, or having thereon an adhesive stamp or stamps, to denote the duty imposed thereon, shall for that cause, if the stamp or stamps required shall be subsequently affixed, be deemed invalid and of no effect:

Instruments executed abroad to be used in the United States to be properly stamped by the party using the same.

And provided, further, That any power of attorney, conveyance, or document of any kind, made or purporting to be made in any foreign country to be used in the United States, shall pay the same duty as is required by law on similar instruments or documents when made or issued in the United States; and the party to whom the same is issued, or by whom it is to be used, shall, before using the same, affix thereon the stamp or stamps indicating the duty required.

Schedule C.

SEC. 164. *And be it further enacted,* That all the provisions of this act relating to dies, stamps, adhesive stamps, and stamp duties shall extend to and include (except where manifestly impracticable) all the articles or objects enumerated in schedule marked C, subject to stamp duties, and apply to the provisions in relation thereto.

Penalty for selling articles in Schedule C without proper stamps.

SEC. 165. *And be it further enacted,* That if any person, firm, company, or corporation shall make, prepare, and sell, or remove for consumption or sale, drugs, medicines, preparations, compositions, articles, or things, including perfumery, cosmetics, lucifer or friction matches, cigar lights, or wax tapers, photographs, ambrotypes, daguerreotypes, or other sun pictures of any description, and playing cards, upon which a duty is imposed by law, as enumerated and mentioned in Schedule C, without affixing thereto an adhesive stamp, or label denoting the duty before mentioned, he or they shall incur a penalty of ten dollars for every omission to affix such stamp: *Provided*, That nothing in this act contained shall apply to any uncompounded medicinal drug or chemical, nor to any medicine compounded according to the United States or other national pharmacopœia, nor of which the full and proper formula is published in either of the dispensatories, formularies, or text-books in common use among physicians and apothecaries, including homœopathic and eclectic, or in any pharmaceutical journal now used by any incorporated college of pharmacy, and not sold or offered for sale, or advertised under any other name, form, or guise, than that under which they may be severally denominated and laid down in said pharmacopœias, dispensatories, text-books, or journals, as aforesaid, nor to medicines sold to or for the use of any person, which may be mixed and compounded specially for said persons, according to the written recipe or prescription of any physician or surgeon.

Not to apply to medicines laid down in the pharmacopœias or dispensatories.

Penalty for removing stamps from articles in Schedule C.

SEC. 166. *And be it further enacted*, That every manufacturer or maker of any of the articles for sale mentioned in Schedule C, after the same shall have been so made, and the particulars hereinbefore required as to stamps have been complied with, who shall take off, remove, or detach, or cause, or permit, or suffer to be taken off, or removed, or detached, any stamp, or who shall use any stamp, or any wrapper or cover to which any stamp is affixed, to cover any other article or commodity than that originally contained in such wrapper or cover, with such stamp when first used, with the intent to evade the stamp duties, shall for every such article, respectively, in respect of which any such offence shall be committed, be subject to a penalty of fifty dollars, to be recovered together with the costs thereupon accruing; and every such article or commodity as aforesaid shall also be forfeited

Forfeiture of articles upon attempt to evade the duty.

SEC. 167. *And be it further enacted*, That on and after the passage of this act every maker or manufacturer of any of the articles or *or* commodities mentioned in Schedule C, as aforesaid, who shall sell, send out, remove, or deliver any article or commodity, manufactured as aforesaid, before the duty thereon shall have been fully paid, by affixing thereon the proper stamp, as provided by law, or who shall hide, or conceal, or cause to be hidden or concealed, or who shall remove or convey away, or deposit, or cause to be removed or conveyed away from or deposited in any place, any such article or commodity, to evade the duty chargeable thereon, or any part thereof, shall be subject to a penalty of one hundred dollars, together with the forfeiture of any such article or commodity.

Articles in Schedule C, intended for exportation, may be manufactured in bonded warehouse.

SEC. 168. *And be it further enacted*, That all medicines, preparations, compositions, perfumery, cosmetics, lucifer or friction matches, and cigar lights, or wax tapers, cordials, and other liquors manufactured wholly or in part of domestic spirts, intended for exportation, as provided for by law, in order to be manufactured and sold or removed, without being charged with duty and without having a stamp affixed thereto, shall, under such rules and regulations as the Secretary of the Treasury may prescribe, be made and manufactured in warehouses similarly constructed to those known and designated in treasury regulations as bonded warehouses, class two: *Provided,* That such manufacturer shall first give satisfactory bonds to the collector of internal revenue for the faithful observance of all the provisions of law and the rules and regulations as aforesaid, in amount not less than half of that required by the regulations of the Secretary of the Treasury from persons allowed bonded warehouses. Such goods, when manufactured in such warehouses, may be removed for exportation, under the direction of the proper officer having charge thereof, who shall be designated by the Secretary of the Treasury, without being charged with duty, and without having a stamp affixed thereto. Any manufacturer of the articles aforesaid, or of any of them, having such bonded warehouse, as aforesaid, shall be at liberty, under such rules and regulations as the Secretary of the Treasury may prescribe, to convey therein any materials to be used in such manufacture which are allowed by the provisions of law to be exported free from tax or duty, as well as the necessary materials, implements, packages, vessels, brands, and labels for the preparation, putting up, and export of the said manufactured articles; and every article so used shall be exempt from the payment of stamp and excise duty by such manufacturer. Articles and materials so to be used may be transferred from any bonded warehouse in which the same may be, under such regulations as the Secretary of the Treasury may prescribe, into any bonded warehouse in which such manufacture may be conducted, and may be used in such manufacture, and, when so used, shall be exempt from stamp and excise duty; and the receipt of the officer in charge, as aforesaid, shall be received as a voucher for the manufacture of such articles. Any materials imported into the the United States may, under such rules as the Secretary of the Treasury may prescribe, and under the direction of the proper officer, be removed in original packages from on shipboard, or from the bonded warehouse in which the same may be, into the bonded warehouse in which such manufacture may be carried on, for the purpose of being used in such manufacture, without payment of duties thereon, and may there be used in such manufacture. No article so removed, nor any article manufactured in said bonded warehouse, shall be taken therefrom except for exportation, under the direction of the proper officer having charge thereof, as aforesaid, whose certificate, describing the articles by their marks, or otherwise, the quantity, the date of importation, and name of vessel, with such additional particulars as may from time to time be required, shall be received by the collector of customs in cancellation of the bonds, or return of the amount of foreign import duties. All labor performed and services rendered under these regulations shall be under the supervision of an officer of the customs, and at the expense of the manufacturer.

May be removed without stamps.

Articles used in such manufacture exempt from duty.

May be removed from ships or bonded warehouse into warehouse where the same are to be used.

Officer in charge of warehouse to give certificate upon removal.

Expenses to be borne by the manufacturer.

SEC. 169. *And be it further enacted,* That any person who shall offer for sale any of the articles named in Schedule C, whether the articles so offered are imported, or are of foreign or domestic manufacture, shall be deemed the manufacturer thereof, and subject to all the duties, liabilities, and penalties

Persons offering for sale articles in Schedule C to be deemed the manufacturers.

imposed by law in regard to the sale of domestic articles without the use of the proper stamp or stamps denoting the duty paid thereon: ***Provided,*** That when any such imported articles shall be sold in the original and unbroken package in which the bottles or other inclosures were packed by the manufacturer, the person so selling said articles shall not be subject to any penalty on account of the want of the proper stamp.

Commissioner may furnish stamps to certain officers for sale.

SEC. 170. *And be it further enacted,* That in any collection district where, in the judgment of the Commissioner of Internal Revenue, the facilities for the procurement and distribution of stamped vellum, parchment, or paper, and adhesive stamps, are or shall be insufficient, the Commissioner, as aforesaid, is authorized to furnish, supply, and deliver to the collector and to the assessor of any such district, and to any assistant treasurer of the United States, or designated depository thereof, or any postmaster, a suitable quantity or amount of stamped vellum, parchment or paper, and adhesive stamps, without prepayment therefor, and shall allow the highest rate of commissions allowed by law to any other parties purchasing the same, and may in advance require of any such collector, assessor, assistant treasurer of the United States, or postmaster, a bond, with sufficient sureties, to an amount equal to the value of any stamped vellum, parchment, or paper, and adhesive stamps which may be placed in his hands and remain unaccounted for, conditioned for the faithful return, whenever so required, of all quantities or amounts undisposed of, and for the payment, monthly, of all quantities or amounts, sold or not, remaining on hand. And it shall be the duty of such collector to supply his deputies with, or sell to other parties within his district who may make application therefor, stamped vellum, parchment, or paper, and adhesive stamps, upon the same terms allowed by law, or under the regulations of the Commissioner of Internal Revenue, who is hereby authorized to make such other regulations, not inconsistent herewith, for the security of the United States and the better accommodation of the public, in relation to the matters hereinbefore mentioned, as he may judge necessary and expedient. And the Secretary of the Treasury may, from time to time, make such regulations as he may find necessary to insure the safe-keeping or prevent the illegal use of all such stamped vellum, parchment, paper, and adhesive stamps.

May require bond.

SCHEDULE B.

STAMP DUTIES.

		Duty.
Agreement.	Agreement or contract, other than those specified in this schedule; any appraisement of value or damage, or for any other purpose; for every sheet or piece of paper upon which either of the same shall be written, five cents	$0 05
	Provided, That if more than one appraisement, agreement, or contract shall be written upon one sheet or piece of paper, five cents for each and every additional appraisement, agreement, or contract.	
Bank check.	BANK CHECK, draft, or order for the payment of any sum of money whatsoever, drawn upon any bank, banker, or trust company, or for any sum exceeding ten dollars drawn upon any other person or persons, companies, or corporations, at sight or on demand, two cents	2

Duty.

Bill of exchange, (inland.)

Bill of exchange, (inland,) draft, or order for the payment of any sum of money, not exceeding one hundred dollars, otherwise than at sight or on demand, or any promissory note, (except bank notes issued for circulation, and checks made and intended to be forthwith presented, and which shall be presented to a bank or banker for payment,) or any memorandum, check, receipt, or other written or printed evidence of an amount of money to be paid on demand, or at a time designated, for a sum not exceeding one hundred dollars, five cents..............................

And for every additional hundred dollars, or fractional part thereof in excess of one hundred dollars, five cents.......................... 5

Bill of exchange, (foreign.)

Bill of exchange, (foreign,) or letter of credit, drawn in but payable out of the United States, if drawn singly, or otherwise than in a set of three or more, according to the custom of merchants and bankers, shall pay the same rates of duty as inland bills of exchange or promissory notes.

If drawn in sets of three or more: For every bill of each set, where the sum made payable shall not exceed one hundred dollars, or the equivalent thereof, in any foreign currency in which such bills may be expressed, according to the standard of value fixed by the United States, two cents 2

And for every additional hundred dollars or fractional part thereof in excess of one hundred dollars, two cents 2

Bill of lading.

Bill of lading or receipt, (other than charter-pay,) for any goods, merchandise, or effects, to be exported from a port or place in the United States to any foreign port or place, ten cents............ 10

Bill of sale of ship.

Bill of sale by which any ship or vessel, or any part thereof, shall be conveyed to or vested in any other person or persons when the consideration shall not exceed five hundred dollars, fifty cents... 50

Exceeding five hundred and not exceeding one thousand dollars, one dollar 1 00

Exceeding one thousand dollars for every additional amount of five hundred dollars, or fractional part thereof, fifty cents 50

Bond.

Bond.—For indemnifying any person for the payment of any sum of money, where the money ultimately recoverable thereupon is one thousand dollars or less, fifty cents 50

Where the money ultimately recoverable thereupon exceeds one thousand dollars, for every additional one thousand dollars or fractional part thereof in excess of one thousand dollars, fifty cents........ 50

Bond for the due execution or performance of the duties of any office, one dollar 1 00

Bond of any description, other than such as may be required in legal proceedings, or used in connexion with mortgage deeds, and not otherwise charged in this schedule, twenty-five cents 25

Certificate.

Certificate of stock in any incorporated company, twenty-five cents. 25

Certificate of profits, or any certificate or memorandum showing an interest in the property or accumulations of any incorporated company, if for a sum not less than ten dollars and not exceeding fifty dollars, ten cents.. 10

Exceeding fifty dollars and not exceeding one thousand dollars, twenty-five cents.. 25

Exceeding one thousand dollars, for every additional one thousand dollars, or fractional part thereof, twenty-five cents............. 25

Certificate.—Any certificate of damage, or otherwise, and all other certificates or documents issued by any port warden, marine surveyor, or other person acting as such, twenty-five cents........ 25

Certificate of deposit of any sum of money in any bank or trust company, or with any banker or person acting as such—

If for a sum not exceeding one hundred dollars, two cents 2

For a sum exceeding one hundred dollars, five cents 5

Certificate of any other description than those specified, five cents.... 5

Charter-party.

Charter-Party.—Contract or agreement for the charter of any ship or vessel, or steamer, or any letter, memorandum, or other writing between the captain, master, or owner, or person acting as agent of any ship or vessel, or steamer, and any other person or persons for or relating to the charter of such ship or vessel, or steamer, or any renewal or transfer thereof, if the registered tonnage of such ship or vessel, or steamer, does not exceed one hundred and fifty tons, one dollar 1 00

Margin	Item	Duty.
	Exceeding one hundred and fifty tons, and not exceeding three hundred tons, three dollars	3 00
	Exceeding three hundred tons, and not exceeding six hundred tons, five dollars	5 00
	Exceeding six hundred tons, ten dollars	10 00
Brokers contract.	CONTRACT.—Broker's note, or memorandum of sale of any goods or merchandise, stocks, bonds, exchange, notes of hand, real estate, or property of any kind or description issued by brokers or persons acting as such, for each note or memorandum of sale, ten cents	10
Conveyance.	CONVEYANCE.—Deed, instrument, or writing, whereby any lands, tenements, or other realty sold shall be granted, assigned, transferred, or otherwise conveyed to, or vested in, the purchaser or purchasers, or any other person or persons by his, her, or their direction, when the consideration or value does not exceed five hundred dollars, fifty cents	50
	When the consideration exceeds five hundred dollars, and does not exceed one thousand dollars, one dollar	1 00
	And for every additional five hundred dollars, or fractional part thereof, in excess of one thousand dollars, fifty cents	50
Entry of goods.	ENTRY of any goods, wares, or merchandise at any custom-house, either for consumption or warehousing, not exceeding one hundred dollars in value, twenty-five cents	25
	Exceeding one hundred dollars, and not exceeding five hundred dollars in value, fifty cents	50
	Exceeding five hundred dollars in value, one dollar	1 00
	ENTRY for the withdrawal of any goods or merchandise from bonded warehouse, fifty cents	50
Gaugers returns.	Gaugers' returns, if for a quantity not exceeding five hundred gallons gross, ten cents	10
	Exceeding five hundred gallons gross, twenty-five cents	25
Insurance.	INSURANCE, (LIFE.)—Policy of insurance, or other instrument, by whatever name the same shall be called, whereby any insurance shall be made upon any life or lives—	
	When the amount insured shall not exceed one thousand dollars, twenty-five cents	25
	Exceeding one thousand dollars and not exceeding five thousand dollars, fifty cents	50
	Exceeding five thousand dollars, one dollar	1 00
	INSURANCE, (MARINE, INLAND, AND FIRE.)—Each policy of insurance or other instrument, by whatever name the same shall be called, by which insurance shall be made or renewed upon property of any description, whether against perils by the sea or by fire, or other peril of any kind, made by any insurance company, or its agents, or by any other company or person, the premium upon which does not exceed ten dollars, ten cents	10
	Exceeding ten and not exceeding fifty dollars, twenty-five cents	25
	Exceeding fifty dollars, fifty cents	50
Lease.	LEASE, agreement, memorandum, or contract for the hire, use, or rent of any land, tenement, or portion thereof, where the rent or rental value is three hundred dollars per annum or less, fifty cents	50
	Where the rent or rental value exceeds the sum of three hundred dollars per annum, for each additional two hundred dollars, or fractional part thereof in excess of three hundred dollars, fifty cents	50
Manifest.	MANIFEST for custom-house entry or clearance of the cargo of any ship, vessel, or steamer for a foreign port—	
	If the registered tonnage of such ship, vessel, or steamer does not exceed three hundred tons, one dollar	1 00
	Exceeding three hundred tons, and not exceeding six hundred tons, three dollars	3 00
	Exceeding six hundred tons, five dollars	5 00
Measurers' returns.	MEASURERS' returns, if for a quantity not exceeding one thousand bushels, ten cents	10
	Exceeding one thousand bushels, twenty-five cents	25
Mortgage.	MORTGAGE of lands, estate, or property, real or personal, heritable or movable whatsoever, where the same shall be made as a security for the payment of any definite and certain sum of money lent at the time or previously due and owing or forborne to be paid, being payable; also any conveyance of any lands, estate, or property whatsoever, in trust, to be sold or otherwise converted into	

	Duty.	
money, which shall be intended only as security, and shall be redeemable before the sale or other disposal thereof, either by express stipulation or otherwise; or any personal bond given as security for the payment of any definite or certain sum of money exceeding one hundred dollars, and not exceeding five hundred dollars, fifty cents	50	
Exceeding five hundred dollars, and not exceeding one thousand dollars, one dollar	1 00	
And for every additional five hundred dollars, or fractional part thereof, in excess of one thousand dollars, fifty cents	50	
Provided, That upon each and every assignment or transfer of a mortgage, lease, or policy of insurance, or the renewal or continuance of any agreement, contract or charter, by letter or otherwise, a stamp duty shall be required and paid equal to that imposed on the original instrument.		
PASSAGE TICKET, by any vessel from a port in the United States to a foreign port, not exceeding thirty-five dollars, fifty cents	50	Passage ticket.
Exceeding thirty-five dollars and not exceeding fifty dollars, one dollar	1 00	
And for every additional fifty dollars, or fractional part thereof, in excess of fifty dollars, one dollar	1 00	
POWER OF ATTORNEY for the sale or transfer of any stock, bonds, or scrip, or for the collection of any dividends or interest thereon, twenty-five cents	25	Power of attorney.
POWER OF ATTORNEY OR PROXY for voting at any election for officers of any incorporated company or society, except religious, charitable, or literary societies, or public cemeteries, ten cents	10	
POWER OF ATTORNEY to receive or collect rent, twenty-five cents	25	
POWER OF ATTORNEY to sell and convey real estate, or to rent or lease the same, one dollar	1 00	
POWER OF ATTORNEY for any other purpose, fifty cents	50	
PROBATE OF WILL, or letters of administration: Where the estate and effects for or in respect of which such probate or letters of administration applied for shall be sworn or declared not to exceed the value of two thousand dollars, one dollar	1 00	Probate of will.
Exceeding two thousand dollars, for every additional thousand dollars, or fractional part thereof, in excess of two thousand dollars, fifty cents	50	
PROTEST.—Upon the protest of every note, bill of exchange, acceptance, check or draft, or any marine protest, whether protested by a notary public or by any other officer who may be authorized by the law of any State or States to make such protest, twenty-five cents	25	Protest.
Receipts for the payment of any sum of money, or for the payment of any debt due, exceeding twenty dollars, not being for the satisfaction of any mortgage or judgment or decree of any court, and a receipt for the delivery of any property, two cents	2	Receipts.
Warehouse receipt for property, goods, wares, or merchandise, not otherwise provided for, in any public or private warehouse, when the property or goods so deposited or stored shall not exceed in value five hundred dollars, ten cents	10	Warehouse receipts.
Exceeding in value five hundred dollars and not exceeding one thousand dollars, twenty cents	20	
Exceeding in value one thousand dollars, for every additional one thousand dollars, ten cents	10	
Warehouse receipt for any goods, merchandise, or property of any kind, not otherwise provided for, held on storage in any public or private warehouse or yard, twenty-five cents	25	
Weighers' returns, if for a weight not exceeding five thousand pounds, ten cents	10	Weighers' returns.
Exceeding five thousand pounds, twenty-five cents	25	
LEGAL DOCUMENTS:		Legal documents.
Writ, or other original process by which any suit is commenced in any court of record, either of law or equity, fifty cents	50	
Where the amount claimed in a writ, issued by a court not of record, is one hundred dollars or over, fifty cents	50	
Upon every confession of judgment, or cognovit, for one hundred dollars or over, (except in those cases where the tax for the writ of a commencent of suit has been paid,) fifty cents	50	

Duty

Writs or other process on appeals from justices' courts or other courts of inferior jurisdiction to a court of record, fifty cents........... 50

Warrant of distress, when the amount of rent claimed does not exceed one hundred dollars, twenty-five cents........................ 25

When the amount claimed exceeds one hundred dollars, fifty cents... 50

Provided, That no writ, summons, or other process issued by and returnable to a justice of the peace, except as hereinbefore provided, or by any police or municipal court having no larger jurisdiction as to the amount of damages it may render than a justice of the *piece* [peace] in the same State, or issued in any criminal or other suits commenced by the United States or any State, shall be subject to the payment of stamp duties: *And provided, further*, That the stamp duties imposed by the foregoing Schedule B on manifests, bills of lading, and passage tickets, shall not apply to steamboats or other vessels plying between ports of the United States and ports in British North America.

Affidavits exempt.

Affidavits in suits or legal proceedings shall be exempt from stamp duty.

SCHEDULE C.

MEDICINES OR PREPARATIONS.

Medicines or preparations.

For and upon every packet, box, bottle, pot, phial, or other enclosure, containing any pills, powders, tinctures, troches, lozenges, sirups, cordials, bitters, anodynes, tonics, plasters, liniments, salves, ointments, pastes, drops, waters, essences, spirits, oils, or other medicinal preparations or compositions whatsoever, made and sold, or removed for consumption and sale, by any person or persons whatever, wherein the person making or preparing the same has, or claims to have, any private formula or occult secret or art for the making or preparing the same, or has, or claims to have, any exclusive right or title to the making or preparing the same, or which are prepared, uttered, vended, or exposed for sale under any letters patent, or held out or recommended to the public by the makers, venders, or proprietors thereof as proprietary medicines, or as remedies or specifics for any disease, diseases, or affections whatever affecting the human or animal body, as follows: where such packet, box, bottle, pot, phial, or other enclosure, with its contents, shall not exceed, at retail price, or value, the sum of twenty-five cents, one cent........................ 1

Where such packet, box, bottle, pot, phial, or other enclosure, with its contents, shall exceed the retail price or value of twenty-five cents, and not exceed the retail price or value of fifty cents, two cents.. 2

Where such packet, box, bottle, pot, phial, or other enclosure, with its contents, shall exceed the retail price or value of fifty cents, and shall not exceed the retail price or value of seventy-five cents, three cents.. 3

Where such packet, box, bottle, pot, phial, or other enclosure, with its contents, shall exceed the retail price or value of seventy-five cents, and shall not exceed the retail price or value of one dollar, four cents.. 4

Where such packet, box, bottle, pot, phial, or other enclosure, with its contents, shall exceed the retail price or value of one dollar, for each and every fifty cents or fractional part thereof over and above the one dollar, as before mentioned, an additional two cents..... 2

PERFUMERY, COSMETICS, PHOTOGRAPHS, MATCHES, AND CARDS.

Perfumery and cosmetics.

For and upon every packet, box, bottle, pot, phial, or other enclosure, containing any essence, extract, toilet water, cosmetic, hair oil, pomade, hair-dressing, hair restorative, hair dye, tooth-wash, dentifrice, tooth-paste, aromatic cachous, or any similar articles, by whatsoever name the same heretofore have been, now are, or may hereafter be called, known, or distinguished, used or applied, or to be used or applied as perfumes or applications to the hair, mouth, or skin, made, prepared, and sold or removed for consumption and sale in the United States, where such packet, box, bottle, pot, phial, or other enclosure, with its contents, shall not exceed, at the retail price or value, the sum of twenty-five cents, one cent...... 1

Duty.

Where such packet, box, bottle, pot, phial, or other enclosure, with its contents, shall exceed the retail price or value of twenty-five cents, and shall not exceed the retail price or value of fifty cents, two cents 2

Where such packet, box, bottle, pot, phial, or other enclosure, with its contents, shall exceed the retail price or value of fifty cents, and shall not exceed the retail price or value of seventy-five cents, three cents 3

Where such packet, box, bottle, pot, phial, or other enclosure, with its contents, shall exceed the retail price or value of seventy-five cents, and shall not exceed the retail price or value of one dollar, four cents 4

Where such packet, box, bottle, pot, phial, or other enclosure, with its contents, shall exceed the retail price or value of one dollar, for each and every fifty cents or fractional part thereof over and above the one dollar, as before mentioned, an additional two cents 2

Friction matches.

FRICTION MATCHES, or lucifer matches, or other articles made in part of wood, and used for like purposes, in parcels or packages containing one hundred matches or less, for each parcel or package, one cent 1

When in parcels or packages containing more than one hundred and not more than two hundred matches, for each parcel or package, two cents 2

And for every additional one hundred matches or fractional part thereof, one cent 1

Cigar lights and wax tapers.

For all cigar lights and wax tapers, double the rates herein imposed upon friction or lucifer matches: *Provided*, That the stamp duties herein provided for on friction or lucifer matches made in part of wood, or cigar lights or wax tapers, shall not be imposed until the first day of September, eighteen hundred and sixty-four; but until that time the tax shall be assessed and collected as heretofore, and on and after said first day of September every package or parcel sold by any person, firm, company, or corporation, shall be stamped as herein required.

Photographs, &c.

PHOTOGRAPHS, ambrotypes, daguerreotypes, or any sun pictures, except as hereinbefore provided, upon each and every picture of which the retail price shall not exceed twenty-five cents, two cents 2

Exceeding the retail price of twenty-five cents, and not exceeding the sum of fifty cents, three cents 3

Exceeding the retail price of fifty cents, and not exceeding one dollar, five cents 5

Exceeding the retail price of one dollar, for every additional dollar or fractional part thereof, five cents 5

Playing cards.

PLAYING CARDS.—For and upon every pack of whatever number, when the retail price per pack does not exceed eighteen cents, two cents 2

Exceeding the retail price of eighteen cents, and not exceeding twenty-five cents per pack, four cents 4

Exceeding the retail price of twenty-five, and not exceeding fifty cents per pack, ten cents 10

Exceeding the retail price of fifty cents, and not exceeding one dollar per pack, fifteen cents 15

Exceeding the retail price of one dollar, for every additional fifty cents, or fractional part thereof, in excess of one dollar, five cents 5

ALLOWANCE AND DRAWBACK.

Drawback on manufactures exported.

SEC. 171. *And be it further enacted*, That from and after the date on which this act takes effect there shall be an allowance or drawback on all articles on which any internal duty or tax shall have been paid, except raw or unmanufactured cotton, refined coal oil, naphtha, benzine or benzole, distilled spirits, manufactured tobacco, snuff, and cigars of all descriptions, equal in amount to the duty or tax paid thereon, and no more, when exported, the evidence that any such duty or tax has been paid to be furnished to the satisfaction of the Commissioner of Internal

Revenue by such person or persons as shall claim the allowance or drawback, and the amount to be ascertained under such regulations as shall, from time to time, be prescribed by the Commissioner of Internal Revenue, under the direction of the Secretary of the Treasury, and the same shall be paid by the warrant of the Secretary of the Treasury on the Treasurer of the United States, out of any moneys arising from internal duties not otherwise appropriated: *Provided,* That no allowance or drawback shall be made or had for any amount claimed or due less than ten dollars, anything in this act to the contrary notwithstanding: *And provided, further,* That any certificate of drawback for goods exported, issued in pursuance of the provisions of law, may, under such regulations as may be prescribed by the Secretary of the Treasury, be received by the collector or his deputy in payment of duties under this act. And the Secretary of the Treasury may make such regulations with regard to the form of said certificates and the issuing thereof as, in his judgment, may be necessary: *And provided, further,* That in computing the allowance or drawback upon articles manufactured exclusively of cotton when exported, there shall be allowed, in addition to the five per centum duty which shall have been paid on such articles, a drawback of two cents per pound upon such articles, in all cases where the duty imposed by law upon the cotton used in the manufacture thereof has been previously paid; the amount of said allowance to be ascertained in such manner as may be prescribed by the Commissioner of Internal Revenue, under the direction of the Secretary of the Treasury.

Method of payment.

No allowance to be less than $10.

Certificates of drawback receivable for duties.

Secretary may make regulations.

Additional drawback on cotton goods.

SEC. 172. *And be it further enacted,* That if any person or persons shall fraudulently claim or seek to obtain an allowance or drawback on goods, wares, or merchandise, on which no internal duty shall have been paid, or shall fraudulently claim any greater allowance or drawback than the duty actually paid, as aforesaid, such person or persons shall forfeit triple the amount wrongfully or fraudulently claimed or sought to be obtained, or the sum of five hundred dollars, at the election of the Secretary of the Treasury, to be recovered as in other cases of forfeiture provided for in the general provisions of this act.

Penalty for fraudulent claim for drawback.

SEC. 173. *And be it further enacted,* That the following acts of Congress are hereby repealed, to wit: The act of July first, eighteen hundred and sixty-two, entitled "An act to provide internal revenue to support the government and to pay interest on the public debt," except the one hundred and fifteenth and one hundred and nineteenth sections thereof; and excepting, further, all provisions of said act which create the offices of Commissioner of Internal Revenue, assessor, assistant assessor, collector, deputy collector, and inspector, and provide for the appointment and qualification of said officers. Also, the act of July sixteenth, eighteen hundred and sixty-two, entitled "An act to impose an additional duty on sugars produced in the United States." Also, the act of December twenty-fifth, eighteen hundred and sixty-two, entitled "An act to amend an act entitled 'An act to provide internal revenue to support the government and to pay interest on the public debt,' approved July first, eighteen hundred and sixty-two." Also, the act of March third, eighteen hundred and sixty-three, entitled "An act to amend an act entitled 'An act to provide internal revenue to support the government and to pay interest on the

Repeal of former acts.

public debt,' approved July first, eighteen hundred and sixty-two, and for other purposes," excepting the provisions of said act which create the offices of deputy commissioner and cashier of internal duties and revenue agents, and provide for the appointment and qualification of said officers. Also, the twenty-fourth and twenty-fifth sections of the act of July fourteenth, eighteen hundred and sixty-two, entitled "An act increasing temporarily the duties on imports, and for other purposes." Also, the second section of the act of March third, eighteen hundred and sixty-three, entitled "An act to prevent and punish frauds upon the revenue, to provide for the more certain and speedy collection of claims in favor of the United States, and for other purposes," so far as the same applies to officers of internal revenue. And, also, the act of March seventh, eighteen hundred and sixty-four, entitled "An act to increase the internal revenue, and for other purposes," together with all acts and parts of acts inconsistent herewith: *Provided*, That all the provisions of said acts shall be in force for levying and collecting all taxes, duties and licenses properly assessed or liable to be assessed, or accruing under the provisions of former acts, or drawbacks, the right to which has already accrued or which may hereafter accrue under said acts, and for maintaining and continuing liens, fines, penalties, and forfeitures incurred under and by virtue thereof. And for carrying out and completing all proceedings which have been already commenced or that may be commenced to enforce such fines, penalties, and forfeitures, or criminal proceedings under said acts, and for the punishment of crimes of which any party shall be or has been found guilty: *And provided further*, That no office created by the said acts and continued by this act shall be vacated by reason of any provisions herein contained, but the officers heretofore appointed shall continue to hold the said offices without reappointment: *And provided further*, That whenever the duty imposed by any existing law shall cease in consequence of any limitation therein contained before the respective provisions of this act shall take effect, the same duty shall be, and is hereby, continued until such provisions of this act shall take effect; and where any act is hereby repealed, no duty imposed thereby shall be held to cease, in consequence of such repeal, until the respective corresponding provisions of this act shall take effect: *And provided further*, That all manufactures and productions on which a duty was imposed by either of the acts repealed by this act, which shall be in the possession of the manufacturer or producer, or of his agent or agents, on the day when this act takes effect, the duty imposed by any such former act not having been paid, shall be held and deemed to have been manufactured or produced after such date; and whenever by the terms of this act a duty is imposed upon any articles, goods, wares, or merchandise manufactured or produced, upon which no duty was imposed by either of said former acts, it shall apply to such as were manufactured or produced and not removed from the place of manufacture or production, on the day when this act takes effect: *And provided further*, That no direct tax whatsoever shall be assessed or collected under this or any other act of Congress heretofore passed, until Congress shall enact another law requiring such assessment and collection to be made; but this shall not be construed to repeal or postpone the assessment or collection of

Provisions to remain in force for collecting taxes already accrued, &c.

Offices not to be vacated by reason of this act.

Former duties to continue until corresponding provisions of this act take effect.

Articles manufactured before the passage of the law.

No further direct tax to be collected until ordered by Congress.

Proceedings to continue for the collection of the

first tax imposed by act of August 5, 1861.

the first direct tax levied, or which should be levied, under the act entitled "An act to provide increased revenue from imports to pay interest on the public debt, and for other purposes," approved August fifth, eighteen hundred and sixty-one, nor in any way to affect the legality of said tax or any process or remedy provided in said acts, or any other acts, for the enforcement or collection of the same in any State or States and Territories and the District of Columbia; but said first tax, and any such process or remedy, shall continue in all respects in force, anything in this act to the contrary notwithstanding.

Commissioner may make necessary regulations.

SEC. 174. *And be it further enacted*, That the said Commissioner of Internal Revenue, under the direction of the Secretary of the Treasury, is authorized to make all such regulations, not otherwise provided for, as may become necessary by reason of the alteration of the laws in relation to internal revenue, by virtue of this act.

Section 119 of act of July 1, 1862, to remain in full force.

SEC. 175. *And be it further enacted*, That the one hundred and nineteenth section of an act entitled "An act to provide internal revenue to support the government and to pay interest on the public debt," approved July first, eighteen hundred and sixty-two, shall remain in full force.

Secretary of the Treasury may establish regulations for certain cases.

SEC. 176. *And be it further enacted*, That when any tax or duty is imposed by law, and the mode or time of assessment or collection is not therein provided, the same shall be established by regulation of the Secretary of the Treasury.

Collector to mark bales of cotton.

To grant permits for removal.

Cotton arriving from insurrectionary districts to be immediately assessed.

SEC. 177. *And be it further enacted*, That every collector to whom any duty upon cotton shall be paid shall mark the bales or other packages upon which the duty shall have been paid, in such manner as may clearly indicate the payment thereof, and shall give to the owner, or other person having charge of such cotton, a permit for the removal of the same, stating therein the amount and payment of [the] duty, the time and place of payment, the weight and marks upon the bales and packages, so that the same may be fully identified. Whenever any cotton, the product of the United States, shall arrive at any port of the United States from any State in insurrection against the government, the assessor or assistant assessor shall immediately assess the taxes due thereon, and shall, without delay, return the same to the collector or deputy collector of said district, and the said collector or deputy collector shall demand of the owner or other person having charge of such cotton the tax imposed by this act, and assessed thereon, unless evidence of previous payment of such tax shall be produced, under such regulations as the Commissioner of Internal Revenue, by the direction of the Secretary of the Treasury, shall from time to time prescribe; and in case the tax so assessed shall not be paid to such collector within ten days after demand, the collector or deputy collector, as aforesaid, shall institute proceedings for the recovery of the tax, as hereinbefore provided, which said tax shall be a lien upon said cotton from the time when said assessment shall be made: *Provided*, That all cotton sold by or on account of the government of the United States shall be free and exempt from duty at the time of and after the sale thereof, and the same shall be marked free, and the purchaser furnished with such a bill of sale as shall clearly and accurately describe the same, which shall be deemed and taken to be a permit authorizing the sale or removal thereof.

Tax to be a lien.

Cotton sold on account of the United States exempt.

SEC. 178. *And be it further enacted,* That consuls of foreign countries in the United States, who are not citizens thereof, shall be, and hereby are, exempt from any income tax imposed by this act which may be derived from their official emoluments, or from property in such countries: *Provided,* That the governments which such consuls may represent shall extend similar exemption to consuls of the United States.

Consuls exempt from income tax in certain cases.

SEC. 179. *And be it further enacted,* That, where it is not otherwise provided for in this act, it shall be the duty of the collectors, in their respective districts, and they are hereby authorized, to prosecute for the recovery of any sum or sums that may be forfeited by virtue of this act; and all fines, penalties, and forfeitures which may be imposed or incurred by virtue of this act shall and may be sued for and recovered, where not otherwise herein provided, in the name of the United States, in any proper form of action, or by any appropriate form of proceeding, before any circuit or district court of the United States for the district within which said fine, penalty, or forfeiture may have been incurred, or before any court of competent jurisdiction; and where not otherwise herein provided for, one moiety shall be to the use of the person who, if a collector or deputy collector, shall first inform of the cause, matter, or thing whereby any such fine, penalty, or forfeiture shall have been incurred, and the other moiety to the use of the United States. And the several circuit and district courts of the United States shall have jurisdiction of all offences against any of the provisions of this act committed within their several districts.

Collectors to prosecute for fines, penalties, and forfeitures.

SEC. 180. *And be it further enacted,* That if any person liable and required to pay any tax upon any article, goods, wares, merchandise, or manufactures, as herein provided, shall sell, or cause or allow the same to be sold, before the tax to which such article, goods, wares, merchandise, or manufacture is legally liable is paid, with intent to avoid such tax, or in fraud of the revenue herein provided, any debt contracted in the sale of such article, goods, wares, merchandise, or manufactures, or any security given therefor, unless the same shall have been bona fide transferred to the hands of an innocent holder, shall be entirely void, and the collection thereof shall not be enforced in any court. And if any such article, goods, wares, merchandise, or manufacture has been paid for, in whole or in part, the sum so paid shall be deemed forfeited, and any person who will sue for the same in an action of debt shall recover of the seller the amount so paid, one half to his own use and the other half to the use of the United States.

Debts contracted through the sale of articles, with intent to evade tax, to be void.

SEC. 181. *And be it further enacted,* That four hundred thousand dollars, or so much thereof as may be necessary for the payment of the expenses incident to carrying into effect the various acts connected with internal revenue which are or may be authorized and payable after the first of July, eighteen hundred and sixty-four, is hereby appropriated for that purpose, payable out of any money in the treasury not otherwise appropriated, to be expended under the direction of the Secretary of the Treasury. And it shall be the duty of the collectors of internal revenue, as the Secretary may direct, to act as disbursing agents to pay the aforesaid expenses, without increased compensation therefor, who shall give good and sufficient bonds for the faithful performance of their duties as such disbursing agents for such sum and in such

Appropriation.

Collectors to act as disbursing agents.

form as shall be prescribed by the First Comptroller of the Treasury, subject to the approval of the Secretary of the Treasury: *Provided*, That the aforesaid appropriation shall continue in force to the thirtieth day of June, eighteen hundred and sixty-five, and thereafter the Secretary of the Treasury shall embrace in his annual estimates the amount which, in his opinion, will be required for the expenses of this branch of the public service.

The word State to include Territories and District of Columbia.

SEC. 182. *And be it further enacted*, That wherever the word State is used in this act, it shall be construed to include the Territories and the District of Columbia, where such construction is necessary to carry out the provisions of this act.

Approved June 30, 1864.

[PUBLIC RESOLUTION NO. 59.]

JOINT RESOLUTION imposing a special income duty.

Joint Resolution.

Be it resolved by the Senate and House of Representatives of the United States of America in Congress assembled, That, in addition to the income duty already imposed by law, there shall be levied, assessed, and collected on the first day of October, eighteen hundred and sixty-four, a special income duty upon the gains, profits, or income for the year ending the thirty-first day of December next preceding the time herein named, by levying, assessing, and collecting said duty of all persons residing within the United States, or of citizens of the United States residing abroad, at the rate of five per centum on all sums exceeding six hundred dollars, and the same shall be levied, assessed, estimated, and collected, except as to the rates, according to the provisions of existing laws for the collection of an income duty, annually, where not inapplicable hereto; and the Secretary of the Treasury is hereby authorized to make such rules and regulations as to time and mode, or other matters, to enforce the collection of the special income duty herein provided for, as may be necessary: *Provided*, That in estimating the annual gains, profits, or income, as aforesaid, for the foregoing special income duty, no deductions shall be made for dividends or interest received from any association, corporation, or company, nor shall any deduction be made for any salary or pay received.

Special income duty of 5 per cent. to be levied and collected October 1, 1864.

Secretary of Treasury authorized to make rules, &c.

No deductions for dividends, interest, &c.

Approved July 4, 1864.

REGULATIONS

FOR

THE COLLECTION OF DIRECT TAXES.

Regulations for the collection of direct taxes in insurrectionary districts, under the act entitled "An act for the collection of direct taxes in insurrectionary districts within the United States, and for other purposes," approved June 7, 1862.

Reason for regulations.

In order that there may be uniformity, as nearly as practicable, in the proceedings of the commissioners, under the act of Congress entitled "An act for the collection of direct taxes in insurrectionary districts within the United States, and for other purposes," the following regulations are adopted, and will be observed by the commissioners until enlarged, modified, or annulled:

I.

Bond to be given by commissioners and approved by the Secretary of the Treasury.

Each of the commissioners appointed under the act of Congress entitled "An act for the collection of direct taxes in insurrectionary districts, and for other purposes," approved June 7, 1862, will give a bond to the United States in the sum of fifty thousand dollars, with two or more sureties, conditioned in conformity with the requirements noted below; to be approved by the Secretary of the Treasury, and to be in form following:

Form of bond.

KNOW ALL MEN BY THESE PRESENTS, That we, as principals, and as sureties, are held and firmly bound unto the UNITED STATES OF AMERICA in the full and just sum of fifty thousand dollars, money of the United States; to which payment, well and truly to be made, we bind ourselves, jointly and severally, our joint and several heirs, executors, and administrators, firmly by these presents. Sealed with our seals, and dated this day of in the year of our Lord one thousand eight hundred and sixty-

The condition of this obligation is such, That whereas the President of the United States hath appointed tax commissioner for the , under an act entitled "An act for the collection of direct taxes in insurrectionary districts within the United States, and for other purposes," approved June 7, 1862: *Now, therefore,* if the said shall faithfully perform, execute, and discharge, and shall continue faithfully to perform, execute, and discharge all the duties of such tax commissioner, and shall well, truly, and promptly account for and pay over all moneys and other property which shall come to his hands as such commissioner, according to law, then the above obligation shall be void and of no effect; otherwise it shall abide and remain in full force and virtue.

Sealed and delivered in presence of—

Particulars to be observed.

The following instructions must be particularly observed and complied with, viz:

1st. The christian names must be written in the body of the bond in full, and so signed to the bond.

2d. A seal of wax or wafer to be affixed to each signature.

3d. Each signature must be made in the presence of two persons, who must sign their names as witnesses.

4th. Each surety must make and sign an affidavit of the amount he is worth after paying his just debts.

5th. A district judge or attorney of the United States, or a clerk of a court of record, under the seal and designation of the court, county, and State, must certify that the sureties are sufficient to pay the penalty of the bond.

6th. The affidavits of the sureties must be taken and signed before an officer authorized to administer oaths generally. The officer must certify that he admistered the oaths. If the magistrate is not a judge of the United States court, his authority to administer oaths must be certified by the clerk of a court of record having official knowledge of that fact.

7th. Bond to be dated.

8th. There must be two or more sureties to the bond.

Oath of commissioners.

I, , having been appointed tax commissioner for the , under an act entitled "An act for the collection of direct taxes in insurrectionary districts within the United States, and for other purposes," do solemnly that I have never voluntarily borne arms against the United States since I have been a citizen thereof; that I have voluntarily given no aid, counsel, or encouragement to persons engaged in armed hostility thereto; that I have neither sought, nor accepted, nor attempted to exercise the functions of any office whatever, under any authority, or pretended authority, in hostility to the United States; that I have not yielded a voluntary support to any pretended government, authority, power, or constitution, within the United States, hostile or inimical thereto. And I do further that, to the best of my knowledge and ability, I will support and defend the Constitution of the United States against all enemies, foreign and domestic; and that I will bear true faith and allegiance to the same; that I take this obligation freely, without any mental reservation or purpose of evasion; and that I will faithfully discharge the duties of the office on which I am about to enter. So help me God.

and subscribed this day of , A. D. 186 . Witness my hand and seal.

[SEAL.]

Certificate of official character of person who administers oath.

I, , do certify that , who administered the above , was, at the time of doing so, duly authorized to administer the same; and that full faith and credit are due to his official attestation.

In testimony whereof, I have hereunto set my hand and affixed the seal of this day of , A. D. 186 .

II.

It will be necessary, in the first place, to obtain, if possible, the aggregate valuation of all the lots or parcels of land subject to taxation within the State or district designated in the President's proclamation of the 1st day of July, A. D. 1862, according to the last State assessment made previous to the 1st day of January, A. D. 1861. When this State assessment cannot be obtained, nor an authentic copy thereof, recourse may be had to other sources of information. 1. Recourse may be had to official documents of such State or district wherein such valuation or assessment is stated or referred to. 2. To the census of the United States for the year 1860, (Preliminary Report, appendix, table No. 35, pp. 194, 195.) 3. To any official document or report made or published by the authority of the respective States or of the United States. 4. To an actual assessment by the commissioners, or by agents or assessors to be specially designated by them for that purpose from time to time, as occasion may require. When such assessment or valuation shall be made by such agents or assessors, or by the commissioners, on view, or upon evidence taken, it is to be made according to the value of such lands on or about the period prescribed by the State law for their assessment next previous to the 1st day of January, A. D. 1861.

Valuation of lands to be obtained according to State assessment.

Means to be adopted when such assessment cannot be obtained.

After the aggregate valuation of all the lands subject to taxation in the State or district named in the President's proclamation aforesaid shall have been ascertained, the valuation of the respective parcels of land subject to taxation will be made in either of the modes above prescribed, reliance in all cases being placed upon the State assessment, if it can be obtained, and if it cannot be obtained, then recourse will be had to the other sources above named.

Valuation of respective parcels.

III.

The commissioners will cause duplicate tax-rolls to be made out, wherein shall be entered a concise, but sufficiently definite and clear, description of each and every tract, lot, or parcel of land subject to taxation within the portion of the State or district in which such assessment can be made, stating the name of the owner or owners of each, respectively, if known; the county, district, and town, city, or parish where situated; the quantity of land in each; the valuation, and the amount of tax, penalty, and charges thereon, each respectively, up to the time of making such tax-roll, and the date of its completion; one copy of which shall be forwarded to the Commissioner of Internal Revenue, and the original to be retained by the commissioners.

Duplicate tax-rolls to be made.

Contents of.

One copy to be forwarded to Commissioner of Internal Revenue.

Commissioners to retain original.

IV.

The commissioners will make out further tax-rolls from time to time, as the advance of the army shall enable them so to do, and from time to time attach such additional tax-rolls to the original roll, and forward a copy of the same to the Commissioner of Internal Revenue, until such original and amended tax-rolls shall embrace

Additional tax-rolls to be made from time to time

all the lands subject to taxation in such insurrectionary State or district, numbering each additional roll successively.

V.

Commissioners to make returns each month of moneys received, and pay over the same from time to time as directed by the Secretary of the Treasury.

The commissioners will make returns of all moneys paid in on account of taxes, or otherwise, to the Commissioner of Internal Revenue on the first day of every month, or oftener when required by the Secretary of the Treasury; which sums of money shall be paid over from time to time, or deposited as the Secretary of the Treasury shall direct.

VI.

Notice to be given of the time when and place where taxes are payable.

Whenever the commissioners shall have completed the tax-rolls of any county, district, city, village, town, or parish, they will give public notice thereof in some newspaper printed in such county, or by posting up notices in three or more public places in such county, district, town, city, village, or parish, to the effect that such tax-roll is completed, and stating the place where such taxes may be paid, and within what time they are due and payable.

VII.

Lands on which taxes may not have been paid to be advertised as having become forfeited, with description of land and amount of tax assessed.

The advertisement of sale of lands on which the taxes have not been paid should state the fact that such lands have become forfeited to the United States by reason of the non-payment of said taxes, a description of said tract, the amount of tax, and penalty charged thereon, each respectively, and the time when and the place where, said lands will be sold.

VIII.

Form of receipt for taxes when paid before advertisement.

UNITED STATES OF AMERICA.

Receipt for direct taxes.

Form of receipt to be given by commissioners.

This is to certify that   has this day paid to the undersigned the sum of   dollars and   cents, that being the amount in full for taxes, penalty, interest, and costs, charged under the act of Congress entitled "An act for the collection of direct taxes in insurrectionary districts within the United States, and for other purposes," approved June 7, 1862, upon the following tract or lot of land, situate in the county of   and State of   , and described as follows:

Witness our hands, at , this day of , A. D. 186 .

Commissioners

[Indorsed.]

UNITED STATES TAX RECEIPT.

Name____________________________________

Date____________________________________

Tax ....

Penalty..........................

Interest..........................

Costs.............................

Total.......................

IX.

The commissioners may continue the sale of lands forfeited by non-payment of taxes from day to day, and may, in their discretion, postpone the same; and, should it be deemed necessary, may, by proclamation, adjourn the same to another place. Commissioners may continue the sale of lands from day to day, and may adjourn the same.

X.

The certificate given to the purchaser at such sale may be in the following form: Form of tax sale certificate.

UNITED STATES OF AMERICA.

Tax sale certificate, No. .

$--------- Acres---------

This is to certify that at a sale of lands for unpaid taxes, under and by virtue of an act entitled "An act for the collection of direct taxes in insurrectionary districts within the United States, and for other purposes," held pursuant to notice, at in the county of , in the State of , on the day of , A. D. 186 , the tract or parcel of land hereinafter described, situate in the of , and State aforesaid, and described as follows, to wit:

containing acres, more or less, was sold and struck off to , for the sum of dollars and cents, he being the highest bidder, and that being the highest sum bidden for the same; the receipt of which said sum in full is hereby acknowledged and confessed.

Given under our hands, at , this day of A. D. 186 .

Commissioners.

[Form of indorsement.]

UNITED STATES.

Tax sale certificate.

[Name of purchaser.]

No.	Amount of sale.	Acres.
	$	--------

XI.

Form of advertisement.

SALE OF LANDS FOR UNPAID DIRECT TAXES IN INSURRECTIONARY DISTRICTS, STATE OF

Form of advertisement.

Notice is hereby given that the several tracts or lots of land situated in the State of , hereinafter described, have become forfeited to the United States, by reason of the non-payment of the direct taxes charged thereon, under the act entitled "An act to provide increased revenue from imports, to pay interest on the public debt, and for other purposes," approved August 5, 1861, and an act entitled "An act for the collection of direct taxes in insurrectionary districts within the United States, and for other purposes," approved June 7, 1862, and that the same will be sold at public auction on the day of , A. D. 186 , at , in the county of , in the State of .

The following is a description of said lands forfeited as aforesaid, together with the amount of the quota of said tax and penalty charged upon each of said tracts or lots of land, respectively:

Description.	Quota of tax.	Penalty.	Amount.

Commissioners.

XII.

Whenever any lands sold for taxes shall be redeemed according to the provisions of said act, the commissioners shall give to the person redeeming the same a certificate substantially in the following form:

Certificate of redemption of lands sold for taxes.

UNITED STATES OF AMERICA.

No *Redemption certificate.* $

Form of.

Whereas, on the day of , A. D. 186 , the following described tract, lot, or parcel of land, situate in the county of , in the State of , and particularly described as follows, to wit:

was sold for the unpaid taxes charged thereon, under an act entitled "An act for the collection of direct taxes in insurrectionary districts within the United States, and for other purposes," for the sum of dollars and cents:

This is to certify that [*the owner thereof, or other person having a valid lien thereon, and stating the nature of the lien, as the case may be,*] having produced satisfactory evidence that he is a loyal citizen of the United States, and having taken an oath to support the Constitution of the United States, and having paid the tax charged on said land under the act aforesaid, together with the penalty, interest, and costs of proceedings, as required by said act, amounting to the sum of dollars, and cents, the receipt whereof in full is hereby acknowledged and confessed, has redeemed the said tract or lot of land from the forfeiture and sale thereof, and the said tract or lot of land is hereby henceforth discharged from all lien, charge, or claim by reason of said tax or penalty, interest, and costs of every kind and nature.

Given under our hands, at , this day of , A. D. 186 .

Direct Tax Commissioners
for the District of ------ .

[Indorsed.]

UNITED STATES.

Redemption certificate, No. .

[Name of person redeeming.]

Amount of tax.............................. $
Penalty......................................
Interest......................................
Costs...

Total..........................

XIII.

Triplicate certificates of sale and redemption. Disposition of.

Triplicate certificates of sale and redemption shall be made and signed by the commissioners, one of which is to be delivered to the purchaser or person redeeming, one to be forwarded to the Commissioner of Internal Revenue, and one to be carefully numbered and filed by the commissioners.

XIV.

Time for redemption may be extended for hearing. Witnesses, &c. Record to be made.

Whenever application shall be made for an extension of the time for redemption of any lands, under the 8th section of said act, reasonable time may be given to any of the parties interested therein for the production of evidence. On the hearing witnesses may be examined orally, whose testimony must be reduced to writing, and other evidence, the best which the nature of the case will admit, may be received. A concise but sufficient record of the proceedings and adjudications of the commissioners under said 8th section must be made and preserved.

XV.

Lands may be leased. Terms and conditions. More than 320 acres may be leased to one person.

On leasing portions of the lands referred to in the 9th section of said act, it is desirable that they should be demised, when practicable, in tracts or lots not exceeding three hundred and twenty acres, and with reference to the subdivision contemplated by the 11th section, so that purchases made by lessees, or others, during the term, or after the expiration of the term, may conform as nearly as possible to the general system of subdivision originally adopted for pre-emption and sale, should the President so direct. It is not intended, however, that not more than three hundred and twenty acres shall be leased to one individual.

XVI.

Contents of leases. Commissioners to have power to cancel. Compensation discretionary.

The temporary rules and regulations in section 10 should be so referred to in the leases, and the leases so drawn, as to retain in the commissioners full and complete power to alter, modify, change, or annul the same, or to add to the same from time to time as the commissioners shall deem necessary or proper, and so that no claim for damage, compensation, or deduction of rent or other allowance can be made by the lessees in consequence of such modification or change. All such compensation or allowance, if any should be necessary, must be wholly discretionary with the commissioners.

XVII.

Books, &c. to be kept within the protection of the army.

The books, papers, and funds in the care, custody, and control of the commissioners should be so kept at all times as to be within the protection of the army, and the commissioners will obtain the aid of commanders when practicable.

Clerk of com-

The clerk of the commissioners will be required to give security

in the form of a bond to the United States, with sufficient sureties in the sum of dollars, conditioned for the faithful discharge of his duties; such bonds and sureties to be approved by the commissioners.

missioners to give bond.

XVIII.

In case the three commissioners shall fail to attend any meetings of the board, of which all shall have had due notice, any two members of the commission shall constitute a quorum for the transaction of business, and for the performance of any duty required by the said act; and the commissioners shall cause to be kept a journal or record of all their proceedings.

A majority of the commissioners to constitute a quorum.

Journal or record to be kept.

XIX.

All expenses incurred for surveying, viewing, measuring, or assessing the said lands shall be charged thereon, and apportioned, according to valuation, to each tract or lot, and collected with other expenses.

Expenses of surveying, viewing, &c., to be charged and apportioned.

XX.

A transcript of the books referred to in section 14 of said act, duly verified, will be returned to the Secretary of the Treasury on the first day of each and every month after the first assessment shall have been completed.

A transcript of the books to be returned to the Secretary of the Treasury.

FORMS.

Form of Valuation Book.

UNITED STATES DIRECT TAX.

VALUATION of land, and lots of land, in ——— County, State of ———, assessed under an "Act of Congress for the Collection of Direct Taxes in insurrectionary districts within the United States, and for other purposes," approved June 7, 1862.

Description.	Contents.			Valuation.		Tax.		Penalty.		10 per ct. Int.		Cost.		Total.		$500 Exemption.		Tax.		By whom paid.	Owner's Name.	To whom paid.	Remarks.
	A.	L.	B.	$	c.	$	c.	$	c.	$	c.	$	c.	$	c.			W. F.	W. P.				
	Acres	Lots	Blocks															When fixed	When paid				

Form of Book of "Abstract of Sales."

UNITED STATES DIRECT TAX.

ABSTRACT of Land and Lots in ——— County, State of ———, sold for Taxes, under an "Act of Congress for the Collection of Direct Taxes in insurrectionary districts within the United States, and for other purposes," approved June 7, 1862.

Description.	Contents.			Valuation.		Tax.		Penalty.		10 per ct. Int.		Costs.		Total.		Date of Adv't.	Date of Sale.	Am't of Bill.		No. of Certificate	Name of Purchaser	When redeemed.	Am't pd. for red'n.		Remarks.
	A.	L.	B.	$	c.	$	c.	$	c.	$	c.	$	c.	$	c.			$	c.				$	c.	
	Acres	Lots	Blocks																						

RULINGS UNDER DIRECT TAX LAWS.

(No. 1.)

* * * * * * * *

* * * *As to the proper construction of the first Section of the Act of Congress for the collection of direct taxes in insurrectionary districts, as to what valuation is to govern the boards of Direct Tax Commissioners in the assessment of the taxes.*

The act requires that the taxes apportioned among the several states and territories shall be apportioned in each state or territory, or part thereof, wherein the civil authority is obstructed, on all lands or lots of ground situate therein, except such as are exempt from taxation by the laws of said state or of the United States, as the lands or lots of ground were enumerated and valued under the last assessment and valuation thereof, made under the authority of the state or territory previous to the first day of January, A. D. 1861. The language of the act appears * * to be perfectly clear, so clear that it is incapable of being misunderstood. The last valuation made under the authority of the state or territory previous to the first day of January, 1861, is the valuation which is to govern in the assessment of the direct taxes in all cases, whether any valuation was made under the state authority at a later period or not. Where the directions of the act are so positive and explicit they ought to be strictly obeyed, and the Commissioners have no cause to heed the valuation of 1861, or 1862, where the valuation of 1860 is accessible. Where that valuation is not accessible, the later valuations may under certain circumstances be referred to, to assist in ascertaining what was the last assessment prior to January 1st, 1861, whatever the actual date of that prior assessment may be.

Tax to be assessed on all lands not exempt by law.

No state assessment made subsequent to Dec. 31, 1860, can be regarded as authority.

(Stat. June 7, 1862, sect. 1.)

Subsequent valuation may be examined to aid in ascertaining last valuation.

(No. 2.)

* * * *Whether, under the 15th section of the same act, the $500 exemption extends to all real estate owners, or but to persons only whose estate is worth $500 or less.*

* * * The $500 is allowed to all persons *resident* on the property within the jurisdiction of the Tax Commissioners, and is not to be allowed in respect to property on which the owner does not reside. In other words, every person who owns property subject to assessment, is to be allowed the prescribed exemption, whatever may be the value of his property, provided he reside on it. If his property is not worth more than $500, the whole is exempt. If worth more, all above $500 is taxable. Where the owner does not reside on his property it is taxable for the whole value, where not otherwise exempt by the laws of the state.

The exemption of $500 is allowed only to persons residing on the estates subject to tax.

If value exceeds $500, the excess is taxable.

13

(No. 3.)

Concerning the sale of lands under the Direct Tax Laws.

* * * * * * * * * * *

If the owner appear in person and request the estate to be struck off to a purchaser for less than two thirds of the assessed value, the Commissioners cannot receive bids for a larger sum.

1st. Where the owner of lots or parcels of ground advertised for sale for the non-payment of direct taxes shall appear in person before the Board of Commissioners, and request the same to be struck off to a purchaser for a less sum than two thirds of the assessed value thereof, the Commissioners would, by force of the provision contained in the amendatory statute, approved February 6th, 1863, be bound by such request, and should not receive bids from other persons who might offer larger amounts.

The power to bid for the United States discretionary, and not a duty.

2d. The authority delegated to Tax Commissioners by the statute aforesaid to bid off property upon certain contingencies therein expressed for the United States, at a sum not exceeding two thirds of the assessed value thereof, is not obligatory in character, but implies only the proper exercise of a discretionary power.

No expense to be allowed except for advertising.

3d. The statute makes no provision for the allowance of any expense whatever in addition to the cost of advertising.

(No. 4.)

In reference to the authority of the Tax Commissioners in States and parts of States where the civil authority is or has been overthrown.

* * * * * * * * * * * * * * * *

Taxes may be assessed in any State where civil authority is overthrown, even in less than a municipal division.

* * * By the 1st section, any part of any State or district where the civil authority of the United States is obstructed, is liable to assessment under the law, and it matters not whether that part constitutes a municipal division of the State or Territory or not.

Military authority must be re-established in one whole parish, county, or district before any assessment can be made.

By the 6th section it is required that the military authority of the government should have become established in one whole parish, county or district before the proper Board of Tax Commissioners shall enter upon the duties of their office. That provision makes the establishment of the military authority over a single municipal division a condition precedent to the exercise of the authority of the Board. But when that condition is once fulfilled there is no limitation of the authority of the Commission as to adjoining districts.

When so established, there is no limit to authority of Commissioners to assess in all parts of the State under military control.

The Commissioners may extend the assessments to the whole or any part of such adjoining districts as may be under the military control of the government, and is no objection to their proceedings. Nor will it affect the titles of purchasers of tracts sold for taxes, that part of such district is occupied by the rebels. * *

(No. 5.)

Word "sailors" defined.

* * * * * * * *

* * * * * * * *

The term "sailors," in section 11, is evidently intended to designate that class of persons who follow the sea as a pursuit, or for a livelihood, and who are mustered into the naval service as such, and certainly does not include those engaged on a vessel which is hired by government for a particular purpose, or for a short time, such as transportation of troops or supplies from place to place.

Stat. June 7, 1862.
Word "sailors" defined with reference to the rights of sailors to purchase lands under the Direct Tax law of June 7, 1862.

LIST OF DIRECT TAX COMMISSIONERS.

SOUTH CAROLINA.

William H. Brisbane,
William E. Wording,
Dennis N. Cooley.

VIRGINIA.

John Hawxhurst,
Gillett F. Watson,
A. Lawrence Foster.

FLORIDA.

William Alsop,
Austin Smith,
Lyman D. Stickney.

TENNESSEE.

Delano T. Smith,
Elisha P. Ferry,
John B. Rodgers.

NORTH CAROLINA.

John R. French,
Charles C. Sholes.

LOUISIANA.

Edwin M. Randall,
George W. Ames,
Maximilian Ferdinand Banzano.

ARKANSAS.

Hulings Cowperthwait,
Josiah Snow,
Enoch H. Vance.

MISSISSIPPI.

Hiram Potter,
James Peckham.

RULINGS.

NOTE.—The Rulings are based upon the correspondence of the office, and, in some cases, the language used in the letters of the Commissioner has been retained. Generally, however, the language has been changed, and in several instances the opinion given has been modified or reversed by the experience of the office. Consequently, the Rulings should not be regarded as binding upon the Office of Internal Revenue, but rather as the opinions of the editor of this volume, aided by the gentlemen whose services are acknowledged in the preface. Some of the questions may seem unimportant, but they are those which have been presented to the Commissioner by parties interested.

AUCTIONEERS.

(No. 1.)

An auctioneer can sell in other districts than that where licensed. Can have but one place of business. May sell for other parties upon their premises.

Under the law of June 30, 1864, section 74, an auctioneer can sell in other districts than that where he has taken out his license.

An auctioneer can have but one place of business at which he may receive consignments of goods. He may, however, sell, either in person or by his employés, for parties upon their premises, and he may sell the goods of licensed dealers at their places of business.—(Stat. June 30, 1864, Sec. 77.)

(No. 2.)

Auction sales under power of sale agreement in mortgage subject to auction tax.

Auction sales by sheriffs, under powers of sale contained in mortgages, in cases where there is not a "judgment or decree of court," are liable to pay a duty of one-fourth of one per centum on the gross amount of such sales.

(No. 3.)

Sales at auction under a standing rule of court are subject to tax.

A rule of court, requiring all sales of real estate under "power" or "trust" to be made by a sheriff, is not such a decree as is contemplated by the law, and therefore such sales are subject to tax, and the seller must be licensed as an auctioneer.—(Sections 77, 98.)

(No. 4.)

Judicial officers may sell property under authority of decree, &c., without taking out license or paying duty on sales. And may deputize others to act for them in making such sales.

The provisos to sections 77 and 98 allow judicial or executive officers to make auction sales by virtue of a judgment or decree of any court, and also allow executors or administrators, as such, to make public sales. Sales so made are exempt from the duty of one-fourth of one per cent. on the amount. Consequently the services of a licensed auctioneer are not required to make such sales, but such judicial or executive officers, executors, and administrators can either sell or employ others to sell without license as auctioneers.

COTTON.

(No. 5.)

(To an Assessor.)

Tax on unginned cotton, how levied.

A letter has been received at this office from Messrs. M. Combie & Child, stating that they are in receipt of a quantity of cotton from New Orleans, in an unginned state, on which an assessment of the excise tax has been levied. They complain upon the ground that the duty applies to cotton in the ginned state only. I am of opinion that their view is correct. You will, however, take note of the number of bales, the marks and weights, in order that no detriment may accrue to the government. Where the cotton cannot be ginned you will use your judgment in determining the amount it would produce if ginned, and levy the tax accordingly.

(No. 6.)

Foreign cotton not subject to excise duty.

Cotton grown without the limits of the United States, and on which an import duty has been paid, is not subject to excise duty under the law.

(No. 7.)

Cotton held by manufacturer, Oct. 1, 1862, is exempt.

The law provides that cotton owned and held by a manufacturer of cotton fabrics on the 1st day of October, 1862, and prior thereto, shall be exempt from tax. This provision must be construed to exempt such cotton while it remains in the hands of the manufacturer by whom it was owned on the first day of October.

If sold to other parties it becomes liable to duty.

If it has been sold in the markets subsequently to that date, and become mixed with the stock on hand in the country, it is liable to taxation as though it had not been so held by a manufacturer on the said first day of October, 1862.

(No. 8.)

Cotton purchased of agents of United States not subject to tax.

Cotton purchased of officers or agents of the United States, on which a tax has not been paid, is exempt from tax, and is not liable to assessment in the hands of the parties holding cotton under purchases so made.—(Stat. June 30, 1864, sect. 177.)

INCOME TAX.*

(No. 9.)

The proceeds of timber when cut is subject to taxation as income.

The fact that the law regards timber standing as a part of the realty cannot be urged as a sufficient reason for the exemption from taxation of the income received from the sale of such timber. For although the timber, while standing, forms a part of the realty, yet, when it is cut down, it becomes personal property, and the

*The Rulings on income tax were made by Commissioner Lewis.

receipts of the owner from such sales go to increase his annual income, and are therefore just as liable to the income tax as is the income received from the sale of other products of the soil, or from mines. A farmer who keeps woodland for the express purpose of cutting and selling firewood, in greater or less quantities every year, would be required to estimate his receipts from that source as a part of his income. And the case is not different with a proprietor who sells to others the privilege of cutting and appropriating the timber on his land.

Income resulting from a sale of standing timber is to be estimated by assessing the value of the land after the removal of the timber and adding thereto the amount received for the timber, and from the sum thus obtained deducting the estimated value of the land immediately prior to the felling of the timber.

(No. 10.)

Discretionary power vested in assessors relative to requiring persons to return income.

In cases where assessors have good reason to believe that persons have not an income of $600, no return need be required.

(No. 11.)

Nature of return of income.

The sources from which the income is derived, whether from any kind of property, or the purchase and sale of property, rents, interest, dividends, salaries, or from any profession, trade, employment, or vocation, or otherwise, shall be particularly stated, and that the claims to deductions allowed by law shall be set forth, each in a specific item, so as to enable the assistant assessor to judge of its validity. If, however, the assessor or assistant assessor has good reason to believe that any return is understated, he may increase the same to such amount as he may think proper; and if then the party is not satisfied, he may obtain relief by making oath to the amount on which he is liable to income duty, and such sworn return is to be accepted by the assessor.

Mode of procedure to be adopted by assessors when insufficient returns are rendered.

Penalty in case of false or fraudulent list or return.

Under section 14, it is the duty of the assessor, whenever in his opinion any list, statement, or return is false or fraudulent, to summon all persons having knowledge of the business of the person making the list, statement, or return, and to pursue the investigation in the manner pointed out in said section. In case the assessor is satisfied that the list or valuation is false or fraudulent, he will add one hundred per centum to the duty.

By the 15th section, persons so offending are liable, upon conviction, to a fine not exceeding one thousand dollars, or to imprisonment not exceeding one year, or both, at the discretion of the court.

These sections relate to the monthly as well as annual lists.

(No. 12.)

Foreign residents subject to taxation for all property in the United States, and for personal property elsewhere.

All foreigners resident in the United States will be required to make return of, and pay income tax on that portion of their income derived from sources within the United States, and from investments elsewhere, other than in real estate.

(No. 13.)

For purposes of taxation husband and wife are to be treated, generally, as one person, on the common law principle of the legal existence of the wife being merged in that of the husband. The husband should therefore return the income derived from the labor of his wife and minor children. Only one allowance of $600 can be deducted from their united incomes. If the husband refuse to return his income, including the items mentioned, the assistant assessor should increase the amount of the list or return. The phrase "separate income," as used in the second proviso to Section 116, is not so construed as to exempt the earnings of the wife and children, or income from sources under the legal control of the husband and father.

Income of married women to be treated as income of husbands; only one deduction to be allowed from united income.

Mode of procedure to be adopted in cases of neglect or omission to render returns.

Meaning of the phrase "separate income."

(No. 14.)

Amounts paid for water rents are not to be considered as taxes, nor should they be allowed as deductions from income.

Water rents not taxes.

(No. 15.)

Local assessments for cleaning or repairing sewers are legitimate deductions from the income of the property upon which such assessments are laid. Assessments for building or improving sewers, being in the nature of improvements to the property, cannot be deducted.

Cleaning sewers and building sewers are improvements.

(No. 16.)

The income tax is entirely independent and irrespective of the license tax, and is imposed upon that portion of the entire sum which exceeds $600, after making deductions allowed by law.

Income tax independent of license tax.

Operation of income tax.

(No. 17.)

Fathers should include salaries, &c., received by minor children in returns of income.

Parents chargeable for income of minor children.

(No. 18.)

The owner of a ship should return as income the entire earnings received in the year 1862, from a voyage completed in that year, no matter when said voyage commenced. The owner of a ship should not return as income for the year 1862 any portion of the earnings received from a voyage completed in the year 1863, the earnings whereof were received in the latter year, no matter when said voyage commenced.

Income returns by ship-owners.

(No. 19.)

In considering the case of whalers, the rule of action should be to assess the tax, when the voyage has terminated, on the total yield. This may appear, at first view, to operate unjustly, but its results will be found equitable, for should a whaler who has

Income tax on whalers to be assessed on total yield of voyage.

recently returned and paid tax on his yield go to sea to-day, his voyage may not be terminated again until our authority to levy a tax upon his future earnings has ceased to exist by the expiration or repeal of the law.

(No. 20.)

Gains may be balanced by losses if incurred.

A person engaged in navigation, and owning vessels, may balance the gains and losses on this branch of his business as a whole, setting the gains of one against the losses of another, including even the entire loss of a vessel by capture, shipwreck, or other disaster, on which there was no insurance.

(No. 21.)

Where it has been the custom of ship-owners to set apart a certain sum on account of the depreciation of vessels, and with no intent to evade the law, the practice may be continued.

Where the custom of the trade has been for years, and is to make a deduction of 5 or 7 per cent. charged off by ship-owners for depreciation of their vessels, such deduction will continue to be set off against the profits of that branch of business, and will not enter into the income return proper. Assessors should be satisfied that a statement of business profits is made bona fide, and with no intent to claim unreasonable and unusual deductions.

(No. 22.)

Premiums paid for insurance not to be deducted from return of taxable income.

Premiums paid for life insurance should not be deducted from the return of taxable income.

(No. 23.)

Income tax upon net gains.

Family and personal expenses not to be deducted.

The income tax is laid upon the net gains, after the expenses of conducting the business are deducted. Family and personal expenses are not to be considered part of the expenses of conducting the business.

Interest and dividends to be treated as income.

The interest and dividends upon all bonds and securities are to be regarded, and are to be assessed, as profits, or income.

(No. 24.)

Trust funds to be applied for general religious purposes of an undetermined character taxable in the hands of the recipient.

If a trust fund be held for general religious purposes, and divided in proportions which are unsettled or which are determined by circumstances, it will not be taxed in the hands of trustees, but in the hands of the persons receiving the income.

If the fund is solely for the support of individuals it is taxable wherever found.

If the fund be solely for the support of some particular person or persons, it is liable to taxation, whether in the hands of the trustees or the beneficiary.

(No. 25.)

Estate of deceased persons dying in April, 1863, subject to tax on income for the year 1862.

The estate of a party who deceased in April, 1863, is liable to tax on income derived in the year 1862, and it will be the duty of his executors or administrators to return the amount and pay the tax.

An executor or administrator of a decedent who died during the year 1862 should, as his representative, make return of the income of the estate which accrued between January 1 and the date of his death, and, as trustee for the beneficiaries under the will, or for the distributees under the intestate law, make return of the income of the estate which accrued during the remainder of the year.

Returns must be made of income received between January 1, 1862, and date of decease, as well as after fiduciary officer obtained possession of estate.

The amount paid by an executor or administrator to a trustee is not liable to a second tax in the hands of the latter as income, but it is considered as principal, the income from which, when derived, must be returned by him. If any accrued to him prior to December 31, 1862, it should be returned during the year 1863.

Not liable to second tax.

(No. 26.)

A salaried officer of the government is entitled to the deduction for house rent in the assessment of income tax. The tax on salaries, provided for in the 123d section of the act of June 30, 1864, must be levied without such deduction, and should not be confounded with the income tax.

House rent, if paid, may be deducted from assessment of income tax by government officials.
Tax on salaries of government officials must be levied as provided by the statute.

(No. 27.)

The assessment paid on a pew in a church should be considered in the nature of a contribution and not as a tax.

Church assessment, contributions not "taxes."

(No. 28.)

All national, State, and local taxes, lawfully assessed and paid, may be deducted without reference to the productiveness or unproductiveness of the property on which they may have been assessed.

National and other taxes deducted whether property taxed is productive or not.

(No. 29.)

Taxes paid by corporations cannot be allowed as deductions from the income of a stockholder.

Corporation taxes not deducted.

(No. 30.)

Marriage fees, gifts from members of a congregation to their pastor, &c., are taxable as income when the gifts or donations are in the nature of compensation for services rendered, whether in accordance with an understanding to that effect at the time of settlement, or with an annual custom.

Gifts from all sources, if made as compensation for services rendered, to be subject to income tax.

Gifts of money from father to son, when clearly not in the nature of payment for services rendered, and also clearly not in pursuance of an attempt to evade the revenue laws, are not liable to taxation as income.

Gifts from parents to children, not made for services nor to evade the law, exempt.

(No. 31.)

As to liability of masters of vessels to be assessed 50 per cent. additional for not rendering returns in due course.

In answer to your letter of the 13th instant, inquiring whether you shall assess fifty per cent. additional upon the income of masters of vessels at sea who left home before May 1, being ignorant of the law, leaving no agent, &c., I have to say that it would seem to be a great hardship to assess the fifty per cent. in such cases; and it is presumed that assessors might find some means of ascertaining their income without proceeding under section eleven.

(No. 32.)

Assessors may require returns from temporary residents and transmit them to assessors of districts in which parties have legal residence.

An assessor may require returns of income from persons sojourning in his district for a few months at a time, and transmit the same to the assessors of the several districts in which the parties reside.

(No. 33.)

Expense of altering buildings so as to render them substantially new ones not to be deducted from income as "repairs."

The removal of a roof of ancient design from a building, and the substitution of one of modern style, raising the walls of the building to conform thereto, should be regarded as an improvement rather than as "repairs," and the expense incurred thereby should not be deducted from the income of the owner of the building.

The mere replacing of a rotten and worthless roof with a new one will be regarded as repairs.

(No. 34.)

Foreign consuls liable to excise duties, except on income from real estate.

A foreign consul residing in this country is not entitled to the privileges accorded by international law to a minister of a foreign state, but only to those that are secured to him by treaty or recognized by the usages of Christian nations. He is liable to excise duties and also to income tax, except as to rents derived from real estate not within our jurisdiction. Foreign consuls are exempt from income tax when similar exemption is accorded by their governments to our consuls.—(Stat. June 30, 1864, sect. 178.)

Exempt in certain cases.

(No. 35.)

Exemption of $600 to each covenanting member of the society of Shakers.

Under the peculiar arrangements of the Shaker institution at Lebanon, New York, it was decided that the statutory allowance of six hundred dollars should be made to each male covenanting member in the assessment of the income tax. The number of persons, male and female, infant and adult, within the organization is about five hundred and twenty—the male covenanting members about one hundred. The number of covenanting members bears, therefore, to the others about the same proportion that the heads of families do to those occupying a subordinate relation in society constituted in the ordinary way.

(No. 36.)

The rate of taxation to which an income is subject will be determined by the net amount after those deductions are made, which are in actual diminution of income, such as rents, taxes, repairs, losses, &c. The rate must be determined before deducting the $600 allowed by law.

Rule for ascertaining rate of tax on income.

LICENSES.

(No. 37.)

The law authorizes assessors to publish the notice that tax lists are open to public inspection in one paper only, in each county of the district.

Annual tax lists to be advertised in one paper only.

In case of licenses embraced in the annual list, the time for payment having expired, collectors will add the ten per cent. and distrain, and they should also enforce the penalty where persons continue business without paying their license taxes.

When the time for payment has expired, the penalty of 10 per cent. may be added.

Penalty to be enforced. (Sect. 73.)

(No. 38.)

An insurance agent can act for any number of companies under one license, but his aggregate receipts must be reckoned in estimating his liability to take license.

Insurance agents can act for any number of companies.

(No. 39.)

While the excise law requires every dealer in liquors to take a license from the United States under the penalty provided in section 73 for selling without license, it is nevertheless expressly provided in section 78 that no such license "shall be construed to exempt any person carrying on the trade, business, or profession specified in said license from any penalty or punishment provided by the laws of any State for carrying on such trade, business, or profession within such State, or in any manner to authorize the commencement or continuance of such trade, business, or profession contrary to the laws of such State, or in places prohibited by municipal law."

The license issued to dealers in liquors will not protect a licensee for violation of the laws of the State where the licensee does business.

The law of the United States does not protect persons who have been licensed as dealers in liquors for acts done in violation of State laws.

The law of the United States does not protect persons who have been licensed as dealers in liquors for acts done in violation of State laws.

(No. 40.)

The owner of a patent is subject to a license tax as a peddler if he sells machines made in conformity therewith while travelling from place to place.

Owner of a patent taxable as a peddler in certain cases.

(No. 41.)

Lawyers' licenses do not authorize their holders acting as claim ag'ts. Lawyers practising as claim agents must take out a license therefor.

The license given an attorney-at-law does not cover the practice of a claim agent. If a lawyer desires to prosecute claims in any of the executive departments of the government he must secure a claim agent's license.

(No. 42.)

Army surgeons do not require a license to practice their professions in the public service.

Surgeons, assistant surgeons, and acting assistant surgeons in the United States army or navy, receiving their appointments as such from the United States government, are not required to take licenses for the practice of their profession in their official capacity, whether engaged in the field, or in hospitals, or on shipboard.

(No. 43.)

Vessels carrying passengers to or from foreign ports not required to take a fifth class hotel license.

The clause referred to in section 79, article 20, requiring steamers and vessels upon waters of the United States, on which passengers and travellers are provided with food or lodging, to take out a license, was not intended for and does not apply to packets or other ships sailing to and from foreign ports.

(No. 44.)

Wool-pulling not a manufacture. A wool-puller making his own sales is subject to taxation to the amount thereof. If he sells through a commission house he is exempt.

A wool-puller is not liable to tax as a manufacturer. If he send his wool for sale to a commission house, he is not liable to a dealer's license; but, if he make his own sales, he is liable to take license as a wholesale or retail dealer.

(No. 45.)

Dealers selling part of their wares require licenses on the basis of their sales.

A person who sells a part of his goods at his place of business, and the remainder through a commission house, requires a license on the basis of his own sales.

(No. 46.)

Manufacturers of articles exempt from duty must be licensed as dealers.

A manufacturer of articles exempt from duty must be licensed as a dealer, in order that he may make sales either at his manufactory or elsewhere, provided his sales exceed $1000 per annum. It is only when the manufacturer makes sales that he is liable for license as a dealer.

(No. 47.)

Stereotypers are manufacturers, and must be appropriately licensed.

Stereotypers are subject to a duty of five per cent. ad valorem tax, under the excise law, upon their productions, and they must take license as manufacturers.

(No. 48.)

Undertakers are to be regarded as manufacturers under the law, and if the coffins and other articles made and sold by a party exceed $1000 per annum, a license is required. Undertakers are manufacturers.

(No. 49.)

Persons engaged in the production of the articles enumerated in section 96 of the excise law, and which are not regarded as manufactures within the meaning of the law, do not require to be licensed as manufacturers. Section 81 does not apply to them, and they must therefore be licensed as retail or wholesale dealers, as the case may be. Liability of producers of articles not regarded as manufactures to dealers' license. Sec. 96.

(No. 50.)

A broker in the State of Indiana cannot employ an agent in the State of Ohio to buy stocks, scrip, &c., under his license. A broker cannot employ agents who will be protected by the license of the principal.

(No. 51.)

A person holding a power of substitution under a power of attorney can act, as far as the original power of attorney gives authority, as real estate agent for both first and second parties without license as a commercial broker. Attorneys by substitution need not take license as commercial brokers.

(No. 52.)

Flour millers are not required to take out license as manufacturers, as the making of flour is not deemed a manufacture under the act. But they should take out license as wholesale or retail dealers whenever they make sale of their products. Millers subject to dealer's license for their sales.

They should also take out license as manufacturers of barrels and bags, and pay the tax thereon; but they do not need license to sell the barrels from the shop, as under the law (section 81) manufacturers can sell their own manufactures on the premises where made, without license as dealers. If they manufacture barrels or bags, must take license therefor.

(No. 53.)

A producer of crude oil, who sells his oil at the well, requires a dealer's license. Crude oil dealers require license.

(No. 54.)

Dentists who buy teeth, put them upon a plate, and fit them, are not manufacturers within the meaning of the law. Dentists are not manufacturers.

They require no license as manufacturers in addition to their license as dentists.

Persons who make teeth for sale are manufacturers.

(No. 55.)

Persons receiving money on deposit, &c., must take license as brokers.

If an individual receives money on deposit for persons other than those for whom he sells produce or merchandise, he must take out a license as a banker, in addition to his license as broker.

Rules for assessors to determine who are bankers and who are brokers.

In deciding whether a person is or is not a broker, assessors will consider—

1. Whether the party does any of the acts which are specified in article 9, section 79; and if satisfied affirmatively, then—

2. Whether it is the business of the party to do the acts or things therein specified. It is not necessary that it should be the sole business, or even the principal business, in order that he may be held liable to license as a broker.

If a person holds out to the public by words, deeds, or writing, that he is engaged in any kind of business requiring license, he must take license therefor, although the business in question may not be his chief or exclusive occupation.

A person who invests his own property may or may not be a broker according to circumstances.

It is not to be inferred from this decision that every person who loans or invests his own capital is to be taxed as a broker. A man having property may invest it as he has opportunity; but if his investments are such in character and amount as to constitute a business, then he becomes subject to the excise law, in relation to license.—(Sect. 79, art. 49.)

Licensed banks and bankers may do brokers' business.

A licensed banker may transact business as a broker without additional license.

(No. 56.)

A person who purchases county and town warrants, and uses them to pay taxes upon lands owned by his correspondents, must be assessed as a broker.

County and town warrants are undoubtedly securities within the meaning of the law. Therefore, a person whose business it is to *purchase* or *sell* these securities is liable to be assessed as a broker. The amount of business done cannot be a satisfactory test, in any case, of a person's liability to license.

If a party, by advertisement or conversation, or by accepting the business whenever it is offered, holds himself out to the public as ready to undertake such business, whatever the aggregate amount of his annual transactions, he is liable to be assessed as a broker.

In the case of the party who professes not to have bought warrants since the excise law was in operation, he has in effect been engaged in the sale of them, inasmuch as upon the receipt of funds from his correspondents, they become the owners of an amount of the warrants in question, which he in good faith must set aside and apply to the payment of their taxes.

In many parts of the west there are persons who purchase town and county warrants and use them in payment of taxes assessed upon lands of non-resident owners.

(No. 57.)

A manufacturer may sell at the place of manufac-

A manufacturer of whips, or other articles, who delivers his goods in large quantities to peddlers, does not require a wholesale dealer's license. He is permitted, by section 81, to sell at the place of manufacture, either at wholesale or at retail.

ture either at wholesale or retail.

Section 79 defines a peddler to be a person who sells goods or merchandise at retail, travelling from place to place. Such persons are to be licensed according to the manner in which they travel. It further provides that any person who sells dry-goods in the original packages, shall pay fifty dollars for a license.

The law is silent respecting the peddling of other articles than "dry-goods," by the piece or package, neither prohibiting nor allowing such sales.

Other articles than "dry goods" may be sold by peddlers according to previous custom.

It would therefore appear that the peddlers of whips should take a peddler's ordinary license, according to their mode of travelling, and they should be permitted to do business, under such a license, according to the previous customs of the trade.

Peddlers of whips must take license based upon mode of travelling.

Article 32 of section 79 provides that garden seeds may be peddled at wholesale, under certain conditions, without license.

Garden seeds may be sold at wholesale by peddlers, without license.

There is no provision of law by which cloth manufactured by the Shakers is exempt from duty.

A country merchant may buy any quantity of produce on his own account, and ship it to another place to be there sold, without subjecting himself to a wholesale dealer's license. If he buys for several parties, he must be licensed as a commercial broker.

A country merchant may buy and ship produce on his own account or for one person without license as a commercial broker.

If he buys for several he is a commercial broker.

The term "commission," in section 86, does not include "guaranty" among the expenses of sale to be deducted from returns of manufacturers.

(No. 58.)

A distiller can sell at his distillery only, under his license as a distiller.

If he becomes a rectifier, he must take a wholesale liquor dealer's license, to enable him to sell his rectified spirits.

A distiller may sell distilled spirits at his distillery without a license.

If he becomes a rectifier he must take a liquor dealer's license.

(No. 59.)

The license of *** as a rectifier expired by limitation when he had rectified 500 barrels. He must take new license, as one who rectifies more than 500 barrels per year, and pay pro rata from the time he reached his maximum, 500 barrels.

Rectifiers required to take new license when business exceeds 500 barrels.

(No. 60.)

Agents of commercial brokers who have offices and solicit orders are liable to license as commercial brokers.

Agents having offices are subject to same duty as principals.

(No. 61.)

The sawing of veneers of mahogany, walnut, &c., is not a manufacture requiring a license.

Sawing of veneers not subject to duty.

(No. 62.)

Purchases may be made by principa's or agents without license, but sales may not be made except in conformity to statute.

Any person may send out his clerks, or he may hire men by the month and send them out, or he may go himself to make purchases of goods, wares, merchandise or produce without license therefor.

So he may go himself, or send his clerks to sell, by samples, goods, &c., the goods sold all being delivered from the store or place of business where he is licensed to sell, without any additional license therefor.

Definition of "broker."

The 14th article of the 79th section of the act of June 30, 1864, defining the kinds of business requiring a license as commercial broker, appears to comprehend two classes of brokers, viz., merchandise brokers and ship brokers. The first of these classes is held to include those persons who offer themselves to the public as ready to buy or sell goods for any person who will employ them.

It is a forced and unnatural construction of this provision of the law to extend its terms to any person, and to denominate him a broker, who is simply employed as the agent of a single person or firm, either to buy or sell goods, by sample, while travelling from place to place.

(No. 63.)

Veterinary surgeons.

Section 79, article 44, applies equally to veterinary surgeons as to other surgeons.

(No. 64.)

License to sell lottery tickets covers only one place for sale.

Article 6 of section 79 authorizes a person, association, firm, or corporation, to sell lottery tickets under a license, as contemplated in said article, at a place of business specified in the license when granted; it cannot, however, be considered as authorizing the agents of such person, association, firm, or corporation, that may have been licensed as aforesaid, to sell at places other than that named in the license.—(See sect. 74.)

Lottery ticket agents also require licenses.

The particular application of this rule would, of course, authorize a corporation, established by a State, to sell lottery tickets at its place of business whenever a license shall have been applied for and granted. If a corporation employs agents in various parts of the State to sell tickets upon commission, such agents will be required severally to take licenses under said article.

(No. 65.)

Job printers may be subject to dealer's license.

A job printer is a retail dealer when he furnishes the paper on which his work is printed; and also when he keeps for sale labels, notices, receipts, drafts, notes, deeds, or other blanks, or articles, when the gross sales of said articles amount to one thousand dollars a year.

(No. 66.)

Mechanics, such as carpenters, masons, and painters, who furnish, respectively, the materials commonly used by them, will be required to take license as dealers, whenever their annual sales of such materials exceed one thousand dollars.

Mechanics who furnish materials are liable to be taxed as dealers when sales exceed $1,000 per annum.

(No. 67.)

If a conveyancer, as known in business, holds himself out as a lawyer or attorney, he must take a license as a lawyer.

A conveyancer who holds himself out as a lawyer must take license as such.

Conveyancing is a branch of the law. Most conveyancers come strictly within the language of the definition furnished.—(Sec. 79, art. 43.)

It is not necessary, however, that a person should actually give such advice; if he holds himself out as ready to do so, he is equally liable.

Conveyancers generally give advice, &c.

As a general proposition, conveyancers are liable to assessment as lawyers.

If, in addition to this, a conveyancer purchases, rents, or sells real estate for others, he must take license as a commercial broker.

If a conveyancer purchases, rents, or sells real estate he is liable to license as a commercial broker.

A person licensed as a lawyer or claim agent may act as a conveyancer without license as such.—(Sect. 79, art. 26.)

Lawyers and claim agents may act as conveyancers.

(No. 68.)

When a person neglects or refuses to make application for a license, he should be assessed in the sum for which he is liable. The return will be made to the collector, and he will tender the license. If the party declines to receive the license and pay therefor, and yet continues the business for which the law requires him to have a license, he will be liable to the penalty under section 73.

Proceedings when a party liable refuses to apply for a license.

(No. 69.)

If a person who sells goods or produce along a railroad has, at any station on the railroad, a temporary place of business—if, for instance, he rents or *uses* a part of the depot or warehouse or a railway car as a place of sale or exchange—he is liable to take a dealer's license.

Persons selling goods along a railroad subject to license as dealers.

(No. 70.)

Boarding-houses are not taxable as hotels. The difference between a boarding-house and a hotel is apparent.

As a general thing, the main point of difference is, that hotels are open, to all who choose to enter, without previous stipulation, expecting entertainment unless the house is full; while a boarding-house is only open to those who, by previous arrangement, have acquired a right to entertainment at such rate of payment as the keeper of the house may fix and agree upon.

Hotels, inns, taverns, boarding-houses, general principles by which to define.

(No. 71.)

A license only covers one exhibition, and is valid only in State where issued.

A circus proprietor, having taken out license as such, cannot include other distinct shows for which a separate ticket is sold, but for each he must take out a separate license; and a license granted in any one State does not authorize the holder to exhibit his circus out of the State in which the license was granted.—(Sect. 79, art. 38.)

(No. 72.)

A letter has been received at this office stating that assessors have issued instructions to the effect that persons crying sales for farmers who sell their stock by auction were not to be considered auctioneers.

Who may sell at auction without taking out license therefor.

All persons who make sales by auction, except those selling by virtue of a judgment or decree of a court, or at sales made by executors and administrators, or as employés of a duly licensed auctioneer, are required to take out licenses as auctioneers, and to pay the tax of one fourth of one per cent. upon their sales.

(No. 73.)

Shot manufacturers need not have a dealer's license for their stores or offices, in certain cases.

A shot manufacturer who has his tower or manufactory three miles from his office or principal place of business, at which his sales are made, need not have a dealer's license for such office. His license as a manufacturer enables him to sell at his office or principal place of business, provided no goods, wares, or merchandise shall be kept for sale at such office or principal place of business.—(Sections 74, 81.)

(No. 74.)

Parties applying for licenses liable therefor, although they may subsequently discontinue the business for which they were required.

A person having made application for license, and continuing the business for a time subsequent thereto, is liable for the amount of the license; and the fact of his having abandoned the business prior to the license having been tendered him does not in the least affect his liability, or present a bar to the commencement of proceedings for the recovery of the amount of the license legally assessed upon him.

(No. 75.)

Taxes paid for licenses may be deducted.

It is presumed that all taxes paid for licenses, and those paid by manufacturers and others making monthly returns, are ordinarily charged as "expenses" in the prosecution of business, or the "cost" of production. Assessors, however, should carefully guard against the same items being deducted a second time in the return of income.

(No. 76.)

Parties purchasing Canada currency and gold to meet notes held by Canadian banks not subject to broker's license.

A person who purchases Canada currency and gold solely for the purpose of meeting notes held by the banks of Canada cannot be held liable for a broker's license therefor.

(No. 77.)

"Mercantile agencies" and "intelligence offices" may be liable to assessment for license under section 79, article 49. Mercantile agencies and intelligence offices.

(No. 78.)

Salaried agents of the Sanitary Commission who prosecute claims for soldiers are liable to license tax as claim agents. Agents of Sanitary Commission who prosecute soldiers' claims.

(No. 79.)

A person whose "business it is to sell medicine by the bottle, and who gives the purchaser an opportunity to draw a ticket from a box which may entitle the holder to some article of jewelry" as a prize, is a lottery ticket dealer under the provisions of article 6, section 79, and liable to a license tax accordingly.—(See also sect. 111, stat. June 30, 1864.) "Gift enterprises" subject to same rules as lotteries.

(No. 80.)

A "gift concert" is held to be a lottery, and the managers, superintendents, and sellers of the tickets are required to take out a license as lottery ticket dealers, and to pay the tax as required in section 111, unless the managers should first obtain the benefits of the first proviso to said section. "Gift concerts" subject to same rules as lotteries, except in certain cases.

(No. 81.)

A person wishing to purchase wool may send agents into different parts of the country to purchase the same. If these agents do not offer themselves to the public for such service, nor accept orders from other parties, a license is unnecessary. If it is their business, as agents of others, to make such purchases, they are commercial brokers, and must be licensed as such. Agents may purchase wool for a principal, provided they are not agents for more than one party.

(No. 82.)

A person who purchases on his own account, or receives from nurserymen, to be sold on commission, fruit-trees, evergreens, flowers, &c., which he sells at his farm, garden, store, shop, or other place of business, is liable for a dealer's license. Nurserymen delivering trees, &c., as agents or principals, must have a license therefor; but agents, merely taking orders which are filled by principals duly licensed, are exempt.

If he delivers such trees by wagons or on foot, travelling from place to place, either selling them at the time or delivering them to fill orders previously solicited, receiving pay therefor, he is liable to a license as a peddler. But if the party is employed by the nurseryman, or dealer in trees, to travel from place to place simply to take orders, which orders are sent to the place of business of his principal that they may be filled, and the trees delivered from said place, such a party would not be held liable to any license therefor.

(No. 83.)

The same principles apply to the buying and selling of corn, wheat, and other grain, as to the purchase and sale of tobacco. Commercial broker's business defined.

Parties who buy and sell those products are dealers, wholesale or retail, as the case may be.

A person who, as agent for others, makes a business of buying corn, wheat, tobacco, &c., is liable to license as a commercial broker. But a person who purchases these products for a single firm or house, or who purchases the same to be forwarded to other markets to be sold on commission, is not liable to take license if he makes no sales himself.

(No. 84.)

Liquor sellers on board steamboats are subject to license independent of hotel license.

If a steamboat owner sells liquor on board his boat, he must take out license as liquor dealer for each boat. This license is independent of his license under article 20, section 79, relating to hotels.

(No. 85.)

Butchers may not sell from carts *and* stalls, without taking out two licenses.

Any person having taken a license to sell butcher's meat from a stall is not authorized, under such license, to make sales from a cart; nor can a person licensed to sell from a cart make sales at a stall under the same license. If sales are made both from a cart and from a stall, two licenses will be required.

(No. 86.)

Owners of stallions and jacks must take license for each animal.
Where to be taken; description; not limited to particular places for use.

The owners of stallions or jacks must take a license for *each* animal kept for purposes as stated in section 79 of the act of June 30, 1864. The license must be taken in the district where the owner resides, and must contain a brief description of the animal, its age, and place or places where to be used. The law does not restrict the use of the animal to the place named in the license.

(No. 87.)

Changes cannot be made of licenses; new ones must be procured when there is a change in business.

If any person holding a license as peddler of the fourth class shall become liable to, or shall desire a license of the second or third class, he should be charged the full amount of such last-named license, the same as though he had previously held no license. Such a change is a change in the business of the party, for which the law affords no remedy.

(No. 88.)

Lottery ticket dealers required to take license notwithstanding such business may be prohibited by the laws of the State in which it is carried on.

Every person or firm that shall make, sell, or offer to sell lottery tickets, should be required to take license under article 6 of section 79, notwithstanding such a business may be prohibited by the laws of the State in which it is carried on.—(Sects. 78, 111.)

(No. 89.)

Peddlers of lightning-rods subject to taxation.

A person who travels from place to place, in the street or through different parts of the country, with one, two, or more horses, transporting lightning-rods, which he sells and puts up as he can find customers, and receives his pay therefor, is liable to a peddler's license.

(No. 90.)

A license as wholesale or retail liquor dealer, granted by a United States collector, does not authorize sales of liquor in violation of State law; but if sales are made in such States without such license, the offenders are liable to the penalties named in section 73.—(See sect. 78.)

Licenses do not authorize sales in violation of State laws, but parties are bound to procure licenses.

(No. 91.)

No license is required of a farmer for the sale of agricultural products of his own farm, unless his gross receipts exceed the sum of $1,000 per annum.—(Sect. 79, art. 49.)

Liability of farmers.

(No. 92.)

It seems that the authority of a licensed auctioneer to make sales is not limited to the district or State where the license was granted.—(Sec. 74.)

Authority of auctioneer not limited territorially.

(No. 93.)

A licensed manufacturer may sell his own products at the place of manufacture without license as a dealer. If, however, he receives other goods, wares or merchandise for sale, he becomes liable as a dealer, and must take license therefor.

Licensed manufacturers may sell their own goods at place of manufacture without license as dealer, but may not sell other goods without license.

(No. 94.)

If a person having a license for the transaction of a particular business desires to take a partner in the same business at the same place, the license may be transferred under section 75 of the excise law, and it will cover the business of the firm so formed for the remainder of the time for which such license was granted. For exceptions to this rule, see section 79.

New partners may be admitted and licenses transferred for remainder of term for which they were granted.

(No. 95.)

Any person who shall sell liquors in quantities of more than three gallons at one time and to the same purchaser, will be required to take license as a wholesale dealer in liquors, although such sales may not amount to twenty-five thousand dollars per annum. Persons selling liquors at retail, whose annual sales each shall exceed twenty-five thousand dollars, will also be required to take license as wholesale dealers in liquors. The amount of license tax in the latter case will be determined by article 4 of section 79.

Parties selling liquor in greater quantities than 3 gallons to one purchaser, are subject to license as wholesale dealers.

(No. 96.)

Parties who advertise themselves as claim agents must take license as such, whether they actually do such business or not.

If persons prepare the papers which are necessary for parties applying for pensions, and send such papers to claim agents at Washington to be used in obtaining pensions, they become claim agents, and must take license accordingly.

Persons advertising themselves as claim agents, must take license accordingly.

(No. 97.)

Butchers who sell by the quarter or carcass, and whose annual sales exceed $25,000.

A butcher's license under article 36, section 79,* does not cover sales by the quarter or by the carcass when the annual aggregate of such sales exceeds twenty-five thousand dollars. He is then liable to a license as a wholesale dealer under article 2, section 79.

(No. 98.)

Tanners may sell wool obtained in their business without further license.

A tanner may sell at his tannery the wool taken from the pelts which he tans under his manufacturers' license, it being a legitimate part of his business.

(No. 99.)

A clerk or agent employed by a person, firm, or corporation, not classed as a commercial broker, though he may manage business matters in regard to vessels, &c. in the ordinary course of the business of such person, firm, or corporation.

A person who is employed by the Western Transportation Company as their clerk or agent, at their cost, and to manage business matters, not for the owners of vessels, nor for the shippers or consignees of the freight carried by the vessels, but for the Western Transportation Company exclusively, is not, on that account, required to take out license as a commercial broker.

(No. 100.)

Right of a farmer to sell his produce by peddling.

A person who sells the products of his farm by travelling from house to house and disposing of the same wherever he finds a purchaser is not, under the law, considered a peddler; but in case he has wheat or other grain raised by him "floured at the mill" before attempting to sell the same, he is then liable to license as a peddler or dealer, as the case may be.

If he sell from store or stall.

Farmers selling the produce of their farms through the medium of a store or a stall are liable to license as "dealers" if their sales thereby exceed $1,000 per annum.

(No. 101.)

Dealers in trees.

Two classes of dealers in trees are required to take license as dealers; those who produce the trees and sell them to dealers or farmers, and those who purchase trees and make sale of them either as dealers or peddlers.

The liability of the latter class to take license as dealers could not be questioned even if the producers should be exempted from license tax.

Growing of trees not considered "farming."

The growing of fruit trees and forest trees for shade or ornament cannot be considered as belonging to the business of farming. Farmers, for the most part, produce those articles only which enter immediately into the consumption of the country; but a fruit tree is rather a means by which the crop of the farmer is to be ultimately obtained.

The arts of budding and grafting, which are essential to the business of a nursery-man, are not necessarily nor generally known to the farmer.

Dealers whose sales are less than $1,000 a year are, of course, exempt.

(No. 102.)

When demand for payment of license is made the collector or deputy should be prepared to deliver the license, if the demand is complied with.

License to be delivered on payment.

(No. 103.)

The owner or lessee of coal lands may sell at the place of production without license.

Owner of coal mine may sell coal at the mine without license.

(No. 104.)

A chiropodist must take out a surgeon's license for a particular place, which must be specified in the license, and under it he may travel and perform surgical operations.—(Sections 74, 79.)

Chiropodist to take surgeon's license. Rights under it.

(No. 105.)

The milk of a farmer's cows is considered as among the products of his farm, and no license is required for the sale thereof.

Farmers do not require licenses for sale of milk.

A person other than a farmer, who keeps cows and makes the sale of milk an occupation, is not embraced in the above ruling and will be required to take a license.

Other persons.

(No. 106.)

Millers selling their flour and meal are liable to license as dealers. If they forward it to commission merchants in New York or elsewhere to be sold for them they are not required to take license as dealers for sales so made.

Millers making sales subject to license.

A person licensed as "commercial broker" may, as the agent of others, purchase spirituous liquors, but he cannot sell such liquors without license as liquor dealer.

A commercial broker may purchase but not sell liquors without license.

(No. 107.)

Licenses may be issued to parties as "dealers in the Washington markets," and under said license they may be authorized to sell in either or any of the recognized markets or market-places in the city without additional license therefor.

Dealers in the markets of Washington.

(No. 108.)

A license to a firm of cattle-brokers will authorize the members thereof to pursue the vocation at different places at the same time. Each member should be able however to exhibit a license, when called upon.—(Sections 74, 79.)

Cattle-broker's license.

(No. 109.)

The fact that a person has taken out a wrong license does not free him from the necessity of taking out the proper one, nor the assessor of the district from seeing that a proper application is made.

When an error is made by an applicant for a license.

Mode of procedure to obtain return of fee.

Where such person has taken out a correct license he can make a claim upon this office for the amount of the incorrect license fee, accompanied by a statement of the facts, indorsed by the assessor of the district.

(No. 110.)

Applicants for license who die.

When a person who may have applied for license shall die before the license is issued, the tax becomes a charge against the estate of the deceased, and should be collected of the administrator or executor. This is especially the case when the license applied for is that of a dealer, and the administrator closes the business of the deceased.

(No. 111.)

Hucksters, &c., where licensed as dealers.

Where as peddlers.

Hucksters, butchers, or peddlers, residing in one district, and making their purchases there, but selling in another district, will require license, if dealers, in the district where sales are made. If they require license as peddlers, they should be licensed where they reside, but they are allowed to travel and sell in any district in the United States, unless prohibited by State laws.

LIQUORS DISTILLED AND FERMENTED.

(No. 112.)

Beer may be removed by brewer without payment of tax in certain cases.

The manufacturer of beer, lager beer, or ale, may, according to the provisions of section 65, remove the same to a depot owned or hired by him, in another collection district, and carried on by the brewer or his agent, in the sole interest of the brewer. He may sell the same, so removed, without being required to take a license. But agents selling beer, lager beer, or ale, at other localities, without a permit for its removal from the place of manufacture as above, must take license.

Payment of the duty at the place of manufacture does not authorize the manufacturer to sell anywhere else without license as a dealer.

(No. 113.)

Distilled spirits not subject to additional tax when rectified.

When the tax has been paid on distilled spirits used by rectifiers, according to the excise law, no further tax can be assessed upon it after rectification.

(No. 114.)

Bonds when cancelled.

All bonds should be sent to this office when cancelled with the evidence upon which the collector cancelled them. When it appears that a bond has been cancelled by the payment of duties, the collector receiving the same will be charged with the amount so paid.

(No. 115.)

Who is a distiller.

The 16th article of the 79th section of the act of June 30, 1864, provides that "every person, firm, or corporation, who distils or manufactures spirits for sale, shall be deemed a distiller under the act."

If a brewer distils liquors for sale, he requires a distiller's license, and he must pay the duty upon the liquor distilled by him, whether it is sold used or consumed on his premises.—(Sec. 93.)

If a brewer distils spirits, he must pay duty.

(No. 116.)

Wines are not classed among spirituous liquors, mentioned in section 93 of the excise law, and are exempt from taxation when the manufacture and sales do not amount to $600 per annum.

Wines not spirituous liquors.

MANUFACTURES.

(No. 117.)

"Chair frames" or "chair seat frames" being complete in themselves, and having a commercial value, must be considered and taxed as manufactures, and the makers thereof must take out manufacturers' license, unless exempt by reason of the provisions of section 93.

Chair frames and chair seat frames are manufactures.

(No. 118.)

The word "premises," which, by the opinion of the solicitor of the treasury of October 1, 1862, is regarded as equivalent to the phrase "place of manufacture," as used in the excise laws, is not susceptible of any broader construction than the "place of manufacture," although, upon ordinary principles of interpretation, a broader construction might be justifiable.

Construction as to the words "premises" and "place of manufacture."

The word "premises" can mean nothing more than the place in which, or the place at which the manufacture is carried on, whether the place be a single room, in a building containing many rooms, or whether it be several buildings, and the ground under and around the same.

Whatever is occupied and used for the purposes of manufacture must be regarded as "premises" or "place of manufacture," and any removal of goods therefrom before the first of September, 1862, which was intended and will clearly serve to distinguish such goods from those afterwards produced, must be held as exempting them from duty.

(No. 119.)

The following regulation has been adopted: "That the process of uniting the parts of a glass lamp, as the foot, the fountain, and the burner, by the use of plaster of paris cement, or other analogous means, is not regarded as a manufacture."

Finishing glass ware exempt.

This decision will apply to glass inkstands, with metallic tops, united by the same or similar means.

(No. 120.)

Lamp manufacturers to be assessed on full value of products.

In the manufacture of lamps, a glass manufacturer who uses brass, or other substances which have paid a tax, must be assessed upon the gross value of his products.

(No. 121.)

Looking-glass plate a manufacture.

The process of preparing looking-glass plate is considered a manufacture, and the plate is subject to a duty of five per cent. ad valorem.

Insertion of plate in a frame exempt from duty.

The mere insertion of a plate in a frame is not a new manufacture.

(No. 122.)

Pearlash and potash deemed to be manufactures.

Pearlash and potash are manufactures, and as such are subject to a duty of five per cent. ad valorem, under section 94 of the excise law.

(No. 123.)

Definition of the term "Roman cement."

The phrase "Roman or water cement" was intended to cover the various hydraulic cements that are used for the same or similar purposes, and they are subject to a duty of three per cent.—(Sect. 94.)

(No. 124.)

Oil-cake exempt.

As "oil-cake" is merely an incident to the process of manufacturing linseed oil, and undergoes no other treatment than what is necessary to extract the oil from the seed, it cannot be taxed as a manufacture.

(No. 125.)

Grinding of salt exempt.

The grinding of salt, to adapt it to culinary and table uses, cannot be considered a manufacture.

(No. 126.)

Stearine a manufacture.

Stearine is subject to a duty of five per centum ad valorem. The opinion concerning the liability of stearine to duty is based upon the belief that it is not a mere residuum obtained in the manufacture of lard oil, but that it undergoes a further process of manufacture.

(No. 127.)

Cake not taxable as confectionery, unless so known to the trade.

Cake cannot be legally taxed as confectionery, even if composed of more than one-fourth sugar, as it is evident that it is not so considered by confectioners.

The rule is to follow the fixed and known customs of the trade, and tax as confectionery only those articles which are known in commerce as such.

Such cake as is made for ornament rather than as an article of food should be regarded as confectionery, and as such taxed.

Cake made for ornament and not for food taxable.

(No. 128.)

Galvanized iron is a distinct and well-known article of commerce, and as such must be treated as a manufacture.

Galvanized iron a manufacture and taxable at its increased value.

This being established, it only remains to inquire whether it is to be taxed at its full value, or only at its increased value over the rough iron used in its manufacture.

A few articles are enumerated in sections 94 and 95, and made subject to taxation on their increased value only. Galvanized iron is among the articles so enumerated, and hence it follows that the tax must be assessed upon its increased value only.

(No. 129.)

Wire cloth is an article of trade, and though it is often made upon order and for special purposes, or to be used in machines that are subject to taxation, the manufacturer of wire cloth is subject to tax upon the amount of his sales.

Wire cloth not exempt.

(No. 130.)

The setting of a horseshoe is no part of its manufacture.

Setting of horseshoes not a manufacture.

The business of toeing and corking old shoes is classed as repairing.

Corking old shoes repairs.

Manufacturers of shoes by machinery must pay an ad valorem tax of five per cent.; and if the shoer afterwards puts toes and corks to them they become a new manufacture, and are subject to taxation.

New shoes, how taxed.

(No. 131.)

The planing of boards for flooring, &c., is not held to be a manufacture. Whenever any operation is performed upon boards by which they lose their distinctive name as "lumber," and assume a new name, as an article of commerce, and not as lumber, then they are liable to taxation as a manufacture. Planing, grooving, and bevelling boards do not make them any the less lumber.

Planing, grooving, and bevelling boards not a manufacture.

(No. 132.)

Charcoal is not a farm product, and any person who sells coal while travelling from place to place in the street, or through different parts of the country, is subject to license tax as a peddler. If he sell at a fixed place, he is liable as a dealer when his sales exceed $1,000 per annum.

Charcoal not a farm product.

Dealers therein subject to license.

(No. 133.)

A cutting apparatus of mowing or reaping machine, being complete in itself, and sold in the market separately, is liable to taxation.

Cutters of mowing machines liable to tax.

(No. 134.)

Tax to be paid in district where mine is located.

If a coal mine is situated in one district, and the office of the company producing the coal in another district, the tax must be paid in the district where the mine is opened.

Owners or lessees of coal land, who take out coal for their own use only as manufacturers, must pay the tax of 5 cents per ton.

Under the original law coal-dealers, whose sales are less than $600 per annum, are liable to duty; but the late act of Congress of June 30, 1864, section 93, contains a provision that producers whose annual product does not exceed $600 are exempt, provided it is produced by the labor of the person claiming exemption, or by the labor of his family.

(No. 135.)

Coke being a residuum and not a manufacture, is not taxable.

Coke, as produced in the manufacture of gas, being rather a residuum than a specific manufacture, is not the subject of taxation under the excise law. If the supposition be correct that coke is not produced as a distinct and leading manufacture, nor as a manufacture known to trade, the production of it as a preparation of coal for the purpose of smelting iron ore cannot be regarded as a manufacture.

For the present, and on the information I now have, I hold that coke produced by manufacturers of pig iron, and for the purpose of smelting iron ore, and so used by the party producing it, is exempt from taxation as a manufacture under the excise law.*

(No. 136.)

Doors, sashes, &c., made by ship-joiners, subject to taxation as manufactures; and if to an extent exceeding $1,000 per annum, liable to license as manufacturers also.

Ship-joiners often manufacture doors, sashes, panels, &c., which they set up and fix in their places on ship-board. These articles have a separate commercial name and value. Those who devote themselves exclusively to their manufacture are merely manufacturers. Those who manufacture them in connexion with other business not taxable, must take license and pay tax on them. Hence ship-joiners, if they manufacture taxable articles, should be taxed therefor; and if they manufacture them to the amount of $1,000 per year, they must take license as manufacturers.—(Sect. 79, art. 31, and sect. 93.)

(No. 137.)

Sashes, doors, &c., taxable.

Articles made from wood, such as sash, doors, blinds, &c., which, though designed for some particular building, have of themselves a distinct and commercial value in the market as articles of traffic, are manufactures, and must pay the tax of five per cent. ad valorem.

Coffins and headboards taxable.

Coffins and headboards, if made in such a manner that they would have a specific value of their own if placed in the market for sale, are to be taxed five per cent. as manufactures.

---

* By the act of June 30, 1864, section 96, coke is exempt; but the principle is applicable to other articles, as oil-cake, for example.

(No. 138.)

Articles made by the use of a saw alone are treated as lumber, and are exempt from taxation. Articles made with a saw alone not taxable.

(No. 139.)

According to section 94 of the act of June 30, 1864, all cotton cloths on which the excise duty has been paid shall, if bleached, be assessed five per centum upon the increased value of the cloth. Cotton cloths subject to duty on their increased value by bleaching.

Bleached cloths manufactured from brown cloths imported, and on which the impost duty has been paid, are subject to duty at the rate of 5 per cent. on their increased value.—(Sect. 95.) Duty on bleached cottons made of imported brown cloths.

(No. 140.)

Enamelled cloth is taxable only on increased value of the cloth of which it is made.—(See 95th section of the excise law.) Enamelled cloth taxable upon increased value only.

It is required that a tax should be paid on the whole value of the manufacture of enamelled cloth, unless it can be shown that the cotton cloth was intended for that use, and that it had previously paid the excise tax, or an import duty, or that it was manufactured prior to September 1, 1862. These conditions existing, the tax would be assessed only on the increased value.—(Sect. 95.)

(No. 141.)

Copper coating is a manufacture, and the assessment must be made upon the increased value of the coated bolts, spikes, and other articles.—(Sect. 95.) Copper-coated bolts, spikes, &c., to be taxed on their increased value.

(No. 142.)

Metallic compositions, made from copper, antimony, tin, sulphur, tar, rosin, and naphtha, and used exclusively for the bottoms of vessels as a substitute for copper sheathings, cannot be regarded as paints, but should be classed as manufactures "not otherwise provided for," and taxed 5 per cent. ad valorem. Composition sheathings, 3 per cent.

(No. 143.)

Sheet-iron stoves and stove furniture are undoubtedly manufactures. Sheet-iron stoves and stove furniture are manufactures.

(No. 144.)

From the statements made it appears that zinc ore, as dug from the mine, is first calcined and crushed, then placed in the furnace, melted, and run out in the form of slabs, or pigs, and in this form is called "*spelter*, or zinc metal." Spelter not subject to duty.

The question arises whether this article, in the form described, is liable to taxation under the excise law. As the law levies duties only on the "oxide of zinc," and "manufactures of zinc," "spelter, or the zinc of commerce," cannot be regarded as a manufacture in the sense of the law, and, therefore, it is not subject to duty as such.

(No. 145.)

Value of iron hoops not to be deducted from articles of which they form a part.

In estimating the value of cooper's work hooped with iron, on which to assess the tax, the value of such iron hoops should not be deducted.

(No. 146.)

A vessel not taxable if keel was laid before March 3, 1863.

Taxable if finished on or after June 30, 1864.

Under the construction which has been given to the law, ships, barks, canal-boats, and other vessels, are exempt from duty, if their keels were laid prior to March 3, 1863; but a vessel finished on or after June 30, 1864, is subject to tax, at the rate of two per cent. on the value of the hull, without reference to the time when her keel was laid.—(Stat. June 30, 1864, sect. 94.)

(No. 147.)

Blacksmiths and *mechanics generally* to be taxed as manufacturers.

Repairing exempt in certain cases.

A blacksmith must be considered as a manufacturer, and subject to taxation, if his business is sufficiently large.

Repairs which do not add ten per cent. to the value of the articles should be deducted in estimating the receipts of mechanics.—(Sect. 95.)

Smith's work on vessels subject to taxation.

The question whether a blacksmith shall pay a duty on the iron work for a vessel which he has contracted for, is not affected at all by the fact that the vessel will or will not be subject to a tax of two per centum when completed, and hence the time of laying the keel has nothing to do with the question of liability of the iron work. All such work, if taxable when offered for sale, is equally taxable when made for use.

(No. 148.)

Binders exempt for books, such as law books, &c.

Bookbinders are exempt from taxation on all printed books they may bind for publishers. The latter are liable to a duty of 5 per cent. ad valorem.—(Sect. 95.)

(No. 149.)

Preparation of corn husks a manufacture.

The preparation of corn husks, consisting in cleaning the husks, hackling them, and putting them up in bales for the market, is deemed a manufacture.

(No. 150.)

Slate in the rough exempt from taxation.

School slates are subject to tax.

Roofing slate, mantels, and table tops, &c., in the rough, are exempt under the 94th section of the excise law, but when finished, they are subject to a duty of 3 per cent. ad valorem. School slates must be considered as manufactures of slate, and, as such, subject to 5 per cent. tax ad valorem.

(No. 151.)

If a person makes gangs of rigging, or parts of gangs, such as stays, guys, shrouds, or other standing rigging which has a separate commercial name and value, he must be considered and treated as a manufacturer.

Ship's rigging taxable in certain cases.

If the customer furnishes the materials, the rigger must pay the tax, but may charge it in his bill for labor, and has a lien upon the rigging until the bill is paid.

(No. 152.)

Cheese is not considered a manufacture within the meaning of the law, consequently no duty is to be assessed upon it; neither is a license required to manufacture it.—(Sect. 96.)

Cheese not a manufacture, and therefore exempt from taxation.

(No. 153.)

Maccaroni and vermicelli are classed as "manufactures not otherwise provided for," and subject to a tax of five per cent. under section 94 of the law of June 30, 1864.

Maccaroni and vermicelli subject to taxation as manufactures.

(No. 154.)

Ice-cream is not a manufacture within the meaning of the law, and it is therefore exempt from taxation.

Ice-cream not a manufacture, and exempt from taxation.

(No. 155.)

Bobbins for cotton and woollen mills are liable to a 5 per cent. ad valorem duty as a manufacture. The party or parties who furnish stock out of which the bobbins are made are liable to license, either wholesale or retail, on the same grounds as dealers in other goods, articles, merchandise, or commodities; but there is no reason why the rough material should be required to pay an ad valorem tax.

Bobbins subject to taxation.

(No. 156.)

Horseshoe nails wrought by machinery should be assessed at the rate of five per centum ad valorem, as a "manufacture not otherwise provided for."

Horseshoe nails subject to duty

(No. 157.)

Articles of manufacture well known and generally used are taxable, though made to order. Such are smoke chimneys, sheet-iron exhaust pipes, blow-off pipes, connecting pipes for steam-engines, &c. A piece of old material wrought into an article substantially new does not exempt the latter from taxation.

Articles taxable, though made to order.

(No. 158.)

Whenever the manufacture of an article liable to stamp duty under Schedule C. makes his own packets, boxes, or cases, and

A manufacturer of articles subject to stamp duty under Schedule C. not liable to tax on the packages if made by himself.

affixes the required stamp answering to the duty imposed, he is not liable to an additional duty as the manufacturer of the packets, boxes, or cases.

(No. 159.)

Oysters put up in kegs not taxable. When in air-tight cans subject to duty.

Oysters put up in kegs, not air-tight, are not liable to tax.

Fresh oysters, put up in air-tight tin cans, are without doubt subject to duty.

(No. 160.)

Pickles and preserves subject to taxation. Not liable to reassessment if put into smaller packages. "Air-tight" bottles defined. Cost of cans not to be included in amount on which tax is levied.

Pickles and preserves are subject to taxation under all circumstances, but are not liable to be again assessed in consequence of removal from casks into smaller packages.

Bottles, whether hermetically sealed or not, are deemed to be air-tight if impervious to air.

The cost of cans is not to be included in the amount on which the tax is levied.

Vegetables in air-tight packages are not liable to taxation, unless desiccated or otherwise prepared.

(No. 161.)

Desiccated vegetables a manufacture.

Mixed, dried, and pressed vegetables, known by the term "desiccated," such as cabbages, turnips, potatoes, beets, carrots, parsnips, onions, tomatoes, celery, parsley, &c., are to be classed among the "articles not otherwise provided for," and the manufacturers must pay a duty of five per cent. ad valorem thereon.

(No. 162.)

Articles manufactured by a State without the intervention of contractors are exempt from taxation.

Articles manufactured by a State in a penitentiary, or elsewhere, if made under the direction of State officers for the benefit of the State, without the intervention of contractors, are not subject to taxation under the excise law.

(No. 163.)

Ornaments, &c., for accoutrements, if, &c., not subject to tax.

Brasses, which are bought by the manufacturer of accoutrements and delivered in original packages with the accoutrements, are not subject to tax as a part of the accoutrements.

Trimmings for harness to be included in assessment when completed.

The trimmings which are buckled into harness become a part thereof, and in such cases the tax must be levied upon the whole value of the manufactures, including the trimmings.

(No. 164.)

Mode of rendering returns of soda-water manufacturers.

Manufacturers of soda-water should make return monthly of all sales in fountains, and the price received for the same. No account should be taken of the fountain. Manufacturers will also return in the same manner the gross amount of sales made in bottles, or other packages. The cost of the bottles and packages should be deducted before the tax of five per cent. ad valorem is levied.

(No. 165.)

Drawbacks can be allowed only upon the article on which a tax has been paid. When alcohol on which the duty has been paid is manufactured into cologne, or perfumed waters, it becomes a new and different article, on which drawback could not be allowed, merely because a tax had been paid on the alcohol.

Drawback can be allowed only on articles on which the duty has been paid.

NOTE.—This ruling is modified by the statute of June 30, 1864, section 168.

(No. 166.)

Articles of clothing made without order or measure, and placed in a store for sale to any person who may desire to purchase, should be regarded as made "for sale generally," and should be taxed at the rate of five per cent. ad valorem.

When goods made to order are taxable.

When boots and shoes made upon special orders are not taken by the persons ordering them, and are placed in a store for general sale, they should be classed as above, and taxed at the rate of five per centum ad valorem.—(Sect. 94.)

(No. 167.)

Tailors, boot and shoe makers, milliners, dress makers, and manufacturers of hats, caps, or bonnets, who make partly for sale generally and partly to order as custom work, are liable to a tax of five per cent. upon their entire sales, when they exceed $600 per annum.—(Sect. 95.)

Tax on clothing made for sale generally, and to order.

(No. 168.)

A manufacturing company having a house in the city where the sales of the company are made, not by an agency, but by the company itself, should be allowed for the expenses of such sales an amount not exceeding three per cent.—(Sect. 86.)

Manufacturing companies making their own sales may deduct for expenses thereof not exceeding three per cent.

(No. 169.)

It has been reported to this office that manufacturers of saddle-trees in the county of ****** are assessed only on their profits, when they should pay an ad valorem duty on their products.

Saddlers subject to ad valorem duty on products as well as tax on profits.

If this is so, you will please instruct your assistant assessors to make their assessments ad valorem.

(No. 170.)

Isinglass made from "sounds" of fish is classed as a manufacture not otherwise provided for, subject to an ad valorem duty of five per cent.

Isinglass a manufacture.

(No. 171.)

The recutting of files is held to be a manufacture, and such files are subject to a duty of five per centum ad valorem.

Recutting files a manufacture.

(No. 172.)

The refining of soda, nitre, and camphor, manufactures.

The refining of crude nitrate of soda, saltpetre, and camphor, is each regarded as a manufacture, and the manufacturer should be assessed five per cent. upon the full value of his products.

(No. 173.)

Bonnets in the rough subject to tax.

A manufacturer who sells bonnets in the rough will pay tax upon the value of the same when sold by him, and the person who finishes them will pay tax upon their increased value when finished.

When finished and trimmed are manufactures.

Hats and bonnets, on which an import or excise duty has been paid, that are trimmed, cut, or changed, in shape or style, are treated as manufactures, and as such are taxable upon the increased value.—(Sect. 95.)

(No. 174.)

Taxation upon tailors, &c.

Tailors, boot and shoe makers, hat, cap, and bonnet makers, milliners and dressmakers, who manufacture any articles for sale generally, are liable to an excise tax of five per centum upon the entire product, although a portion may be made to order as custom work. When the entire product is made to order and as custom work, the rate is three per cent. upon the excess above the sum of six hundred dollars per annum.

(No. 175.)

Hoop-poles exempt.

Hoop-poles, split and trimmed for box-straps, should not be held as a manufacture, nor liable to duty.

(No. 176.)

Preparing hair for upholsterer's use a manufacture.

Hatchelling and twisting of hair into ropes, to curl and lighten the hair preparatory to its use in upholstering, is a manufacture, and taxable under section 94.

(No. 177.)

Sized or bleached wrapping cotton a manufacture.

Sized or bleached wrapping cotton twine and cord are liable to an ad valorem duty of 5 per cent., and this liability is not at all affected by the fact that the twine or cord or thread has previously been assessed and paid tax in the raw state.

(No. 178.)

"Tin roofing" is not a manufacture, nor taxable.

"Tin roofing" is not a manufacture, nor taxable.

(No. 179.)

Patentees employing other parties to manufacture patented articles subject to taxation therefor.

By decision No. 77, whenever a person is the owner of a patent or of the right to manufacture a patented article, and employs other parties to make such patented articles, the patentee or owner of the patent right will be regarded as the manufacturer, and the tax will be assessed upon the sales as made by him or his agents.

This decision, it seems to me, covers the case referred to. The exclusive right to manufacture and sell these sewing-machines is vested in Mr. ——, by virtue of his patent.

He must be regarded as the manufacturer, not simply by construction, but legally, though the entire mechanical labor and the materials used in the production of these machines are furnished by other parties.

Mr. ——, then, being legally the manufacturer, all the liability for taxes on the sewing-machines attaches to him, and the tax must be assessed upon the sales as made by him or his agents.

(No. 180.)

Manufacturers of shirts must pay an ad valorem duty of 3 or 5 per cent., as the case may be, though the materials used may have paid an import duty.

Shirts, though made of foreign materials, subject to duty.

Parties who manufacture shirt-bodies are liable, if the increased value added to the material exceeds the amount of 5 per cent. ad valorem.

Liability of manufacturers of shirt-bodies.

There is no clause other than the 96th section of the act of June 30, 1864, by which they can claim exemption, and they can claim it by that section only on the condition stated above.

(No. 181.)

Railroad chairs manufactured by rolling the iron at once into the chair-shaped bar, and not into the ordinary bar and then into shape and size for the chair, must be taxed at the rate of three dollars per ton.

Wrought railroad chairs, $3 per ton.

(No. 182.)

Two thousand pounds are deemed the equivalent of a ton in all cases under the excise law.—(Sect. 94.)

A ton 2,000 lbs. in all cases.

(No. 183.)

Railroad iron, made partly of old and partly of new iron, is to be regarded as new, and is liable to the duty of three dollars per ton.

Railroad iron made partly of old and partly of new iron to be regarded as new.

(No. 184.)

Every new car or locomotive must be regarded as a manufacture, and taxable as such, even though it be made to take the place of a car or locomotive which is worn out and thrown aside.

Articles made to replace similar articles which have been worn out not exempt as repairs.

An old car or engine is liable to an *ad valorem* tax on account of repairs made thereon, when such repairs increase its value ten per cent. or more; and all articles used in such repairs, or new parts furnished, which have in themselves a commercial value, and which would be liable to tax if sold, or removed from the place of manufacture for sale, are equally liable to tax when made for and used in the repairs of old cars or engines.

Old cars and engines when repaired to be taxed if the repairs increase the value 10 per cent. or more.

(No. 185.)

Tailors are manufacturers. The clothing which they manufacture is well known as an article of commerce.

Tailors manufacturers.

Clothing taxable.

If made to order, it still has a commercial value, independent of the fact that some one person is intended as the purchaser.

(No. 186.)

Muskets. Tax on the parts and on the full value of musket in certain cases.

The manufacturer of parts of muskets, as barrels, locks, &c., which have a commercial value, is liable to a tax thereon. If the assembling or putting the various parts together adds more than 5 per cent. to the value of the parts on which taxes have been assessed, a tax should be assessed upon the value of the musket.

(No. 187.)

Manufacturers of sorghum molasses need not be licensed. · Sorghum molasses not subject to duty

A person who manufactures molasses from sorghum need not be licensed as a manufacturer, and the molasses thus produced is not subject to a duty.

(No. 188.)

Yellow ochre a manufacture.

The production of yellow ochre is a manufacture, and subject to duty, as such, under the general clause, section 94.

(No. 189.)

The compounding of maple sugar with other sugar is held to be a confectory process, rendering the compound liable to the duty imposed upon sugar candy and other confectionery. And all sugars so compounded since the passage of the act of March 3d, 1863, must be assessed and returned to the collector.

Merely melting maple sugar not chargeable.

The mere melting of maple sugar, without compounding, is held not to be a confectory process, rendering it liable to tax.

(No. 190.)

Essential oils, 5 per cent.

Essential oils are subject to an ad valorem tax of 5 per cent. under the excise law.

(No. 191.)

Handles finished taxable as a manufacture.

A person who manufactures shovel and fork handles, with the exception of boring the head and fitting the lower end of the handle to the shovel, and boring the end of the handle to receive the fork, cannot claim exemption from the tax as a manufacturer. The law exempts from taxation partially wrought handles; that is, handles in the block, or rough form. Such as are finished, but not fitted, have a known and commercial value of their own, and must therefore be considered and taxed as manufactures.—(section 96.)

(No. 192.)

Box-making a manufacture.

The making of boxes is a manufacture of wood. Those making boxes will be considered and treated accordingly.

Barrels, when made by manufacturers of whatsoever article for the purposes of their business, are taxable as separate manufactures.

(No. 193.)

Millers and distillers who manufacture barrels for their own use, must pay duty on the entire product. When the annual product does not exceed the rate of $600, and is produced by the labor of the person or firm making the same, or by his or their family, the product is exempt from duty.—(Sect. 93.)

Barrels taxable as a separate manufacture.

When the annual product does not exceed the rate of $600.

(No. 194.)

Staves, hoops, and heading are not regarded as manufactures under the law. If, therefore, a person makes flour barrels from them, he must pay a tax of five per cent. ad valorem on the amount manufactured. When staves which have been prepared and set up, or fitted as casks, are sold in sets, they are not taxable as shooks, whether with or without hoops and heading. If a person uses barrel shooks, and sets them up as flour barrels, he would be considered a manufacturer, and liable to taxation.—(Sec. 96.)

Staves, hoops, and heading, not regarded as manufactures.

Shooks exempt. Barrels made from shooks taxable.

(No. 195.)

The sorting, cleaning, and tying of bristles into bundles cannot be considered a manufacture.

Sorting, &c., of bristles not a manufacture.

(No. 196.)

Coal is a production, and not a manufacture.

Coal a product.

All coals mined, except pea and dust coal, regardless of the use to which they are applied, are subject to duty under section 94.

The process of grinding and granulating pea and dust coal, reducing it to a uniform fineness, that it may be used by founderymen in forming their moulds, appears to be a manufacture, both by reason of the process involved and because a new article of trade is produced.

Coal ground for use of founderymen taxable as a manufacture.

(No. 197.)

A person engaged in the manufacture of salt, or any other article, who uses coal of his own production for fuel, is liable to taxation on such coal, as provided in the 94th section of the excise law.

If a person engaged in the manufacture of salt, also packs pork, and uses salt of his own manufacture, he is liable to tax on the salt so used, in the same manner as on that which he sells to other parties.

Persons producing coal and consuming it in the manufacture of salt, are liable to taxation upon the coal. If they manufacture barrels for packing salt, the barrels are taxable.

If the person above referred to manufactures the barrels in which he puts his salt, and also those used by him in packing pork, he is liable to tax on the barrels in the same manner as any one would be who might have manufactured them for him.—(See proviso to sect. 93.)

A pork packer who makes his own barrels should be assessed thereon.

(No. 198.)

Fire-bricks.

Fire-bricks are subject to a duty of five per cent. *ad valorem*, not being included under the term "bricks," as used in the 94th section of the excise law.

(No. 199.)

Oil-dressed leather defined.

The phrase "oil-dressed leather" is a technical term, applied by the trade to a certain kind of leather which is used in making gloves, mittens, moccasins, covering for the hammers moved by piano keys, and for several other like purposes. It does not apply to leather in which oil is used as a dressing, indiscriminately.

(No. 200.)

Neat's-foot oil a manufacture.

The making of neat's-foot oil is a manufacture.

(No. 201.)

Soles, &c., made from shavings, subject to tax.

Soles, stiffenings, &c., for shoes, made from the shavings pro duced by curriers of leather, should be regarded as manufactures, and taxed as such.

(No. 202.)

Finished or curried upper leather on which a tax has been paid in the rough, taxable on the increased value.

Finished or curried upper leather made from rough leather, on which the tax has previously been paid, is subject to an additional tax of five per cent. on the increased value in consequence of finishing or currying.

Harness leather.

The tax on harness leather is levied according to the same rule.

(No. 203)

The finisher of goat and sheep skins to be deemed a manufacturer.

The finisher of goat, kid, and sheep skins is to be regarded as the manufacturer, and the tax should be assessed upon the value of the finished skins. If they have been taxed previously in the rough, the tax is assessed on the increased value only.

(No. 204.)

Rule for assessing cloth dyed, printed, &c.

Under the proviso to section 94 the tax on cloths dyed, printed, or bleached, is to be assessed on the difference between the fair market value of the cloth before it is dyed, printed, &c., and its value when dyed, printed, &c., as shown by actual sales.

Thus, if the brown cloth sold at 15 cents, and the tax was assessed and paid on that valuation, and if the same cloth, when dyed, printed, &c., sold for 25 cents, ten cents must be considered the increased value, and the tax must be assessed accordingly.

(No. 205.)

Manufactured goods in the hands of an agent of the

If goods are sold through an agent, under salary, the tax will be levied upon the sale of goods from month to month. The transfer from the factory to the care of the agent for sale will not be considered such a removal as to require payment of tax within the same month unless the goods are sold also. manufacturer not liable to tax.

In other words, goods sent to an agent are regarded as still in the factory, and in such case the tax is due, when the goods are actually sold or removed from the agent's custody. To be taxed when sold or removed.

(No. 206.)

Cement pipe should be regarded as a manufacture and as such subject to tax. Cement pipe a manufacture.

(No. 207.)

The grinding of drugs is not a manufacture, unless they are compounded with some other drug or medicine. Grinding drugs not a manufacture unless compounded with another

(No. 208.)

If a railroad company refuse to make monthly returns and pay taxes, as it is held they are bound by law to do, under section 93, the assistant assessor will proceed to assess the company, upon such information as he may have, and the collector will collect such taxes in the same manner as is provided for the collection of taxes from delinquent persons, viz.: by distraint and sale of goods, chattels, or effects of said company. Railroad companies may be distrained for non-payment of taxes upon their manufactures.

(No. 209.)

Barges built by a railroad company for the transportation of freight across a river, should pay a duty of two per cent. ad valorem. Barges built by railroad companies, 2 per cent.

(No. 210.)

A rifle cannon is not in any commercial sense, or in the sense intended by the framers of the law, a "casting." Cannon subject to a duty of 5 per cent.

A cannon is a manufacture, and it would be a misnomer to call it anything else, and a failure to comprehend the requirements of the law to tax it as anything else. All manufacturers of cannon are required to pay thereon an ad valorem duty of 5 per cent.

Shot and shell may be taxed as castings under the act of June 30, 1864, section 94. Shot and shell taxable as castings.

(No. 211.)

"Piano actions" are not so peculiar in shape, size, or manner of construction as to entitle them to exemption from tax. Piano actions and strings taxable.

They have a commercial name; and if offered for sale, purchasers for them could easily be found.

For these reasons they must be treated as manufactures, and subject to 5 per cent. ad valorem tax. For similar reasons, the strings must be held liable to tax. If the value added to the wire does not exceed 5 per cent. ad valorem, the strings would be exempt under the 96th section of the act of June 30, 1864. The fact that the pianos are taxed on their full value in the finished state does not at all affect the question.

(No. 212.)

Duty on nails and spikes.

All articles that were commercially known and sold as cut nails and cut spikes at the time of the passage of the excise law are subject to the specific duty.

Tacks and brads.

Tacks and brads, not commercially known as nails and spikes at the time aforesaid, are to be taxed as unenumerated articles, subject to a duty of 5 per cent. ad valorem.

Usage determines the class to which articles belong.

The usage when the law was passed should determine the class to which any of these articles belong.

(No. 213.)

Definition of articles included in the phrase "stoves and hollow ware."

The phrase "Stoves and hollow-ware" is to be construed to include fire-frames, open grates for fire-frames, and registers.

(No. 214.)

Stereotype plates not deemed manufactures, and are, consequently, exempt from taxation.

Persons engaged in making stereotype plates are liable to license under section 79, article 49, and the plates are liable under the law to the tax of 5 per cent. ad valorem.

(No. 215.)

Metallic burial cases a manufacture.

"Metallic burial cases" are taxable as a manufacture, viz: 5 per cent. ad valorem, under the general provision of section 94, taxing "all manufactures of iron, steel, lead," &c., at that rate.

(No. 216.)

Silver consumed in plating goods not to be deducted in assessing.

Silver used in the manufacture of silver-plated ware is not to be deducted from the value of the manufactured article before assessing the tax.

Mode of procedure for determining as to "bullion used in the manufacture of silver ware."

The law provides only for the exemption of "bullion used in the manufacture of silver ware." Assessors should be satisfied upon two points before allowing the exemption in any specified case:

1st. That it is the material technically known to the trade as "bullion" which is used, and not any mixture or alloy; and,

2d. That the article produced is classed by the trade as "silver ware."

(No. 217,)

Value of bullion may be deducted from silver ware, but not from plated ware.

Silver ware is to be taxed for the value of the ware over the value of the bullion used in its manufacture.—(Sect. 96, stat. June 30, 1864.)

Silver bullion rolled or prepared for platers' use exclusively, is not taxable when so rolled or prepared; but the plated ware is taxable on in its full value.—(Stat. June 30, 1864, sect. 96.)

(No. 218.)

A coal-miner cannot be permitted to deduct a percentage for the pea and dust coal he has sold mixed with taxable coal. He must separate the two classes, or pay duty upon the whole amount sold.

Coal-miners cannot deduct a percentage for pea & dust coal when it is sold mixed with other coal.

(No. 219.)

Bone coal is subject to a duty of five per cent. ad valorem, as a manufacture not otherwise provided for.

Bone coal.

(No. 220.)

Vinegar should be taxed five per cent. without regard to the articles from which it is made.

Vinegar.

(No. 221.)

Crude turpentine, or pitch, should be classed as a manufacture, subject to a duty of five per cent.

Crude turpentine a manufacture.

(No. 222.)

There is no provision in the excise laws requiring shipping-masters to be licensed.

Shipping-masters.

STAMPS.

(No. 223.)

The manufacturer of a medicine who has or claims to have any private formula or occult secret or art of making or preparing the same, must cause the appropriate stamp to be affixed to each bottle or package, although he may intend to administer, and shall actually administer the same to patients who are under his personal charge.

Proprietary medicines must be stamped if administered by maker.

(No. 224.)

A renewal of a promissory note subjects it to the same amount of stamp as an original note.

A note renewed must be stamped.

(No. 225.)

Deeds of land made under the decree of a master in chancery are subject to stamp duty as conveyances.

Deeds by master in chancery must be stamped.

(No. 226.)

The date of execution and not the date of record determines the question of liability to stamp duties, of deeds or other instruments of writing, subject to the payment of stamp duty under the provisions of the internal revenue laws.

Liability to stamp duty dates from execution of instrument.

(No. 227.)

Citation from surrogate's court not an "original process."

A citation from the surrogate's court is not an original process, (a surrogate's court not being a court of record,) and is not subject to stamp duty.

(No. 228.)

Dedimus potestatem not subject to stamp duty.

A "*dedimus potestatem*" or commission issued out of any court in one State to take the deposition of a witness in any other State, or in the same State, to be used on a trial of a cause pending, is not subject to stamp duty.

(No. 229.)

Power of attorney in a mortgage not subject to stamp.

A mortgage or trust deed being duly stamped as "mortgage" is not subject to further stamp duty by virtue of a power of attorney or power of sale contained therein.

The stamp duty required upon assignment of mortgage is the same as that imposed upon the original instrument.

(No. 230.)

Indorsement on a writ is a bond, if under seal. When not under seal an agreement.

If the indorsement upon a writ required in an action brought by a citizen of another State is under seal, it is a bond, and will require a twenty-five cent revenue stamp.

If not under seal, it is liable to stamp duty as an agreement.

(No. 231.)

Official bonds subject to stamp duty of 50 cents.

The official bonds of sheriffs, constables, executors, administrators, trustees, guardians, &c., come within the meaning of the third clause of Schedule B, title "Bond," and are each subject to stamp duty of one dollar.

Letters of guardianship are exempt from stamp.

(No. 232.)

Certificate of ownership in a cemetery subject to stamp.

A certificate of ownership of a burial lot in a cemetery is subject to stamp duty.

(No. 233.)

"Warehouse receipts."

All receipts for grain or other property of any kind, held on storage in any public or private warehouse or yard, are "warehouse receipts" within the meaning of the excise law, and are each subject to a stamp duty according to the value of the property stored.

(No. 234.)

"Plantation Bitters" are a proprietary medicine, and subject to a proprietary stamp. "Bourbonia Whiskey," "Wolfe's Schiedam Schnapps," and "Bininger's Gin," if not claimed as proprietary, and stamped as such, must be regarded the same as other liquors, subjecting the person who sells them to the liability of a liquor-dealer's license.

Plantation Bitters subject to stamp duty.

Bourbonia Whiskey, &c., not subject.

(No. 235.)

Every foreign bill of exchange must be stamped by the party accepting it in this country, if the acceptor be not a fiscal agent or other public officer of the United States acting in his official capacity in accepting the bill. If the bill be drawn abroad and be negotiated before acceptance, it must be stamped at the time of its negotiation. If it be drawn at sight and paid on presentation, it must be stamped by the party paying it at the time of payment.

Foreign bills of exchange must be stamped when accepted or negotiated.

(No. 236.)

If the manufacturer of proprietary articles, acting in good faith, and upon such information as he can obtain, affixes a stamp answering to the retail price in the market where he deals, or in the vicinity thereof, he will be exempt from proceedings for penalty, even though in other parts of the country the articles so manufactured and stamped may be sold at enhanced prices.

Articles in schedule C to be stamped to answer to ordinary "retail price."

Articles enumerated in Schedule C, when sold in bulk or in quantities greater than specified or contemplated in the part of the excise law relating to said schedule, will be taxed as manufactures. If such articles are afterwards prepared and sold in such packages as are mentioned or described in Schedule C, the appropriate stamps must be affixed to the packages.

When sold in bulk to be taxed as manufactures.

(No. 237.)

"Are sterling bills drawn in a foreign country, and sent to the United States for sale, and sold here, liable to the tax law requiring stamps?"

The law is not clear upon this point; but I am of opinion that any person who should issue such a bill in this country unstamped would be subject to the penalty prescribed in section 100 of the excise law of July 1, 1862.*

Bills of exchange drawn and payable in foreign countries, negotiated in the United States, subject to taxation.

It is also provided in section 100 that no bill of exchange shall be paid or negotiated without such stamp; and by the same section any person who shall pay or negotiate, or offer in payment any such draft or order without stamp, shall forfeit the sum of $100.

The provisions seem to be sufficient for the case suggested, and, I think, it will be a violation of the law for any person to negotiate in this country bills of exchange drawn in England, and payable there, unless they are stamped as required in Schedule B, under the head of "inland bills of exchange."

---

* See section 158 of the act of June 30, 1864.

(No. 238.)

Value of property in jurisdiction, measure of stamp.

The value of all the property of the testator, whether real or personal, which, under the law or by virtue of the terms of the will, can be administered upon, and is within the jurisdiction of the court wherein the will is approved, is the measure of the stamp duty chargeable upon the will when proved.

Addition'l stamps if reproved in other jurisdictions.

Should the will be proved in another jurisdiction, it will then be necessary to affix an additional stamp proportionate to the value of the property within such jurisdiction, and subject to the law and terms of the will.

(No. 239.)

Proprietary medicins given to the poor.

Proprietary medicines, given to the poor, are exempt from taxation.

(No. 240.)

Agreements for leasing subject to stamp duty as leases.

Both agreements, that held by the tenant as well as that held by the landlord, are subject to stamp duty, under the head of "Lease."

(No. 241.)

Conveyance by an executor to heirs subject to stamp duty.

The conveyance of property to heirs, by an executor, administrator, or trustee, should be stamped, according to the full value of the property.

Bond, on appeal from one court to another, exempt.

The bond, on an appeal from a lower to a higher court, is exempt from stamp duty, as a bond "required in legal proceedings."

(No. 242.)

What bonds are subject to taxation and what are exempt defined.

All bonds required in legal proceedings are exempt from stamp tax; but this does *not* exempt bonds of guardians, administrators, assignees, trustees, &c.

(No. 243.)

Notes payable in merchandise subject to stamp duty.

A note payable in corn is subject to stamp duty.

The party making the note, and the party receiving the same, must estimate the value of the corn at the date of the note, and affix a stamp thereto proportionate to the value thereof, agreeably to Schedule B.

Penalty for issuing or receiving such notes without stamp.

The party receiving the note, without an adequate stamp, will do so at his peril, and the party making and issuing it, without an adequate stamp, will be subject to the penalties of section 158 of the excise law.

(No. 244.)

Clearing-house receipts exempt from stamp duty, if not allowed to pass into circulation.

Clearing-house receipts, *if used exclusively in the business of the clearing-house, and if they are not allowed to pass into the hands of third parties*, will be regarded as ordinary receipts, which do not come within the provisions of the stamp act, and which are therefore exempt from tax.

(No. 245.)

The stamps affixed to letters of administration on intestate estates should correspond in value to the duties on probate of will. (See Schedule B.

Stamps on letters of administration of intestate estates.

(No. 246.)

Any power of attorney, conveyance, or document of any kind, made and issued in foreign countries, which is to have effect in the United States, and which, if made and issued within the United States, would require a stamp, may be stamped, and the stamp cancelled by the maker, at the time and place of issue, as provided in the excise law, or by the party to whom the same is issued or by whom it is to be used.—(Sect. 163.)

Legal documents drawn abroad, but operative in the United States, require stamps as though made here.

(No. 247.)

The certificate of a master in chancery, in the case of a debtor, that the plaintiff has good cause of action, &c., and the certificate of the master in chancery that he has administered the oath to a poor debtor, are both subject to stamp as certificates.

Certificates of masters in chancery.

Certificates of sheriffs upon processes, that such processes have been duly served, are exempt from stamp tax.

Certificates of sheriffs.

(No. 248.)

Papers filed in court, on which there is an indorsement made by the clerk or register that they were filed at a certain time, do not require a certificate or other stamp.

Legal papers indorsed by clerk or register, showing date of filing, exempt.

If copies of papers which have been filed in court are issued with certificate, a certificate stamp will be required on such copies

Certified copies require stamp.

(No. 249.)

The tax of five cents per sheet on "agreements" applies to agreements, appraisements, &c., and not to deeds and mortgages.

Agreem'nt stamps not to apply to bonds and mortgages.

(No. 250.)

Executory agreements, for purchase of real estate, should be stamped as "agreements."

(No. 251.)

A chattel mortgage, made prior to 1st October, 1862, is valid without stamp; and the renewal thereof, by notice entered upon the record, as provided by the laws of several States, does not render the use of a stamp necessary. Upon the same principle, it must be held that when a mortgage has been stamped, agreeably to the act of July 1, 1862, its revival or renewal, in the same manner, does not render the use of the stamp necessary.

Chattel mortgages made prior to October 1, 1862, valid without stamps.

Also, exempt on renewal.

(No. 252.)

Prepared chalk, how taxable.

As prepared chalk is used almost exclusively as a cosmetic, each packet, bottle, pot, phial, or other enclosure or envelope, in which it is contained, is subject to stamp duty, as provided in Schedule C.

If not sold as a cosmetic, it will be subject to a duty of five per cent. ad valorem, under section 94, as a manufacture not otherwise provided for.

(No. 253.)

Stamp on deeds must answer to the *value* of the estate. See Schedule B.

In all conveyances of real estate by deed, the law provides that the stamp or stamps affixed must answer to the *value* of the estate conveyed. If the *consideration* specified does not correspond with the *value*, the grantee will accept the title with all its perils. If the consideration named in a deed be "natural love and affection," and the grantor neglect to affix stamps corresponding in amount to the value of the estate, it is not easy to see how the title could be sustained, when it appears from the deed itself that there was a sale of the estate, although the consideration named is not such as to require a stamp under the excise law.

(No. 254.)

As to stamping legal instruments to be used in other countries.

Do powers of attorney for foreign countries for the collection of moneys abroad, or the sale of property there, require stamps?

If such powers of attorney are so prepared and authenticated as to conform to the laws of the country in which moneys are to be collected or property sold by virtue thereof, I am of opinion that the transaction would be valid as between the principal and attorney, and that the rights of third parties could not be questioned, upon the ground that such powers were not stamped according to the laws of the United States.

The law provides that bills of exchange drawn in, but payable out of, the United States shall be stamped. No such provision exists with regard to powers of attorney; nor is there reason to suppose, from the language employed, that stamps are required upon such instruments when made in this country, but which could be operative and of value only in another country.

(No. 255.)

A special claim to the manufacture of an article renders it liable to stamp duty under Schedule C.

It appears from the evidence submitted that the article sold as "Husbands's Calcined Magnesia" is an uncompounded medicinal chemical; but inasmuch as it is offered for sale under a name not laid down in the pharmacopœias, dispensatories, text-books, or journals mentioned in section 166 of the excise law, and inasmuch as it is advertised and offered for sale under a form or guise not described or denominated in said text-books, it is subject to stamp duty under Schedule C. The maker claims upon the label that the article is prepared by no other person than said "Husbands," which is, in substance, a claim to an exclusive right for making or preparing the article advertised and sold by him.

(No. 256.)

Brokers' memorandums of purchase and sale subject to stamp duty.

Memorandums of purchase and sale must be regarded as within the meaning of the clause pertaining to contracts or brokers' notes, (Schedule B, excise law,) and therefore subject to a stamp tax of ten cents.

(No. 257.)

Administrators, &c., bonds, tax on. Probate of Will subject to tax. Letters testamentary issued thereupon exempt.

Bonds of administrators, executors, and guardians should *each* have a one dollar stamp affixed.

"Probate of Will" is subject to stamp tax, but letters testamentary issued thereupon are exempt.

(No. 258.)

Checks drawn by bank proprietors or employés subject to stamp tax. Checks drawn against collections also subject to tax.

Checks drawn on a bank by one of its proprietors for his daily expenses, or by its employés for their wages, must be stamped.

The check of a correspondent, on money to his credit, to transfer an amount of money collected for him, is also subject to stamp duty.

(No. 259.)

Cologne taxable.

Cologne water is subject to stamp tax under Schedule C.

(No. 260.)

Messages for railroad or express companies, if free or paid for in kind, or if for individuals or corporations, if treated as free, though paid for quarterly or yearly, or if sent over lines which they do not exclusively own, must be accounted for in return of gross receipts.

Telegraphic messages forwarded free of charge, by railroad or express companies, or which are paid for in kind, must be accounted for in gross receipts of company.

Messages forwarded in the same manner for corporations or individuals, treated as free messages in their transmission, but paid for quarterly or yearly, must also be accounted for.

Messages of a railroad company sent over a line which they do not own and work exclusively for railroad purposes, although the stock of the telegraph line over which their messages pass may be partly or chiefly owned by the railroad company, must also be accounted for.

Only such messages as are covered by the following are entitled to exemption as "free messages:"

If over their own lines, and not paid for, exempt.

"Messages transmitted by telegraph and railroad companies over their own wires, on their own business, for which they receive no pay.

(No. 261.)

Act of March 3, 1863, changes amount of stamps only in those cases in which the premium or assessment exceeds $10. Definition of the words "premium or assessment."

* The act of March 3, 1863, has changed the stamp required from twenty-five to ten cents, only in those cases in which the premium or assessment upon a policy of insurance shall not exceed ten dollars.

The words "premium or assessment" are held to include as well cash payments as the amount of premium or deposit notes upon which assessments are actually made.

---

* The act of June 30, 1864, contains the same provision.

Interest or annual payments not affected by the amended act.

The law does not appear to apply to the case of an interest or annual payment, which must necessarily be contingent and variable.

(No. 262.)

A sheriff's deed requires a stamp, notwithstand'g the writ or original process was duly stamped.

Although the writ or original process in a suit may have been properly stamped, a sheriff's deed under an execution issued upon the judgment will require to be stamped under the head of "conveyance."

Date of deed determines the liability to stamp, not the date of original process.

The date of the deed must determine its liability to stamp duty, independently of the date of the original process.

(No. 263.)

Bonds issued by the State, and executive warrants on the treasurer of the State, are exempt from stamp duty.

State bonds and checks exempt from duty.

It follows also, from the same decision, that the check of the State treasurer, for moneys belonging to the State, is exempt from stamp duty.

Town treasurers' orders on State treasurer not exempt.

The orders of a town treasurer upon the State treasurer for money due to or belonging to the town are not exempt.

(No. 264.)

Deeds made prior to June 1, 1863, without stamp, no void, but may be stamped in court whenever necessary.

By the first proviso of the sixteenth section of the excise law, passed March 3, it is declared that no instrument, document, or paper, made, signed, or issued prior to the 1st day of June, 1863, without being duly stamped, or having thereon an adhesive stamp to denote the duty imposed thereon, shall, for that cause, be deemed invalid and of no effect, and by the second proviso the stamp may be affixed whenever it is necessary to use the instrument or document as evidence in any court.

A deed executed and delivered prior to June 1, 1863, is not void, nor even voidable, for the reason that the same has not been stamped. See also sect. 163, stat. June 30, 1864.

(No. 265.)

Originals and duplicates of brokers' contracts must have a stamp.

The clause of Schedule B, imposing a stamp duty upon brokers' contracts, is construed to include both the original and the duplicate—the one issued to the seller as well as that given to the buyer.

(No. 266.)

Demand loans made on checks an evasion of law, and liable to penalty therefor, if made, &c.

Demand loans made on checks stamped as such, are an evasion of the law, if made with an understanding that the check is not to be presented, or not to be presented till a day future.

Notes, whether on demand or on time, are subject to stamp duty as "inland bills of exchange."

(No. 267.)

The masters' inward and outward manifests of the whole cargo are subject to stamp duty under the provisions of the internal revenue excise law, except in the case of vessels plying between the United States and British North America. Masters' inward and outward manifests are alone subject to duty.

(No. 268.)

When parties have complied with the terms required for a permit to export distilled spirits, there is no authority by which the collector can claim the right to reinspect the same, and charge an additional inspection fee. Collectors not authoriz'd to claim to reinspect where parties have already complied with the law.

Neither does the law authorize a fee for issuing permits for exports of distilled spirits, &c.; or for filling out the bonds and necessary papers for such permits. No fees authorized for issuing permits for exportation of distilled spirits.

(No. 269.)

Certificates of dismission and recommendation of church members are *not* subject to stamp tax. Certificates of dismissal and recommendation of members require no stamp.

(No. 270.)

The annual payment of interest on a premium note is not a renewal of the policy. If payment be delayed beyond the day when due, its acceptance afterwards would be a renewal and subject the party to a stamp on the policy. Annual payment of interest on premium note not renewal of policy. If payment is delayed, its acceptance afterwards would be a renewal and require a stamp.

(No. 271.)

Every conveyance, whether by quit-claim or warranty-deed, must bear a stamp, or stamps, corresponding to the value of the estate conveyed, whether the conveyance be made by quit-claim or warranty-deed. Deeds should carry stamps proportioned to the interest they cover. In several States it is the custom to discharge a mortgage or deed of trust by a quit-claim deed from the mortgagee to the mortgagor. A quit-claim deed, in such a case, does not operate to convey the estate; it is merely in substance a release of the mortgage under it. Being, therefore, equivalent to a discharge of the mortgage, it has been held that such a quit-claim deed is exempt from stamp duty. Quit-claim deeds, or mere releases of mortgages, exempt from tax.

(No. 272.)

When "bills of sale," or deeds of vessels, are given as security for money, they must be treated as conveyances in trust, and stamped under head of Mortgage. Bills of sale of vessels, if given as security for money, are subject to stamp tax as mortgages.

(No. 273.)

When a note is made payable at a certain bank, and a check is drawn upon the same bank for the amount of it, a check stamp is required for the check. Checks drawn to meet notes at same bank must have stamps.

If notes are charged to promisors, and no checks are used, stamps are not required.

When the note is charged at the bank to the account of the promisor, and a check is not used, then a stamp is not required.

(No. 274.)

Stamps on letters of administration of intestates' estates must be in proportion to the value of interest included.

The stamp used upon letters of administration upon the estates of intestates must answer to the value of the real and personal estate within the jurisdiction of the court.

(No. 275.)

Sheriffs' deeds are subject to stamp duty.

Deeds of real estate sold by a sheriff under process of law are subject to stamp duty.

(No. 276.)

Certificates of witnesses as to possession being taken by mortgagees require general certificate stamps.

If possession of real estate is taken by the mortgagee, or surrendered by the mortgagor, the certificate of the witnesses will require a general certificate stamp.

(No. 277.)

Powers of attorney executed prior to October 1, 1862, are exempted, subsequently thereto must be stamped.

Powers of attorney to sell and transfer stock executed prior to October 1, 1862, are exempt from stamp duty; but if such powers of attorney were executed subsequently to that date, they are liable to stamp duty.

(No. 278.)

All articles enumerated in Schedule C must be stamped, whether proprietary or not; stamp to be proportioned to retail price.

All articles enumerated in Schedule C, under head of "perfumery and cosmetics," must be stamped, whether "proprietary" or not.

The retail price of articles subject to proprietary stamp duty is in all cases, except of friction or lucifer matches, the measure of that duty. The stamp duty upon this class of articles, as well as medicines, &c., is one cent generally for every twenty-five cents or any fractional part thereof of the retail price; two or more stamps of a smaller denomination may be used in numbers, sufficient to make a required stamp duty.

(No. 279.)

Appraisements in sheriffs' cases subject to stamp duty, amount of.

An appraisement of property made by freeholders selected by the sheriff of a county, in accordance with the law providing for the sale of real estate, under executions issued by a court, as well as appraisements of personal property taken in actions of replevin, are in each case subject to a stamp duty of five cents for each sheet.

Bonds, when exempt and when subject to taxation.

Bonds required in legal proceedings, are not subject to stamp duty; if, however, a bond is not absolutely indispensable, as a part of such proceedings, but only incidental or voluntary, it is subject to stamp duty.

Certificate of justice of the peace to transcript to district court subject to stamp duty, amount of.

A certificate of a justice of the peace certifying a transcript to the district court is subject to a stamp duty of five cents.

(No. 280.)

If parties making articles known as essences, such as cinnamon, peppermint, lemon, cloves,&c., do not claim a private formula or occult secret or art for the manufacture, nor an exclusive right or title by letters patent, and if they are not used or applied as perfumes or applications to the hair, mouth or skin, the articles are exempt from stamp duty.

What preparations, &c., are exempt from duty.

(No. 281.)

The design of the stamp offered by Mr. ——— cannot be approved. He has proceeded under a misconstruction of the law.

Proprietary articles not subject to duty require no stamps.

Stamps are not issued to be used upon articles which are exempt from duty; it however appears from Mr. ——— letter that the article prepared by him is subject to stamp duty. He should use either the general proprietary stamp, or furnish a suitable design for a stamp, for which, when engraved and printed, he will be required to pay to the government the customary stamp duties.

The letter of Mr. ———, the assistant assessor, sets forth that the eye salve prepared by Mr. ——— is fully described in the American Eclectic Dispensatory, printed in 1851, at Cincinnati; but it also appears from the letter of Mr. ——— that the eye salve is advertised and sold as "Petitt's eye salve," and that Mr. ——— claims to have a private formula for the making or preparing the same. It is also apparent that this article is offered for sale under a name, form, or guise different from that in which it is laid down or described in the dispensatory mentioned.

Proprietary articles to be exempt must have the formulas from which they are prepared strictly recorded in dispensatories in common use among physicians.

Either of these circumstances, if true, will deprive Mr. ——— of the right to sell the article without affixing upon each package the stamp, as required in Schedule C.

It does not appear that the dispensatory referred to is in common use among physicians and apothecaries. If it be not in such use, then the fact of the publication of the formula would not exempt the manufacturer of the medicine from liability to duty.

Upon the evidence presented, I am obliged to rule that the article prepared by Mr. ——— is subject to a stamp duty, and that the sale of such article, without the use of stamps, renders him liable to the penalty prescribed in the 165th section of the excise law.

(No. 282.)

If A, as the grantee of the widow and heirs of B, conveys the interest granted to him by their deed, together with his own interest, to another party, the stamp duty upon his deed must answer to the entire value of his estate.

Value of interest conveyed governs the amount of stamp on deed.

A quitclaim deed, made to A by the widow and heirs of B, must be stamped, according to the value of the interest conveyed by them.

(No. 283.)

Suits are commenced in many States by other process than

Original processes of whatever

form. must be appropriately stamped. writ, viz: summons, warrant, petition, &c.; in which cases, these, as the original processes, severally, require stamps.

(No. 284.)

Entry of cargo exempt from stamp duty in certain cases. The entry by the captain should include the manifest of the cargo, and the entry is therefore exempt from stamp duty, under the proviso of Schedule B of the excise law, when the vessel plies between ports of the United States and ports of British North America. If the owners enter the goods owned by them, respectively, the "entry" stamp will be required.

(No. 285.)

Checks or drafts, intended to serve as memorandums of a partner to his firm, exempt from taxation, but if given to third parties liable to stamp duty. If your check or draft on your bookkeeper is used merely as a memorandum to show your liability to the firm of which you are a member, it is exempt from stamp duty; but if used for any other purpose, and especially if paid out, or transferred, or negotiated to a third party without being duly stamped, you will be liable to the penalty provided in section 158 of the excise law.

(No. 286.)

Mortgages must be stamped sufficiently to cover amount of risk or of liability. A "general indemnity mortgage," or a mortgage made to secure indorsements, past and future, must be stamped at the time of delivery; and the mortgage cannot be enforced for any sum greater than the amount covered by the stamps so affixed and cancelled at the time of the execution and delivery of the mortgage.

(No. 287.)

Perfumery and cosmetics subject to stamp tax. All perfumery and cosmetics enumerated in Schedule C of the excise law are subject to stamp duty, whether manufactured with or without a private formula. They are also equally subject to stamp duty when sold in irregular packages and quantities, or when sold in regular packages. Perfumery and cosmetics put into and sold in bottles or packages, furnished by the purchasers, are also subject to stamp duty.

(No. 288.)

Promissory notes executed prior to July 1, 1862, and subsequently extended, renders them subject to duty. A promissory note which was executed prior to the passage of the excise law, and the payment of which has been, subsequently to the passage of that law, extended by agreement, is subject to stamp duty, under the head of "inland bills of exchange."

(No. 289.)

Promissory notes given for sums under twenty dollars subject to stamp duty. A promissory note, given for payment of twenty dollars, or less, is, by the act of March 3, 1863, subject to stamp duty, under head of "inland bills of exchange." See also Schedule B, stat. June 30, 1864.

(No. 290.)

If the duplicate copy of a contract is required as evidence, it must be stamped as well as the original.

Duplicates, to have legal value, must be stamped.

(No. 291.)

This office has no power to decide whether corporations or stockholders shall pay the cost of the stamp used upon certificates. The law subjects a party issuing an instrument without a stamp to a penalty.

Stamps upon certificates issued by corporations, who shall pay.

(No. 292.)

Manufacturers of "playing cards" must affix stamps upon each pack of cards corresponding to the price at which they are sold at retail.*

Amount of stamp required on playing cards.

(No. 293.)

The actual value of an estate conveyed is the measure of the stamp duty required upon a deed conveying it.—(See "conveyance" in Schedule B, in the act of June 30, 1864.)

Value of estate determines amount of stamp required on a conveyance.

A stamp should be affixed to an instrument subject to stamp duty, by the party executing the instrument, at the time of its execution; and the stamp should be cancelled by the party affixing it, by writing his initials and the date thereof upon the stamp.

Time and method of affixing stamp.

A party executing an instrument, and failing to stamp it, is liable to a penalty of $200, which penalty should be enforced by the local collector of internal revenue.—(Sec. 158.)

Penalty for neglect to stamp deed.

(No. 294.)

In reply to your queries respecting the additional liability of promissory notes payable at bank, to stamp duty as bank checks, I have to state, that although the words "promise to pay at bank" may be accepted by the bank as sufficient authority to pay the note at maturity, and to charge the amount thereof to the account of the maker, they nevertheless do not constitute or convey any pledge, or guarantee on the part of the maker that he has the money in bank to meet the note when it falls due.

Promissory notes payable "at bank" not subject to duty as checks

A check, on the other hand, is always supposed to be drawn against funds, and is to be regarded as an absolute appropriation of so much money as it calls for, in the hands of the banker, to the holder thereof, and, in ordinary practice, is payable on presentation.

I therefore hold that said form of note does not come within the meaning of the stamp act pertaining to bank checks, but is only liable to tax as a promissory note.

* See ruling No. 278 in reference to proprietary articles.

(No. 295.)

Stamps required on the various documents pertaining to the common school system of Pennsylvania

I have duly considered the several forms of papers issued and used by you as superintendent of common schools of Pennsylvania, together with your several queries in regard to their respective liability to stamp duty under the provisions of the excise law, and now beg to enclose you my decision thereon.

	Stamp duty.
1. Diplomas and certificates issued by the State Normal School to teachers	5 cents.
2. Certificates to teachers, issued by county superintendents	5 cents.
3. Certificates or returns of unpaid tax on unseated lands, to county commissioners, by district tax collectors	5 cents.
4. Certificates or returns of unpaid balance of school tax against district tax collector to prothonotary, by secretary of the board of directors	5 cents.
5. Certificates by president and secretary of the board of directors to county superintendent, that schools have been open and in operation according to law	5 cents.
6. Certificates of election of county superintendents, by president and secretary of county convention of directors	5 cents.
7. Warrants or authorities to collectors to collect school tax	Exempt.
8. Bonds of collectors of school tax	$1 00
9. Bonds of treasurers of school districts	$1 00
10. Deeds of ground for school-houses must bear a conveyance stamp, according to the consideration expressed in the deed or the value of the property conveyed. (Schedule B.)	
11. Leases of houses and lots for schools, if rent does not exceed $300 per annum	50 cts.
For each additional $200, or fractional part thereof	50 cts.
12. Agreements or contracts with contractors to build school-houses and repair them, when there is a written agreement for this purpose—on every sheet	5 cents.
13. Warrants or drafts by the State superintendent of common schools on the State treasury, for the annual State appropriation to the common school districts are	Exempt.
14. Warrants or drafts by the State superintendent on the State treasury, quarterly, for the salaries of county superintendents are	Exempt.
15. Orders or drafts by board of school directors on the district treasurer, for the payment of teachers' salaries and the other debts of the district, are	Exempt.
16. Checks by the district treasurer on banks to pay orders on the district treasury by the board of directors	2 cents.
17. Agreements or contracts between teachers and boards of directors to teach	5 cents.

18. Monthly reports by teachers to boards of directors, of the condition of their schools are.......... Exempt.
19. Petition to court for the formation of a new school district or change in a district................ Exempt.
20. Petition to court for the removal of school directors Exempt.

(No. 296.)

The *employés* of a State government, are not 'officers' within the meaning of section 154 of the act approved June 30, 1864. Nor can their affidavit to the correctness of personal accounts be considered as "official papers," under the same section and act.

Employés of a State government not "officers" under the act of December 25, 1862.

(No. 297.)

Every bond issued by a city must bear a stamp as inland bills of exchange, whether issued in redemption of an old bond or for a new debt.

Bonds issued by a city require to be stamped, whether issued in redemption of an old bond or for a new debt.

If the Baltimore and Ohio Railroad Company assume payment of interest and principal of bonds issued by the city of Baltimore in aid of the railroad company, then the five per cent. upon the interest should be withheld, on the ground that the bonds are, in fact, the bonds of the railroad. The city is, in such case, substantially the indorser. If the road pays the city, then the road will deduct the five per cent. from such payment.

If a railroad company assumes the liability of a city's bonds, 5 per cent. should be deducted from the accruing interest.

If the road pays the city, 5 per ct. deduction is required therefrom.

(No. 298.)

If a subscription list for the payment of a clergyman's salary, or for the building of a church, or for any benevolent purpose, is in the form of an agreement, it is subject to a stamp duty of five cents per sheet.

Subscription list an agreement.

If it be in the form of a promissory note, it is subject to stamp duty under the head of "inland bills of exchange."

Any agreement of trustees or others with regard to the disposition of the funds raised on such subscription is subject to a further stamp duty of five cents.

(No. 299.)

The phrase "Letter of Credit," as used in the excise law, Schedule B, is construed to refer to such letters as are equivalent to a "Bill of Exchange," the payment of which is not contingent upon any other transaction.

"Letter of credit" defined.

(No. 300.)

In the case of conveyance of property subject to a ground rent, the rent is to be regarded as a separate and distinct estate in the land from that held by the owner of the property.

Ground rent lease is a separate estate.

(No. 301.)

Applications for prize-money subject to stamp.

The act of June 30, 1864, section 160, cannot be construed to exempt from stamp duty applications or claims for prize-money or papers relating to such applications or claims.

(No. 302.)

An "appeal" an original process in certain cases.

An appeal or instrument by which a suit is transferred from a justice of the peace to a superior court is an original process, and subject to stamp duty as such.

If, by the laws of a State, a suit is commenced against a non-resident defendant, by an order or application under authority of the court, such order or application is subject to stamp duty as an original process.

Writ of *habeas corpus*, "error," *certiorari*, exempt.

A writ of "habeas corpus," of "error," or of "certiorari," not being an "original process," is not subject to stamp duty.

Alias and pluries writs, and counterpart, are not original processes, and are, therefore, exempt from stamp duty.

Writs of scire facias, in either civil or criminal causes, are original processes, and subject to stamp duty.

Certificates issued to grand and petit jurors should be stamped as certificates.

(No. 303.)

Conveyance of widow's dower, stamp duty on.

When an estate is conveyed subject to widow's dower, actually assigned, the following rules should be observed in ascertaining the amount of stamp duty imposed by law upon the deed:

The present value of the portion of the estate covered by the dower should be ascertained by appropriate tables; that sum deducted from the value of the estate, estimated free of all encumbrances, and the stamp duty upon the deed measured by the remainder.

In most cases the consideration named in a conveyance of an estate subject to dower, as above, would indicate the value of the required stamps.

(No. 304.)

"Trust deeds" stamped as mortgages.

In all cases of deeds given for real estate, they should be stamped under head of "Conveyance," in "Schedule B," except in case of "trust deed" for security for the payment of money. In the latter case the deed must be stamped as a "mortgage."—(See "Bond of any description," Schedule B.

(No. 305.)

Who may affix stamps in certain cases.

When several persons are the parties of the first part, executing an instrument which is subject to stamp duty, either of said parties may affix and cancel the revenue stamp or stamps required thereon.

(No. 306.)

Stamp duty upon demand notes.

The stamp duty required upon a demand note is the same as upon a note for a designated time.

(No. 307.)

In addition to the stamp duty required upon notes drawn according to the forms you enclose, (as notes,) the power of attorney to sell stock, which is incorporated in each of them, is subject to a stamp duty of twenty-five cents, and the power of attorney to transfer stock, which is appended to one of them, is also subject to a stamp duty of twenty-five cents.

Power of attorney to sell stock, when incorporated in a promissory note, must be stamped.

TOBACCO.

(No. 308.)

The Mode of estimating the Tax on Cigars.

Tax on Cigars.

By the 86th section of the act of June 30th, manufacturers are required to return the full amount of actual sales as the basis on which the assessment of taxes is to be made, or in case the manufactured articles have passed beyond the custody or control of the manufacturer or his agent, no sale having been made, the value for purposes of taxation shall be estimated at the average of the market value of the like goods at the time when the same became liable to duty. The taxable value in all cases is to be determined by one or the other of the above modes, and in no case is the cost of production to be taken as the basis for estimating or assessing the tax. This is plainly evident from the deductions allowed by the same section when goods, wares, and merchandise are sold by the manufacturer or producer, or his agent. No such deductions would be allowed if the cost of production were taken as the taxable value of the goods.

In the clause of the 94th section, relating to cigars, it is declared that "the valuation of the cigars herein mentioned shall in all cases be the value of the cigars exclusive of the tax." This provision requires a value to be sought other than that immediately indicated by actual sales, by which to determine the different rates of tax on cigars. Under the limited series of *values* and *rates*, a schedule has been prepared of *sales* and *rates*. Since the tax on cigars valued over $45 per M. is $40, it follows that all cigars that are sold for more than $85 per M. are taxable at the highest rate provided by law, viz., $40. The next grade below are cigars valued at $30, the tax on which is $25. Now, whenever the manufacturer sells his cigars for more than $55, but less than $85, he is liable to pay thereon a tax of $25 per M., as they come within the next to the highest grade provided by law. Pursuing this course with the other grades, we obtain the following schedule:

Rate per M. according to salable value.

Cigars less than $14 per M., known as cheroots, -	$ 3 00
Cigars selling at not over $13, - - -	3 00
Cigars selling at over $13, and not over $30, - -	8 00
Cigars selling at over $30, and not over 55, -	15 00
Cigars selling at over $55, and not over $85, - -	25 00
Cigars selling at over $85, - - -	40 00

Cigarettes in like manner.

If this schedule does not, in all cases, give to the government the full amount of tax intended, it obviates the difficulty that would constantly be meeting the assessor without such a schedule indicating sales value, namely, the problem of finding from the sales price in each given case the two unknown quantities, the value of the cigars exclusive of the tax, and the tax itself.

The tax is to be paid when the cigars are sold or consumed or used, or removed for consumption, or for delivery to others than the agents of the manufacturer.

MISCELLANEOUS.

(No. 309.)

Repairing vessels, amounting substantially to a rebuilding, subjects the owner to duty.

Repairing vessels, amounting substantially to rebuilding, subjects the owner to ad valorem duty of 2 per cent. thereon.

(No. 323.)

Bookbinders not required to pay tax on books made for other parties in certain cases.

In the case where the paper and other materials are furnished to the bookbinders, by the stationer, for the purpose of having the same manufactured into blank books, such bookbinders may not be required to pay the tax of five per cent. on the value thereof, provided that, at the request of the assistant assessor, they make out a list, subscribed and sworn, which list shall contain the quantity of books so made, during each month, and, as near as may be, the value thereof, together with the name and residence of the person for whom the labor has been performed.—

(No. 310.)

Persons in the civil service of the government subject to taxation on all excess of salary over $600 per annum.

The ruling of this office has been that the tax on the salaries of persons in the civil service of the United States must be on the whole amount of the salary which such officer receives above the rate of six hundred dollars per annum.

(No. 311.)

Tax to be withheld from commutation for expenses incurred by public officers in travelling.

When public officers incur expenses in travelling which are not returned, but a substitute of commutation is made therefor, the tax must be withheld from the amount paid.

Actual payments not subject to deduction.

It may be observed as a rule, that actual payments made by an officer in the service of the government are not subject to a deduction of the tax when the government refunds the money so advanced.

(No. 312.)

7.30 Treasury coupons not liable to 3 per cent. tax.

The United States interest coupons attached to the 7.30 notes are not liable to any deduction.

(No. 313.)

Assessors cannot require prepayment of freight passing into foreign countries.

By the 10th section of the act of March 3, on and after the 1st day of April, 1863, express companies are to pay, in lieu of stamp duties, two per centum on their gross receipts, and they are subject to the same provisions, rules, and penalties as are prescribed in section 80 of the excise law. An assessor has no right to require the prepayment of freights on express matter passing into Canada. By section 104 of the act of June 30, 1864, the rate is fixed at three per centum.

(No. 314.)

Railroad corporations taxable for receipts of their own roads, and not for money received on account of other roads.

The distributive share of each railroad is to be regarded as liable to taxation. Each road is expected to pay a tax upon its own receipts, and upon them only.

The fact that one road by selling tickets over several roads, and is in original receipt of amounts belonging to several roads, does not affect the question.

(No. 315.)

Steamboats chartered by government exempt.

Steamboats chartered by the government for the transportation of troops and munitions of war are exempt from the duty imposed upon steamboats, &c., under section 103 of the excise law, while under such charter.

(No. 316.)

Cities or towns owning tollbridges are liable to tax under section 80.

The language of section 80, applicable to toll bridges is as follows: "Any person or persons, firms, companies, or *corporations*, owning, possessing, or having the care or management of any bridge, &c., shall be subject to and pay a duty of three per centum on the gross amount of all their receipts of every description." The word "corporation," as used in this section, undoubtedly includes cities and towns. It must be assumed that Congress understood, when using this word without limitation, that public corporations, as they are defined in law, as well as private corporations, were included.

It must further be assumed that Congress was aware that cities and towns, as corporations, are frequently the owners of bridges on which tolls are collected.

Upon this construction of the word "corporation," which appears reasonable, and upon this knowledge on the part of Congress, reasonably assumed, it is held, in the absence of any constitutional inhibition, that a city which is the owner of a bridge is liable to assessment, under the said 80th section, upon the receipts from tolls collected upon such bridge. See section 103 of the act of June 30, 1864.

(No. 317.)

Stage proprietors to pay duty on receipts from carrying packages.

Proprietors of stage lines are liable to a duty of 3 per centum on the gross receipts from carrying packages and express matter.—(See section 104 act of June 30, 1864.)

(No. 318.)

Railway companies owning estates cannot withhold a tax from interest on mortgages given by former owners of such estates.

In the case of ordinary mortgages given by prior owners of estates now owned by a railway, the corporation cannot legally withhold three per cent. of the interest.

(No. 319.)

Perpetual insurance companies.

In principle, mutual insurance companies and stock insurance companies are substantially the same. In one case the insured are the stockholders, for the purpose of receiving the profits and sustaining the losses, as circumstances may dictate; in the other case the stockholders, who take the risks of the association, are not necessarily the parties insured; but this difference is of no importance as affecting the principle of the two organizations. The principle of doing business is the same; the organizations, only, differ.

Their character.

Nor is there any difference in principle between a mutual insurance company, that takes risks for one, five, or seven years, and a mutual company which issues policies for an indefinite period of time, which is the fact with those risks that are called perpetual.

It may be true that the company pays each policy holder a stipulated sum when the policy is cancelled, without special regard to its pecuniary condition. But it would be no longer true if the company were insolvent, or embarrassed, or its credit seriously impaired.

The money paid by the insured for a perpetual policy is, in fact, a premium. When the policy is cancelled, and a sum, large or small, is paid to the insured, the payment is made upon the theory, if not upon computation, that that sum is actually due to the holder of the particular policy as his share of the profits.

It may be, and, probably, often is, the fact that the premium paid in the beginning by the several policy holders is more than is needed to meet ordinary losses.

This, however, is a business question exclusively within the control of the companies themselves, and it is not necessary or proper for this office to make any inquiry in relation thereto.

It may be proper to add that the companies are allowed to deduct returned premiums in one case only, viz: when open policies are issued for a certain sum, and the premium paid, and the policy is used only in part, it is customary for the underwriters to make a pro rata return of the premium, and by the regulations of this office such return premiums are recognized.

(No. 320.)

Where taxes should be assessed.

When a man's residence is in a different district from his place of business, his business should be taxed where it is located, and only such articles as properly appertain to his residence should be taxed in that district.

(No. 321.)

Assessors' lists.

After the time for appeals has passed, assessors have nothing to do with the annual list but to copy and hand it to the collector.

Yet it might be proper to correct a very obvious error, though it is doubtful whether an assessor can remit penalties.

There must be extraordinary reasons to justify any changes in the lists after appeals are heard.

Monthly lists are also subject to correction, for good reasons, prior to the delivery of them to the collector.

(No. 322.)

Assessors cannot take possession of a manufacturer's books. May examine books. Party required to produce his books.

It does not appear that an assessor has the legal right to take possession of and keep, for purposes of evidence, the books of any person suspected of making false returns. But under section 37 he has the right to demand and make an inspection of the accounts kept by such person, and such inspection could be made in a way to answer all practical purposes. In case of trial or suit, the party can be required to produce the accounts in court, where it could be readily determined by the officer who inspected the accounts whether they had been changed or tampered with.

(No. 323.)

Frauds in the returns of manufactured oil.

As there is a reasonable doubt as to the guilt of ———, and as there are strong reasons for believing that the other members of the firm are innocent of any fraudulent intent, I am of the opinion that it is judicious to release the property seized, the oil in transitu, as well as the distillery and fixtures, upon payment by ——— ——— of all taxes due, and all costs incurred by you, including counsel fees.

The policy of the government

It should, however, be understood by them, and by all persons engaged in the manufacture of oil in your district, that, while the office has dealt leniently with the parties concerned in this transaction, hereafter the rights of the government will be strictly enforced against all violators of the law.

It must also be understood that persons engaged in the manufacture of oil, but who do not themselves superintend the business, must share the responsibility of any violation of the law by their agents or partners who are intrusted with the management of their affairs.

(No. 324.)

Assessors may remove assistants, and report the reasons therefor to Commissioner.

The assessor of each district, being held responsible for the faithful performance of the duties of his assistants, has the power to remove them for cause, but he is expected to report such removals, with the reasons therefor, to this office.

(No. 325.)

Yachts defined.

The provisions of section 100, providing for the taxation of yachts, are construed to apply only to vessels so known, technically, in the maritime language of the country; and to such of that class as are used for racing or purposes of pleasure.

(No. 326.)

Right of a town or city to issue fractional notes.

A town or city, being a public corporation, is not prohibited by the act of July 17, 1862, from issuing notes for circulation of

18

a less denomination than one dollar. Whether a town or city has a right to issue such notes is a different question, and may depend upon the laws of the several States.

(No. 327.)

An illegitimate child a stranger, and legacy from reputed father taxable accordingly.

An illegitimate son, being in the eye of the law a stranger in blood to the person who may be his reputed father, the tax imposed upon a legacy to such son from the father will be at the rate of six dollars for each and every hundred dollars of the clear value of such legacy.

(No. 328.)

Rule for levying tax on advertisements.

The tax on advertisements is to be paid on the cash receipts for advertisements published during the period covered by the return.

The tax dates from September 1, 1862.

(No. 329.)

Interest coupons payable in foreign countries not subject to tax.

Whenever coupons are payable in a foreign country, no deduction can be made legally by virtue of our excise laws.

On dividends and coupons payable in this country, the deduction will be made in conformity with the excise law.

The residence of the holder not to be considered.

In neither case is the residence of the holder to be regarded.

(No. 330.)

Additions to surplus and contingent funds by banking and other corporations taxable.

Dividends and all additions to surplus and contingent funds are held by this office to be taxable. In dealing justly with the government you will carry over any profits on hand, after declaring dividends to your contingent fund, and pay the tax upon it as such.

May then be divided.

You can divide the contingent fund among the stockholders directly or indirectly as suggested in your letter.

Surplus used for construction of a railway liable to taxation.

To use surplus profits for construction, and divide the shares issued therefor, would not relieve the stockholders from taxation.

(No. 331.)

No tax upon interest coupons or railroad bonds due on or before Sept. 1, 1862.

The three per cent. tax upon the interest on railroad bonds does not apply to coupons matured and unpaid prior to the 2d of September, 1862.

(No. 332.)

It was not the intention of Congress to levy a tax upon States.

If bonds were issued by the State of Missouri on its own account, and without special relation to any railway, bank, or other corporation, mentioned in sections 81 and 82 of the excise law, the withholding of three per cent. of the interest is clearly without authority. The law does not contemplate a tax upon States, or upon their securities.

If a State issues bonds to aid a railway company,

If, however, such bonds were issued in aid of a railway company which has undertaken to pay the interest and principal thereof, the case would be essentially changed, and the deduction of three per cent. on the payment of interest would be in conformity to the decisions of this office.

such company agreeing to pay the interest and principal thereof, the deduction of 3 per cent. from the interest thereof should be made.

(No. 333.)

Penalty of fifty per cent. under direct tax law.

An owner of land charged with direct tax, the amount of which has been fixed by the tax commissioners, and to which the penalty of fifty per cent. has been added, may obtain a certificate of the commissioners discharging his land of the lien of the tax and fifty per cent. penalty. This may be done by paying to the commissioners, within sixty days of the tax being fixed, the amount of the tax.

Title to land forfeited in sixty days.

If the tax is not paid within the sixty days the title of the land becomes forfeited to the United States.

To be sold.

If the tax charged on land shall not be paid within sixty days from the time of the amount being fixed by the commissioners, the land shall be advertised by them for sale and sold to the highest bidder for a sum not less than the taxes, penalty, and costs, and ten per centum per annum interest on the tax, the interest to be computed from the date of the ascertainment of the amount of tax by the commissioners. The former owner may become a purchaser at such sale, and on payment of the tax, penalty, interest, and cost, may have a deed for his land.

Former owner may redeem.

If the former owner fails to appear till after the sale, he may still redeem his land from the sale within sixty days, but in such case must pay the tax, the penalty, all costs, and interest at the rate of fifteen per cent., from the date of the President's proclamation, on the aggregate amount of the tax and penalty, and also take an oath before the commissioners to support the Constitution of the United States.

Further time may be allowed to owners who have not taken part in rebellion.

Within a year of the sale by the commissioners, an owner who shall prove to their satisfaction that he has not, after June 7, 1862, taken part in or abetted the present insurrection against the United States, and that he, by reason of said insurrection, has been unable to pay the tax or to redeem the lands from sale within sixty days from the sale, the commissioners may allow him further time, not exceeding two years, to redeem the same. The redemption in such case is to be effected only by paying the tax, penalty, fifteen per cent. interest, and costs, and taking an oath to support the Constitution.

Conditions.

Minors and others may redeem in two years.

To a minor, non-resident, alien, or loyal citizen beyond seas, a person of unsound mind, or under other legal disability, two years from the date of sale are allowed for the redemption of the land on terms last mentioned, to be complied with by the guardian, trustee, or other person representing the owner.

(No. 334.)

Property held by trustees for the use of widows or married women of foreign birth and residence.

Property held by trustees, as the separate estate and for the benefit of a widow, a person of foreign birth, and who is now a resident of another country, but whose husband was a citizen of the United States, is exempt from income tax.

The same rule applies to a married woman of foreign birth and residence whose husband is a citizen of the United States.

(No. 335.)

In case of bond or note secured by mortgage, one instrument only subject to stamp duty.

Under section 160 of the act of June 30th, 1864, it is provided that whenever any bond or note shall be secured by a mortgage, but one stamp duty shall be required on such papers, provided that the stamp duty placed thereon shall be the highest rate required for said instruments, or either of them. If the bond, note or notes, (where more than one bond or note accompanies the mortgage,) require a higher stamp than the collateral instrument, the stamp or stamps must be such as are appropriate to the bond, note, or notes. If the mortgage requires the higher stamp, as can seldom happen, the stamp must be such as is appropriate to the mortgage. When the instrument requiring the higher stamp is appropriately stamped the other is exempt.

(No. 336.)

Certificate of stock not subject to stamp duty.

As a certificate of stock is neither money, nor property, within the meaning of the word, as used in the act of Congress, a receipt for the same, (of the form furnished by you,) is not chargeable with stamp duty. (See Schedule B.)

(No. 337.)

Stamp duty on leases when the rental is contingent.

Where the rental of a lease is contingent, as in the case of a certain share of oil being stipulated as rent for the use of wells, as just an estimate as possible under the circumstances should be made of the probable amount of annual rent to be received, and the stamps be affixed in accordance therewith. I may remark, that if a fair and just estimate be made of the amount, with a view to attain as accurate result as the circumstances will allow, it is all that can be done by the parties, and the law will exact no more. In case of a future litigation between the parties, it will be to the interest of the person seeking to enforce the contract that the stamp shall be large enough to preclude all question as to the intent being to affix the proper stamp; for if the stamp should represent a value so far below that of the rent as to raise a presumption of fraud, the court trying the cause might refuse to admit the lease in evidence.

(No. 338.)

Stamps on bills of lading and receipts.

Bills of lading or receipts (other than charter party) for any goods, merchandise, or effects to be transported from any port or place in the United States, to be delivered at any other port or place in the United States, are chargeable with a stamp duty of two cents. Where receipts are issued for the benefit or use of the United States government, no stamp duty is chargeable where payment of the same would be a direct charge on the treasury of the United States.

When issued for the benefit of the U. S. not taxable.

(No. 339.)

Copies of instruments stamped under sect. 163.

When unstamped instruments are rendered operative by a compliance with section 163 of the act of June 30, 1864, in order to make a certified copy of the record evidence, it will be necessary that the instrument be re-recorded.

(No. 340.)

Under the act of June 30, 1864, articles manufactured or produced by any railroad for their own use on or after July 1st, are liable to tax; and by section 173 all such articles which were on the 1st of July in the possession of such railroad or its agents, which had not previous to that date been subjected to use, are equally liable. Tax on articles made by railway companies for their own use.

(No. 341.)

A life lease of lands is subject to stamp duty as a conveyance, and the assignment of such lease is equally liable. A life lease subject to stamp duty as a conveyance.

(No. 342.)

The extent of an execution by a sheriff upon real estate is not a conveyance, nor liable to stamp duty as such. Under the terms used in the excise law, there must be a contract of sale as an essential element of a conveyance. Extent of an execution upon real estate not subject to stamp duty.

(No. 343.)

Where sums were held by a person deceased in trust, and such trust fund was held by the deceased separate and distinct from his own property, such trust fund should be deducted in estimating the value of the estate to determine the amount of stamp duty on the letters of administration. Funds in hands of a deceased person as trustee, not estimated as part of his estate.

Where the deceased invested such trust fund in his own name, without any designation as trustee, so that the executor or administrator cannot separate it from his individual estate without the aid of extrinsic evidence, it is not to be deducted. If invested as his private estate, the rule is otherwise.

(No. 344.)

A butcher selling from a shop or stand, may sell other articles than butcher's meat. If his sales from both sources do not amount to $1,000, his license fee is $5. If they exceed that sum, it will be $10. A dealer who sells butcher's meat, must take license as a butcher, although not liable to license as a dealer because his sales do not exceed $1,000. A farmer, who kills for his own use is not liable, although he may occasionally sell a portion to his neighbor. Butchers. Liability to take license. Liability of farmers.

A butcher licensed to sell from a cart, cannot, under such license, sell other articles, but is confined to butcher's meat exclusively. Butcher cannot sell any thing but butcher's meat from a cart.

(No. 345.)

The tax imposed on transportation companies by section 103, is upon the gross receipts; and the canal tolls paid to the State of New York cannot, therefore, be deducted. Transportation companies must pay on gross receipts.

CORRESPONDENCE.*

(No. 1.)

THE INCOME TAX.

Income tax.

"SIR: I have the honor to acknowledge the receipt of your letter, 7th instant, relative to the assessment of income tax. You make two points:

Dividends from which the deduction of 3 per cent. has been made to be taxed 2 per cent. additional in case the total income of the party amounts to $10,000.

"1st. That the deduction of income from sources named in section 91, on which a tax of 3 per cent. has been already paid, is to be made in ascertaining the amount of taxable income and the rate of tax thereon, and is then to be excluded from all further computation.

"2d. That there is no authority of law for requiring an additional two per cent. upon portions of income derived from the sources above named, when the taxable income of the person proves to be in excess of $10,000.

"I think you have not fully weighed the provisions of the law, or its manifest intent. Section 90 divides into two classes the taxable incomes of persons residing in the United States: one, 'whose annual gains, profits, or income exceed $600,' and do not exceed $10,000, is liable to a duty of 3 per cent. on the excess over $600; the other, whose income exceeds $10,000, is liable to a duty of 5 per cent. on the excess over $600. Previous sections of the law impose a tax of 3 per cent. on payments of interest and dividends by specified corporations, on salaries of United States officials, and on income derived from advertisements. Section 91, in its first clause, provides 'that in estimating said annual gains, profits, or income, whether subject to a duty as provided in this act of three per centum or five per centum, all other national, State, and local taxes * * * shall be first deducted.' In its second clause it provides that salaries or payments from the United States, and interest or dividends from banks and other corporations, the taxes on which shall have been assessed and paid by said banks and other corporations, and income from advertisements, upon which specific, stamp, or ad valorem duties shall have been assessed or paid, shall also be deducted.

"You hold that all the income from all these sources shall be first deducted in determining the taxable income and the rate of tax. I cannot see that the law justifies your opinion. It certainly

* The letters without signature were written or dictated by the editor of this manual.

does not so provide in terms. The 91st section gives to every person residing in the United States an absolute deduction of other national, State, and local taxes paid by him. The 11th section of the act of March 3, 1863, as if to make this distinction more emphatic, provides 'that in estimating the annual gains, profit, or income of any person under the act to which this act is an amendment, the amount actually paid by such person for the rent of the dwelling-house or estate on which he resides shall be first deducted from the gains, profits, or income of such person.'

"This office has also authorized, as by the equity of the statute, a deduction, in this as in all cases, of necessary repairs, &c., upon the property yielding the income. These comprise all the deductions authorized by law or equity to be made in determining the amount of taxable income and the rate of tax. The second clause of section 91, which is wholly independent of the first, is distinct in form, and on no reasonable construction can be made to mean more than it expresses, authorizes the deduction of income received from the other sources therein named, but for a reason expressed therein, viz: that the taxes due thereon have been assessed and paid. This interpretation exhausts the phraseology, and gives the reason for the deduction—not as a means of determining the rate of tax, but to avoid re-imposition of three per cent. tax. Your claim ignores facts, and assumes, what cannot be granted, that there is but one class of deductions. There are two. One consists of those which are absolutely exempt from taxation, without reference to the amount of income, and which are first deductions, and are made in estimating the income and the rate of tax. The other consists of those which have been already taxed, which may be taxed an increased rate in case the taxable income exceeds $10,000, and which are simple deductions, either absolute or contingent, as the case may be.

"Your construction, besides not being literal, would have the obviously unjust effect of relieving from 5 per cent. taxation one class of citizens whose chief sources of income are made taxable under section 91, and of imposing 5 per cent. on the same amount of income derived from rents, professions, trades, commerce, and stocks and bonds not reached by section 91. This, surely, cannot be considered the intent of Congress, whose division of income, of all persons residing in the United States, is into two great classes, with a rate of taxation proportioned thereto, and whose fundamental idea is, or should be, equality of taxation upon the citizens.

"There is one other consideration which bears heavily against your construction. Congress imposed a duty of 1½ per cent. on that portion of income derived from United States securities, but that source of income is not named in section 91 among those to be deducted. Hence, were your construction correct, the patriotic citizen with a gross income exceeding $10,000, one-half of which is derived from United States securities, would be placed at a disadvantage, and made to pay 5 per cent. on the remainder; while another with like gross income, one-half of which is derived from the sources named in section 91, which you propose to deduct in ascertaining the taxable income and the rate of tax, would escape with but 3 per cent. on the remainder. And this, too, while

Congress at every point manifestly sought to put the holders of government securities in a better position than any other class of citizens. Your construction must be wrong, or Congress has wholly failed to do what it manifestly and in the clearest language intended.

"The construction of this office is natural and reasonable. It is in harmony with the general scope of the law. It is reasonable, in placing upon one footing all residents of the United States whose taxable incomes are over $10,000, and in maintaining the broad distinction of rate expressly enacted in section 90, and in harmonizing that with the merely directory provisions of section 91.

"Where taxable income is ascertained to be in excess of $10,000, it becomes liable to a 5 per cent. tax, and must be made to bear it, whatever its sources. If some of them have already paid 3 per cent., at the hands of corporations paying interest or dividends or otherwise, 2 per cent. additional must be imposed upon them as a necessary means, and the only practicable means, of carrying out the mandatory provisions of the law. To fail to require this, would be to make the law an engine of inequality and oppression. This, I am sure, you are too good a citizen to desire.

"I am, very respectfully, your obedient servant,

"EDWARD McPHERSON,

"*Deputy Commissioner.*"

(No. 2.)

Coal land leases treated as "conveyances," and subject to stamp duty as such.

SIR: Your letter of February 5 was duly received, but as a decision upon the stamp duty required upon "coal land leases," or upon assignments thereof, has been withheld for careful consideration, yours, with other letters upon the same subject, has not been answered ere this.

In reply thereto I have the honor to state that those leases are construed to be "conveyances," and as such to be stamped under head of "conveyance," as per "Schedule B," in the act of July 1, 1862. The assignment of such a lease should also be stamped under the head of "conveyance," as above, the consideration paid being the measure of stamp duty. If the consideration in such an assignment is $33,000, the stamp duty required is $60.

In the case presented of a price per ton of coal mined, there being nothing in the contract to indicate more accurately its probable value, the practical difficulty of ascertaining the value will be met, should it arise, by the resident revenue officers.

Very respectfully,

EDWARD McPHERSON,

Deputy Commissioner.

To J. BRISBIN, Esq., *Superintendent, &c.*

(No. 3.)

Powers of attorney to be used abroad not subject to stamp duty.

SIR: The communication from the honorable Secretary of State, under date of January 14, and the letter of C. F. Hagedorn, esq., consul of Baden, dated Philadelphia, January 10, have been considered, and I respectfully submit the following reply:

Mr. Hagedorn inquires, first, "whether powers of attorney for foreign countries for the collection of moneys abroad, or the sale of property there, require stamps?" If such powers of attorney are so prepared and authenticated as to conform to the laws of the country in which moneys are to be collected or property sold by virtue thereof, I am of opinion that the transaction would be valid as between the principal and attorney, and that the rights of third parties could not be questioned, upon the ground that such powers were not stamped according to the laws of the United States.

The law provides that "bills of exchange," drawn in but payable out of the United States, shall be stamped. No such provision exists with regard to powers of attorney, nor is there reason to suppose, from the language employed, that stamps are required upon such instruments when made in this country, but which could be made operative and of value only in another country.

Mr. Hagedorn next inquires, "whether the certificates of notaries public attached to such powers require stamps, and to what amount?"

In all cases the certificate of the notary, that the party appeared and duly executed the power, &c., is exempt from duty.

To Hon. S. P. CHASE,
Secretary of the Treasury.

(No. 4.)

Tax on receipts for advertising may be added to the amount chargeable to the United States.

SIR: I have received your communication of December 29, in relation to certain claims made by publishers of the laws of the United States.

In section 88 of the excise law it is "provided that in all cases where the rate or price of advertising is fixed by any law of the United States, State, or Territory, it shall be lawful for the company, person, or persons publishing said advertisements, to add the duty or tax imposed by this act to the price of said advertisements, any law as aforesaid to the contrary notwithstanding."

Assuming that in the cases to which you have called my attention, the rate of advertising is fixed by a law of the United States, I think the publishers are justified in adding the amount of the tax to their bills, if they satisfy the officers of the Department of State that the sum so claimed has been paid.

I will mention that it is the practice of this office in similar cases to require the certificate of the collector in proof of the payment of the tax.

To G. E. BAKER, Esq.,
Department of State.

(No. 5.)

Bonds issued by a State in aid of a railway to be treated as railway bonds.

SIR: Your letter of the 4th instant is received.

In reply to your inquiry in regard to sterling bonds of the Commonwealth of Massachusetts, issued in aid of the Western Railroad

Corporation, and if the semi-annual interest warrants are subject to the tax of three per centum, I have to say that the sterling bonds to which you refer must be treated as issued by the Western Railroad Corporation, and the three per centum must be reserved upon all coupons payable in the United States. If payable in foreign countries, the tax cannot be reserved. If payable here or abroad at the option of the holder, and the holder has chosen or chooses to receive the interest here, the tax must be withheld.

If interest is payable abroad the tax cannot be withheld.

To STEPHEN FAIRBANKS, Esq., *Boston.*

(No. 6.)

The stamp upon a deed given by several tenants in common to one of the number must answer to the value of the estate conveyed.

SIR: Your letter of the 29th instant has been received, giving the statement of Charles Remelin, esq., attorney for the heirs of Jacob Lohweigsehop, esq., deceased, on which you ask an opinion.

Said Jacob Lohweigsehop died about ten years since, leaving a widow and four daughters. He left his property to the former, during her life, and then it was to revert to the heirs, as aforesaid. He further states that these heirs have now agreed to a partition among themselves, and have made quitclaim deeds to each other, in each of which the consideration is one dollar. Mr. Remelin desires to know whether these deeds are subject to stamp duty, and if so, to what stamp.

In reply, I would say that if, as I presume from your letter, the heirs are tenants in common, and are making an equal division of the property among themselves, each deed will be a conveyance of three-fourths of the estate described in the deed, and must be stamped to answer to three-fourths of the value of the property so described.

In all cases, whether a conveyance is a "quitclaim," or a "warranty deed," stamps, as prescribed under the head of conveyance, are required.

To R. M. W. TAYLOR, Esq., *Cincinnati, Ohio.*

(No. 7.)

The stamp tax upon a will must answer to the value of the estate which can be administered upon.

SIR: In your letter of the 17th ultimo you make the following inquiries:

"In the probate of wills, under the national tax law, is the duty chargeable upon the value of the real estate devised, as well as upon the personalty?"

I am of opinion that the value of all the property of the testator, whether real or personal, which, under the law, or by virtue of the terms of the will, can be administered upon, and which is within the jurisdiction of the court wherein the will is approved, is the measure of the stamp duty chargeable upon the will when approved.

If the will is approved in another jurisdiction an ad-

Should the will be approved in another jurisdiction, it will then be necessary to affix an additional stamp, proportionate to the value of the property within such jurisdiction, and subject to the law, and terms of the will.

ditional stamp required.

This latter remark is in reply to your second inquiry, in which you say:

"If the real estate is embraced in the law requiring a stamp duty, and there are pieces of real property lying in different counties and in different States, in each of which the will must be admitted to probate, is the stamp duty to be affixed for the whole value on the first probate, or must the stamp be affixed for the portion of the estate within the jurisdiction of each particular court of probate?"

To L. ANDERSON, Esq., *Cincinnati, Ohio.*

(No. 8.)

SIR: I have received a letter dated at Philadelphia, March 12, from Abel Reed and others, a committee representing various firms engaged in making window and door frames, sash, doors, blinds, mouldings, &c.

Contractors who make doors, &c., to be used in buildings, must pay tax upon such doors, &c., if the articles are salable.

This committee complain that by the operation of the tax law as administered in Philadelphia, carpenters and builders, who, in the construction of buildings taken on contract, make, instead of purchasing, window and door frames, sashes, doors, blinds, and mouldings, have an advantage over manufacturers of these articles equal to eight per cent. on the labor employed. In answer, I have to say that it has been decided by the Commissioner that window and door frames, sashes, doors, blinds, mouldings, &c., being in themselves manufactures, and liable to taxation when removed for sale, are equally liable to taxation when the carpenter or builder makes the same and uses them on houses built under contract.

By section 79, article 46, of the act of June 30, 1864, builders and contractors are required to pay a license tax of $25 when their building contracts exceed $2,500 in any one year.

If the assessor applies the law as thus written and interpreted, (and it is to be presumed that he will,) I see not how the contractor or builder who makes the above enumerated articles can have any advantage over the special manufacturer of the same.

No article held to be a manufacture will be allowed exemption from taxation under the plea of its having been made to special order, unless it fully satisfies the conditions of the above-named decision.*

To ——— ———, *Assessor.*

(No. 9.)

SIR: I have received your letter, together with a copy of a letter from the Quartermaster General, and of a charter-party, and

* See proviso to section 93.

of a contract. It is stated that the army regulations, approved June 2, 1862, require all contracts with the government to be made in quintuplicate.

Upon this state of facts the question arises whether each part of the contract is subject to stamp duty under the provisions of Schedule B, of the act of July 1, 1862.

Contracts made in quintuplicate, according to army regulations, require stamps for every copy.

It has been held by this office, in the case of papers which are usually prepared in several parts, but which would be valid under the law if executed in one part only, that the parties interested might exercise a discretion, and affix a stamp to each part when several were made, or to one part only. It has been a custom, however, to inform parties that the enforcement of their legal rights must depend entirely upon the stamped instrument.

The case presented differs from those which have been considered heretofore by the Commissioner of Internal Revenue, in the circumstance that the regulations of the War Department, which have, as I suppose, the force of law, require each contract to be executed in five parts. It may reasonably be assumed that it is the purpose of the regulation to make each part of full legal value. It therefore follows that the proper stamps should be affixed to each part of every contract.

To WM. WHITING, Esq.,
Solicitor of the War Department,
Washington, D. C.

(No. 10.)

I have received your letter, with form of lease of land for ninety-nine years, with right of renewal forever, and assignment of the same by the lessee or his representatives, enclosed.

Leases operating as conveyances subject to appropriate stamp.

Method of determining values of rents, &c.

I am of opinion that the assignment, or deed as it more properly is, must be stamped as a conveyance. The lease must also be regarded as a conveyance, and when made, it must bear stamps proportionate to its value. This valuation may be fixed by the market price, or by converting the annual rent into a capital sum at the legal rate of interest at which money may be obtained upon such security.

Assignment of leases subject to same taxes as original.

The assignment of a lease is subject to the same stamp as the original.

GEORGE E. SANGSTON, Esq.,
Clerk of the Superior Court, Baltimore, Md.

(No. 11.)

Act of March 3, 1863, relating to stamps on powers of attorney, soldiers' bounty papers, &c., does not apply to claims for prize-money.

SIR: In your letter you call my attention to the following provision of the amendments to the excise law approved 3d March, 1863: "No stamp duty shall be required on powers of attorney or any other paper relating to applications for bounties, arrearages of pay, or pensions, or to the receipt thereof from time to time."*

I am of opinion that this provision exempts from stamp duty all papers relating to applications for bounties, arrearages of pay,

* This language is retained in section 160 of the act of June 30, 1864.

or pensions, made by or on behalf of officers or privates of the army, or officers, marines, or sailors of the navy, who are, or at the time of such application may have been, in the service of the United States; but it cannot be construed to exempt from stamp duty applications or claims for prize-money or papers relating to such applications or claims.

(No. 12.)

Advances by a testator to his sons previously to passage of act July 1, 1862, not subject to taxation at his death subsequently thereto unless notes had been given as security therefor.

SIR: Your letter of March 27, enclosing a communication addressed to you by ** **, esq., inquiring whether he is liable as executor to pay tax on advances made by testator to his sons during his lifetime, has been received.

In reply, I have the honor to say that the tax cannot be levied upon advances that were made in the lifetime of the testator, and previous to July 1, 1862. If the advances had been made since that time, the case might have been different, but on this point I express no opinion.

If the testator had taken notes for the sums advanced, and those notes had been appraised as a part of the assets of the estate, and charged to the executor, the full amount of the legacies, including such advances, would be liable to the tax specified in section 111.*

It is not stated that notes were taken by the testator for the sums advanced in this case, nor does it appear that such sums were counted among the assets of the estate and charged to the executor; and if neither the one nor the other was done, then the tax is to be levied only on the amounts actually paid by the executor to the legatees.

To ——— ———, *Assessor.*

(No. 13.)

A bridge company authorized by law to receive tolls must pay 3 per cent. to the government.

SIR: If there is, in your district, a bridge owned by a company, and the company is authorized by law to receive toll for the transit of passengers, beasts, carriages, &c., over such bridge, then the person, or persons, or parties having the care and management of the bridge must pay to the government three per centum on the gross amount of all their receipts of every description.

Immaterial whether the company was chartered as a turnpike or bridge company.

It is entirely immaterial whether the company was chartered as a turnpike company or as a bridge company. It is sufficient for the purposes of the government that the parties having the control of it are authorized by law to receive tolls.

To ——— ———, *Assessor.*

(No. 14.)

SIR: Accepting your statement that the George's Creek Coal and Iron Company was chartered for mining purposes, and that the

* Stat. July 1, 1862.

A company, not chartered as a railway company, having issued bonds for the construction of a railway, must deduct 3 per cent. of the interest paid on such bonds.

construction of the railway was incidental to the main business of the corporation, I am of opinion that the interest upon those bonds which were issued especially for or in aid of the construction of the railway is liable to taxation, under the 81st section of the excise law, passed July 1, 1862.*

It follows from the same statement that the bonds issued previous to the construction of the railway, as well as those issued since, for general purposes, are not subject to the provisions of said section.

(No. 15.)

Your letter of February 24, in regard to the tax on gun-barrels of a peculiar description, made by * * * *, has been received.

Gun-barrels made by a patentee or his licensee may be subject to taxation.

The question is, whether they are liable to pay a tax on gun-barrels forged by them, upon an order from a manufacturer for the specific purpose of being used by him in the construction of a patent fire-arm, and which could be used only by the party owning the patent, or one having a license from the owner of the patent.

I reply, first, that the fact that the owner of the patent sells to others the right to use and manufacture the gun, settles the question that the article has a commercial character and will find sale as an article of commerce; and, therefore, it must be regarded as a manufacture, and subject to taxation as such.

Secondly: If the patentable feature of the gun-barrel may be removed so as not to injure the barrel, and it may thereby be converted into one of ordinary form, it would thus clearly have a commercial value, be salable in market, and therefore should be regarded as a manufacture.

(No. 16.)

SIR: Your letter of the 26th ultimo, relative to the course to be pursued in collecting unpaid taxes has been received.

Taxes to be collected by distraint

You will collect taxes by distraint in all cases. If they cannot be collected in that manner, there would be but little use in resorting to the courts.

If suits are instituted they are to be brought in United States courts.

All suits must be brought in the United States courts. The employment of counsel will be authorized, in proper cases, on application to this office.

(No. 17.)

DECEMBER 27, 1862.

The communication of the honorable the Secretary of State, of the 24th instant, addressed to yourself, together with despatch No. 134, from the United States consul general at Frankfort-on-the-Main, has been received at this office, agreeably to the reference you were pleased to make.

No deduction made from payments of interest on United States bonds.

In reply, I have the honor to say that neither under the excise law, nor under any other law of the United States, is a deduction to be made from the interest payable upon United States bonds.

* See section 122, act of June 30, 1864.

The income tax is levied only upon residents of the United States and upon citizens of the United States residing abroad. Hence the subjects and citizens of other governments, and residents in foreign countries not citizens of the United States, who are holders of United States bonds, are not liable to the payment of income tax under our laws, and they will receive the interest on such bonds without tax, charge, or deduction in any form.

To Hon. S. P. CHASE,
Secretary of the Treasury.

(No. 18.)

SIR: You are correct in assuming that the dividend to stockholders in a bank or railway of 4½ per cent. of ascertained profits is subject to the duty of 5 per cent.; and I am of the opinion, further, that the additional payment of 3½ per cent., called by you a payment "for six months interest on the capital stock," must be treated as a dividend also, and, of course, subject to the duty of 5 per cent.

Any payment of profits to a stockholder must be regarded as a dividend. It cannot be said, properly, that a stockholder, by his investment in a company, for which he receives as evidence a certificate that he owns a certain number of shares, stands in the relation of a lender of money to such company; and as he does not lend money to the company, it cannot with truth be said that a payment made to him out of the profits of the company is a payment of interest. It is, in fact, a dividend on the stock.

Dividends to stockholders in companies cannot be regarded as payments of interest. Are therefore liable to taxation. Section 122.

By the 120th section of the excise law a tax of 5 per cent. is levied upon all scrip issued by insurance or other companies named in said section; and I am of opinion that payments made for the redemption of scrip, which has been so issued, and which, if issued since the 31st day of August, 1862, was liable to duty, are exempt from further taxation.

Scrip issued by insurance companies taxable.

No tax levied upon the redemption.

To ——— ———, *Assessor.*

(No. 19.)

FEBRUARY 16, 1863.

SIR: I have received and considered your letters of the 16th and 31st days of January, 1863, together with the printed communication of S. S. Moffit, esq., comptroller of the treasury of Maryland, under date of January 7, 1863; also, your argument upon the questions presented, and a copy of the mortgage made by the Northern Central Railroad Company to the State of Maryland.

Dividends upon railway and bank stocks owned by a State are not liable to deduction under secs. 81, 82.

From these several communications and documents it appears that the State of Maryland receives an annuity of $90.000 from the Northern Central Railroad Company, secured by the mortgage referred to; the right existing on the part of the corporation, by virtue of an act of the State of Maryland, to quiet the annuity by the payment of a million and a half of dollars. It also appears that the State is further entitled to receive from the Baltimore and Ohio Railroad Company a yearly sum of $180,000. This sum is charged on the gross earnings of the company, in consideration of a subscription of three millions of dollars to the capital stock of said company, under the provisions of an act of the legislature of the year 1835. I conclude, from the statements made, that, to the extent of the subscription, the State is distinguished from ordinary stockholders by the fact that the payment of six per cent. is a lien upon the gross earnings of the road, and is of course to be paid in full, without regard to the ability of the company to pay dividends to other stockholders.

It also appears that the State of Maryland is a stockholder in various banking corporations, and that from these sources a large portion of its revenue is derived.

By the excise law of July 1, 1862, section 82, dividends made by banks are subject to a duty of three per centum; and by the 81st section of the same act every railroad company or railroad corporation, being indebted for any sum or sums of money for which bonds or other evidences of indebtedness have been issued, is authorized and required to deduct and withhold from all payments made to any person, persons, or party, on account of any interest on coupons, a like duty of three per cent. The word party might be so construed as to include State; but I am of opinion that it was not the intention of Congress to levy a tax upon States; but it is clear, from the uniform language of the law, that it was the intention of Congress to levy a tax upon the business and property of the people of the several States, and the corporations and companies therein existing.

Accepting this statement of the intentions of Congress, it only remains to consider whether a requisition upon the officers of the railway companies named, and upon the several banks in which the State of Maryland is a stockholder, to withhold three per centum of the annuities, interest, and dividends, is, in form or effect, a tax upon the State. It cannot be doubted that the deduction of three per centum on the several sums which may be due and payable to the State of Maryland, is, to that extent, a deduction from the revenue of the State, and is, in fact, if not in form, a tax upon the State.

It follows, then, as a further inference, that the officers of the railroad corporations named, and of the several banks in which the State of Maryland is a stockholder, will continue to pay to the proper authorities of the State the annuities, interest, and dividends which may be now due, or which may hereafter become due, as such annuities, interest and dividends would have been paid if the excise law of July 1 had not been passed. It only remains for me to say, in conclusion, that the excise law of July 1, 1862, does not contemplate or authorize the assessment or collection of a tax or duty upon the property or revenues of a State.

THOMAS S. ALEXANDER, Esq.
Baltimore, Maryland.

(No. 20.)

DECEMBER 31, 1862.

The phrase "articles of traffic" defined.

SIR: Articles manufactured and known to dealers in such or similar articles as articles of traffic, and having as such a commercial value independent of and greater than the value of the materials used, are to be treated as manufactures, and subject to taxation under the excise law.

It is not sufficient, however, that an article should be valuable to a particular individual: it must be known to, dealt in, and be valuable to many persons, or to a class of dealers or consumers, in order that it may be considered an article of commerce.

For example, if an inventor produce a machine different in its parts, or as a whole, from any machine previously or elsewhere known or used, and in the construction of such machine prepares patterns, or parts thereof, and procures castings therefrom, such castings* could not be taxed as manufactures, for it cannot be said that they are known to trade; that any number or class of persons are accustomed to buy or sell such castings; and consequently they cannot have a commercial value, inasmuch as no one but the inventor has a right to make and use the articles in question.

The same reasoning would apply and the same rule exist in regard to an article the use of which, by the customs of trade, was restricted to one person, or a small number of persons, and which consequently was not the subject of unrestricted purchase and sale.

This might be true of parts of sewing-machines, for instance, such as are peculiar in their character, and used for the manufacture of a particular kind of machine. If, however, the part were common to two or more machines, so that if offered in market there would be purchasers for it as for other articles of commerce, it would be liable to taxation.

Cotton machinery which is in general or common use in the manufactories of the country would undoubtedly possess a commercial value, and be subject to taxation, inasmuch as it might be used by many persons engaged in that branch of business.

Whenever a particular kind of machine is so well known and so generally used that manufacturers make provision for supplying parts of such machine, the presumption arises that such parts are articles of traffic in the community, and consequently must be considered as manufactures in themselves.

In the case presented by you, if the said boiler possess a commercial value, (and this the assessor must determine,) it is not exempt because of its belonging to a marine engine any more than a pipe or faucet that is used in the construction of the engine.

If the boiler had been made by the makers of the engine, it would have been equally liable to taxation.

To ——— ———,
Assessor of ———

(No. 21.)

JANUARY 7, 1863.

Certificates issued by a collector of customs not subject to stamp duty unless collector is acting as port warden or surveyor.

SIR: Your letter of the 2d instant was duly received.

In reply thereto I have to state that, in my opinion, the certificates and other papers signed and issued by custom-house collectors cannot be regarded as coming within the meaning of the third clause of the excise law, pertaining to "certificate" of damages

---

*This ruling is changed by the act of June 30, 1864, section 94, by which castings are subject to taxation, without inquiring whether such castings are articles of traffic. The reasoning still applies generally.

and all other certificates or documents issued by any port warden, marine surveyor, or other person acting as such, except when such certificates are signed and issued by the collector at a port to which no warden or surveyor is appointed, or in the absence of, and under authority from, said warden or surveyor.

(No. 22.)

JANUARY 28, 1863.

Debts due to a mutual life insurance company from policy-holders treated as capital.

SIR: The insurance company to which you refer must make return for the dividend of 7 per cent. upon its whole capital of $100,000.

It is stated in a letter of the secretary that a part of this capital is secured by the notes of certain persons who are called guarantors.

It is understood that these parties are policy-holders; but this circumstance does not change the obligation of the company to account for the entire dividend paid. These parties are debtors to the company, pay an annual interest of 6 per cent. upon their notes, and receive a dividend of 7 per cent. as stockholders.

The payment by the company is an actual payment of dividend, as truly as though it was paid to parties who were not indebted to the corporation; and being a dividend, the officers are required to withhold the tax, and account for the same to the government.

To ——— ———, *Assessor.*

(No. 23.)

NOVEMBER 17, 1862.

Person acting under a power of attorney, either as principal or substitute, does not require license as commercial broker.

SIR: If Mr. Parrish holds a power of attorney, with power of substitution, from Honorable Edward Ellice, of England, and if Mr. Parrish has gone abroad, leaving two persons as his salaried agents or clerks attending to the property which he holds in his own right and by power of attorney, I think Mr. Parrish needs no license as commercial broker, as he acts for but one person beside himself; nor do his salaried clerks, if they do no other than his business.

If liquor is sold on steamers, the owner must take license as liquor dealer.

If Mr. Wooley is the agent of three steamers the principal offices of which are at Oswego, he should take out a retail liquor dealer's license for such steamers at Oswego. If his steamers supply passengers with food and lodging, and he has taken out hotel licenses, (article 20, section 79,) the before-mentioned liquor dealer's license must be taken out in addition thereto.

Returns may be required of persons claiming that their annual product is less than $600.

In cases where persons claim to manufacture a less amount than at the rate of $600 per year, the assessor may at his discretion require from them monthly returns if he has a suspicion that the amount manufactured exceeds that sum.

To ——— ———, *Assessor.*

(No. 24.)

I cannot hold with you that the term "port warden," as used in the clause of Schedule B under consideration, is synonymous with that of "collector of customs."

Had Congress, in framing the law, intended to have included, under this head, such certificates and other documents as are ordinarily issued by custom-house collectors, it would scarcely have been left a matter for conjecture.

Section 1, article 567, of the revenue regulations, (1857,) sets forth in full the general duties of collectors or surveyors.

After due consideration of the article referred to, and of the several papers submitted by you, I hold that they are respectively subject to stamp duty as follows, viz:

Stamp tax on papers issued by custom-house officers.

1st, certificate of enrolment; 2d, certificate of license; 3d, transit certificate; 4th, certificate to cancel transportation bond; each requires the general (five cent) certificate stamp. Nos. 5, 6, being certificates of clearance, and partial discharge of cargo of vessels bound for inland (American) ports, are exempt from tax.

No. 7, certificate of clearance for a Canadian port, is also exempt under the last clause of Schedule B, which provides that the stamp duties imposed upon manifests, bills of lading, and passage tickets *shall not apply to vessels plying between ports of the United States and ports in British North America.*

No. 8, oath to an invoice, is exempt.

No. 9, the certificate of the master builder, requires the general (five-cent) certificate stamp.

No. 10, certificate of admeasurement. This paper, as I understand, is issued by the surveyor in his official capacity, and, as such, is subject to the twenty-five-cent stamp.

Stamp tax on custom-house bonds.

I am also of the opinion that three several bonds, numbered and named, respectively, 11, warehouse bond; 12, enrolment bond; 13, license bond, (and all other penal bonds of a similar character required in the transaction of the business of the custom-house,) come within the meaning of the third clause of Schedule B, relating to "bond," and are therefore subject to stamp duty of 25 cents.

In reply to your queries respecting certificates issued in duplicate and triplicate, I refer you to the enclosed copy of official regulations.

If these or any of these papers are signed by the collector, or surveyor, or warden, they will require the twenty-five-cent stamp, as provided in clause No. 3.

To EDWIN PALMER, Esq., *Collector of Customs,*
Milwaukie, Wis.

(No. 25.)

Manufacturers of gas must pay tax upon quantity consumed as well as upon quantity sold.

SIR: Your letter of the 16th instant, in regard to the tax upon gas you manufacture, and in part sell, was duly received.

If the annual product does not exceed the rate of $600, no tax can be assessed. If it does, the tax must be paid upon the whole product, whether sold or consumed.

The same principle applies to what you make in your shop. All manufactures are subject to tax, whether consumed or sold.—(Sect. 93.)

(No. 26.)

JANUARY 3, 1863.

Clothing made for gratuitous distribution not subject to tax.

SIR: I have received a letter from Mr. Yeatman, president of the Western Sanitary Commission, in which it is stated that Mr.

Sleuth was employed by the commission to make from their own materials a large number of shirts and drawers, and that he has been required by the assessor to pay three per cent. upon their value under the excise law.

By reference to decision No. 36, you will see that when one person makes clothing for another person, the owner of the cloth is regarded as the manufacturer, and that the employé should make returns to the assistant assessor of the number and value of the garments, and of the name and residence of the owner of them.

In this case the return will show that the Sanitary Commission is the manufacturer. But as the commission makes a gratuitous distribution of the garments in question to others than members of their own body, I do not see that they can be taxed for the value of the garments, as taxes are levied only on goods when sold or removed for sale, or when removed for consumption by the owners.

To T. PAPIN, Esq., *Assessor 1st District, St. Louis, Mo.*

(No. 27.)

JANUARY 2, 1863.

Payment to stockholders in a railway, of money received for the use of the same, under a lease, is payment of a dividend.

SIR: From your letter it appears that the Stockbridge and Pittsfield railroad is leased to the Housatonic Railroad Company, at a rent of seven per centum upon the cost.

From your statement, I am of opinion that the lease, as described by you, does not, in fact, amount to a sale and transfer of the franchise and property of the Stockbridge and Pittsfield railroad to the Housatonic Railroad Company; for, should the Housatonic Railroad Company neglect or refuse to comply with the stipulated conditions, there is no reason why the Stockbridge and Pittsfield Railroad Company may not legally enter into possession and enjoyment of the property and franchise of its road.

If this view of the contract be correct, then it follows that the stipulated payment of three and a half per centum semi-annually is a dividend to the stockholders of the Stockbridge and Pittsfield railroad, and, as such, subject to the tax.

It is entirely immaterial to the stockholders of the Stockbridge and Pittsfield railroad whether their dividend is derived from the annual rent, or from the proceeds of business transacted by the corporation.

To Hon. J. Z. GOODRICH, *Stockbridge, Mass.*

(No. 28.)

MARCH 19, 1863.

The United States has power to levy a tax upon banks incorporated by a State.

SIR: I have examined your arguments, numbered 1 and 2, in which you set forth the views you entertain as counsel for the Bank of the State of Indiana, concerning the right of the United States to levy a tax upon banks chartered by a State legislature.

After due reflection, upon the arguments presented by you, I am of opinion that there is but one question to be considered, viz: Has the United States government power, under the Constitution, to levy a tax upon banks incorporated by a State?

The Constitution gives to Congress power to lay and collect taxes, duties, imposts, and excise; and it must follow, as a necessary result, that this power may be applied, in its exercise, to every object and subject of taxation in the country. It is undoubtedly true that the States have authority, by long practice, if not by recognized constitutional right, to create corporations for banking purposes. The excise law does not question this right, nor interfere in any way with its exercise by the several States.

If it is said, as it is said in your argument, that the power to tax a bank is a power which may be so exercised in degree as to deprive the bank itself of the capacity to exist, and thereby defeat the will and the legislation of the State, so it is also true that if the general government has the power, as it has, undoubtedly, to tax individuals, that power of taxation may become, by the force of events, so onerous as to deprive individuals of their whole estate; but it is to be presumed that the government will exercise the power of taxation with all the moderation that circumstances will permit. It cannot be alleged, with any show of truth, that the taxation of banks under the excise law is objectionable upon this ground.

In many States corporations have been chartered for manufacturing purposes, and all the products of such corporations are subject to a tax under the excise law. Indeed, a large portion of the revenues of the government is derived from taxes levied upon the business of corporations; and I see not why the reason offered in support of the claim of the Bank of Indiana might not be offered, with equal force, in support of a similar claim on behalf of any bank, railroad, insurance, or manufacturing corporation in the country.

If the views you present are to be accepted as sound constitutional doctrine, the general government is at once deprived of a large portion of its revenues.

It has been held by this office that it was not the intent of Congress to levy a tax upon States, or the property of States; but with this exception, the general government has asserted its right to levy a tax upon the property and business and income of the persons, partnerships, firms, associations, and corporations of the country, to the same extent that a State might levy taxes upon the persons, partnerships, firms, associations, and corporations within its jurisdiction.

If the charter authorizes the bank to do the business of a broker, the bank must take license as a broker.

In the course of your argument you question the right of Congress to levy a tax upon the Bank of the State of Indiana, for the transaction of business which, by its charter, it is authorized to transact, but which, by the excise law of July 1, 1862, is described as the business of a broker, as distinguished from the business of a banker. You proceed to show, historically, that the business of banking in Italy, England, and this country, includes those transactions which, in the excise law, are regarded as the business of a broker. The result of your historical researches may be entirely accurate; but, as it seems to me, it is not in any degree pertinent to this inquiry. If Congress had the power to levy a tax upon the business of banking, it had power also to describe and define the nature of that business under the law. Such a declaration and definition were necessary to its proper administration. Congress has also the power to define the business of a broker, not historically, nor for the world at large, but for the purpose of assessing a tax upon those branches of business.

That definition is consequently binding upon the officers of the government, and upon the parties engaged in those pursuits. Congress has declared what the business of banking is; it has fixed the amount of the license to be paid by private bankers, and it has exempted from the license fee all incorporated banks and all banks legally authorized to issue notes as circulation. The Bank of the State of Indiana is, consequently, exempted, as far as its business as a banker is described and defined by the law. But the bank, as appears from your argument and from the statements made by the assessor of the district, is also engaged in business which, by the law, is declared to be that of a broker, and for which the license fee of $50 is required. This claim by the general government does not, in any manner, infringe upon the sovereignty of the State of Indiana, nor are the chartered rights of the bank impaired. The bank is taxed, in common with other corporations, and without burdensome or unjust discrimination.

In your admission that the general government has the power of taxation under the Constitution, you admit all that is claimed or contemplated.

Under the Constitution, Congress has the power to levy taxes; that power is coextensive with the subjects of taxation. In most, if not all of the States of the Union banks have been taxed, and they have everywhere, I believe, been regarded as proper subjects of taxation; therefore, the act of Congress is no departure from the settled policy of the country, as exhibited in the legislation of a great majority of the States.

Each branch of a bank treated as a separate institution.

I have only to add, in accordance with the rulings of this office, that each branch of the State Bank of Indiana must, for the purposes of taxation, be regarded as a separate institution.

HON. DAVID KILGORE, *Indiana.*

(No. 29.)

OCTOBER 8, 1862.

City bonds issued for the benefit of a railway company treated as though issued by the company.

SIR: Your letter of the 3d instant, asking a reconsideration of my decision in regard to the payment of the tax upon the coupons of the Milwaukie city bonds issued in payment of subscriptions to railroads, has been received.

The subject to which you call my attention was carefully considered. The party in interest is the railway company, which in fact is the promisor. The loan was for the benefit of the company. The effect of the opinion you desire would be to relieve the holders of the railway bonds of a tax which is paid by the bond-holders of other railways, although they have already the good fortune to enjoy the security which the faith and property of the city of Milwaukie furnish. The ruling already made, if the facts have been truly presented, seems to be sustained by law, and it is compatible with justice. The fact that the bonds are held by foreigners cannot affect the question as one of law or justice.

To Messrs. MORAN BROTHERS, *New York.*

(No. 30.)

WASHINGTON, *July* 9, 1863.

Duties on manufactured sugars.

It is, I am assured, the purpose of the head of this department to execute the several acts of Congress prescribing the duties of the Secretary of the Treasury in their true intent and meaning.

In the existing condition of the country, doubtless the proper enforcement of the laws must occasion sometimes inconveniences and sometimes hardships to individuals whose interests under other circumstances would be carefully guarded and efficiently protected.

To limit these inconveniences and hardships, and to mitigate, whenever and wherever possible, the calamities of civil war, is, I am sure, among the most earnest wishes of the honorable Secretary; and representatives of parties who think they suffer unjustly are always willingly received and attentively considered.

The papers submitted on behalf of the persons concerned in the sugar culture and trade in Louisiana have been examined by the Secretary in this spirit, and the following conclusions have been reached:

When liability to duty commences.

1st. That the proviso to the first section of the act of July 16, 1862, practically limits the effect in Louisiana of the act taxing sugar, to the time subsequent to the appointment and commissioning of a collector and assessor for that district.

The proviso requires the collection of internal taxes in the States and parts of States declared to be in insurrection in such manner and by such officers as the President may direct. The action of the President was therefore essential to putting the act in force in districts formed from States in insurrection. As to such districts, therefore, the general rule established by the act, that the tax shall be collected on all sugars in the hands of the producer and manufacturer at the date of the act, (July 16, 1862,) was practically suspended from operation by the proviso, until the manner in which and the officers by whom the collection should be made had been directed by the President.

The appointment of collector and assessor, so far as Louisiana is concerned, was a direction that internal taxes shall be collected in the manner and by the officers prescribed in the internal revenue and supplementary acts, which, so far as then enacted, may therefore be regarded as having taken effect on the 12th day of March, 1863, the date of the commission of William H. Higgins, the officer last appointed.

2d. The act directs the tax on sugar to be levied and collected on all sugar not made for family use, in the hands of the producer or manufacturer or of his agent or factor. An actual purchaser, in good faith, having possession of the sugar purchased, is not an agent or factor within the meaning of the law. When sugar, therefore, has been delivered to such a purchaser it ceases to be subject to the tax, though the producer or manufacturer in whose hands it was before delivery, and after the taking effect of the act, remains liable to pay the tax, and the tax to a lien on his property.

These conclusions, I believe, cover all the questions raised on the subject of sugars except those which have been already answered, and there will, I presume, be no difficulty in making the proper application of this interpretation of the acts of Congress to the circumstances of each particular case. You are at liberty to communicate the contents of this letter to such persons as have an interest in the questions considered.

Very respectfully,

JOSEPH J. LEWIS,
Commissioner.

(No. 31.)

JULY 26, 1864.

SIR:

Each person giving a receipt upon a pay roll, and receiving $20, must affix a stamp.

Under the act of June 30th, 1864, (which, so far as stamp duties are concerned, takes effect on the 1st day of August, 1864,) where several parties sign a pay roll, each for a separate and distinct amount of money, a stamp will be required for each signature, provided each amount of money exceeds $20. The law requires that each person who receipts for $20, or more, should affix and cancel a two-cent stamp. Receipts on pay rolls are the separate receipts of each person that signs the roll. The pay *roll* is not a single instrument, but an assemblage or agglomeration of instruments, without a single principle of legal unity to hold them together. The instrument is complete as to the parties, the railroad company and the employé, when executed by the employé, without waiting for the signature or concurrence of any other employé. If a single stamp should be affixed, and that stamp sufficient only for a hundred, and the roll should be signed by an hundred and two, how could it be said that it was stamped for any certain *hundred* of the signers, and not for any certain *two?* It would be impossible to appropriate the stamp, and therefore impossible to stamp the paper in that way.

I speak of the ordinary pay rolls, and give no opinion as to any other.

The same rule applies to receipts for dividends, on dividend sheets.

SCHEDULE OF STAMP DUTIES,

FROM AND AFTER AUGUST 1, 1864.

	Stamp Duty.
Acknowledgment of deeds, ...	exempt.
Affidavit, ...	5 cents.
" in suits or legal proceedings, ...	exempt.
Agreement or appraisement, (for each sheet, or piece of paper on which the same is written,)	5 cents.
Assignment or transfer of mortgage, lease, or policy of insurance, the same duty as the original instrument.	
" of patent right, ...	5 "
Bank Checks, drafts, or orders, &c., at sight or on demand, .	2 "
Bills of Exchange, (Foreign,) drawn in, but payable out of, the United States, each bill of set of three or more, must be stamped.	
For every bill of each set, where the sum made payable does not exceed $100, or the equivalent thereof in any foreign currency in which such bills may be expressed, according to the standard of value fixed by the United States, ...	2 "
For every additional $100, or fractional part thereof in excess of $100, ...	2 "
(Foreign,) drawn in, but payable out of, the United States, (if drawn singly or in duplicate,) pay the same duty as Inland Bills of Exchange.	
[The acceptor or acceptors of any Bill of Exchange, or order for the payment of any sum of money drawn, or purporting to be drawn, in any foreign country, but payable in the United States, must, before paying or accepting the same, place thereupon a stamp indicating the duty.]	
Bills of Exchange, (Inland,) draft, or order, payable otherwise than at sight or on demand, and any promissory note, whether payable on demand or at a time designated, (except bank notes issued for circulation, and checks made and intended to be, and which shall be, forthwith presented for payment,) for a sum not exceeding $100, . .	5 "
For every additional $100, or fractional part thereof,	5 "
[The warrant of attorney to confess judgment on a note or bond is exempt from stamp duty, if the note or bond is properly stamped.]	
Bills of Lading, of vessels for ports of the United States or British North America, ...	exempt.
" or receipt for goods, to any foreign port, . .	10 cents.
Bill of Sale of any vessel, or part thereof, when the consideration does not exceed $500, ...	50 "
" exceeding $500, and not exceeding $1,000, . .	$1 00
" exceeding $1,000, for each $500, or fractional part thereof,	50 cents.
" of personal property, (other than ship or vessel,) .	5 "

	Stamp Duty.
Bond, personal, for the payment of money. (See *Mortgage*.)	
" official, ...	$1 00
" for indemnifying any person for the payment of any sum of money, where the money ultimately recoverable thereupon is $1,000, or less, ...	50 cents.
" where the money recoverable exceeds $1,000, for every additional $1,000, or fractional part thereof, .	50 "
Bonds.—County, city, and town bonds, railroad and other corporation bonds, and scrip, are subject to stamp duty. (See *Mortgage*.)	
" of any description, other than such as are required in legal proceedings, and such as are not otherwise charged in this Schedule, ...	25 "
Certificates of deposit in bank, sum not exceeding $100, .	2 "
" of deposit in bank, sum exceeding $100, . .	5 "
" of stock in an incorporated company, . .	25 "
" general, ...	5 "
" of record upon the instrument recorded, . .	exempt.
" of record upon the book, ...	"
" of weight or measurement of animals, coal, wood, or other articles, except weighers' and measurers' returns,	"
" of a qualification of a justice of the peace, commissioner of deeds, or notary public, ...	5 cents.
" of search of records, ...	5 "
" that certain papers are on file, ...	5 "
" that certain papers cannot be found, ...	5 "
" of redemption of land sold for taxes, ...	5 "
" of birth, marriage, and death, ...	5 "
" of qualification of school teachers, ...	5 "
" of profits of an incorporated company for a sum not less than $10 and not exceeding $50, . . .	10 "
" exceeding $50, and not exceeding $1,000, . .	25 "
" exceeding $1,000, for every additional $1,000, or fractional part thereof, ...	25 "
" of damage, or otherwise, and all other certificates or documents issued by any port warden, marine surveyor, or other person acting as such, ...	25 "
Certified Transcripts of judgments, satisfaction of judgments, and of all papers recorded or on file, ...	5 "
[N. B.—As a general rule, every certificate which has, or may have, a legal value in any court of law or equity, will require a stamp duty of 5 cents.]	
Charter Party, or letter, memorandum, or other writing between the captain, owner, or agent of any ship, vessel, or steamer, and any other person, relating to the charter of the same, if the registered tonnage of said ship, vessel, or steamer does not exceed 150 tons, ...	$1 00
" exceeding 150 tons, and not exceeding 300 tons, . .	3 00
" " 300 tons, and not exceeding 600 tons, .	5 00
" " 600 tons, ...	10 00
Check, draft, or order for the payment of any sum of money exceeding $10, drawn upon any person other than a bank, banker, or trust company, at sight or on demand, .	2 cents.
Contract. (See *Agreement*.)	
" broker's, ...	10 "

	Stamp Duty.
Conveyance, deed, instrument, or writing, whereby lands, tenements, or other realty sold, shall be conveyed, *the actual value* of which does not exceed $500, ...	50 cents.
" exceeding $500, and not exceeding $1,000, . .	$1 00
" for every additional $500, or fractional part thereof in excess of $1,000, ...	50 cents.
Endorsement of any negotiable instrument, ...	exempt.
Entry of any goods, wares, or merchandise at any custom-house, either for consumption or warehousing, not exceeding $100 in value, ...	25 cents.
" exceeding $100, and not exceeding $500 in value, .	50 "
" exceeding $500 in value, ...	$1 00
" for the withdrawal of any goods or merchandise from bonded warehouse, ...	50 cents.
Gaugers' returns, if for quantity not exceeding 500 gallons, gross,	10 "
" exceeding 500 gallons, ...	25 "
Insurance, (Marine, Inland, and Fire,) where the consideration paid for the insurance, in cash, premium notes, or both, does not exceed $10, ...	10 "
" exceeding $10, and not exceeding $50, . . .	25 "
" exceeding $50, ...	50 "
Insurance, (Life,) when the amount insured does not exceed $1,000,	25 "
" exceeding $1,000, and not exceeding $5,000, .	50 "
" exceeding $5,000, ...	$1 00
" limited to injury to persons while travelling, . .	exempt.
Lease of lands or tenements, where rent does not exceed $300 per annum, ...	50 cents.
" exceeding $300, for each additional $200, or fractional part thereof in excess of $300, ...	50 "
" perpetual, subject to stamp duty as a " conveyance," the stamp duty to be measured by resolving the annual rental into a capital sum.	
" clause of guaranty of payment of rent, incorporated or indorsed, five cents additional.	
Manifest, for custom-house entry or clearance of the cargo of any ship, vessel, or steamer for a foreign port, if the registered tonnage of such ship, vessel, or steamer does not exceed 300 tons, ...	$1 00
" exceeding 300 tons, and not exceeding 600 tons, .	3 00
" " 600 tons, ...	5 00
Measurers' Returns, if for quantity not exceeding 1,000 bushels,	10 cents.
" exceeding 1,000 bushels, ...	25 "
Mortgage, trust deed, bill of sale, or personal bond for the payment of money exceeding $100, and not exceeding $500, .	50 "
" exceeding $500, for every additional $500, or fractional part thereof in excess of $500, ...	50 "
Pawners' Checks, ...	5 "
Pension Papers.—Powers of attorney, and all other papers relating to applications for bounties, arrearages of pay, or pensions, or to receipt thereof, ...	exempt.
Passage Ticket from the United States to a foreign port, costing not more than $35, ...	50 cents.
" costing more than $35, and not exceeding $50, .	$1 00
Passage Ticket, for every additional $50, or fractional part thereof in excess of $50, ...	$1 00

	Stamp Duty.
Power of Attorney to sell or transfer stock, or collect dividends thereon,	25 cents.
" to vote at election of incorporated company, . .	10 "
" to receive or collect rents, ...	25 "
" to sell, or convey, or rent, or lease real estate, . .	$1 00
" for any other purpose, ...	50 cents.
Probate of Will, or letters of administration, where the value of both real and personal estate does not exceed $2,000,	$1 00
" for every additional $1,000, or fractional part thereof in excess of $2,000, ...	50 cents.
" bonds of executors, administrators, guardians, and trustees, are each subject to a stamp duty of . .	$1 00
" certificate of appointment, ...	5 cents.
Protest upon bill, note, check, or draft, ...	25 "
Promissory Note.—(See *Bills of Exchange*, Inland.)	
" deposit note to mutual insurance companies, when policy is subject to duty, ...	exempt.
" renewal of, subject to same duty as an original note.	
Quit Claim Deed, to be stamped as a conveyance, except when given as a release of a mortgage by the mortgagee to the mortgagor, in which case it is exempt.	
Receipt for the payment of any sum of money or debt due exceeding $20, or for the delivery of any property, . .	2 cents.
" for satisfaction of any mortgage or judgment, or decree of any court, ...	exempt.
Sheriff's return on writ, or other process, ...	"
Trust Deed, made to secure a debt, to be stamped as a mortgage.	
" conveying estate to uses, to be stamped as a conveyance.	
Warehouse Receipt for any goods, wares, or merchandise, not otherwise provided for, deposited or stored in any public or private warehouse, not exceeding $500 in value, .	10 cents.
" exceeding $500, and not exceeding $1,000, . .	20 "
" exceeding $1,000, for every additional $1,000, or fractional part thereof in excess of $1,000, . .	10 "
" for any goods, &c., not otherwise provided for, stored or deposited in any public or private warehouse or yard, .	25 "
Writs and Legal Documents.	
Writ, or other original process by which any suit is commenced in any court of record, either of law or equity,	50 "
Writ, or other original process issued by a court not of record, where the amount claimed is $100, or over,	50 "
Upon every confession of judgment or cognovit for $100, or over, except in cases where the tax for a writ has been paid, ...	50 "
Writs, or other process on appeals from justices' courts, or other courts of inferior jurisdiction, to a court of record,	50 "
Warrant of distress, when the amount of rent claimed does not exceed $100, ...	25 "
Warrant of distress, when amount exceeds $100, .	50 "
Writs, summons, and other process issued by a justice of the peace, police or municipal court, of no greater jurisdiction than a justice of the peace in the same State, .	exempt.
Writs, and other process in any criminal or other suits commenced by the United States in any State, .	"
Official documents, instruments, and papers issued or used by officers of the United States government, .	"

GENERAL REMARKS.

Revenue stamps may be used indiscriminately upon any of the matters or things enumerated in Schedule B, except proprietary and playing-card stamps, for which a special use has been provided.

Proprietary stamps cannot be used as revenue stamps.

Postage stamps cannot be used in payment of the duty chargeable on instruments.

Same of postage stamps.

It is the duty of the maker of an instrument to affix and cancel the stamp required thereon. If he neglects to do so, the party for whose use it is made may stamp it before it is used; but in no case can it be legally used without a stamp; and if issued after the 30th of June, 1864, and *used* without a stamp, it cannot be afterwards effectually stamped. Any failure upon the part of the maker of an instrument to appropriately stamp it, renders him liable to a penalty of two hundred dollars.

Cancellation of stamps.

Suits are commenced in many States by other process than writ, viz., summons, warrant, publication, petition, &c., in which cases these, as the original processes, severally require stamps.

Legal papers requiring stamps

Writs of scire facias are subject to stamp duty as original processes.

Writs of scire facias.

The jurat of an affidavit, taken before a justice of the peace, notary public, or other officer duly authorized to take affidavits, is held to be a certificate, and subject to a stamp duty of five cents, except when taken in suits or legal proceedings.

Jurat.

Certificates of loan, in which there shall appear any written or printed evidence of an amount of money to be paid on demand, or at a time designated, are subject to stamp duty as "Promissory Notes."

Certificates of loan to be stamped in certain cases.

The assignment of a mortgage is subject to the same stamp duty as that imposed upon the original instrument; that is to say, for every sum of five hundred dollars, or any fractional part thereof of the amount secured by the mortgage at the time of its assignment, there must be affixed a stamp or stamps denoting a duty of fifty cents.

Assignment of mortgage.

When two or more persons join in the execution of an instrument, the stamp to which the instrument is liable under the law may be affixed and cancelled by any one of the parties.

Either one of parties executing an instrument jointly may affix a stamp.

In conveyances of real estate, the law provides that the stamp affixed must answer to the *value* of the estate or interest conveyed.

Stamp upon deeds to answer to value of estate.

No stamp is required on any warrant of attorney accompanying a bond or note, when such bond or note has affixed thereto the stamp or stamps denoting the duty required; and whenever any bond or note is secured by mortgage, but one stamp duty is required on such papers, such stamp duty being the highest rate required for such instruments, or either of them. In such case, a note or memorandum of the value or denomination of the stamp affixed should be made upon the margin or in the acknowledgment of the instrument which is not stamped.

Stamp upon bonds and mortgages.

20*

SCHEDULE

OF

ARTICLES AND OCCUPATIONS SUBJECT TO TAX UNDER THE EXCISE LAW OF THE UNITED STATES,

APPROVED JUNE 30, 1864.

MANUFACTURES AND PRODUCTIONS.

No.		Rate of Tax.
1.	Barytes, sulphate of, per 100 pounds, . .	12 cents.
2.	Bill-heads, cards, and circulars, printed, . .	5 per cent.
3.	Books, magazines, pamphlets, reviews, and similar publications, printed, ...	5 "
4.	Boots and shoes, ...	5 "
5.	Brandy, distilled from grapes, per gallon, . .	25 cents.
6.	Brass and copper, rolled, and yellow sheathing metal in rods or sheets, (see No. 35,) . . .	3 per cent
7.	Brass and copper, rolled, and yellow sheathing metal in rods or sheets, on which a duty of 3 per cent. has not been previously paid, ...	5 "
8.	Brick, draining tiles, earthen and stone water pipes,	3 "
9.	Bullion, in lumps, ingots, or bars, as assayed, .	½ of 1 "
10.	Candles, ...	5 "
11.	Carriages and other vehicles, . . .	5 "
12.	Cassia, ground, and all imitations, per pound, . .	1 cent.
13.	Chemical productions uncompounded, not otherwise provided for, ...	5 per cent.
14.	Chocolate and cocoa, prepared, per pound, . .	1½ cent.
15.	Cigars, less than $13 per M, known as cheroots, .	$3 00
16.	Cigars selling at not over $13, ...	3 00
17.	Cigars selling at over $13, and not over $30, .	8 00
18.	Cigars selling at over $30, and not over $55, . .	15 00
19.	Cigars selling at over $55, and not over $85, .	25 00
20.	Cigars selling at over $85, ...	40 00
21.	Cigarettes in paper wrappers, not over $6 per 100 packages, of 25 each, per 100 packages, . .	1 00
22.	Cigarettes in paper wrappers, over $6 per 100 packages, of 25 each, per 100 packages, ...	3 00
23.	Cigarettes, made wholly of tobacco, per M, . .	3 00
24.	Clocks, timepieces, and clock movements, . .	5 per cent.
25.	Cloth, and all textile, knitted, or felted fabrics of materials other than cotton or wool, ...	5 "
26.	Cloth, painted, enamelled, shirred, tarred, varnished, or oiled, ...	5 "
27.	Clothing, ready-made, or other articles of dress, .	5 "
28.	Clothing, or other articles of dress, made to order, as custom-work, ...	3 "
29.	Cloves and clove stems, ground, and all imitations, per pound, ...	1 cent.

No.		Rate of Tax.
30.	Coal, mineral, per ton, ...	5 cents.
31.	Coffee, ground, and all substitutes, per pound, .	1 cent.
32.	Confectionery, not over 20 cents per pound in value, per pound, ...	2 cents.
33.	Confectionery, over 20 cents and not over 40 cents per pound, ...	4 "
34.	Confectionery, over 40 cents per pound in value, or when sold otherwise than by the pound, ...	10 per cent.
35.	Copper and lead, in ingots, pigs, or bars, spelter and brass, ...	3 "
36.	Copper, manufactures of, not otherwise provided for, .	5 "
37.	Cotton fabrics, woven, knit, or felted, and all manufactures of cotton, ...	5 "
38.	Cotton, raw, per pound, ...	2 cents.
39.	Cutlery, ...	5 per cent.
40.	Diamonds, emeralds, precious stones, and imitations, and all other jewelry, ...	10 "
41.	Distilled spirits, per gallon, until February 1, 1865, .	1 50
	Distilled spirits, per gallon, after February 1, 1865, .	2 00
42.	Fermented liquors, per barrel, ...	1 00
43.	Furs, when made up or manufactured, . . .	5 per cent.
44.	Furniture, or other articles made of wood, . .	5 "
45.	Gas, monthly product not over 200,000 cubic feet, per 1,000 cubic feet, ...	10 cents.
46.	Gas, monthly product over 200,000 cubic feet and not over 500,000 cubic feet, per 1,000 cubic feet, .	15 "
47.	Gas, monthly product over 500,000 cubic feet and not over 5,000,000 cubic feet, per 1,000 cubic feet, .	20 "
48.	Gas, monthly product over 5,000,000 cubic feet, per 1,000 cubic feet, ...	25 "
49.	Ginger, ground, and all imitations, per pound, . .	1 "
50.	Glass, manufactures of, ...	5 per cent.
51.	Gloves, mittens, and moccasins made from leather or skins on which a duty has been paid, upon the increased value, ...	5 "
52.	Glue and cement, liquid, per gallon, ...	40 cents.
53.	Glue, solid and gelatine, per pound, ...	1 cent.
54.	Gold, manufactures of, not otherwise provided for, .	5 per cent.
55.	Gold foil, per ounce troy, ...	2 00
56.	Gold leaf, per pack, ...	18 cents.
57.	Gunpowder, not over 28 cents per pound in value, per pound, ...	1 cent.
58.	Gunpowder, over 28 cents and not over 38 cents in value, per pound, ...	1½ cent.
59.	Gunpowder, over 38 cents per pound in value, per pound,	8 "
60.	Gutta-percha, manufactures of, ...	5 per cent.
61.	India-rubber, manufactures of, ...	5 "
62.	Iron, advanced beyond blooms, slabs, or loops, and not beyond bars, per ton of 2,000 pounds, . . .	3 00
63.	Iron, band, hoop, and sheet, not thinner than No. 18, wire gauge, per ton, ...	3 00
64.	Iron, band, hoop, and sheet, thinner than No. 18, wire gauge, per ton, ...	5 00
65.	Iron, bars, rods, &c., made from iron on which a duty of $3 has been paid, per ton, ...	2 00

No.		Rate of Tax.
66.	Iron, blooms, slabs, or loops, per ton, . . .	$3 00
67.	Iron, castings used for bridges and other permanent structures, per ton, ...	3 00
68.	Iron, castings, exceeding 10 pounds in weight, per ton,	3 00
69.	Iron, cut nails and spikes, per ton, ...	5 00
70.	Iron, pig, per ton, ...	2 00
71.	Iron, plate, not less than ⅛ of an inch in thickness, per ton, ...	3 00
72.	Iron, plate, less than ⅛ of an inch in thickness, per ton,	5 00
73.	Iron, railroad, per ton, ...	3 00
74.	Iron, railroad, rerolled, per ton, ...	2 00
75.	Iron, rivets, nuts, washers, and bolts, per ton, .	5 00
76.	Iron, rivets, nuts, &c., made from iron on which a duty of not less than $3 per ton has been paid, per ton, in addition only, ...	2 00
77.	Iron, stoves and hollow ware, per ton, . .	3 00
78.	Iron, advanced beyond pigs, blooms, &c., on which no duty has been paid in the form of blooms, slabs, &c., in addition to the foregoing rates, per ton, . .	3 00
79.	Iron, manufactures of, not otherwise provided for, .	5 per cent.
80.	Lead, sheet, lead pipes, and shot, (see No. 35,) .	3 "
81.	Lead, sheet, lead pipes, and shot, on which a duty of 3 per cent. has not been previously paid, . .	5 "
82.	Lead, white, per 100 pounds, ...	35 cents.
83.	Leather, of all descriptions, curried or finished, .	5 per cent.
84.	Leather of all descriptions, tanned in the rough, .	5 "
85.	Leather, manufactures of, not otherwise provided for,	5 "
86.	Lime, and Roman or water cement, ...	3 "
87.	Marble, or other monumental stones, ...	5 "
88.	Masts, spars, and vessel blocks, ...	2 "
89.	Materials, not otherwise provided for, manufactures of, .	5 "
90.	Molasses, produced from the sugar-cane, per gallon,	5 cents.
91.	Molasses, sirup of, melado, and cistern bottoms, per pound, ...	1¼ cent.
92.	Mustard, ground, and all imitations, per pound, . .	1 "
93.	Naphtha, known as gasoline, of specific gravity exceeding 80°, ...	5 per cent.
94.	Oils, essential, of all descriptions, ...	5 "
95.	Oil, coal illuminating, refined naphtha, benzine, benzole, produced by the distillation of petroleum, &c., per gallon, ...	20 cents.
96.	Oil, coal illuminating, refined, produced by the distillation of coal, asphaltum, or shale, exclusively, per gallon, ...	15 "
97.	Oil, lard, linseed, mustard-seed, and all animal and vegetable, not otherwise provided for, per gallon, .	5 cents.
98.	Paints and painters' colors, ...	5 per cent.
99.	Paper of all descriptions, including pasteboard, binders' board, and tarred paper, ...	3 "
100.	Pepper and pimento, ground, and all imitations, per pound, ...	1 cent
101.	Photographs, or other sun-pictures, beings copies of engravings or works of art, ...	5 per cent.
102.	Pianos and other musical instruments, ...	5 "

No.		Rate of Tax.
103.	Pickles, preserved fruit, vegetables, meat, fish, and shell-fish,	5 per cent.
104.	Pins,	5 "
105.	Pottery-ware, manufactures of,	5 "
106.	Quicksilver, produced from the ore,	2 "
107.	Repairs of engines, cars, carriages, or other articles, on increased value,	3 "
108.	Repairs of ships, steamboats, or other vessels, on increased value,	2 "
109.	Sails, tents, shades, awnings, and bags, of whatever materials made,	5 "
110.	Saleratus, and bicarbonate of soda, per pound,	5 mills.
111.	Salt, per 100 pounds,	6 cents.
112.	Screws, commonly called wood-screws,	10 per cent.
113.	Ships, and all other vessels or water-craft, on hulls of,	2 "
114.	Silk, manufactures of,	5 "
115.	Silver, manufactures of, not otherwise provided for,	5 "
116.	Slate, freestone, sandstone, &c., when hewn, finished, or dressed,	3 "
117.	Snuff, of all descriptions, per pound,	35 cents.
118.	Soap, soft,	5 per cent.
119.	Soap, Castile, &c., not over 5 cents per pound in value, per pound,	2 mills.
120.	Soap, Castile, &c., over 5 cents per pound in value, per pound,	1 cent.
121.	Soap, fancy, scented, &c.,	5 cents.
122.	Starch, made of potatoes, per pound,	2 mills.
123.	Starch, made of corn or wheat, per pound,	3 "
124.	Starch, made of rice or other materials, per pound,	1 cent.
125.	Steam engines, including locomotives and marine engines,	3 per cent
126.	Steel, not over 7 cents per pound in value, per ton,	5 00
127.	Steel, over 7 cents and not over 11 cents per pound in value, per ton,	10 00
128.	Steel, over 11 cents per pound in value,	12 50
129.	Steel, rolled in sheets, rod or wire made of steel, on which a duty has been paid, on increased value,	5 per cent.
130.	Steel, manufactures of, not otherwise provided for,	5 "
131.	Stereotypers, lithographers, and engravers, productions of,	5 "
132.	Sugar, brown, per pound,	2 cents.
133.	Sugar, clarified or refined, above 12 and not above 18, Dutch standard, in color, per pound,	2½ "
134.	Sugar, clarified or refined, above number 18, Dutch standard, in color, per pound,	3½ "
135.	Sugar refiners, on gross amount of sales of,	2½ per ct.
136.	Thread, yarn, and warps for weaving,	5 "
137.	Tobacco, Cavendish, &c., from which the stem has been taken, per pound,	35 cents.
138.	Tobacco, smoking, prepared with all the stems in, and fine-cut shorts, per pound,	25 "
139.	Tobacco, smoking, made exclusively of stems, per pound,	15 "
140.	Tobacco, fine-cut chewing, per pound,	35 "
141.	Turpentine, spirits of, per gallon,	20 "

No.		Rate of Tax.
142.	Umbrellas and parasols, ...	5 per cent.
143.	Varnish or Japan, ...	5 "
144.	Water, artificial mineral, soda, sarsaparilla, . .	5 "
145.	Water, mineral or medicinal, per bottle containing not more than 1 pint, ...	½ cent.
146.	Water, mineral or medicinal, per bottle containing more than 1 pint and not more than 1 quart, . .	1 "
147.	Water, mineral or medicinal, containing more than 1 quart, for each additional quart, . .	1 "
148.	Wine made of grapes, per gallon, ...	5 cents.
149.	Wine produced by being mixed with other spirits, per gallon, ...	50 "
150.	Woollen fabrics woven, knit, or felted, and all manufactures of wool, ...	5 per cent.
151.	Zinc, oxide of, per 100 pounds, ...	35 cents.

Animals Slaughtered.

152.	Cattle over 3 months old, per head, . . .	40 cents.
153.	Cattle not over 3 months old, per head, . .	5 "
154.	Sheep and lambs, per head, ...	5 "
155.	Sheep slaughtered for pelts, per head, . .	2 "
156.	Swine, per head, ...	10 "

Gross Receipts.

157.	Advertisements, ...	3 per cent.
158.	Bridges and toll-roads, ...	3 "
159.	Canals, ...	2½ "
160.	Express companies, ...	3 "
161.	Ferries, ...	3 "
162.	Insurance companies, ...	1½ "
163.	Lotteries, ...	5 "
164.	Railroads, ...	2½ "
165.	Ships, barges, &c., ...	2½ "
166.	Stage coaches, wagons, &c., ...	2½ "
167.	Steamboats, ...	2½ "
168.	Telegraph companies, ...	5 "
169.	Theatres, operas, circuses, and museums, . .	2 "

Sales.

170.	Auction sales, ...	¼ of 1 per cent.
171.	Broker's sales of merchandise, produce, &c., .	⅛ of 1 "
172.	Broker's sales of stocks and bonds, on par value thereof,	$\frac{1}{20}$ of 1 "
173.	Broker's sales of gold and silver bullion and coin, foreign exchange, &c., ...	$\frac{1}{20}$ of 1 "

Licenses.

174.	Apothecaries, ...	$10 00
175.	Architects and civil engineers, ...	10 00
176.	Assayers, annual assays not over $250,000 in value,	100 00
177.	Assayers, annual assays over $250,000 and not over $500,000, ...	200 00

No.		Rate of Tax.
178.	Assayers, annual assays over $500,000,	$500 00
179.	Auctioneers, annual sales not over $10,000,	10 00
180.	Auctioneers, annual sales over $10,000,	20 00
181.	Bankers, capital not over $50,000,	100 00
	Bankers, capital over $50,000, $2 for each additional $1,000 in addition to the $100.	
182.	Billiard rooms, for each table,	10 00
183.	Brewers, annual manufacture less than 500 barrels,	25 00
184.	Brewers, annual manufactures not less than 500 barrels,	50 00
185.	Bowling alleys, for each alley,	10 00
186.	Brokers, cattle, annual sales not over $10,000,	10 00
	Brokers, cattle, over $10,000, $1 for each additional $1,000 in addition to the $10.	
187.	Brokers, commercial,	20 00
188.	Brokers, custom-house,	10 00
189.	Brokers, land warrant,	25 00
190.	Brokers, pawn, capital not over $50,000,	50 00
	Brokers, pawn, capital over $50,000, $2 for every $1,000 in addition to the $50.	
191.	Brokers, produce,	10 00
192.	Brokers, stock,	50 00
193.	Builders and contractors, annual contracts not over $25,000,	25 00
	Builders and contractors, annual contracts over $25,000, $1 for every $1,000 in addition to the $25.	
194.	Business, trade, or profession, not otherwise provided for,	10 00
195.	Butchers, who sell butcher's meat at retail,	10 00
196.	Butchers, annual sales not over $1,000, &c.,	5 00
197.	Circuses,	100 00
198.	Claim agents,	10 00
199.	Confectioners,	10 00
200.	Conveyancers,	10 00
201.	Dentists,	10 00
202.	Distillers of coal oil,	50 00
203.	Distillers of spirituous liquor,	50 00
204.	Distillers of spirituous liquor, annual manufacture less than 300 barrels,	25 00
205.	Distillers of apples, grapes, and peaches, annual manufacture less than 150 barrels,	12 50
206.	Eating houses,	10 00
207.	Exhibitions not otherwise provided for,	10 00
208.	Gift enterprises,	50 00
209.	Horse dealers,	10 00
210.	Hotels, yearly rental $200 or less,	10 00
	Hotels, yearly rental over $200, $5 for every $100 in addition to the $10.	
211.	Hotels, steamers, and vessels boarding passengers,	25 00
212.	Insurance agents, domestic,	10 00
213.	Insurance agents, foreign,	50 00
214.	Intelligence office keepers,	10 00
215.	Jugglers,	20 00
216.	Lawyers,	10 00
217.	Livery stable keepers,	10 00
218.	Lottery ticket dealers,	100 00

No.		Rate of Tax.
219.	Manufacturers,	$10 00
220.	Patent agents,	10 00
221.	Patent-right dealers,	10 00
222.	Peddlers, 1st class,	50 00
223.	Peddlers, 2d class,	25 00
224.	Peddlers, 3d class,	15 00
225.	Peddlers, 4th class,	10 00
226.	Peddlers who peddle jewelry or dry goods,	50 00
227.	Photographers, annual receipts not over $500,	10 00
228.	Photographers, annual receipts over $500 but not over $1,000,	15 00
229.	Photographers, annual receipts over $1,000,	25 00
230.	Plumbers and gas fitters,	10 00
231.	Physicians and surgeons,	10 00
232.	Real estate agents,	10 00
233.	Rectifiers of any quantity not exceeding 500 barrels,	25 00
	Rectifiers of any quantity exceeding 500 barrels, for every 500 barrels in addition to, $25.	
234.	Retail dealers,	10 00
235.	Retail dealers in liquor,	25 00
236.	Stallions and jacks,	10 00
237.	Theatres, museums, and concert halls,	100 00
238.	Tobacconists,	10 00
239.	Wholesale dealers, annual sales not over $50,000,	50 00
	Wholesale dealers whose annual sales are over $50,000, $1 for every $1,000, in addition to the $50.	
240.	Wholesale dealers in liquor, annual sales not over $50,000,	50 00
	Wholesale dealers in liquor, annual sales over $50,000, $1 for every $1,000, in addition to the $50.	

INCOME.

241.	Income exceeding $600 and not exceeding $5,000,	5 per cent.
242.	Income exceeding $5,000 and not exceeding $10,000, on excess over $5,000,	7½ "
243.	Income exceeding $10,000, on excess over $10,000,	10 "
244.	Bank dividends and addition to surplus funds,	5 "
245.	Bank profits not divided or added to surplus,	5 "
246.	Canal companies, dividends, interest on bonds, and addition to surplus funds,	5 "
247.	Insurance companies, dividends, and addition to surplus funds,	5 "
248.	Railroad companies, dividends, interest on bonds, and addition to surplus funds,	5 "
249.	Salaries of United States officers,	5 "
250.	Turnpike companies, dividends, interest on bonds, and addition to surplus funds,	5 "

LEGACIES AND SUCCESSIONS.

251.	Legacies, lineal issue or ancestor, brother or sister,	1 "
252.	Legacies, descendant of brother or sister,	2 "
253.	Legacies, uncle or aunt, or descendant of same,	4 "

No.		Rate of Tax.
254.	Legacies, great uncle or aunt, or descendant of same, .	5 per cent.
255.	Legacies, stranger in blood, ...	6 "
256.	Successions, lineal issue, or ancestor, . . .	1 "
257.	Successions, brother or sister, or descendant of same,	2 "
258.	Successions, uncle or aunt, or descendant of same, .	4 "
259.	Successions, great uncle or aunt, or descendant of same,	5 "
260.	Succession, stranger in blood, ...	6 "

Articles in Schedule A.

261.	Billiard tables, kept for use, ...	$10 00
262.	Carriages, kept for use, over $50 and not over $100, .	1 00
263.	Carriages, kept for use, over $100 and not over $200,	2 00
264.	Carriages, kept for use, over $200 and not over $300, .	3 00
265.	Carriages, kept for use, over $300 and not over $500,	6 00
266.	Carriages, kept for use, over $500, . . .	10 00
267.	Piano-fortes, and other musical instruments, kept for use, over $100 and not over $200 in value, each, .	2 00
268.	Piano-fortes, and other musical instruments, kept for use, over $200 and not over $400 in value, each, . .	4 00
269.	Piano-fortes, and other musical instruments, kept for use, over $400, each, ...	6 00
270.	Plate of gold, kept for use, per ounce troy, . .	50
271.	Plate of silver, kept for use, per ounce troy, . .	5
272.	Watches, gold, kept for use, not over $100 in value, .	1 00
273.	Watches, gold, kept for use, over $100 in value, .	2 00
274.	Yachts, 10 tons or less, each, ...	5 00
275.	Yachts, over 10 tons and not over 20 tons, each, .	10 00
276.	Yachts, over 20 tons and not over 40 tons, each, .	25 00
277.	Yachts, over 40 tons and not over 80 tons, each, .	50 00
278.	Yachts, over 80 tons and not over 110 tons, each, .	75 00
279.	Yachts, over 110 tons, each, ...	100 00

Bank Circulation and Deposits.

280.	Bank deposits, per month, ...	$\frac{1}{24}$ of 1 per cent.
281.	Bank capital, per month, ...	$\frac{1}{24}$ of 1 "
282.	Bank circulation, per month, ...	$\frac{1}{12}$ of 1 "
283.	Bank circulation, exceeding 90 per cent. of capital, in addition, ...	$\frac{1}{6}$ of 1 "
284.	Bank circulation, exceeding average of six months preceding July 1, 1864, in addition, . . .	$\frac{1}{6}$ of 1 "

Passports.

285.	Passports, each, ...	5 00

LIST OF ASSESSORS AND COLLECTORS

OF

INTERNAL REVENUE IN THE UNITED STATES.

MAINE.

Assessors.			Collectors.		
Dist.	Name.	Address.	Dist.	Name.	Address.
1	Nath'l G. Marshall	Portland.	1	Nathaniel J. Miller	Portland.
2	Hannibal Belcher	Farmington.	2	Jesse S. Lyford	Lewiston.
3	George W. Wilcox	Gardiner.	3	Peter F. Sanborn	East Readfield.
4	George P. Sewall †	Oldtown.	4	Aaron A. Wing	Bangor.
5	Nathaniel A. Joy	Ellsworth.	5	John West	Ellsworth.

NEW HAMPSHIRE.

Dist.	Name.	Address.	Dist.	Name.	Address.
1	George M. Herring	Farmington.	1	James M. Lovering	Exeter.
2	Isaac W. Smith	Manchester.	2	John Kimball	Concord.
3	Bolivar Lovell	Paper Mill Village, Cheshire County.	3	Daniel P. Wheeler	Orford.

VERMONT.

Dist.	Name.	Address.	Dist.	Name.	Address.
1	Wm. C. Kittredge	Fairhaven.	1	Joseph Poland	Montpelier.
2	Thomas E. Powers	Woodstock.	2	George A. Merrill	St. Johnsbury.
3	Henry C. Adams	East Alburgh.	3	Carlos Baxter	Burlington.

MASSACHUSETTS.

Dist.	Name.	Address.	Dist.	Name.	Address.
1	Charles G. Davis	Plymouth.	1	Walter C. Durfee	Fall River.
2	Elias S. Beals	North Weymouth.	2	Chas. P. Huntington	Boston.
3	James Ritchie	Boston.	3	E. L. Pierce	Boston.
4	Otis Clapp	Boston.	4	John Sargent	Boston.
5	Amos Noyes	Newburyport.	5	J. Vincent Browne	Salem.
6	Charles Hudson	Lexington.	6	George Cogswell	Haverhill.
7	C. C. Esty	Framingham.	7	John Nesmith	Lowell.
8	Ivers Phillips	Worcester.	8	Adin Thayer	Worcester.
9	Amasa Norcross	Fitchburg.	9	Daniel W. Alvord	Greenfield.
10	C. N. Emerson	Pittsfield.	10	E. R. Tinker	North Adams.

RHODE ISLAND.

Dist.	Name.	Address.	Dist.	Name.	Address.
1	Thomas G. Turner	Providence.	1	L. B. Frieze	Providence.
2	William A. Pirce	Johnston.	2	William D. Brayton	Warwick.

Assessors and Collectors, &c. — Continued.

CONNECTICUT.

Assessors.			Collectors.		
Dist.	Name.	Address.	Dist.	Name.	Address.
1	Alphonso C. Crosby	Rockville.	1	J. G. Bolles	Hartford.
2	John B. Wright . .	Clinton.	2	John Woodruff . . .	New Haven.
3	Jesse S. Ely	Norwich.	3	Ezra Dean	East Woodstock.
4	Reuben Rockwell . .	Colebrook.	4	David F. Hollister .	Bridgeport.

NEW YORK.

Dist.	Name.	Address.	Dist.	Name.	Address.
1	Henry W. Eastman	Roslyn, Queens Co.	1	George F. Carman .	Patchogue, Suffolk [Co.
2	John Williams . . .	Brooklyn.	2	A. M. Wood	Brooklyn.
3	William E. Robinson	Brooklyn.	3	Henry C. Bowen . .	Brooklyn.
4	Pierre C. Van Wyck	New York.	4	John Mack	New York.
5	George F. Bellows .	New York.	5	Joseph Hoxie . . .	New York.
6	John F. Cleveland .	New York.	6	William Orton . . .	New York.
7	Geo. F. Steinbrenner	New York.	7	Marshall B. Blake .	New York.
8	Anthony J. Bleecker	New York.	8	George P. Putnam .	New York.
9	Homer Franklin . .	New York.	9	Edgar Ketchum . .	New York.
10	Abram Hyatt	Sing Sing.	10	John M. Macon . .	Yonkers.
11	James C. Curtis . .	Cochecton, Sullivan [Co.	11	John G. Wilkin . .	Middletown.
12	James Mackin . . .	Fishkill Landing.	12	Joshua T. Waterman	Hudson.
13	Frederick Cooke . .	Catskill.	13	William Masten . .	Kingston.
14	John G. Treadwell .	Albany.	14	Theodore Townsend	Albany.
15	Philip H. Neher . .	Granville, Washington County.	15	Gideon Reynolds . .	Troy.
16	Lawrence Myers . .	Plattsburg	16	Walter A. Faxon . .	Glen's Falls.
17	Uriah D. Meeker . .	Malone.	17	Erasmus D. Brooks	Potsdam.
18	George T. Hanford .	Schenectady.	18	James H. Burr . . .	Gloversville, Fulton [Co.
19	Haskell Ransford, Jr.	Norwich, Chenango, [Co.	19	George W. Ernst . .	Cooperstown.
20	Nelson J. Beach . .	Watson, Lewis Co.	20	Lawrence L. Merry	Ilion, Herkimer Co.
21	Charles M. Dennison	Rome.	21	Thomas R. Walker .	Utica.
22	Leonard Ames . . .	Mexico, Oswego Co.	22	Ralph H. Avery . .	Canastota, Madison [Co.
23	William Candee . .	Syracuse.	23	Alfred Wilkinson .	Syracuse.
24	Joseph W. Gates . .	Lyons.	24	William A. Halsey .	Port Byron, Cayuga [Co.
25	Lewis Peck	Phelps.	25	Myron H. Clark . .	Canandaigua.
26	Alfred Wells	Ithaca.	26	Simon C. Hitchcock	Binghamton.
27	John I. Nicks . . .	Elmira.	27	Seymour F. Denton	Elmira.
28	John W. Graves . .	Medina, Orleans Co.	28	Samuel P. Allen . .	Rochester.
29	James P. Murphy .	Lockport.	29	John B. Halsted . .	Batavia, Wyoming [Co.
30	Otis P. Presbrey . .	Buffalo.	30	Philip Dorsheimer .	Buffalo.
31	Henry S. Woodruff .	Franklinville, Cattaraugus Co.	31	Milton Smith	Mayville, Chautauque Co.
32	S. P. Gilbert	New York.	32	Sheridan Shook . .	New York.

NEW JERSEY.

Dist.	Name.	Address.	Dist.	Name.	Address.
1	Josiah C. Sparks . .	Carpenter's Landing, Gloucester Co.	1	William S. Sharp . .	Salem, Salem Co.
2	G. W. Cowperthwait	Tom's Riv., Ocean Co.	2	Stephen B. Smith .	Trenton.
3	Robert Rusling . . .	Hackettstown, Warren Co.	3	Elston Marsh . . .	Plainfield.
4	Nathaniel Lane . . .	Paterson.	4	Eugene Ayres . . .	Morristown.
5	George A. Halsey .	Newark.	5	Daniel M. Wilson .	Newark.

PENNSYLVANIA.

Dist.	Name.	Address.	Dist.	Name.	Address.
1	Washington Keith .	Philadelphia.	1	Jesper Harding . .	Philadelphia.
2	Thomas W. Sweney	Philadelphia.	2	John H. Diehl . . .	Philadelphia.
3	J. Fletcher Budd . .	Philadelphia.	3	Wm. J. Wainwright	Philadelphia.
4	Delos P. Southworth	Philadelphia.	4	John M. Riley . . .	Philadelphia.
5	Edwin T. Chase . .	Germantown.	5	John W. Cowell . .	Doylestown.
6	Samuel McHose . .	Allentown.	6	David Newport . . .	Norristown.
7	Thomas W. Cheyney	Westchester.	7	William Baker . . .	Westchester.
8	Alexander P. Tutton	Reading.	8	Diller Luther	Reading.
9	James K. Alexander	Lancaster.	9	Alexander H. Hood	Lancaster.
10	J. W. Killinger . . .	Lebanon, Lebanon County.	10	James A. Inness . .	Pottsville.

Assessors and Collectors, &c.—Continued.

PENNSYLVANIA.

Assessors.			Collectors.		
Dist.	Name.	Address.	Dist.	Name.	Address.
11	Samuel Oliver . . .	Easton, Northampton County.	11	Edgar T. Foster . .	Bethlehem, Northhampton Co,
12	William H. Jessup .	Montrose, Susquehanna County.	12	Joseph H. Scranton	Scranton, Luzerne County.
13	Benjamin P. Fortner	Catawissa, Columbia County.	13	H. Lawrence Scott .	Towanda, Bradford County.
14	Daniel Kendig . . .	Middletown.	14	Adam K. Fahnestock	Harrisburg.
15	Horace Bonham . .	York.	15	Levi Kauffman . . .	Mechanicsburg.
16	Robert G. Harper .	Gettysburg.	16	Edward Scull	Somerset.
17	John Dean	Holidaysburg.	17	Samuel J. Royer . .	Johnstown.
18	George Boal	Boalsburg, Centre County.	18	George Bubb	Williamsport, Lycoming Co.
19	Daniel Livingston .	Curwensville, Clearfield County.	19	John W. Douglass .	Erie.
20	Joseph H. Lenhart .	Meadville.	20	William F. Clark . .	Meadville.
21	D. W. Shryock . . .	Greensburg.	21	Jasper M. Thompson	Uniontown.
22	Henry A. Weaver .	Pittsburg.	22	William Little . . .	Pittsburg.
23	Samuel Marks . . .	Freeport.	23	David N. White . . .	Alleghany.
24	Samuel Davenport .	Beaver.	24	David Sankey . . .	Newcastle.

DELAWARE.

1	John P. McLear . .	Wilmington.	1	Charles H. B. Day .	Dover.

MARYLAND.

1	George M. Russum .	Denton, Caroline Co.	1	Jas. T. McCullough	Elkton.
2	John W. Webster .	Baltimore.	2	Joseph J. Stewart .	Baltimore.
3	William E. Beale . .	Baltimore.	3	Peter G. Sauerwein	Baltimore.
4	Elias Davis	Boonsborough.	4	Frederick Schley . .	Frederick.
5	William Welling . .	Clarksville, Howard County.	5	George W. Dawson .	Poolesville, Montgomery Co.

DISTRICT OF COLUMBIA.

1	Peter M. Pearson . .	Washington.	1	Lewis Clephane . . .	Washington.

VIRGINIA.

1	John Parkinson . .	Cameron, Marshall County.	1	James C. Orr	Wheeling.
2	A. G. Leonard . . .	Parkersburg.	2	Andrew S. Core . .	Ellenboro'.
3	Josiah Millard . . .	Alexandria.	3	N. D. Keneaster . .	Alexandria.
4	J. M. Donn	Norfolk.	4	George C. Tyler . .	Onancock, Accomac County.

KENTUCKY.

1	Charles S. Todd . .	Owensboro', Daviess County.	1	George D. Blakey .	Bowling Green.
2	William M. Spencer	Greensburg, Greene County.	2	Willard Davis. . . .	Richmond.
3	Edgar Needham . .	Louisville.	3	Philip Speed	Louisville.
4	William S. Rankin .	Williamstown, Grant County.	4	John S. Nixon . . .	Covington.

Assessors and Collectors, &c.—Continued.

MISSOURI.

Assessors.			Collectors.		
Dist.	Name.	Address.	Dist.	Name.	Address.
1	Theophile Papin . .	St. Louis.	1	Samuel H. Gardner	St. Louis.
2	Daniel Q. Gale . . .	Washington, Franklin Co.	2	J. B. Maupin	Washington.
3	Joseph A. Hay . . .	La Grange, Lewis County.	3	C. B. Wilkinson . .	St. Joseph, Buchanan County.

OHIO.

Dist.	Name.	Address.	Dist.	Name.	Address.
1	Charles R. Fosdick .	Cincinnati.	1	Thomas Spooner . .	Cincinnati.
2	James Pullan	Cincinnati.	2	Reub. M. W. Taylor	Cincinnati.
3	William Miner . . .	Lebanon. [Co.	3	John L. Martin . . .	Dayton.
4	James Walker . . .	Bellefontaine, Logan	4	F. M. Wright . . .	Urbana, Champaign
5	George W. Beery . .	Upper Sandusky.	5	Shelby Taylor . . .	Lima. [Co.
6	Daniel H. Murphy .	Ripley, Brown Co.	6	David Sanders . . .	Wilmington, Clinton
7	Isaae M. Barrett . .	Spring Valley, Greene Co.	7	A. P. Stone	Columbus. [Co. [Co.
8	C. S. Hamilton . . .	Marysville, Union Co.	8	Isaac Ranney	Delaware, Delaware
9	Luther A. Hall . . .	Tiffin, Seneca Co.	9	John F. Dewey . . .	Norwalk, Huron Co.
10	E. Graham	Perrysburg, Wood County.	10	S. A. Raymond . . .	Toledo.
11	Daniel McFarland .	Portsmouth.	11	John Campbell . . .	Ironton, Lawrence
12	Charles F. Shaeffer .	Lancaster. [Co.	12	Nathan Denny . . .	Circleville. [Co.
13	Benjamin Grant . .	Mt. Vernon, Knox	13	Albert A. Guthrie .	Zanesville.
14	Aaron Pardee	Wadsworth, Medina	14	N. B. Gates	Elyria, Lorain Co.
15	Israel R. Waters . .	Marietta. [Co.	15	Eliakim H. Moore .	Athens, Athens Co.
16	John H. Barnhill . .	New Philadelphia, Tuscarawas Co.	16	Charles J. Albright .	Cambridge, Guernsey County.
17	Joseph C. McCleary	Warrenton, Jefferson Co.	17	Joseph R. Arter . .	New Lisbon, Columbiana Co.
18	Joseph E. Hurlbut .	Cleveland.	18	Richard C. Parsons .	Cleveland.
19	Horace Y. Beebe . .	Ravenna, Portage County.	19	Henry Fassett . . .	Ashtabula, Ashtabula County.

INDIANA.

Dist.	Name.	Address.	Dist.	Name.	Address.
1	Jas. G. Hutchinson	Vincennes. [Co.	1	Horace B. Shepard .	Vincennes.
2	Thos. C. Slaughter .	Corydon, Harrison	2	Henry Crawford . .	New Albany.
3	Wm. F. Browning .	Bloomington, Monroe County.	3	John S. S. Hunter .	Bloomington, Monroe County.
4	U. V. Kyger	Brookville, Franklin County. [Co.	4	James L. Yater . . .	Aurora, Dearborn County.
5	John Yaryan	Richmond, Wayne	5	Samuel W. Harlan .	Muncie, Delaware Co.
6	Wm. A. Bradshaw .	Indianapolis, Marion County.	6	Theod. P. Haughey	Indianapolis, Marion County.
7	James Farrington .	Terre Haute.	7	John G. Crain . . .	Terre Haute.
8	Joseph Potter . . .	Delphi, Carroll Co.	8	John L. Smith . . .	Stockwell, Tippecanoe County.
9	David Turner	Crown Point, Lake County.	9	John F. Dodds . . .	Logansport, Cass Co.
10	James S. Frazer . .	Warsaw, Kosciusko County.	10	Warren H. Withers	Fort Wayne, Allen County.
11	Winburn R. Pierse .	Anderson, Madison County.	11	Dewitt C. Chipman .	Noblesville, Hamilton County.

ILLINOIS.

Dist.	Name.	Address.	Dist.	Name.	Address.
1	Peter Page	Chicago.	1	George Schneider . .	Chicago.
2	Duncan Ferguson . .	Rockford.	2	Wait Talcott	Rockford.
3	Lester H. Robinson	Morrison, Whitesides Co.	3	Henry A. Mix . . .	Oregon, Ogle Co.
4	Wm. D. Henderson	Aledo, Mercer Co.	4	Seth C. Sherman . .	Quincy.
5	Thomas C. Moore .	Peoria.	5	John H. Bryant . .	Princeton. [Co.
6	Eri L. Waterman . .	Ottawa.	6	Lewis Ellsworth . .	Napierville, Du Page
7	George W. Rives . .	Paris, Edgar Co.	7	W. T. Cunningham .	Danville, Vermillion
8	Peter Folsom	Bloomington, McLean County.	8	Turner R. King . .	Springfield. [Co. [Co.
9	Amos C. Babcock . .	Canton, Fulton Co.	9	Milton B. Harrison .	Petersburg, Menard
10	John Moses	Winchester, Scott Co.	10	Jediah F. Alexander	Greenville, Bond Co.
11	Peter Smith	Sumner, Lawrence	11	Robert D. Noleman .	Centralia, Marion Co.
12	Fred'k H. Pieper . .	Belleville. [Co.	12	Willard C. Flagg . .	Alton, Madison Co.
13	Dewitt C. Barber . .	Tamaroa, Perry Co.	13	Daniel G. Hay . . .	Cairo.

Assessors and Collectors, &c. — Continued.

MICHIGAN.

Assessors.			Collectors.		
Dist.	Name.	Address.	Dist.	Name.	Address.
1	Joseph R. Bennett	Detroit.	1	L. G. Berry	Detroit.
2	Elisha J. House	Paw Paw, Van Buren County.	2	Alex'r H. Morrison	St. Joseph, Berrien County.
3	Whitney Jones	Lansing, Ingham Co.	3	Ira Mayhew	Albion, Calhoun Co.
4	Alonzo Sessions	Ionia, Ionia Co.	4	Aaron B. Turner	Grand Rapids, Kent County.
5	Luther Stanley	Birmingham, Oakland County.	5	Dexter Mussey	Romeo, Macomb Co.
6	Townsend North	Vassar, Tuscola Co.	6	Samuel N. Warren	Flint, Genesee Co.

WISCONSIN.

Dist.	Name.	Address.	Dist.	Name.	Address.
1	Charles A. Bronson	Milwaukie.	1	Thomas J. Emerson	Milwaukee.
2	David Atwood	Madison.	2	Edwin R. Wadsworth	Madison.
3	Bernard W. Brisbois	Prairie du Chien.	3	J. H. Warren	Albany, Green Co.
4	Orrin Hatch	Oakfield Centre, Fond du Lac Co.	4	Joseph H. Babcock	Beaver Dam, Dodge County.
5	George Gary	Oshkosh, Winnebago County.	5	Horace Meriam	Berlin, Green Lake County.
6	Lute A. Taylor	Prescott, St. Croix County.	6	William T. Price	Black River Falls, Jackson Co.

IOWA.

Dist.	Name.	Address.	Dist.	Name.	Address.
1	R. M. Pickel	Mount Pleasant, Henry Co.	1	J. C. Walker	Fort Madison, Lee County.
2	Pliny Fay	Muscatine, Muscatine County.	2	George W. Ells	Davenport, Scott Co.
			3	Levi Fuller	West Union, Fayette Co.
3	Jesse T. Jarrett	Dubuque.			
4	G. H. Jerome	Iowa City, Johnson Co.	4	William F. Cowles	Ottumwa, Wapella C.
5	Cole Noel	Adel, Dallas Co.	5	Horace Everett	Council Bluffs, Pottawatomie Co.
6	Delos Arnold	Marshalltown, Marshall County.	6	S. B. Hewitt, Jr.	Eagle Grove, Wright County.

MINNESOTA.

Dist.	Name.	Address.	Dist.	Name.	Address.
1	George W. Baker	Rochester, Olmstead County.	1	John Norris Hall	Mankato, Blue Earth County.
2	H. G. O. Morrison	St. Paul.	2	Thomas G. Jones	Anoka, Anoka Co.

KANSAS.

Dist.	Name.	Address.	Dist.	Name.	Address.
1	Thomas Steinburg	Lawrence.	1	John Speer	Lawrence.

CALIFORNIA.

Dist.	Name.	Address.	Dist.	Name.	Address.
1	Caleb T. Fay	San Francisco.	1	William Y. Patch	San Francisco.
2	Richard Savage	Santa Cruz, Santa Cruz County.	2	James H. Morgan	San José, Santa Clara County.
3	N. M. Orr	Stockton.	3	John Sedgwick	Stockton, Tuolumne Co.
4	J. M. Avery	Sacramento.	4	Alfred Briggs	Sacramento.
5	W. A. Eliason	Petaluma, Sonoma County.	5	Charles Maltby	Napa City,

Assessors and Collectors, &c.—Continued.

OREGON.

Assessors.			Collectors.		
Dist.	Name.	Address.	Dist.	Name.	Address.
	Thomas Frazer . . .	Portland.	. . .	Medoram Crawford .	Portland.

NEBRASKA TERRITORY.

Dist.	Name.	Address.	Dist.	Name.	Address.
	Joseph H. Burbank	Falls City.	. . .	James Sweet	Nebraska City.

TERRITORY OF NEW MEXICO.

Dist.	Name.	Address.	Dist.	Name.	Address.
	Vincent St. Vrain . .	Maro.	. . .	Charles Blummer . .	Santa Fe.

UTAH TERRITORY.

Dist.	Name.	Address.	Dist.	Name.	Address.
	Jesse C. Little . . .	Great Salt Lake City.	. . .	Robert T. Burton . .	Great Salt Lake City.

COLORADO TERRITORY.

Dist.	Name.	Address.	Dist.	Name.	Address.
	Daniel Witter . . .	Denver.	. . .	George W. Brown .	Denver.

NEVADA TERRITORY.

Dist.	Name.	Address.	Dist.	Name.	Address.
	Warren Wasson . .	Carson City.	. . .	James S. Dilley . . .	Silver City.

WASHINGTON TERRITORY.

Dist.	Name.	Address.	Dist.	Name.	Address.
	J. G. Sparks	Olympia.	. . .	P. D. Moore	Olympia.

TENNESSEE.

Dist.	Name.	Address.	Dist.	Name.	Address.
1	Halsey F. Cooper . .	Memphis.	1	R. Hough	Memphis.
2	Jno. McClelland . .	Nashville.	2	H. L. Nowell	Nashville.

LOUISIANA.

Dist.	Name.	Address.	Dist.	Name.	Address.
	W. H. Higgins . . .	New Orleans.	. . .	W. R. Whittaker . .	New Orleans.

LIST OF ASSISTANT TREASURERS AND DEPOSITARIES

OF THE

UNITED STATES,

Including such National Banks as have been designated as Depositories of Public Moneys (except Receipts from Customs) and Financial Agents of the United States, under the Provisions of the fifty-fourth Section of the National Currency Act.

NOTICE.—The Assistant Treasurers and designated Depositaries of the United States are authorized to detach, at and after maturity, the coupons from the two-years' Treasury Notes. These officers will pay such coupons as they thus detach, and no other, at the time they are separated from their connected notes.

NOTE.—It is requested that Heads of Bureaus, instead of directing that funds be placed to the credit of a Disbursing Officer with a particular Assistant Treasurer or Depositary, will specify only the location of such Disbursing Officer, and direct that the funds be placed to his credit in some Depository convenient to the place where the disbursement is to be made.

TREASURER OF THE UNITED STATES.

FRANCIS E. SPINNER,* . . Washington, District of Columbia.

ASSISTANT TREASURERS.

John J. Cisco,	New York, New York.
T. P. Chandler,	Boston, Massachusetts.
Archibald McIntyre,	Philadelphia, Pennsylvania.
Ben. Farrar,	St. Louis, Missouri.
D. W. Cheesman,	San Francisco, California.
Thomas P. May,	New Orleans, Louisiana.
G. W. Lane,	Denver City, Colorado Territory.

Deposits how made.

* Deposits may be made with the Treasurer, an Assistant Treasurer, or a Depositary, to the credit of the Treasurer of the United States, specifying the account on which the same is made, and the original certificate thereof will be received in payment of taxes or for the purchase of stamps.

Mode of proceeding by depositors.

REGULATIONS CONCERNING DEPOSITS OF PUBLIC MONEYS.—Every National Bank, which may now be, or that may hereafter become, a depository of public moneys, will, upon the receipt of any such money, place the same to the credit of the Treasurer of the United States, and will immediately issue therefor, to the officer or other person making such deposit, certificates in triplicate for each and every amount so received. The original will be, by the then next mail, forwarded, addressed to the "Treasurer of the United States" at *Washington, D. C.*, marked "*Official Business*," over the signature of the President or Cashier as "Designated Depositary." The duplicate and the triplicate will be handed to the person making the deposit, who will immediately forward the former to the "Commissioner of Internal Revenue" at *Washington, D. C.*, retaining the latter.

President and Cashier of—

Bank	Place	State
Third National Bank,	Boston,	Massachusetts.
First " "	Lowell,,	"
" " "	Cambridge,	"
" " "	Adams,	"
" " "	Dorchester,	"
First National Bank of	Hartford,	Connecticut.
" " "	New Haven,	"
Second " "	New Haven,	"
First " "	New London,	"
" " "	Stamford,	"
" " "	Bridgeport,	"
Second " "	Norwich,	"
National Exchange Bank of Hartford,		"
First National Bank of	Albany,	New York.
" " "	Albion,	"
" " "	Binghamton,	"
" " "	Buffalo,	"
" " "	Bath,	"
" " "	Cooperstown,	"
Second " "	Cooperstown,	"
First " "	Chittenango,	"
" " "	Dansville,	"
" " "	Ellenville,	"
" " "	Elmira,	"
Second " "	Elmira,	"
First, " "	Fishkill Landing,	"
" " "	Havana,	"
" " "	Lockport,	"
" " "	Morrisville,	"
" " "	New York, City of—	"
Second " "	New York, City of—	"
Sixth " "	New York, City of—	"
First " "	Oswego,	"
Second " "	Oswego,	"
First " "	Palmyra,	"
" " "	Rondout,	"
" " "	South Worcester,	"
" " "	Seneca Falls,	"
" " "	Syracuse,	"
Third " "	Syracuse,	"
First " "	Sandy Hill,	"
" " "	Troy,	"
Second " "	Utica,	"
First " "	Watertown,	"
Tenth " "	New York City,	"
New York National Exchange Bank,		"
Fourth National Bank of City of New York,		"
Second " "	Syracuse,	"
First " "	Warwick,	"
Ninth " "	City of New York,	"
Fifth " "	City of New York,	"

UNITED STATES DEPOSITARIES.

H. W. Hoffman, . . .	Baltimore, Maryland.
C. Metz., Jr., . .	Buffalo, New York.
Enoch T. Carson, . .	Cincinnati, Ohio.
Luther Haven, . .	Chicago, Illinois.
H. K. Sanger, ...	Detroit, Michigan.
C. W. Batchelor, . .	Pittsburgh, Pennsylvania.
W. D. Gallagher, . .	Louisville, Kentucky.
C. Nichols, . . .	St. Paul, Minnesota.
B. M. Trumbull, . . .	Omaha City, Nebraska Territory.
John Greiner, . .	Santa Fe, New Mexico.
W. T. Matlock, . . .	Oregon City, Oregon.
Joseph Cushman, . .	Olympia, Washington Territory.
Benjamin W. Reynolds, . .	St. Croix, Wisconsin.

NATIONAL BANKS DESIGNATED AS DEPOSITORIES.

President and Cashier of—

First National Bank of Bath, . . .	Maine.
" " " Brunswick, . .	"
" " " Bangor, . . .	"
" " " Portland, . . .	"
" " " Augusta, . . .	"
" " " Lewiston, . . .	"
First National Bank of Portsmouth, . . .	New Hampshire.
" " " Concord, . . .	"
" " " Nashua, . . .	"
National Mechanics and Traders Bank of Portsmouth,	"
First National Bank of Bennington, . .	Vermont.
" " " North Bennington, . .	"
" " " Springfield, . .	"
Brandon National Bank, Brandon, . . .	"
First National Bank of St. Albans, . .	"
First National Bank of Providence, . . .	Rhode Island.
First National Bank of Amesbury, . .	Massachusetts.
" " " Boston, . . .	"
" " " Barre, . . .	"
" " " Fall River, . . .	"
" " " Grafton, . . .	"
" " " Marlboro', . . .	"
" " " New Bedford, . .	"
" " " Newburyport, . .	"
" " " Springfield, . .	"
Second " " Springfield, . . .	"
Third " " Springfield, . .	"
First " " Worcester, . . .	"
Second " " Boston, ...	"
National Bank of the Republic of Boston, . .	"
First National Bank of Northampton, . .	"
" " " Salem, ...	"
Boston " " Boston, ...	"

President and Cashier of—

Bank			Place	State
First	National	Bank of	Canandaigua,	New York.
"	"	"	Hudson,	"
Central	"	"	City of New York,	"
First	"	"	Kingston,	"
Third	"	"	City of New York,	"
Farmers and Mechanics	National	Bank of	Buffalo,	"
First	National	Bank of	Cortland,	"
"	"	"	Batavia,	"
Eighth	"	"	City of New York,	"
First	National	Bank of	Newark,	New Jersey.
"	"	"	Trenton,	"
"	"	"	Jersey City,	"
Second	"	"	Newark,	"
First	"	"	Plainfield,	"
First	National	Bank of	Carlisle,	Pennsylvania.
"	"	"	Danville,	"
"	"	"	Erie,	"
"	"	"	Marietta,	"
"	"	"	Meadville,	"
"	"	"	Philadelphia,	"
"	"	"	Scranton,	"
Second	"	"	Scranton,	"
First	"	"	Strasburg,	"
"	"	"	Towanda,	"
Second	"	"	Wilkes Barre,	"
First	"	"	West Chester,	"
"	"	"	York,	"
"	"	"	Alleghany,	"
Second	"	"	Philadelphia,	"
First	"	"	Wilkes Barre,	"
Third	"	"	Philadelphia,	"
"	"	"	Pittsburgh,	"
First	"	"	Pittsburgh,	"
"	"	"	Allentown,	"
"	"	"	Altoona,	"
"	"	"	Milton,	"
"	"	"	Chester,	"
Fourth	"	"	Pittsburgh,	"
"	"	"	Philadelphia,	"
First	"	"	Gettysburgh,	"
"	"	"	Franklin,	"
First	National	Bank of	Baltimore,	Maryland.
First	National	Bank of	Washington,	Dist. of Columbia.
First	National	Bank of	Norfolk,	Virginia.
First	National	Bank of	Parkersburgh,	West Virginia.
"	"	"	Wheeling,	"

First National Bank of Bridgeport, . . . Ohio.
" " " Canton, ... "
" " " Cincinnati, . . . "
Third " " Cincinnati, . . "
First " " Cleveland, . . . "
Second " " Cleveland, . . "
First " " Circleville, . . . "
" " " Cadiz, . . . "
" " " Columbus, . . . "
" " " Dayton, . . . "
Second " " Dayton, . . . "
First " " Fremont, . . "
" " " Gallipolis, . . . "
" " " Hamilton, . . "
" " " Ironton, . . . "
" " " Lodi, . . . "
" " " McConnelsville, . . "
" " " Oberlin, . . . "
" " " Portsmouth, . . . "
" " " Sandusky, . . "
Second " " Sandusky, . . . "
First " " South Charleston, . "
" " " Upper Sandusky, . . "
" " " Troy, . . . "
" " " Toledo, . . . "
Second " " Zanesville, . . "
First " " Akron, . . . "
Fourth " " Cincinnati, . . "
First " " Zanesville, . . . "
Second " " Springfield, . . "
First " " Findlay, . . . "
Second " " Toledo, . . . "
" " " Cincinnati, . . . "

First National Bank of Evansville, . . Indiana.
" " " Fort Wayne, . . "
" " " Indianapolis, . . "
" " " Lafayette, . . . "
" " " Madison, . . "
" " " Terre Haute, . . "
" " " Indianapolis, . . "

First National Bank of Aurora, . . . Illinois
" " " Cairo, . . . "
" " " Chicago, . . . "
Second " " Chicago, . . . "
Third " " Chicago, . . . "
First " " Peoria, . . . "
Second " " Peoria, . . . "
First " " Springfield, . . "
Fourth " " Chicago, . . . "
First " " Quincy, . . . "
" " " Galesburg, . . . "

President and Cashier of—

First National Bank of Ann Arbor, . .	Michigan.
" " " Fenton, . . .	"
Second " " Detroit, . . .	"
First National Bank of Janesville, . . .	Wisconsin.
" " " Milwaukee, . .	"
" " " Madison, . . .	"
" " " Monroe, . .	"
First National Bank of St. Paul, . . .	Minnesota.
First National Bank of Davenport, . .	Iowa.
" " " Keokuk, . . .	"
" " " Mount Pleasant, . .	"
" " " Lyons, . . .	"
" " " Iowa City, . .	"
" " " Burlington, . . .	"
First National Bank of St. Louis, . .	Missouri.
Second " " St. Louis, . . .	"
Third " " St. Louis, . .	"
First National Bank of Louisville, . . .	Kentucky.
First National Bank of Nashville, . .	Tennessee.
" " " Memphis, . . .	"
First National Bank of New Orleans, . .	Louisiana.

CIRCULAR

TO RAILROAD, CANAL, CANAL NAVIGATION, SLACKWATER, AND TURNPIKE COMPANIES, CONCERNING INTEREST ON BONDS AND OTHER EVIDENCES OF INDEBTEDNESS, AND DIVIDENDS TO STOCKHOLDERS.

TREASURY DEPARTMENT,
OFFICE OF INTERNAL REVENUE,
WASHINGTON, July 1, 1864.

Corporations, tax on interest paid by, and dividends of.

The Internal Revenue act of June 30, 1864, fixes the rate of taxation upon interest and dividends at five (5) per centum. This applies only to interest and dividends *payable* on or after July 1, 1864. The usual quarterly return (at three per cent.) to that date will be made directly to the Commissioner of Internal Revenue as heretofore. In future, quarterly returns will not be required unless tax has accrued, but the following regulations will be observed: The company will notify the Commissioner of Internal Revenue in what months the interest and dividends are payable; and a list or return will be made and rendered to the assessor or assistant assessor in duplicate, and one of said lists or returns will be transmitted by the company, and the duty paid to the Commissioner of Internal Revenue, within thirty (30) days after the time when said interest and dividends are payable, and as often as every six months.

The returns of tax on interest will be made on Form No. 68, and of dividends and undivided gains or profits used for construction, upon Form No. 65.

Assessors will be particularly careful not to receive returns under *the old law*, and will bear in mind that the date when the interest and dividends are payable determines the rate of taxation.

The blank Forms, Nos. 65 and 68, will be furnished to the assessors, and by the assessors to the companies, as soon as they can be prepared.

The return and the payment should, in all cases, be sent to the Commissioner of Internal Revenue at the same time.

JOSEPH J. LEWIS, *Commissioner.*

CIRCULAR No. 16.

TO ASSESSORS AND COLLECTORS

CONCERNING TAXES IMPOSED UPON BANKS, INSURANCE, RAILROAD COMPANIES, &c.

TREASURY DEPARTMENT,
OFFICE OF INTERNAL REVENUE,
WASHINGTON, July 6, 1864.

Tax on corporations.

The particular attention of the local officers of internal revenue is directed to sections 105, 110, 120, 121, and 122 of the act approved June 30, 1864, wherein sundry changes are made in the mode of assessment and collection of the taxes imposed upon the above-named corporations.

Taxes prior to July 1, 1864.

With respect to all taxes under the old law of the nature referred to hereafter, and due prior to July 1, 1864, your duties remain unchanged; and collectors will be particularly careful not to receive them, as their receipt will involve errors, which must, in all cases, be corrected.

Under the new Internal Revenue act, (approved June 30, 1864,) insurance companies will report gross receipts monthly to the assessor, and pay the duty thereon to the collector. The first return is for the month of July, 1864, and the blank form to be used for this purpose is numbered 64.

Tax on and after July 1, 1864.

Banks, trust companies, savings institutions, insurance, railroad, canal, canal navigation, slackwater, and turnpike companies are to report all dividends *payable* on or after July 1, 1864, to the assessor in duplicate; and are to transmit one of the said returns, with payment of the amount of tax, to the Commissioner of Internal Revenue at Washington. (Form No. 65.)

Railroad, canal, canal navigation, slackwater, and turnpike companies will report all interest on bonds, or other evidences of indebtedness, to the assessor in duplicate; and the tax will be paid, as above, to the Commissioner of Internal Revenue. (Form No. 68.) All plank roads, and roads upon which tolls are taken, are deemed turnpikes within the meaning of the act.

Tax on banks.

Banks issuing notes for circulation as currency, neglecting or omitting to make dividends as often as once in six months, will make return to the assessor of the profits which have accrued during the six months preceding the first days of January and July in each year, and pay the duty thereon to the collector of the district. The first return will be for the half-year ending June 30, 1864. (Form No. 66.)

Capital, deposits, and circulation.

The return of duties imposed upon capital, deposits, and circulation of banking-houses, (except National Banks, which will make return and payment to the Treasurer of the United States,) is to be made monthly to the assessor in duplicate, and the tax paid to the Commissioner of Internal Revenue. (Form No. 67.)

Duties of assessors.

The assessors are required to make careful examination of the returns to them, and to report at once to this office any misstatement or fraudulent evasion they may discover, either from such examination or from their knowledge of the business of the company otherwise obtained. They will, in all cases, require statements of whatever dividends were payable after June 30, 1864, without regard to the time when such dividends were declared. They will pursue the same course in regard to interest upon bonds payable after the same date.

In communicating with this office, assessors will observe the regulation requiring that but a single subject shall be treated in a single letter, and great care should be used in allowing claims for reduction of amount of tax due. The necessary blanks will be forwarded as soon as they can be prepared.

JOSEPH J. LEWIS, *Commissioner.*

CIRCULAR No. 17.

REGULATIONS

UNDER WHICH COLLECTORS MAY IMPRESS STAMPS UPON INSTRUMENTS.—(SECTION 162, ACT OF JUNE 30, 1864.)

TREASURY DEPARTMENT,
OFFICE OF INTERNAL REVENUE,
WASHINGTON, July 13, 1864.

Duty of collectors in reference to the stamp tax upon instruments.

The 162d section of the act of June 30, 1864, provides that any person may present to the collector of the district, subject to the rules and regulations of the Commissioner of Internal Revenue, any instrument not previously issued or used, and require his opinion whether or not the same is chargeable with any stamp duty. If such instrument is determined to be exempt, the collector is to impress thereon a stamp indicating that fact; if the instrument is determined to be chargeable with a stamp duty, the collector may, upon payment therefor, affix and cancel the proper stamp, and he will then impress thereon a stamp indicating that the instrument is chargeable only with the duty denoted by the stamp affixed.

The fact, whether exempt or not, to be stamped upon the instrument.

In furtherance of the aim of this section, each collector will be furnished by this office with the requisite stamps for the impressions described. A blank will be left within each impression, upon which the collector will write his name whenever it is placed upon any instrument.

In no case will any collector thus decide upon the stamp duty chargeable upon an instrument unless one of the parties to the instrument is a resident of his collection district, or unless the subject-matter of the instrument is real estate situated within his district.

Whenever a collector is in doubt as to the liability of an instrument to stamp duty, or as to the amount of such stamp duty, either the instrument or a copy thereof (at the option of the holder) should be transmitted to this office for instructions before any stamp is impressed. It will be proper to adopt this course in all instances where the instrument is of a nature with which the collector is unfamiliar.

In case of doubt, the instrument, or a copy, to be sent to department.

Each collector will keep a record of all instruments upon which either stamp is impressed, in which must be given the names of the parties to the instrument, the date of its execution, and a sufficient description of its nature to show the reasons for impressing the particular stamp. A copy of this record will be transmitted to this office at the close of each month during which any entry is made. If, however, during any month, the only instruments impressed with either stamp shall have been first submitted to this office for instructions, the transmission of the record may be deferred until a subsequent month.

Collector to keep a record and transmit copy monthly.

It will be improper for any collector to impress his stamp upon an instrument in which he is interested, or which may be made by or for the use of a corporation of which he is a member, or in which he is a stockholder, without first receiving special instructions from this office.

If collector interested he cannot act.

When a collector has any reason to suppose that the consideration expressed in an instrument which is subject to an *ad valorem* duty is less than the actual consideration passing between the parties, he should require evidence upon the point before impressing any stamp; and where the amount of stamp duty is dependent upon the estimated value of any property or estate, he should in like manner require evidence before impressing the stamp.

Evidence of value of property to be required in certain cases.

JOSEPH J. LEWIS, *Commissioner*.

REGULATIONS

FOR THE ASSESSMENT AND COLLECTION OF THE SPECIAL INCOME TAX UPON THE INCOME OF 1863.

TREASURY DEPARTMENT,
WASHINGTON, July 20, 1864.

Special income tax.

The joint resolution imposing a special income duty, approved July 4, 1864, provides that there shall be levied on the 1st of October, 1864, upon the gains, profits, or income, for the year 1863, of all persons residing in the United States, or of citizens of the United States residing abroad, a duty of 5 per cent. on all sums exceeding $600. It is also provided that, in estimating income for this purpose, no deductions shall be made for dividends or interest received from any association, corporation, or company, nor shall any deduction be made for any salary or pay received.

In order to facilitate the assessment of this tax, assessors are directed to scrutinize carefully the returns of income heretofore made to them for the year 1863 by persons residing within the United States, and to select all such as have been made in detail, in the manner provided upon Form No. 24, issued by the Commissioner of Internal Revenue, and with the accuracy and correctness of which they are thoroughly satisfied. When deductions have been made from any such return on account of dividends or interest received from any corporation, or on account of any salary or pay as an officer of the United States, the amounts thus deducted will be added to the amount heretofore assessed, and any income derived from interest upon United States securities will be included in the same total. The income thus determined may be entered in the list as the amount upon which the special duty of 5 per cent. is to be assessed.

Assessors will direct their assistants to procure returns from all persons residing in their several divisions who have heretofore made no return in detail, or with whose returns as heretofore made they have any reasons to be dissatisfied, and from the agents of all citizens of the United States residing abroad and belonging in their several divisions. Notice should be left with all such persons at least ten days before the first day of October, requiring them to make return, under oath or affirmation, on or before said first day of October, in the manner provided by the act of June 30, 1864. By the terms of that act, the return must state the sources from which the income is derived — whether from any kind of property, or the purchase and sale of property, rents, interest, dividends, salaries, or from any profession, trade, employment or vocation, or otherwise. The distinction heretofore made between the incomes of residents and of non-resident citizens is set aside, and the latter are to be treated in all respects in the same manner as the former.

Assistant assessors will transmit the returns to the assessors of their respective districts as rapidly as they are received, and in all cases within ten days after the first day of October. If any person shall have neglected to give in a return in the form required, or if any person shall have given in a return which, in the opinion of the assessor, is false or fraudulent, or contains any understatement or undervaluation, it will be the duty of the assessor to summon such person, or his agent, to appear and produce all books of account containing entries relating to the trade or business of such person, and to summon any other persons, as he may deem proper, to give testimony, in the manner prescribed in section 14 of the act of June 30, 1864.

If, upon such examination, it shall appear that any person has made a false or fraudulent return, the assessor will estimate the income of such person according to the best information which he can obtain, and assess the duty thereon, and enter the same in the list, adding one hundred per centum to such duty. The assessor will, in like manner, estimate the income of all persons who shall have neglected to make return on or before the first day of October, and assess the duty thereon; and, except in cases of sickness or absence, he will add fifty per centum to such duty. No return can be accepted which is not verified by oath or affirmation; and if any such return is transmitted to the assessor, he will proceed in the same manner as if no return had been received.

Immediately thereafter the assessor will make up an alphabetical list of all persons who have been assessed for the special income duty in each division of his district, and will then advertise in some newspaper published in each county in his district, if any such there be — if not, in some newspaper nearest thereto in the same collection district — the time and place, within said county, where said list may be examined; and the list shall remain open for ten days for the inspection of all persons who may apply for the same.

No relief from assessments which are made after the examination of witnesses, as provided in section 14 of the act of June 30, 1864, can be given by the assessor; but any persons aggrieved will have a right of appeal to the Commissioner of Internal Revenue. In all other cases the assessor may revise any assessment, including those made upon the basis of returns heretofore received, at any time before the first day of November, 1864.

It is explicitly provided by the act of June 30, 1864, that copies of all lists returned to the collector shall remain in the office of the assessor, and *shall be open to the inspection of all persons who may apply to inspect the same.* It is of especial importance that assessors give full effect to this provision with reference to the lists heretofore made up and containing the assessments upon the income for the year 1863, in order that the amplest opportunity may be given for the detection of any fraudulent returns that may have been made, and any omissions that may have occurred; and for this purpose assessors should seek the co-operation of all tax-paying citizens.

Assistant assessors will be particularly careful to obtain returns from persons employed in the service of the United States whose names may not appear on the annual assessment list, as the special income duty upon their salaries, imposed by the joint resolution of July 4, is not to be withheld by paymasters, but must be assessed in the same manner as income from other sources.

Immediately after the first of November the lists made in accordance with these regulations will be returned to the several collectors in the manner provided by law, and the subsequent proceedings for the collection of the duty will be in all respects similar to those for the collection of taxes assessed in the annual list.

W. P. FESSENDEN, *Secretary of the Treasury.*

CIRCULAR

TO PAYMASTERS AND DISBURSING OFFICERS OF THE UNITED STATES GOVERNMENT CONCERNING THE INTERNAL REVENUE TAX UPON SALARIES.

TREASURY DEPARTMENT.
OFFICE OF INTERNAL REVENUE,
WASHINGTON, July 1, 1864.

Tax on salaries. By the 123d section of the Internal Revenue act of June 30, 1864, the rate of tax upon salaries is fixed at five per centum. The particular attention of Paymasters and Disbursing Officers is requested to the following

REGULATIONS.

Rate. 1. The duty of five per centum is to be withheld from all salaries of officers or payments for services to persons in the civil, military, naval, or other employment or service of the United States, including senators, representatives, and delegates in Congress, when exceeding the rate of six hundred dollars per annum.

Where persons are transiently employed. 2. Where persons are transiently employed, the tax will be computed on a basis of three hundred working days in each year. In such cases, the amount of two dollars per day will consequently be exempt from taxation.

Officers of the army. 3. Each commissioned officer in the army receives from a paymaster compensation at a rate exceeding six hundred dollars; therefore, all payments to commissioned officers made by a quartermaster, or disbursing agent other than a paymaster, will be in excess of the rate of six hundred dollars per annum, and the duty of five per centum must be withheld from such payments.

Return. 4. An accurate return should be made upon Form No. 10, which will be furnished by this office, showing the names of the person or persons to whom the payments were made, and from whom the tax was withheld, and also the month or months for which the salaries were due.

5. This return, in all cases accompanied by payment of the amount of tax, must be transmitted to the Commissioner of Internal Revenue at Washington. Payment.

6. If the payment is remitted by certificate of deposit with an assistant treasurer or designated depositary of the United States, or with a National Bank duly authorized to receive such moneys, special care must be exercised to forward the proper certificate in accordance with the note upon its margin. Certificate in case of deposit.

JOSEPH J. LEWIS, *Commissioner.*

CIRCULAR

TO BANKS, TRUST COMPANIES, SAVINGS INSTITUTIONS, AND INSURANCE COMPANIES, CONCERNING DIVIDENDS AND UNDIVIDED PROFITS.

TREASURY DEPARTMENT,
OFFICE OF INTERNAL REVENUE,
WASHINGTON, July 1, 1864.

The Internal Revenue act, approved June 30, 1864, fixes the rate of taxation upon dividends and surplus gains at five (5) per centum. All dividends payable on or after July 1, 1864, no matter when declared, are subject to the duty of five (5) per centum; and a list or return is to be made and rendered to the assessor or assistant assessor in duplicate; and one of said lists or returns is to be transmitted, and the duty paid to the Commissioner of Internal Revenue, by the company, within thirty (30) days after the time when said dividends become due or payable.

When any dividend is made which includes any part of the surplus fund which has been assessed and the duty paid thereon, the *amount of duty so paid* on that portion of the surplus or contingent fund may be deducted from the duty on such dividend.

The full amount of profit is subject to taxation, without any regard to the manner in which it was acquired.

As soon as they can be prepared, the blank form for returns (No. 65) will be furnished to the assessors, and by the assessors to the companies.

A complete return of all dividends not payable until on or after July 1, 1864, must be made to the assessor. It is very desirable that the company should transmit the duplicate return and the payment to the Commissioner of Internal Revenue at the same time.

JOSEPH J. LEWIS, *Commissioner.*

RETURN BY PAYMASTERS AND DISBURSING OFFICERS OF THE UNITED STATES.

(SECTION 123.)

Certificate of money paid as salary to officers, or payments to persons in the civil, military, naval, or other employment or service of the United States, including Senators and Representatives and Delegates in Congress, with the amount of tax thereon withheld, conformably to the provisions of the 123d section of an act entitled "An act to provide internal revenue to support the government, to pay interest on the public debt, &c., approved June 30, 1864.

NAME OF PERSON.	OFFICE UNDER THE GOVERNMENT.	AMOUNT TAXABLE.		RATE.	AMOUNT OF TAX.	
				5 per cent.		
				do.		
				do.		
				do.		
				do.		
				do.		
				do.		
				do.		
				do.		
				do.		
				do.		
				do.		
				do.		
				do.		
				do.		
				do.		
				do.		
				do.		
				do.		
				do.		
				do.		
				do.		
				do.		
				do.		
				do.		
				do.		
	Total, ...			5 per cent.		

(Signed) ________________________________

Dated at ________________________________,
this ________ day of ____________________, 186 .

CIRCULAR

TO BANKS, ASSOCIATIONS, CORPORATIONS, COMPANIES, AND INDIVIDUALS ENGAGED IN THE BUSINESS OF BANKING.

TREASURY DEPARTMENT,
OFFICE OF INTERNAL REVENUE,
WASHINGTON, July 1, 1864.

Concerning returns by banks and bankers.

The 110th section of the Internal Revenue act, approved June 30, 1864, requires all parties engaged in the business of banking (except associations organized under the National Currency act, which are elsewhere taxed) to pay a duty of one twenty-fourth ($\frac{1}{24}$) of one per centum each month on the average amount of deposits held by them.

It is further provided in the act that all deposits subject to payment on check or draft, or represented by certificates of deposit, or otherwise, whether payable on demand or at a future day, shall be taxable.

There is also imposed by this act a duty of one twenty-fourth ($\frac{1}{24}$) of one per centum each month on the average amount of capital employed beyond the amount invested in United States bonds.

A further duty of one twelfth ($\frac{1}{12}$) of one per centum each month is levied upon the average amount of circulation outstanding for the month, including all certified checks and all notes or other obligations calculated or intended to circulate or to be used as money.

Where the amount of such circulation exceeds ninety (90) per cent. of the capital, an additional tax of one-sixth ($\frac{1}{6}$) of one per centum each month is imposed upon such excess; and should the circulation at any time during the month exceed the average circulation for the six months prior to July 1, 1864, (which amount must be clearly stated on each return,) a further duty of one-sixth ($\frac{1}{6}$) of one per centum must be paid on such excess. And on the first Monday of August next, and of each month thereafter, a true and accurate return of the amount of circulation, deposits, and capital as aforesaid for the previous month, is to be made and rendered in duplicate to the assessor or assistant assessor, and the company will transmit the duplicate of said return to the Commissioner of Internal Revenue, at Washington, and pay to the said Commissioner the duties.

The return and payment should, in all cases, be forwarded at the same time. In the case of banks with branches, the duty is imposed upon the circulation of each branch severally, and the amount of capital of each branch is to be considered as the amount allotted thereto.

For any refusal or neglect to make and render the return and payment as aforesaid, the party in default will be subject to a penalty of two hundred dollars, besides the additions, penalties, and forfeitures provided in this act; and the amount of circulation, deposits, and capital aforesaid will be estimated by the assessor or assistant assessor upon the best information he can obtain.

These returns will be made upon Form No. 67, which will be forwarded to the assessor as soon as they can be prepared.

JOSEPH J. LEWIS, *Commissioner*.

265 *MONTHLY RETURN by Banks, Associations, Corporations and Individuals engaged in the business of Banking.*

(SECTION 110.)

ACCOUNT of the average amount of Capital, Circulation, and Deposits of the ______________________ in the ______________ of ______________________, and in the ______________ Collection District of the State of ______________ for the month of ______________________, 186 , with the tax thereon, pursuant to an act entitled "An act to provide internal revenue to support the Government, to pay interest on the public debt, and for other purposes," approved June 30, 1864, viz.:

		AMOUNT.	RATE.	TAX.
	Average Capital . . . . $			
	Less Amount invested in U. S. Bonds		$\frac{1}{24}$ of 1 per ct.	
	Average amount of deposits held		$\frac{1}{24}$ of 1 per ct.	
	Average amount of circulation		$\frac{1}{12}$ of 1 per ct.	
	Average amount of circulation in excess of 90 per cent. of capital		$\frac{1}{6}$ of 1 per ct.	
	Average circulation for the six months preceding July 1, 1864			
	Highest circulation at any time during the month in excess of this amount		$\frac{1}{6}$ of 1 per ct.	
	Total			

(Signed) ______________________

I, ______________________, do swear that this account contains, to the best of my knowledge and belief, a true and faithful statement of the amount of tax which has accrued during the time, and according to the provisions of the act aforementioned.

SWORN and subscribed before me, this ____________ day of ______________________, 186 . } (Signed) ______________________

____

Assistant Assessor.

NOTE.—This Statement is to be prepared in accordance with Circular issued by the Commissioner of Internal Revenue.

RETURN BY BANKS, &c., OF SEMI-ANNUAL PROFITS.

(Section 121.)

Account of all Earnings, Profits, or Gains of the ____________________ in the ________ of ____________________, and ____________________ Collection District of the ____________________ of ____________________, for the six months preceding the first day of ____________________, 186 , pursuant to an act entitled "An act to provide internal revenue to support the Government, to pay interest on the public debt, and for other purposes," approved June 30, 1864, viz.:

		AMOUNT.		RATE.	TAX DUE.	
	Net Profits for the six months.			5 per cent.		

(Signed) ____________________

I, ____________________, do swear that the above account contains, to the best of my knowledge and belief, a true and faithful statement of all the gains of the said ____________________, together with the amount of taxes which have accrued thereon, or should accrue, and not accounted for, during the time and according to the provisions of the act aforementioned.

(Signed) ____________________

Sworn and subscribed before me, this ________ day of ____________________, 186 .

____

Assistant Assessor.

SALES OF REVENUE STAMPS. RETURNS BY COLLECTORS.

MONTHLY RETURN of Internal Revenue Stamps sold during the month of ----------------,
186 , and amount remaining on hand at its close, by ----------------------------------,
Collector, --------- District of ---------------------, at ---------------------------.

Collectors are entitled to receive stamps equal to *three-fourths* of the *penal sum* designated in their bonds, subject to the following regulations, which have been approved by the Secretary of the Treasury.

"1st. Each Collector shall be allowed a commission of five per cent. on all remittances made by him.

"2d. Each Collector shall deposit stamps, in suitable quantities, with his deputies, and allow to such deputies the commission provided in the regulations of this office, issued under date of January 12, 1863.

"3d. Each Collector, on or before the 15th day of *each month*, shall make return to this office of the amount of stamps sold during the preceding month, and, *at the time of rendering such return, shall make payment therefor.*"

			Dr.		*Cr.*	
		By balance of stamps on hand from last month's account.				
		" stamps received on order No				

RULES

FOR THE REDEMPTION OF MUTILATED UNITED STATES NOTES, UNITED STATES TREASURY NOTES, AND FRACTIONAL CURRENCY.

TREASURY DEPARTMENT,
WASHINGTON, May 18, 1862.

To guard against frauds upon the Government, and to secure the just rights of holders, the following rules, for the redemption of mutilated United States notes, are hereby established: —

RULES.

Rules for the redemption of mutilated United States notes.

FIRST. — Mutilated notes, which have been torn, no matter how much, but of which it is evident that all the fragments are returned, — or defaced, no matter how badly, but certainly satisfactorily genuine, — will be redeemed at their full face value on presentation.

SECOND. — Fragments of notes will be redeemed *in full* only when accompanied by an affidavit stating the cause and manner of the mutilation, and that the *missing part of the note is* TOTALLY DESTROYED. The good character of the affiant must also be fully vouched by the officer before whom the affidavit is taken.

THIRD. — In the absence of such affidavit, fragments of notes will not be paid in full, but the parts presented will be redeemed in their proportion to the whole note; reckoning, as a general rule, by twentieths.

FOURTH. — Less than half of a note will not be redeemed, except by payment of the full value of the note under the second rule, or by the payment of the proportional value of the missing part, when presented under the fifth rule.

FIFTH. — Fragments of notes, for which less than the full face value has been paid, will be retained for a year, to the end that the owners, who have received less than the value of a full note, may have opportunity to return the missing part, and receive the amount previously withheld.

SIXTH. — Until further order, mutilated notes and fragments will be redeemed only at the Treasury of the United States at Washington, whither they can be sent, addressed to the "*Treasurer of the United States.*" A draft on the Assistant Treasurer at New York, for the amount allowed, will be returned by mail to the address of the person remitting the same.

S. P. CHASE,
Secretary of the Treasury.

TREASURY DEPARTMENT,
WASHINGTON, D. C., Oct. 9, 1862.

The Rules promulgated on the 18th of May last, for the redemption of mutilated United States Notes, are not intended to apply to such notes of which the abrasion or loss of substance from the corners or edges does not exceed one-twentieth of their original proportions. Such are not understood to be mutilated notes within those Rules. They are regarded as entire notes, and, when of the issue known as Demand Notes, are receivable for Customs duties.

No United States Notes, which have lost more than one-twentieth part of their original proportions, have ever been received for Customs duties. They can only be paid, therefore, as ordinary claims, in ordinary notes, under the Rules heretofore established.

S. P. Chase,
Secretary of the Treasury.

REDEMPTION OF UNITED STATES TREASURY NOTES.

Rules for the redemption of mutilated United States Treasury Notes.

The same rules in force for the redemption of mutilated United States Notes, that are embodied in circulars of the Department dated May 18, 1862, and October 9, 1862, are applied to mutilated one and two years' five per cent. United States Treasury Notes.

Separation of a coupon from a two years' five per cent. United States Treasury Note renders such note no longer a legal tender, until interest commences on the next succeeding coupon attached to the note; and the separation is such a mutilation of the note as to make it redeemable only at its face value, without interest, at this office.

Coupons of two years' five per cent. United States Treasury Notes, that have been separated from the notes of which they constitute a part, are of no value, and will not be redeemed. Coupons must not be detached from the notes to which they belong, except by a Government officer authorized to redeem them at maturity.

RULES FOR REDEMPTION OF FRACTIONAL CURRENCY.

Rules for the redemption of Fractional Currency.

1. All Fractional Currency, *not mutilated*, when presented to an Assistant Treasurer or Designated Depositary of the United States, or a National Bank designated as a Depository of the United States, for redemption, must have been assorted by the holder, according to denominations, with the faces and upper sides in corresponding order in the packages.

2. When presented in sufficient numbers, each package must contain one hundred pieces; it must be securely pinned, with a paper strap at least one inch wide, and on the strap must be written, in ink, the number of pieces, denomination, date of deposit, and the name of the owner.

3. The entire deposit must be securely done up in one package, and upon the wrapper, endorsed with ink, the date of the deposit, the amount contained, and the name and residence of the owner.

4. No less sum than three dollars will be redeemed, and packages will be paid for in lawful money of the United States, in the order as to time in which they shall have been received, as soon as the currency can be counted and passed upon.

RULES FOR REDEMPTION OF MUTILATED FRACTIONAL CURRENCY.

Rules for the redemption of mutilated fractional currency.

Fractional notes can be exchanged, if not mutilated, with any Assistant Treasurer or designated Depositary of the United States, or a National Bank designated as a Depository of the United States, in sums not less than three dollars. Defaced notes, if whole, are not considered as mutilated; nor is an evidently accidental injury, not reducing the note by more than one-tenth its original size, regarded as a mutilation. Mutilated fractional notes will be redeemed at the Treasury of the United States, at the city of Washington, under the following regulations, established as necessary guards against fraud:—

I. Fragments of a note will not be redeemed unless it shall be clearly evident that they constitute one-half, or more, of one original note; in which case, notes, however mutilated, will be redeemed in proportion to the whole note, reckoning by fifths.

II. Mutilations less than one-tenth will be disregarded, unless fraudulent; but any mutilation which destroys more than one-tenth the original note will reduce the redemption value of the note by one-fifth its face value.

III. Mutilated notes, presented for redemption, must be in sums not less than three dollars of the original full face value.

All Government Officers will receive for public dues all United States Notes of the several kinds, and on account for which they are respectively receivable, as per Treasury Circular of October 9, 1862, in explanation of the Rules promulgated May 18, 1862; no matter how badly defaced or torn they may be, so long as their genuineness can be clearly ascertained, and so that it is certain that not one-twentieth part thereof is missing. But all such notes as are unfit for re-issue, so received, should be kept separate and distinct, and, as occasion may require, be returned to the Treasury of the United States to be retired from circulation. Fractional currency, from which not *one-tenth* part is missing, will be received in the same manner.

F. E. SPINNER,
Treasurer U. S.

WASHINGTON, D. C., March 7, 1862.

[SPECIAL No. 1.]

TO COLLECTORS OF CUSTOMS AND COLLECTORS OF INTERNAL REVENUE.

TREASURY DEPARTMENT,
OFFICE OF INTERNAL REVENUE,
WASHINGTON, July 6, 1864.

Concerning the levy and collection of duties on distilled spirits.

The fifty-fifth section of the act of June 30, 1864, provides that all spirits which may be in the possession of the distiller, or in public store or bonded warehouse, on the first day of July, 1864, no duty having been paid thereon, shall be held and treated as if distilled on that day; and the duty of one dollar and fifty cents per gallon shall be paid by the owner, agent, or superintendent of the still, or other vessel, in which the said spirits shall have been distilled.

Collectors will observe that this clause applies to all distilled spirits which were on the first day of July, 1864, in the possession of the distiller, or in any public store or bonded warehouse, and the tax of one dollar and fifty cents per gallon must be collected on the same when removed, unless removed for exportation, or in transportation bonds under section 61 of the act of June 30, 1864. For this purpose there is no difference between the different kinds of bonded warehouses.

If, in any case, collectors have, before July 1, 1864, received money on account of spirits or other manufactures which had not, in fact, been sold, removed, or consumed, but were on that day in the possession of the manufacturer, or in public store or in bonded warehouse, such payment cannot be considered as the payment of a tax, inasmuch as the articles were not subject to a tax, and therefore does not relieve the articles from liability to the taxes imposed by the act of June 30.

Collectors of customs will take notice that distilled spirits placed in public store prior to July 1, 1864, pursuant to the instructions contained in the "circular to collectors of customs and collectors of internal revenue, in reference to the act of Congress approved March 7, 1864," issued by the Secretary of the Treasury, and dated March 30, 1864, may, by virtue of the act of June 30, 1864, be removed from said public store upon the payment of the duty upon the same, at the rate of one dollar and fifty cents per gallon, notwithstanding such spirits were originally allowed to be removed for the purpose of exportation only. But collectors of customs will not permit such spirits to be removed, except for exportation, until the owner produces a receipt or certificate in duplicate from the collector of internal revenue for the district in which the public storehouse is situated, showing that the duties have been paid on said spirits at the rate of one dollar and fifty cents per gallon, one of which receipts must be forwarded to the Commissioner of Internal Revenue.

The circular of March 30, 1864, above referred to, will continue in force, so far as applicable, until new regulations are issued. The bond for transportation of spirits and coal oil will be taken by the collector, as heretofore, but the applicant for a permit to remove spirits and coal oil is no longer required to swear that "the spirits or oil are designed for transportation to the said port *for exportation*," &c. The same form of bond, with the proper changes, may be taken for the removal of tobacco, and for the removal of spirits for re-distillation.

Section 46 of the act of July 1, 1862, was not re-enacted, and, therefore, spirits can no longer be shipped from one district to another in bills of lading.

Section 57 of the act of June 30, 1864, provides that distillers who distil or manufacture less than 150 barrels of spirits per year, may make monthly returns instead of tri-monthly.

The regulations concerning leakage, prescribed in Circular 13, will continue in force until otherwise directed, excepting paragraph II., which, of course, becomes inoperative by the repeal of section 46, act of July 1, 1862.

When spirits are removed, after payment of duties, from a bonded warehouse established under section 44 of the act of July 1, 1862, only one per cent. can be allowed for leakage.

New forms for distiller's book and tri-monthly return will be issued shortly. In the mean time, the old forms can be used by changing the headings of two columns thus, viz.: the words "removed to other collection districts" should be erased, and the words "removed to bonded warehouse" substituted therefor; and the words "removed in bond" must be substituted for the words "removed for export." The oaths on the old form of distiller's book must be made to correspond to the oaths prescribed in sections 62 and 63 of the act of June 30, 1864.

JOSEPH J. LEWIS, *Commissioner*.

Approved July 8, 1864.

W. P. FESSENDEN, *Secretary of the Treasury*.

DECISION

WITH REFERENCE TO PRINTED BOOKS, MAGAZINES, PAMPHLETS, REVIEWS, &c.

TREASURY DEPARTMENT,
OFFICE OF INTERNAL REVENUE,
WASHINGTON, July 30, 1864.

Duty 5 per cent.

The act of June 30 provides that on all printed books, magazines, pamphlets, reviews, and all similar printed publications, except newspapers, a duty of five per centum *ad valorem* shall be levied, collected, and paid.

Manufacturer or producer to render an account.

Section 86 of the same act provides that the manufacturer or producer of any article on which a duty is imposed by law shall, in his return of the value and quantity, render an account of the full amount of actual sales made by the manufacturer, producer, or agent thereof; and section 95 further provides that when any manufactured articles, on which an excise or import duty has been paid, are increased in value by being more completely finished or fitted for use or sale, without changing the original character or purposes for which the same are intended to be used, there shall be levied, collected, and paid a duty of five per centum *ad valorem* upon the amount of such increased value, to be ascertained by deducting from the finished article when sold, or removed for sale, delivery, or consumption, the cost or value of the original article to the person, firm, or company liable to the duty imposed upon the increased value thereof.

Tax to be levied on increased value in certain cases.

Publisher, if owner of the copyright, deemed the manufacturer.

Under these several provisions it is held that when the publisher of any book, magazine, pamphlet, review, or other similar printed publication, is the owner of any copyright stereotype plates, and carries on the business of printing and binding books, he is to be held and deemed the manufacturer, and as such must take license, and pay the *ad valorem* duty on the amount of his sales; but if the publisher, though owning the copyright, the stereotype plates, and furnishing the materials, employs other parties on commission, or by contract, to print any book, magazine, &c., such printer may be held to be the manufacturer, and required to pay the tax on the value of the finished book, in case the same is bound and finished by the printer. In such case he is entitled to collect the amount thereof of the publisher or owner.

Printer the manufacturer in certain cases.

If the printing is done by one party, and the binding by another, under contract with the publisher, then the printer may be assessed for the value of the printed sheets or signatures, and the binder on the increased value, which increased value must be determined by deducting from the trade prices of the publisher the cost or value of the printed sheets or signatures previously assessed in the hands of the printer.

Tax on increased value in certain cases.

In either case, whether the tax is assessed to the publisher on the finished book, &c., or primarily on the printed sheets or signatures, and afterwards on the increased value from binding and finishing, the assessment must be so made as to cover the trade value of the books, magazines, pamphlets, reviews, &c., and not simply the cost of production.

The trade price the value for purposes of taxation.

The tax is an *ad valorem* tax of five per centum on the value of the books, &c., exclusive of any tax previously assessed and paid on the materials used, and in no case should a higher rate of tax be imposed or assessed.

DECISION

IN REGARD TO THE LIABILITY OF DISTILLED SPIRITS, COAL OIL, AND TOBACCO.

TREASURY DEPARTMENT,
OFFICE OF INTERNAL REVENUE,
WASHINGTON, July 30, 1864.

Liability on spirits, tobacco, and oil, on which no duty had been paid on the 1st of July, 1864.

From various letters received at this office, it seem that great diversity of opinion exists among the officers of Internal Revenue, and other parties interested, in regard to the construction given to the 55th section of the act of June 30, in the Circular of July 6.

By the 55th section, all spirits which may have been in the possession of the distiller, or in public store or bonded warehouse, on the 1st day of July, no duty having been paid thereon, shall be held and treated as if distilled on that day. By the 173d section, it is also provided that "all manufactures and productions on which a duty was imposed by either of the acts repealed, which shall be in the possession of the manufacturer or producer, or of his agent or agents, on the day when this act takes effect, shall be held and deemed to have been manufactured or produced after such date."

These provisions are to be construed together, as the last includes the first, and both cover the same ground. They plainly apply to all distilled spirits which were, on the 1st of July, in the possession of the distiller or manufacturer, or in any public store or bonded warehouse, and spirits shipped under the old law in bills of lading. If no tax had been paid prior to July 1, no question of sale or removal could intervene, if the spirits on that day were in the possession of the distiller, or in public store or bonded warehouse, but he must pay the increased rate. Coal oil and tobacco, when bonded, are, by both the old and new law, subject to the same regulations and liabilities as distilled spirits.

The old law provided that spirits and oil should become subject to tax when sold, consumed, or removed for consumption or sale; and tobacco when sold, or removed for consumption, or for delivery to others than agents of the manufacturer or producer, but not when bonded for export.

When either of the conditions stated occurred, the law imposed the duty, the manufacturer became bound to pay, and officers of internal revenue to enforce the collection; if such duty was paid prior to July 1, there was no liability to the increased rate, the payment having been made as required by law.

If liability to duty had not accrued a receipt by collector not recognized as payment.

But, until the condition occurred on which the manufacturer became chargeable, he was under no liability to the government for tax on his product, and the collector had no authority to collect. Of course, any receipt he might give for tax would be in anticipation of an obligation not yet devolved, and would not operate as a discharge of a duty to accrue afterward.

If the manufacturer was liable to pay the duty, and had actually paid no increase of duty to be assessed.

When, therefore, under the provisions of the law and the regulations of this office, any manufacture had become liable to the duty, and the manufacturer, being bound to pay, had, prior to July 1, actually paid the duty according to the former law, no liability accrues for the increased duty imposed by the recent law.

A payment not a bar to additional duty if liability to payment did not exist when payment was made.

But if, under the same law and regulations, the article had not become liable to duty, no payment by the manufacturer to the collector could be made on account of duty, or operate as a legal discharge of a liability thereafter to accrue. Of course, it could not avail to defeat any increased liability created by the change in the law.

If collectors have failed to collect under circular of March 30, 1864, no increase of duty to be claimed.

Under the circular of the Secretary of the Treasury of March 30, 1864, in relation to bonded warehouses, collectors were required to enforce the payment of the duties on spirits which were not removed to a bonded warehouse, or shipped under a bill of lading; and when, in accordance with that circular, collectors did not enforce the payment of the duty, and such duty was paid prior to July 1, such spirits must be held to be exempt from the increased rate.

Spirits in bonded warehouse subject to increase of duty, although payment of previous duty may have been made.

Where spirits, on the 30th of June, were in a bonded warehouse, and on that day the manufacturer paid to the collector an amount equal to the duties on the same at the then rate of tax, but such spirits remained in such warehouse on the 1st of July, without any change of possession, there was no payment of the duty within the meaning of the law, and they still remain subject to the increased rate prescribed by the new law.

Spirits, &c., in hands of manufacturer, July 1, 1864, subject to duty under act of June 30, 1864.

If the spirits or other manufactured articles were in the possession of the distiller or manufacturer, or his agent or agents, on the 1st of July, and no tax had previously been paid, the law is clear and explicit that such spirits or other articles must be held and treated as if distilled or manufactured on that day, and subject to the increased rate of tax. The non-payment of the tax is conclusive, and no inquiry need be made further.

TREASURY DEPARTMENT,
OFFICE OF INTERNAL REVENUE,
WASHINGTON, July 14, 1864.

Duties of inspectors of cigars.

SIR: Enclosed you will find commissions for the persons named as Inspectors of Cigars in your District. You will deliver the commissions to the several inspectors, after they shall have taken the oath of office in the form prescribed, as by the copy herewith enclosed.

Stamp upon cigars.

It will be the duty of each inspector to examine all cigars manufactured, within the limits of the territory assigned to him, before the same pass out of the hands of the manufacturer, to see that the bundles, boxes, or packages are correctly labelled with the number and kind contained therein; and, unless the same shall be removed to a bonded warehouse for exportation, to affix a stamp denoting the tax thereon, in such a manner that the bundle or box cannot be opened without effacing or destroying the stamp. A quantity of stamps, appropriate to the several rates of tax imposed by law, are forwarded to you by this day's mail, and you will distribute such portion of them to the several inspectors as you may find necessary. The stamps now forwarded are —

For cigars taxed at $3 per thousand.
" " $8 "
" " $15 "
" " $25 "
" " $40 "

As soon as possible you will make a requisition for such additional stamps of the several kinds as you may need for immediate use, and you will further state what number, in your opinion, will be wanted for your district during the coming year.

You will require each inspector to make return to you, monthly, of the number and quality of cigars inspected for each manufacturer, and of the number of stamps of each kind affixed.

It is to be distinctly understood, and you will so instruct your assistants and all manufacturers, that the stamp affixed by the inspector expresses merely the opinion of that officer as to the rate of tax to which the cigars are liable, and is not, of itself, conclusive.

The 86th section of the revenue law provides that the value and quantity of the goods, wares, and merchandise required to be stated, shall be estimated by the actual sales made by the manufacturer, or by his agent, or persons acting in his behalf. In relation to cigars, the special provision is made in the 94th section that the amount of the tax shall be deducted from the price at which the cigars are sold, and that the value exclusive of the tax shall be the value in accordance with which the tax shall be assessed.

Although, on a first view, these two provisions, when taken

together, leave it uncertain, in some cases, to which class cigars are to be assigned, the construction which has been reached, and which is the most favorable for the manufacturer, leads to the adoption of the following schedule as a convenient guide for assessors, assistant assessors, and inspectors in determining the rate of tax to which any cigars are liable: —

Rate of tax.

* Cigars selling at not over $13,	$3.
" " over $13 and not over $30,	$8.
" " " $30 " " $55,	$15.
" " " $55 " " $85,	$25.
" " " $85,	$40.

You will, therefore, instruct your inspectors, when affixing stamps upon cigars, to be governed by the rule thus established.

The 58th section of the revenue law provides that the fees of the inspector shall be such as may be fixed and prescribed by the Commissioner, and that they shall be paid by the owner or manufacturer of the articles inspected. Under this provision, I have given a careful consideration to the circumstances of the trade in your district, and have concluded that a fee of cents per package inspected will be reasonable and just, and that fee is, therefore, hereby fixed and prescribed.

If, in any case, a manufacturer shall declare, under oath or affirmation, that certain cigars are to be immediately removed to a bonded warehouse for exportation, the inspector will not affix the stamp above described; but, in such case, he will put a brand or mark upon the box in which the cigars are packed, which will indicate the number and quality of the cigars contained therein; and he will, also, in like manner, place upon the box his name and official designation, with the date of inspection.

Before taking a bond for the removal of any cigars to a bonded warehouse, either for exportation or for storage, the assessor will require a return from the manufacturer, under oath or affirmation, setting forth the number of cigars which he wishes to remove, and the market value of the same, and will cause the inspector to affix a brand or mark which will indicate such value and the appropriate tax.

JOSEPH J. LEWIS, *Commissioner.*

---

* See Circular No. 19.

[CIRCULAR No. 19.]

REGULATIONS

CONCERNING THE INSPECTION AND STAMPING OF CIGARS.

TREASURY DEPARTMENT,
OFFICE OF INTERNAL REVENUE,
WASHINGTON, August 9, 1864.

Inspector to affix stamp exclusive of the tax.

The law provides no mode by which the Inspector shall be legally informed of the value of the cigars he is called upon to inspect. He is, therefore, required in making his valuation to act upon his own knowledge of the market value of the inspected article, exclusive of the tax, of which value he should be careful to keep himself well informed. After the cigars have been packed in bundles, boxes, or packages, in the shape in which they are exhibited for sale, or sold, the Inspector will affix the stamp, indicating the rate of tax according to the value of the cigars, EXCLUSIVE OF THE TAX, pursuant to the 94th section of the act of Congress. In estimating the value he will include the cost of production, packing, boxing, inspecting, and whatever may be properly regarded as a part of the expense of putting the commodity into a complete and final condition for the market. And when the cigars have once been packed, labelled, and stamped, the packages cannot be broken, or the cigars repacked, or divested of the stamps affixed to such packages or boxes, while in the possession, control, or custody of the manufacturer, or his agent or agents, without rendering them liable for a re-inspection; and, where the value of the cigars is found to be more than was fixed on the first inspection, stamps denoting higher rates of tax must be affixed; and any such re-packing or removal of the Inspector's stamp without such re-inspection must be regarded as a fraudulent transaction, rendering such cigars liable to seizure and forfeiture.

Rate.

For reasons stated above, the Inspector will affix to all cigars, which he values at $3, $4, and $5, a stamp denoting a tax of $3. On cigars which he values above $5 and up to $15, he will affix a stamp denoting a tax of $8. On cigars which he values above $15 and up to $30, he will affix a stamp denoting a tax of $15. On cigars which he values above $30 and up to $45, he will affix a stamp denoting a tax of $25; and on cigars which he values above $45, he will affix a stamp denoting a tax of $40 per thousand.

To visit manufactories.

The Inspector will visit, as often as may be deemed necessary by the Assessor, each manufactory of cigars in his district. Before stamping he will satisfy himself that each package or box is entirely made up of cigars of one quality. Care will be exercised in affixing the stamps to so attach them to the bundle, package, or box, that they cannot be opened or broken without effacing or destroying the stamps. When a single stamp will not sufficiently protect a box, bundle, or package, the Inspector is required to attach so many stamps as will. No other person than an Inspector, duly appointed by the Secretary of the Treasury, is authorized to affix stamps, and the affixing of stamps by any other person will render the cigars liable to forfeiture under section 94, and any Inspector who may consent to or may have knowledge of such fraudulent stamping, will, on the facts being brought to the knowledge of this office, be dismissed.

Disability of inspector.

Whenever an Inspector, by sickness or otherwise, becomes disqualified for the performance of his duty, and his place cannot be conveniently supplied by another Inspector, notice must immediately be given, by the Assessor, to this office, and, if necessary, the nomination of another person as Inspector forwarded to take his place.

Inspector not to affix stamp to cigars of his own manufacture.

In no case will it be proper for an Inspector to inspect or affix stamps on cigars of his own manufacture.

Record of inspection.

The Inspector will also keep a record of all cigars which he inspects, and the rates of tax to which they are liable, giving at the same time the names and places of business of the persons or firms for whom the same are inspected, and the number for each, and at the end of each month he will render to the Assessor of the district, on the form provided by this office, a full account of all the cigars he has thus inspected and stamped.

Circular of July 14th.

The Circular of July 14th, relating to stamps on cigars, &c., is hereby superseded so far as relates to the schedule by which Inspectors shall determine the rate of tax.

JOSEPH J. LEWIS, *Commissioner.*

[SPECIAL, No. 5.]

INSTRUCTIONS

CONCERNING THE ASSESSMENT OF TOBACCO, SNUFF, AND CIGARS.

TREASURY DEPARTMENT,
OFFICE OF INTERNAL REVENUE,
WASHINGTON, August 9, 1864.

Instructions relating to fraudulent sales of tobacco, cigars, and snuff.

Information has been given to this office that many manufacturers have made returns — as for the month of June or for previous months — of tobacco, snuff, and cigars not *bona fide* sold, or removed for consumption or sale, during those months. It has been stated that colorable sales have been made, and taxes paid according to the rates under the former acts, with the view of avoiding the additional tax required by the act of June 30, 1864.

Sales made by a manufacturer to his foreman, or to some convenient friend or man of straw, with the view of a re-transfer to the manufacturer, or of a sale afterwards to his use, though possession may have been delivered to such foreman or other person, will not affect the right of the Government to the increased tax. Such sale is fraudulent, so far as the Government is concerned, whatever it may be between the parties, and ought not to be recognized as valid by the officers of Internal Revenue. Upon the sale, or consumption, or removal for consumption or sale, or removal from the place of manufacture of such articles after the 1st of July, the tax thereon became due and must be paid at the increased rates, pursuant to the last act.

Articles which in June or previous months were the subjects of such colorable sales, remaining actually the property of the manufacturer, though in other hands for his use, and actually sold during the month of July, ought to have been returned as belonging in the weekly returns of that month; and Assessors and Assistant Assessors should be careful to see that those returns include all such articles as really belonged to the manufacturer, though they may have been subjects of pretended sales and deliveries.

There may be articles on hand, which, in order to avoid the increased tax, were pretended to be sold, and which may be hereafter actually sold. These ought to be hereafter returned, and the same caution, herein enjoined as to the returns for the month of July, ought to be observed as to the returns of subsequent months.

This course is rendered necessary in order to secure to the Government its just dues, and to protect the fair dealer from fraudulent competition. It is therefore the duty of Assessors to scrutinize carefully all returns which have been made by manufacturers of tobacco, snuff, and cigars, since the 1st of July, or which may hereafter be made.

Under section 90, manufacturers of tobacco, snuff, and cigars are required to make weekly returns of the amounts of each made or manufactured, and sold or consumed, or removed for consumption or sale, or removed from the place of manufacture, during the week; and also render an account of the full value of the same as shown by actual sales. Whenever it shall appear that cigars have actually been sold by the manufacturer at prices which would render them liable to a higher rate of tax than that denoted by the Inspector's stamp, or when it shall be discovered that articles have been fraudulently returned under former rates, and that the manufacturer is legally liable to the increased tax under the instructions herein given, the assessor will immediately proceed to reassess such cigars for the additional tax to which *actual sales* show them to have been liable. The assessment and collection of such additional tax may be enforced as provided in section 84, or proceedings may be commenced under section 48, or section 89, as either may be applicable, and an investigation may be had under section 14.

The enclosed declaration, required by section 91, has been prepared by the Commissioner. This declaration should have been made and signed by every manufacturer of tobacco, snuff, and cigars, on the last day of July. In all cases where it has not yet been made and signed substantially in the form now prescribed by the Commissioner, Assessors must be particular to require it now as of that time, and at the end of every month hereafter. It is evidently contemplated by the law that this declaration may be an essential aid in the discovery of possible fraud, and it is therefore of the utmost importance that it be strictly required of every manufacturer of tobacco, cigars, &c. Each declaration will be carefully dated and filed in the office of the Assessor, subject to the inspection of any officer of Internal Revenue.

JOSEPH J. LEWIS, *Commissioner.*

TO BE LEFT WITH PARTY SIGNING DECLARATION.

DECLARATION BY THE MANUFACTURER OF TOBACCO, SNUFF, OR CIGARS.

Declaration by manufacturer of tobacco, cigars, and snuff.

I ____ do solemnly declare, that during the period commencing on the 1st day of July, 1864, and ending on the 31st day of July, 1864, no tobacco, snuff, or cigars, of any description whatsoever, which were subject or liable to any tax under the act to provide internal revenue to support the Government, to pay interest on the public debt, and for other purposes, approved June 30, 1864, and which, during that time, were made or manufactured or owned by, or were in the possession of the undersigned, or of the firm of __________________ ______________________ of which I am a member, doing business at ____ were removed, carried, or sent, or caused or suffered or known to have been removed, carried, or sent, from the premises of the undersigned, or of the firm of which I am a member, either by myself, or any member, agent, or employé of myself or the firm aforesaid, except such of said articles as were *duly assessed*, according to the provisions of said act, and the duties imposed on said articles by said act fully paid, and except also such as were removed under bond, according to law.

____

Signed this ______ day of ________________ 1864,
in presence of

____

Assistant Assessor.

NOTE.—When a person requires time to make a special or additional return to the assessor, in order to enable him consistently to sign the above declaration, further and reasonable time should be given for that purpose.

INVENTORY OF TOBACCO, SNUFF, AND CIGARS

(SECTION 90, ACT OF JUNE 30, 1864.)

Inventory of the Quantity and Description of Manufactured and Unmanufactured Tobacco, including Snuff, Snuff Flour, Cigars, Licorice, Tin Foil, and Stems held or owned by ______________, of ______________, County of ______________, and State of ______________, whose Factory is at No. ________, ______________ Street, on this ______________ day of ______________, A. D. 186 .

	Pounds of Leaf Tobacco for cutting or plug.	Pounds Spanish Leaf Tobacco.	Pounds Seed Leaf Tobacco.	Pounds Tobacco Stems.	Pounds Snuff Flour.	Pounds Prepared Snuff.	Pounds Inspected Plug or Twist.	Pounds Plug or Twist not inspected.	Pounds Tobacco in process of manufacture.	Pounds Cut Chewing Tobacco.	Pounds Cut or prepared Smoking.	Pounds Cut Stem with no Leaf in.	Pounds Fine-Cut Shorts.	Pounds Pressed Tobacco.	Pounds Licorice.	Pounds Tin Foil.
Amount manufactured, or produced and held, or stored at Factory as above																
Amount purchased from others, and held or stored at Factory as above																
Amount manufactured or produced, and held or stored elsewhere than at Factory																
Amount purchased from others, and held or stored elsewhere than at Factory.																
Total Amount held or owned																

	Cigarettes not over $6 per 100 packages of 25 each.		Cigarettes or Cheroots, not over $13 per M.		Cigars from $13 to $30.		Cigars from $30 to $55.		Cigars from $55 to $85.		Cigars over $85.		Total Quantity Cigars.	Total Value Cigars.
	Quantity.	Value.	Quantity.	Value.	Quantity.	Value.	Quantity.	Value.	Quantity.	Value.	Quantity.	Value.		
Cigars of own manufacture and stored at Factory as above														
Cigars of own manufacture and stored elsewhere than at Factory														
Cigars purchased of others and stored at Factory as above														
Cigars purchased of others and stored elsewhere than at Factory														

Extract from Section 90, *Act June* 30, 1864.

Any person, firm, company, or corporation, now or hereafter engaged in the manufacture of Tobacco, Snuff, or Cigars, of any description whatsoever, shall be, and hereby is, required to make out and deliver to the Assistant Assessor of the Assessment District a true *statement* or *inventory* of the quantity of each of the different kinds of Tobacco, Snuff Flour, Snuff, Cigars, Tin Foil, Licorice, and Stems held or owned by him or them *on the day this act takes effect*, or at the time of commencing business under this act, setting forth what portion of said goods was manufactured or produced by him or them, and what was purchased from others, whether chewing, smoking, fine-cut, shorts, pressed, plug, snuff flour, or prepared snuff, the several kinds of Cigars, and the market price thereof; which statement or inventory shall be verified by the oath or affirmation of such person or persons, and be in manner and form as prescribed by the Commissioner of Internal Revenue. And on the first day of January in every year hereafter, shall make out and deliver a true statement or inventory in manner and form as aforesaid.

(Signed) ______________________

I, ______________________, do swear that the above is, to the best of my knowledge and belief, a complete and correct account of all the Tobacco, Snuff, Snuff Flour, Cigars, Stems, Licorice, and Tin Foil held or owned by ______________________, on the ________ day of ______________, 186 , and that I have taken all the means in my power to make this account complete and correct in each and every particular.

SWORN and subscribed before me, this ________ day of ______________, A. D. 186 .

(Signed) ______________________

____

TOBACCO AND SNUFF MANUFACTURERS' WEEKLY RETURN.

Account of the quantity and description of Tobacco of all descriptions, including Snuff, manufactured and sold, or consumed, removed for sale or consumption, or removed from the manufactory, or removed under bond, and of all purchased, by ____________ __________, of the ________ of ____________________, in the County of ____________________, and State of ____________________, in the __________ Assessment Division of the ____________, Collection District, at No. _______________________ Street, in said _______ of ____________________, with all Leaf and Stemmed Tobacco, and Stems, Licorice, and Tin Foil purchased and sold, or removed to said Factory, during the week commencing on the ________ day of ________________, and ending on the _________ day of ____ __________, 186 , both days inclusive.

MANUFACTURED TOBACCO.	Total Manufact'd.	Amount Purchased.	Removed in Bond.	Sold, or Removed for Sale, of Amount purchased.	Sold, Consumed, or Removed for Sale, &c., after Manuf're.	Rate of Tax.	Amount of Tax.	
	Pounds.	Pounds.	Pounds.	Pounds.	Pounds.	Cents.	Dolls.	Cts.
Cavendish, Plug, Twist, and all other kinds of manufactured Tobacco, not otherwise specified, sweetened, with stem out in part or in whole						35		
Fine-cut Chewing of all descriptions .						35		
Smoking, with all Stems in						25		
" exclusively of Stems						15		
Fine-cut Shorts						25		
Snuff, Maccaboy						35		
" Scotch						35		
" Coarse						35		
" of other kinds						35		
Snuff Flour								
						Total . . .		

RAW MATERIAL.	Leaf Tobacco, Pounds.	Stemmed Tobacco, Pounds.	Stems, Pounds.	Licorice, Pounds.	Tin Foil, Pounds.
Amount Purchased					
" Sold					
" taken into Factory					

(Signed) ________________________________

I, ____________________________, do swear that the above is, to the best of my knowledge and belief, a true and complete account of all the Tobacco and Snuffs manufactured, purchased, sold, consumed, or removed for consumption or sale, or removed from the manufactory, or removed in bond, during the period specified; and also all the Leaf and Stemmed Tobacco, Stems, Licorice, and Tin Foil purchased and sold, or taken into the manufactory, during the same period; and that I have taken all the means in my power to make said account complete and correct in each and every particular.

SWORN before me, this _________ day of ____________________, A. D. 186 .

(Signed) ________________________________

____

Assistant Assessor.

CIGAR MANUFACTURER'S WEEKLY RETURN.

(SECTION 90, ACT OF JUNE 30, 1864.)

Account of the quantity and description of Cigars, Cheroots, or Cigarettes of all descriptions, purchased, manufactured, removed in bond, sold, consumed, or removed for consumption or sale, or removed from the manufactory, by ——————, of the ——— of ———, County of ———, and State of ———, at No. ——— Street, in said ——— of ———, in the ——— Assessment Division of the ——— Collection District in said State; and also all the material purchased, sold, or taken into the manufactory during the week commencing on the ——— day of ———, and ending on the ——— day of ———, 186 , both days inclusive.

Names of persons making Cigars this week, and the No. made by each.	No.
No. 1	
2	
3	
4	
5	
6	
7	
8	
9	
10	
11	
12	
13	
14	
15	
16	
17	
18	
19	
20	
Total Number made . . .	
Total quantity exported this week . .	Thousands.

Kind or Description.	No. removed in bond.	No. purchased during the week.	No. sold or removed of those purchased.	No. sold, consumed or removed, &c. of those manufactured.	Prices at which sold.	Rate of Tax.	Amount of Tax. Dolls.	Amount of Tax. Cts.
Cigarettes, paper wrappers, No. of hundred packages, not over 25 in each pack. .					Not over $6 per hundred packages	$1.00		
Do. Do.					Over $6 per hundred packages	3.00		
Cheroots and Cigars					Not over $13 per thous.	3.00		
Cigars					Over $13 and not over $30	8.00		
Do.					Over $30 and not over $55	15.00		
Do.					Over $55 and not over $85	25.00		
Do.					Over $85	40.00		
Total quantity					Total Tax			

(Signed) ——————————

RAW MATERIAL.	Leaf Tobacco, Pounds.	Stemmed Tobacco, Pounds.	Stems, Pounds.			
Purchased during week						
Sold " "						
Taken into Factory . .						

I, ——————, do swear that the above is, to the best of my knowledge and belief, a complete and correct account of all the Cigars, Cheroots, or Cigarettes, made or manufactured by or for ——————, or for any other person or persons, during the period aforesaid; and also of the quantities and descriptions thereof purchased, removed in bond, sold, consumed, or removed for consumption or sale, or from the manufactory, by ——— or ——— agents; and also all the material purchased, sold, or taken into said manufactory, during the same period; and that I have taken all the means in my power to make said account complete and correct in each and every particular.

SWORN and subscribed before me, this ——— day of ———, A. D. 186 .

(Signed) ——————————

——————————, *Assistant Assessor.*

[SPECIAL, No. 4.]

REGULATIONS CONCERNING LICENSES.

ASSESSMENT AND REASSESSMENT OF LICENSES.

Treasury Department,
Office of Internal Revenue,
Washington, July 30, 1864.

Section 80 of the act of June 30, 1864, prescribes that "where the amount of any license, or the rate has been increased, or is liable to be increased by law above the amount of any existing license to any person, firm, or company, or has been understated or underestimated, such person, firm, or company shall be again assessed, and pay the amount of such increase, which shall be endorsed on the original license, which shall thereafter be held good and sufficient."

License fee may be increased if too low under existing law.

Under this provision, assessors will at once proceed to reassess all persons, firms, and corporations assessed for licenses where, under the act of June 30, the rate has been or is liable to be increased, or where any existing license has been understated or underestimated.

Duty of assessors to assess additional under act of June 30, 1864.

They will also notify all persons engaged in any trade, business, or profession for which a license is required under the provisions of the new law, though not liable to be assessed for a license under the former laws, to take out the appropriate license.

To notify persons liable to license under said act.

Licenses, whether reassessed or newly issued under the act of June 30, will take effect from the 1st of July, and the assessment will be *pro rata* — ten-twelfths of the rate or amount fixed for such new license, or of the increase upon the old rate.

Assessment to be pro rata from July 1, 1864, to May 1, 1865.

Where any person was, on the 1st of May, engaged in any occupation for which a license was then required, and continued such occupation after that date, and made no application for a license, and no license tax was assessed prior to July 1, such party will be required to take license, as of May 1, for one year, and be charged with the then existing rate; and, if by the new law the rate is increased, such license will be reassessed, and the amount of such increase endorsed thereon.

Persons liable under former laws to be assessed under such laws, and also under act of June 30, 1864.

The endorsement will be made by the collector, and no reassessed license will protect the party carrying on the business mentioned in it without such endorsement.

Collector to endorse facts on license.

The law provides for a reassessment and the payment of the increase, where the rate has been or is liable to be increased; but it does not provide for any remission of the excess where the rate has been diminished, or where the law is so changed that any existing license becomes unnecessary, or a new license of a different character is required. Under the old law lottery ticket dealers were required to pay a license fee of $1,000; by the present law the fee is fixed at $100. An incorporated bank,

If license reduced by act of June 30, 1864, excess cannot be refunded.

under the old law, was required, in certain cases, to take a broker's license; by the present law it is required to take a banker's license, which covers the business of a broker. Yet the law gives no authority to refund any part of the fee in either case.

Same of wholesale liquor dealers who have license as general dealers.

Under the old law wholesale liquor dealers, who were also wholesale dealers in other goods, were required to take out a license for each business; while, under the present law, a license as a wholesale liquor dealer, by special provision, covers the business of a wholesale dealer; where, therefore, a party is now assessed or reassessed as a wholesale liquor dealer, his license as a wholesale dealer becomes unnecessary; yet the fee paid for that license cannot, as the law now stands, be refunded.

Rules in regard to retail liquor dealers.

The law defines a wholesale liquor dealer to be, first, a person who shall sell spirits in quantities of three gallons and upwards; and, second, one whose annual sales, including sales of other merchandise, shall exceed twenty-five thousand dollars; and, by express provision, a person licensed as a wholesale liquor dealer is not required to take out an additional license for the sale of other merchandise on the same premises. This exemption from additional license for the sale of other merchandise is not, by the law, extended to a retail liquor dealer; but a person holding a license as a retail liquor dealer cannot sell other merchandise without a license as a retail dealer. A person holding a license only as a retail dealer may sell merchandise to the amount of twenty-five thousand dollars, and, under a license as a retail liquor dealer only, he may sell spirits in quantities less than three gallons to the same amount; but, if he holds both licenses, the instant his sales of spirits and other merchandise exceed twenty-five thousand dollars, he ceases to be a retail liquor dealer, but comes within the definition of a wholesale liquor dealer, and must take license as such.

Lawyers, conveyancers, and others doing business in firms, require individual licenses.

Lawyers, conveyancers, claim agents, physicians, surgeons, dentists, cattle brokers, horse dealers, and pedlers, under the new law, though associated in business, must take license individually, and cannot be licensed as a firm. Where persons belonging to either class have taken license as a firm, such license, with the approval of the collector, may be transferred to a member of the firm, and the others must take a new license.

In regard to lawyers acting as claim agents.

A party holding a license as a lawyer or claim agent is not required to take license as a conveyancer; but a claim agent cannot carry on the business of a lawyer, nor a conveyancer that of a claim agent or lawyer, without a separate license. In towns having a population of less than six thousand persons, one license may cover the business of land warrant broker, claim agent, and real estate agent, upon the payment of a fee of twenty-five dollars, the highest fee applicable to either business; but such license must specify the three occupations.

Auctioneers.

Auctioneers are not, by the act of June 30, restricted in their business to the district in which they have taken out their license. Their monthly returns, however, must be made, and the tax on their sales paid in the district where they have taken out their license. The license should be taken out in the district where they have their office or place of business; but no auctioneer can have an office or place of business in more than one district under one license.

Where any person shall claim an exemption from a license tax as dealer, manufacturer, apothecary, confectioner, eating house keeper, tobacconist, cattle broker, builder, contractor, or insurance agent, because of his annual receipts being less than the sum which determines the liability according to the act, it will devolve on him to show to the satisfaction of the assistant assessor that his annual sales or receipts do not exceed that sum; and the assistant assessor may demand of him a statement in writing of his actual and estimated receipts. If he shall fail to satisfy the assistant assessor of the amount of his receipts or sales, the assistant assessor may make whatever examination may be in his power, and assess the license tax as in his judgment may appear just. If he should be unable to obtain evidence sufficient to justify him in making an assessment, it will be his duty to report the case to the assessor, who may proceed under the 14th section of the act to elicit the necessary evidence, on the basis of which the assessment may be made.

Rules in regard to persons who claim exemption upon the ground of insufficiency of receipts.

The license of a wholesale dealer will not be for a less amount than his sales for the previous year, except in the case specified in paragraph two of section seventy-nine. The year will be the year next preceding the 1st day of May.

License of a wholesale dealer not to be based upon a less sum than his sales for the previous year.

Where the amount of the license fee is fixed, and not graduated by the amount of sales or otherwise, the reassessment may be made upon the application for the existing license.

Where the license fee is fixed.

By the forty-ninth paragraph of the seventy-ninth section of the act of June 30, a license fee of ten dollars is "required of every person, firm, or corporation engaged in any business, trade, or profession whatsoever, for which no other license is herein required, whose gross annual receipts therefor exceed one thousand dollars."

License required of every one whose gross receipts exceed $1,000.

This is a very general and sweeping provision. It applies —

1st, To "every person, firm, or corporation" engaged as stated.

A license, though procured by a firm, will not protect a person belonging to the firm and prosecuting an independent business; nor will a license to a corporation protect its corporate members or employés. A man may be one of a firm requiring a license, one of a corporate company requiring a license, and, at the same time, a clerk of the same or of another firm or corporation, and be compelled to pay a license fee as such clerk. His business, as employé, is separate from that of the firm or corporation so far as concerns him individually. The license fee is the purchase of a personal privilege, or rather, perhaps, a tax on the personal employment of the taxpayer, and inures to the benefit of no third person, whatever may be the relation between the parties. The act regards corporations in their legal character as artificial persons, and partnerships as *quasi* corporations having a legal existence separate and distinct from the individuals by the aggregation of whom they are respectively constituted. In States where the local law allows a married woman to act as a *femme sole*, she will be subject to the license duty if she pursues a business which yields the prescribed amount. Minors in business incur the same liabilities for licenses as adults.

Regulations in reference to licenses under article 49 of section 79

2d. The business, trade, or profession mentioned in the act is limited to such as no other license is required for. But if a person already licensed for one business pursues another, which yields him more than one thousand dollars, he is obliged to pay a separate license fee. The business, trade, or profession requiring a license fee, must be one which of itself yields over a thousand dollars. If a person should carry on two trades — one of a tailor, for instance, and one of a shoemaker — or should pursue the profession of a clergyman, and at the same time teach school, from each of which pursuits his receipts should not exceed one thousand dollars, he would not be required to pay a license fee. For though the license is to the person, it is for the business, and the business which demands it must, without aid from other sources, produce a sum in excess of that mentioned in the statute. Different varieties, or branches of the same kind of business, do not come within this principle, and care on the part of the revenue officers is necessary to distinguish between what is and what is not a kind of business different from some other kind.

Enumeration of persons liable.

Among those persons who may be liable to take license under this paragraph may be enumerated the following, as examples, to wit: Clergymen, teachers, farmers, artists, boarding-house keepers, bookkeepers, gardeners, nursery men, express men, teamsters, truckmen, bricklayers, bank tellers, presidents and cashiers of banks, substitute brokers, painters, and blacksmiths (when not manufacturers); persons carrying on saw mills, clover, grist, or other mills (when not manufacturers); superintendents, managers, agents or officers of companies or corporations; firms, companies, or corporations organized for any business not requiring any other license, such as railroad and insurance companies, &c., &c.

Exceptions.

An office held under the Federal or under a State government is not either a business, trade, or profession, in the meaning of the act. The commission which the officer holds of the executive authority, or appointing power, is his sufficient license.

Assessment of licenses assessed or reassessed returnable in monthly lists.

The licenses assessed or reassessed will, by regulation of this department, be returned by the assessors in their regular monthly lists.

Omissions to be returned in special lists.

In cases where it is discovered that the names of persons, or objects liable to tax or duty, were omitted from the annual list of May, 1864, the same should be returned on a special list, and the assessment and collection will be made as on a monthly list. Such special list should be attached to and returned with a monthly list, and the aggregate amount of both should be stated in the accompanying aggregate list.

JOSEPH J. LEWIS, *Commissioner*.

WARRANT.

UNITED STATES OF AMERICA.

______________________________ *Collection District, State of* ____________________

To ______________________________________ *Deputy Collector:*

Warrant of distraint.

Whereas, in pursuance of the provisions of the Acts of Congress of the United States to provide Internal Revenue to support the Government, to pay interest on the public debt, and for other purposes, the several persons and firms named in the list or schedule signed by me, and hereto annexed, have become chargeable with, and are indebted to the United States for, the taxes assessed against them, respectively, in the amount set forth opposite the name of each in the aforesaid list or schedule, together with the penalty as therewith stated, amounting in the aggregate to ________________ $\frac{}{100}$ dollars, for neglect to pay the said tax when the same became due; AND WHEREAS more than ten days have elapsed since payment of said taxes was demanded of each of said persons or firms, and as they still neglect and refuse to pay the same: *You are hereby commanded* to distrain upon so much of the goods, chattels, and effects of each of them, respectively, if any such can be found, as may be necessary for the payment of the taxes and penalties due and owing by them, respectively, as set forth in the aforesaid schedule, and also for the payment of all necessary and reasonable fees and expenses of each said distraint, with the commission chargeable by law. And you will safely keep all property so distrained, and do all things needful and necessary to be done in the premises, as required by law, before the sale thereof. But in case sufficient goods, chattels, and effects cannot be found, then you are hereby commanded to seize so much of the real estate of each of said persons or firms as may be necessary for the purposes aforesaid. And for so doing, this shall be your WARRANT; of which make due service, and return to me at this office.

WITNESS my hand and official seal, at ______________________, this ___________ day of __________________ Anno Domini 186 .

____

Collector of Internal Revenue,

____________ *District of* _______________

SCHEDULE.

NAME.	LOCATION.	DESCRIPTION OF TAX.		AMOUNT OF TAX.	PENALTY.	TOTAL.	REMARKS.
							Collector of Internal Revenue *District of*

DECISION

IN REFERENCE TO BILL HEADS PRINTED, PRINTED CARDS, AND PRINTED CIRCULARS.

The act of June 30, under the 94th section, provides that on bill heads printed, printed cards, and printed circulars, a duty of 5 per centum shall be levied, assessed, and collected. Bill heads, cards, and circulars, printed.

As the law is particular in enumerating these three different kinds or specimens of job printing, without reference to any other, the inference is clear that all articles of job printing not included under either the head of bill heads, cards, or circulars, are exempt from tax.

Bill heads can refer only to the printed headings used by merchants, manufacturers, and others in rendering accounts of goods or services, &c., and does not refer to printed headings of official or other letter paper. Definition of.

Printed cards include cards of business and cards of civility, railway tickets and checks, tickets for theatres, concerts, exhibitions, shows, &c., whether printed on pasteboard, card board, card paper, or any other kind of paper.

Printed circulars include not only circulars intended to be sent through the mails, but also printed notices, programmes, posters, &c., whether circulated through the mail or by carriers, or posted upon the streets, highways, in stores, hotels, inns, or taverns, or in any other public place.

DEMAND FOR TAX ON INCOME, SECTION 92.

OFFICE OF THE COLLECTOR OF INTERNAL REVENUE,

_______ *Collection District, State of* _______________

*M*____186

The tax assessed upon your income for the year ending December 31, 186 , amounting to _______________________ $\frac{}{100}$ dollars, has been transmitted to me by the Assessor of the District, and for payment of which, demand is hereby made. If unpaid for thirty days after the 30th day of June last, and for ten days after this demand, five per centum will be added to the amount unpaid; and the amount of said tax, with such addition, together with interest and the costs that may accrue, will become a lien on all the property, rights, and interests from which such income accrued; which lien will be enforced by distraint, if necessary. Demand for income tax.

Payment may be made to ____________________ at __________

No. ______ *Collector* ______ *District.*

INDEX.

A.

B.

C.

D.

E.

F.

G.

H.

I.

J.

K.

L.

PAGE

M.

N.

O.

P.

Q.

R.

S.

T.

U.

V.

W.

Y.

Z.

www.ingramcontent.com/pod-product-compliance
Lightning Source LLC
LaVergne TN
LVHW010208110826
845151LV00002B/641
9781425535896